Foreign Investments in BRIC Countries

MÜNSTERANER SCHRIFTEN ZUR INTERNATIONALEN UNTERNEHMENSRECHNUNG

Herausgegeben von Peter Kajüter

Band 10

Zu Qualitätssicherung und Peer Review der vorliegenden Publikation

Die Qualität der in dieser Reihe erscheinenden Arbeiten wird vor der Publikation durch den Herausgeber der Reihe geprüft.

Notes on the quality assurance and peer review of this publication

Prior to publication, the quality of the work published in this series is reviewed by the editor of the series.

Thomas Poplat

Foreign Investments in BRIC Countries

Empirical Evidence from Multinational Corporations

PL ACADEMIC RESEARCH

Bibliographic Information published by the Deutsche Nationalbibliothek
The Deutsche Nationalbibliothek lists this publication in the Deutsche Nationalbibliografie; detailed bibliographic data is available in the internet at http://dnb.d-nb.de.

Zugl.: Münster (Westfalen), Univ., Diss., 2013

D 6
ISSN 1868-7687
ISBN 978-3-631-64887-2 (Print)
ISBN 978-3-653-03928-3 (E-Book)
DOI 10.3726/978-3-653-03928-3

This book is part of an editor's series of PL Academic Research and was peer reviewed prior to publication.

www.peterlang.de

Preface

In the course of their internationalization strategies, multinational companies undertake significant investments to establish subsidiaries and production sites in foreign countries. In 2012, worldwide foreign direct investment flows more than doubled compared to 2002 accounting for USD 1.4 trillion. Investments in emerging economies were a main driver of the significant increase of worldwide foreign investment flows in recent years. In particular during the times of stagnating growth in North America and Europe, emerging economies offer substantial opportunities for multinational companies, but they also entail significant risks. Specifically investments in BRIC countries are exposed to various challenges, as institutional voids, host governments and national champions dictate the local business conditions for multinationals. A systematic investment decision process is necessary to anticipate upcoming opportunities and mitigate arising risks.

In spite of the high failure rate of cross-border investments the design of foreign investment decision processes in multinational corporations is largely unexplored. The work of Thomas Poplat is therefore addressing an important research gap. His focus on investment projects in BRIC countries further enhances the practical relevance of his study. Based on a multiple-case study design involving two multinational companies, Thomas Poplat interviewed more than 50 managers, business developers and management accountants about their experiences with decision processes for BRIC investments. The author analyzes the empirical data on the firm- and country-level and consolidates his findings in a cross-level analysis.

On the firm-level, Thomas Poplat reconstructed the two company specific investment decision processes in their real-life context based on a pre-developed foreign investment decision process model. The author analyzes the two firm-specific decision processes from various perspectives and provides explanations for cross-company differences based on his conceptual framework. Thomas Poplat argues that decision process speed and decision process comprehensiveness are the two adjusting screws for efficient investment decision-making. Thereby, he shows how industry specifics and organizational characteristics determine the investment decision uncertainty and complexity which in turn influence the underlying decision process speed and comprehensiveness. Finally, the author recommends that a troika of power, process and technology promoters represents a reasonable role constellation to balance decision process speed and comprehensiveness.

The country-level analysis is focused on identifying political-economic and socio-cultural challenges for foreign multinational corporations in each of the four BRIC countries. Thomas Poplat combines his archival analysis with the interview evidence and thereby provides valuable insights for corporations which consider investing in the BRIC countries. In the cross-level analysis he finally consolidates the firm- and country-level in order to evaluate whether the identified country-specific challenges demand for higher decision process speed or comprehensiveness.

Overall, the empirical findings provide interesting insights into corporate investment decision-making in MNEs. They are highly relevant to both researchers and practitioners. Moreover, the study presents several suggestions how to improve foreign investment decision processes. It thereby significantly contributes to the research stream of foreign investments. Considering the valuable scientific contribution and the practical relevance of Thomas Poplat's work, I wish that his thesis will gain a lot of attention in academia and practice.

Münster, July 2013 Prof. Dr. Peter Kajüter

Acknowledgement

This study was conducted during my time as a PhD student at the Chair of International Accounting at the University of Münster. The thesis was accepted as a dissertation by the Münster School of Business and Economics in July 2013.

In this acknowledgment I want to express my sincere gratitude to everyone who supported me during my thesis. First of all, I would like to thank my academic teacher Prof. Dr. Peter Kajüter who has always been approachable for discussions and proposed both effective ideas as well as solutions. He greatly contributed to the success of this study and I deeply appreciate the amount of time and energy he invested in my work. I would also like to thank Prof. Dr. Gerhard Schewe who reviewed and evaluated my study as a second referee. My sincere thanks are further given to Prof. Dr. Ulrich van Suntum for being the third referee at my disputation.

The empirical part of this thesis is based on case studies with multinational corporations. I am grateful for the support and energy all the interviewed persons dedicated to my study. Particularly, I want to thank Tom Blades who established the research partnerships for my study and enabled me to conduct this research project in the first place. I would further like to thank my sister Sabine Poplat and my colleagues Julius Hannemann and Gregor Hagemann for reviewing my thesis. Furthermore, I also want to thank Martin Merschdorf who has always been willing to discuss the research design during our frequent coffee breaks. Moreover, I am grateful to all the student assistants who transcribed the interview data for my thesis and supported me in literature research.

Nonetheless, my thesis would not have been possible without the mental support of my dear friends at the Chair of International Accounting. They made my time at the chair really enjoyable. With great pleasure I remember and will never forget the sailing cruises on the Ijsselmeer, chair excursions, the WiWi-Cup, spontaneous office parties as well as various nightlife trips in Münster, Amsterdam and Berlin. Specifically, I would like to thank Marcel Baki for the entire administrative support at the final stages of my thesis, in particular prior to my disputation. Special thanks are dedicated to Daniel Blaesing who is a perfect host for doctorial seminar preparations. Moreover, I want to thank Max Saucke and Stefan Hannen for great soccer matches which helped to clear my mind. My sincere thanks are further given to Moritz Schröder and Gregor Hagemann for spontaneous half-marathons and distracting cycling workouts. Also, I would like to thank our IUR ladies Christina Voets, Stephanie Eckerth and Daniela Peters who enriched the entire working atmosphere at our chair. I want to thank Martin Merschdorf, Kristian Bachert and Martin Nienhaus for legendary nights at Jüdefelder Street. With great joy I remember fun times at the chair with Ashly Bills, Leila Prousch and Christian Reisloh. Finally, I want to thank Matthias Moeschler for providing me with fruitful comments in accounting.

Finally but foremost, this thesis would not have been possible without my beloved family who helped me through the difficult times of my research project. I owe my deepest gratitude to my fiancé Kristin Blades. Her endless love, understanding and patience motivated me to never give up. With great anticipation I look forward to our common future in Dubai. In this regard, I also want to thank her parents Heike and Tom for their great encouragement over the past seven years and for the warm welcome into their family. Moreover, I want to thank my sister Sabine and my grandmother Emma for their great support and their positive attitudes during the final stages of my study. Most importantly, I would like to thank my parents Monika and Klaus Poplat who accompanied me during my entire life and showed great enthusiasm in my projects. I am deeply grateful for their trust, unconditional support and love. To my entire family I dedicate this thesis.

Münster, July 2013 Thomas Poplat

Overview of contents

1 Foundation 1

1.1 Introduction 1

1.2 Terms and definitions 10

1.3 Investment decision processes 16

1.4 The BRIC phenomenon 42

1.5 Prior research 51

2 Theoretical perspectives 68

2.1 Relevant firm-level theories 68

2.2 Relevant country-level theories 80

3 Research design 88

3.1 Qualitative research 88

3.2 Research process 104

3.3 Firm-level case design 100

3.4 Country-level case design 102

4 Empirical results 127

4.1 Firm-level cases 127

4.2 Country-level cases 195

4.3 Cross-level synthesis 260

5 Conclusions 270

5.1 Main results 270

5.2 Managerial implications 275

5.3 Limitations and perspectives 276

Table of contents

Index of figures .... **XVI**

Index of tables .... **XVIII**

Index of abbreviations .... **XIX**

1 Foundation **1**

1.1 Introduction 1

1.1.1 Motivation and research goals 1

1.1.2 Outline of the investigation 5

1.1.3 Scientific positioning 6

1.2 Terms and definitions 10

1.2.1 Foreign investment projects 10

1.2.2 Multinational corporations 12

1.2.3 Emerging markets 13

1.3 Investment decision processes 16

1.3.1 Corporate context 16

1.3.1.1 Corporate goals 16

1.3.1.2 Value based management 19

1.3.1.3 International management philosophies 21

1.3.2 Single phases and decision process success 22

1.3.2.1 Initialization 24

1.3.2.2 Approval 25

1.3.2.3 Implementation 27

1.3.2.4 Start-up and control 29

1.3.2.5 Investment decision process success 31

1.3.3 Specific foreign investment decisions 33

1.3.3.1 Target market decision 34

1.3.3.2 Timing decision 35

1.3.3.3 Allocation decision 37

1.3.3.4 Coordination decision 39

1.4 The BRIC phenomenon 42

1.4.1 Economic prospects 43

1.4.2 FDI prospects ... 44
1.4.3 Political power ... 46
1.4.4 Institutional environment ... 47
1.4.5 Emerging market multinationals ... 50
1.5 Prior research ... 51
1.5.1 Research field characteristics ... 51
1.5.2 Investment decisions ... 54
1.5.3 Investment decision processes ... 59
1.5.4 Conclusions ... 64

2 Theoretical perspectives ... 68
2.1 Relevant firm-level theories ... 68
2.1.1 Behavioral decision theory ... 69
2.1.2 Behavioral theory of foreign investments ... 71
2.1.3 Agency theory ... 74
2.1.4 Promotor model ... 76
2.1.5 Summary ... 79
2.2 Relevant country-level theories ... 80
2.2.1 Cost of doing business abroad and liability of foreignness ... 81
2.2.2 Liability of outsidership ... 85
2.2.3 Disadvantage of foreignness ... 86
2.2.4 Summary ... 87

3 Research design ... 88
3.1 Qualitative research ... 88
3.1.1 Overview ... 88
3.1.2 Case study research ... 93
3.1.3 Selection rationale ... 97
3.2 Case study design ... 98
3.2.1 Case company selection ... 99
3.2.2 Firm-level case design ... 100
3.2.3 Country-level case design ... 102
3.3 Research process ... 104
3.3.1 Data collection ... 105

3.3.1.1 Firm-level data ... 113
3.3.1.2 Country-level data ... 116
3.3.2 Data analysis ... 118
3.3.3 Review of the research process ... 123

4 Empirical results ... 127
4.1 Firm-level cases ... 127
4.1.1 GasCo Case ... 127
4.1.1.1 Company profile ... 127
4.1.1.2 Investment profiles ... 127
4.1.1.3 Foreign investment decision process ... 129
4.1.1.3.1 Initialization ... 129
4.1.1.3.2 Approval ... 135
4.1.1.3.3 Implementation ... 140
4.1.1.3.4 Start-up and control ... 146
4.1.2 TechCo Case ... 149
4.1.2.1 Company profile ... 149
4.1.2.2 Investment profiles ... 150
4.1.2.3 Foreign investment decision process ... 151
4.1.2.3.1 Initialization ... 151
4.1.2.3.2 Approval ... 157
4.1.2.3.3 Implementation ... 160
4.1.2.3.4 Start-up and control ... 164
4.1.3 Cross-company analysis ... 169
4.1.3.1 Phase-specific analysis ... 169
4.1.3.1.1 Initialization ... 170
4.1.3.1.2 Approval ... 175
4.1.3.1.3 Implementation ... 180
4.1.3.1.4 Start-up and control ... 184
4.1.3.2 Discussion ... 187
4.1.3.2.1 Decision process speed ... 188
4.1.3.2.2 Decision process comprehensiveness ... 189
4.1.3.2.3 Conclusion ... 191

4.2 Country-level cases ... 195
4.2.1 Brazil case ... 195
4.2.1.1 Political-economic characteristics ... 195
4.2.1.1.1 Domestic economy ... 195
4.2.1.1.2 Foreign investment projects ... 198
4.2.1.1.3 Infrastructure ... 200
4.2.1.2 Socio-cultural characteristics ... 202
4.2.1.2.1 Education ... 202
4.2.1.2.2 Society ... 203
4.2.1.2.3 Informal networks ... 204
4.2.1.3 Summary ... 205
4.2.2 Russia case ... 206
4.2.2.1 Political-economic characteristics ... 206
4.2.2.1.1 Domestic economy ... 206
4.2.2.1.2 Foreign investment projects ... 209
4.2.2.1.3 Infrastructure ... 212
4.2.2.2 Socio-cultural characteristics ... 214
4.2.2.2.1 Education ... 214
4.2.2.2.2 Society ... 215
4.2.2.2.3 Informal networks ... 217
4.2.2.3 Summary ... 219
4.2.3 India case ... 219
4.2.3.1 Political-economic characteristics ... 219
4.2.3.1.1 Domestic economy ... 219
4.2.3.1.2 Foreign investment projects ... 221
4.2.3.1.3 Infrastructure ... 224
4.2.3.2 Socio-cultural characteristics ... 227
4.2.3.2.1 Education ... 227
4.2.3.2.2 Society ... 229
4.2.3.2.3 Informal networks ... 231
4.2.3.3 Summary ... 233
4.2.4 China case ... 234

4.2.4.1 Political-economic characteristics 234

4.2.4.1.1 Domestic economy 234

4.2.4.1.2 Foreign investment projects 237

4.2.4.1.3 Infrastructure 241

4.2.4.2 Socio-cultural characteristics 242

4.2.4.2.1 Education 242

4.2.4.2.2 Society 245

4.2.4.2.3 Informal networks 250

4.2.4.3 Summary 253

4.2.5 Cross-country discussion 253

4.2.5.1 Political-economic characteristics 253

4.2.5.2 Socio-cultural characteristics 256

4.3 Cross-level synthesis 260

4.3.1 Overview 260

4.3.2 Phase-specific comparison 261

4.3.2.1 Initialization 261

4.3.2.2 Approval 263

4.3.2.3 Implementation 264

4.3.2.4 Start-up and control 266

5 Conclusions 270

5.1 Main results 270

5.2 Managerial implications 275

5.3 Limitations and perspectives 276

Appendix A: Prior Research 281

Appendix B: Kick-off interview questions 289

Appendix C: List of interviews 300

List of references 301

Index of figures

Figure 1-1: Outline of the investigation ... 5
Figure 1-2: Foreign market entry modes ... 11
Figure 1-3: Corporate goal and management layers ... 17
Figure 1-4: Shareholder value network and the influence of investments ... 20
Figure 1-5: The investment process and related management accounting tasks 23
Figure 1-6: Success of investment decision processes ... 32
Figure 1-7: International investment timing strategies ... 36
Figure 1-8: Geographic configuration alternatives ... 38
Figure 1-9: Coordination mechanism in MNCs ... 40
Figure 1-10: Population and share of world GDP of G7 and BRIC countries ... 44
Figure 1-11: Inward Greenfield investment value: BRIC vs. Germany ... 45
Figure 1-12: Research field characteristics ... 52
Figure 1-13: Classification of prior research ... 54
Figure 2-1: Main agency relationships in the capital allocation process ... 75
Figure 2-2: The promotor model in the context of foreign investments ... 78
Figure 2-3: Theoretical firm-level framework ... 79
Figure 2-4: Liability of foreignness and cost of doing business abroad approach ... 83
Figure 3-1: Basic types of case study research designs ... 94
Figure 3-2: Visualization of firm-level analysis dimensions ... 100
Figure 3-3: Firm-level case study design ... 101
Figure 3-4: Visualization of country-level analysis dimensions ... 103
Figure 3-5: Country-level case study design ... 104
Figure 3-6: Interview process ... 106
Figure 3-7: Interviewee identification process ... 107
Figure 3-8: Development of the pool of interview questions ... 109
Figure 3-9: Interview data sorted by company ... 114
Figure 3-10: GasCo interview statistic by informants' position ... 115
Figure 3-11: TechCo interview statistic by informants' position ... 115
Figure 3-12: Interview data sorted by country ... 116
Figure 3-13: Interview data by country and company ... 117

Figure 3-14: Schematic illustration of the data analysis process 121
Figure 4-1: Initialization phase at GasCo 129
Figure 4-2: Approval phase at GasCo 135
Figure 4-3: Implementation phase at GasCo 140
Figure 4-4: Start-up & control phase at GasCo 146
Figure 4-5: Initialization phase at TechCo 152
Figure 4-6: Approval phase at TechCo 157
Figure 4-7: Implementation phase at TechCo 161
Figure 4-8: Start-up & control phase at TechCo 165
Figure 4-9: Example explanation for process-related differences between GasCo and TechCo 170
Figure 4-10: Internal investment drivers GasCo and TechCo 173
Figure 4-11: Approval processes and agency relations 176
Figure 4-12: Promotor troikas in the implementation phases of GasCo and TechCo 182
Figure 4-13: Trade-off between decision process speed and decision process comprehensiveness 187
Figure 4-14: Context dependent investment decision process model 192
Figure 4-15: Influences of promotors on decision process speed and comprehensiveness 193
Figure 4-16: Country balance of speed and comprehensiveness 260
Figure 4-17: Country-specific initialization process speed and comprehensiveness 261
Figure 4-18: Country-specific approval process speed and comprehensiveness 263
Figure 4-19: Country-specific implementation process speed and comprehensiveness 264
Figure 4-20: Country-specific start-up and control process speed and comprehensiveness 267
Figure 5-1: Firm-level results 271
Figure 5-2: Cross-level results 274

Index of tables

Table 1-1: BRIC country classification by major international institutions 15

Table 1-2: Composite Index of National Capabilities (percent of world total) and population 47

Table 3-1: Differences between qualitative and quantitative research 89

Table 3-2: Principles of qualitative research 90

Table 3-3: Quality factors for qualitative research designs 92

Table 3-4: Qualitative content analysis approaches 118

Table 4-1: Initialization process influences of GasCo and TechCo 170

Table 4-2: Approval process influences of GasCo and TechCo 175

Table 4-3: Implementation process influences of GasCo and TechCo 180

Table 4-4: Start-up and control process influences of GasCo and TechCo 184

Table 4-5: Political-economic characteristics of BRIC countries 254

Table 4-6: Socio-cultural characteristics of BRIC countries 256

Index of abbreviations

ARR	Accounting rate of return
BB	Betriebs-Berater (journal)
BCG	Boston Consulting Group
Bd.	Band
BRIC	Brazil, Russia, India and China
Capex	Capital expenditures
CAPM	Capital asset pricing model
CDBA	Costs of doing business abroad
CEO	Chief Executive Officer
Cf.	Compare for
CFO	Chief Financial Officer
CFROI	Cash flow return on investment
CIMA	Chartered Institute of Management Accounting
CINC	Composite Index of National Capabilities
CMA	Comparative management accounting
COO	Country of origin
CPI	Corruption Perception Index
CSF	Critical success factor
DAC	Development assistance committee
DAX	Deutscher Aktienindex
DCF	Discounted cash flow
DPC	Decision process comprehensiveness
DPS	Decision process speed
EBIT	Earnings before interest and taxes
E.G.	Exempli gratia
EMNC	Emerging market multinationals
EVA	Economic value added
FDI	Foreign direct investment
FiCo	Finance & Controlling
GAINS	Gestalt approach of international business strategies
GDP	Gross domestic product
GNI	Gross national income
HR	Human resources

I-proposal	Investment proposal
IC	Investment Committee
IMF	International Monetary Fund
IPC	Intellectual property rights
IPO	Initial Public Offering
IRR	Internal rate of return
IT	Information technology
KPI	Key performance indicators
LOF	Liability of foreignness
LOO	Liability of outsidership
M&A	Mergers and acquisitions
MAS	Management Accounting Systems
MNC	Multinational corporations
MNE	Multinational enterprise
MRTP	Monopoly and Restrictive Trade Practices Act
NPV	Net Present Value
OECD	Organization of Economic Development and Cooperation
OPEX	Operational expenditures
P	Page
P&L	Profit and loss
p-proposal	project proposal
PAC	Growth Acceleration Program
PESTEL	Political, Economic, Social, Technological, Environmental
PPP	Purchasing power parity
QDA	Qualitative data analysis
R&D	Research and development
ROCE	Return on capital employed
ROIC	Return on invested capital
RTE	Free and Compulsory Education Act
SCM	Supply chain management
SMART	Simple, maintenance-friendly, affordable, reliable, timely-to-market
SME	Small and medium-sized enterprise
SOE	State-owned enterprises
SVA	Shareholder Value Added
TFS	TechCo financial services

TRE	TechCo real estate
TSR	Total shareholder return
UN	United Nations
UNCTAD	United Nations Conference on Trade and Development
US	United States
WACC	Weighted average cost of capital
WTO	World Trade Organization
WWW	Worldwide web

1 Foundation

1.1 Introduction

1.1.1 Motivation and research goals

> *"Today the changing nature of competition and the increasing pressure of globalization make investment the most critical determinant of competitive advantage."*[1]

In 1998, *Michael E. Porter* – who is one of the most-cited strategy researchers – already highlighted the importance of investment decisions within increasingly globalized economies for creating and defending competitive advantages. In 2013, globalization has entered a new phase in which the global economic power is shifting to emerging economies.[2] As a consequence, this **rebalancing of the global economy** creates new challenges for internationally operating companies.

According to the *International Monetary Fund* (IMF), 2013 is expected to be a turning point within the world economy. In this year the industrial production of emerging markets will overtake those of the developed economies[3] for the first time in history. In 2020, almost 50% of the worldwide GDP growth will be attributed to the **BRIC** countries[4]. The dynamic economic development will inevitably create emerging market multi-nationals (EMNCs)[5] which are serious competitors in their host markets. Moreover, these national champions will seek to dominate their industries on a global scale.[6]

In return, multinational corporations (MNCs) take their business overseas to the developing world in order to strengthen their positions in growth markets. However, developing markets also entail **significant risks**. In particular, BRIC investments are exposed to various challenges, as institutional voids, host governments and "national champions" dictate local business conditions for MNCs.[7] The failure of the *ThyssenKrupp* investment in a steel plant in Brazil is a current example in this respect.[8] Therefore, it seems necessary to design systematic investment decision processes to mitigate these arising risks and exploit upcoming opportunities.

---

1 *Porter* (1998), p. 431.

2 Cf. *Roberts* (2011), p. 6. The terms "emerging" and "developing" economies, markets or countries will be used interchangeably hereafter.

3 The terms "developed" and "advanced" economies, markets or countries will be used synonymously in the following.

4 The acronym BRIC means Brazil, Russia, India and China and was invented by Jim O'Neill, a chief economist at *Goldman Sachs* in 2001; cf. *O'Neill* (2001).

5 Emerging market multinational (EMNC) will be used for multinational corporations having their origin in one of the BRIC countries.

6 Cf. *Khanna/Palepu* (2006), p. 62.

7 Cf. *Holtbrügge/Baron* (2011), p. 109.

8 For a documentation of *ThyssenKrupp's* investment project in Brazil see *Blasberg/Kotynek* (2012).

Yet, investment decision-making is not solely germane to implement corporate strategies and create future performance potentials from a firm-level perspective but is also a main determinant for the overall **economic development** and **social well-being**, e.g. by creating new employment.[9] Foreign investment projects are not always positively perceived in the home country due to the associated negative consequences for domestic corporate locations, such as relocations of labor to foreign low-wage countries. But in particular **German MNCs** are able to offset or even overcompensate their domestic declining demand by strengthening their international presence in emerging economies, as it can be observed during the recent European sovereign-debt crisis. This illustrates that foreign investment projects may have positive influences on the domestic position of MNCs and their environment due to stabilizing effects from foreign activities and growth markets.

The increasing practical relevance of foreign investments in Germany is also underpinned by the significantly increasing **foreign direct investment (FDI) activity** of German firms. The total outward FDI flows of German companies rose from USD 39 billion in 1995 to its peak of USD 164 billion in 2007.[10] The cumulative outward stock of German FDI amounted to USD 1.4 trillion in 2011.[11] These numbers indicate Germany's long-term globalization process. In contrast to small and midsize companies (SMEs) from other countries, German SMEs managed to emerge as world leaders in their niche markets.[12] This tendency may explain that the country was the world export champion between 2003 and 2008.[13] Thereby, exporting generally represents a preliminary stage of internationalization with further resource commitments – such as Greenfield investment or cross-border acquisitions – as foreign market know-how increases.[14] Therefore, the number and volume of FDIs is expected to further increase in the future.

However, as opposed to foreign entry modes with lower resource commitments, FDIs involve **complex decision processes**. A variety of investment configuration decisions has to be made, e.g. the target market selection, which are not relevant for domestic investments. Due to the international dimensions further external influences, such as exchange or inflation rates, have to be controlled.[15] Process complexity and **uncertainty** are driven by multiple agency-relations, unfamiliar economic environments or cultural distances, to name just a few.[16] Surprisingly, the review of prior research indicates that foreign investment decision processes within MNCs are almost unexplored. *Swoboda* criticized that the international management literature fails to provide practical recommendations concerning the design of internationalization processes.[17] From a

9 Cf. *Harris/Raviv* (1996), p. 1139.
10 Cf. *OECD* (2010b), p. 81.
11 Cf. *UNCTAD* (2012), p. 173.
12 Cf. *Simon* (2007a), p. 11.
13 Cf. *Jeremias* (2012), p. 239.
14 Cf. *Mutinelli/Piscitello* (1998), p. 495.
15 Cf. *Becker* (2005), p. 2.
16 Cf. *Fox* (1999), p. 47.
17 Cf. *Swoboda* (2001), p. 4.

theoretical point of view, foreign investment decision processes offer a variety of interesting research aspects due to their multidisciplinary nature.

Nonetheless, prior research is biased by focusing too narrowly on the investment decision evaluation with more or less sophisticated capital budgeting techniques. However, the investigated theory-practice gap of the 1970s – between theoretically proposed and practically applied capital budgeting models – was closed by the development of computer technologies and the rise of consulting firms which accelerated the **diffusion of sophisticated capital budgeting tools.**[18] Furthermore, this work takes the view that shareholder value is not solely created by applying sophisticated capital budgeting methods, but particularly through the investment case development in creating shareholder value accumulation. For this reason, this study is primarily interested in gaining a deeper understanding of the investment decision process as well as the underlying critical success factors.[19]

Certainly, investment decisions rely on business experience and intuition. But irreversible strategic investments involving high capital expenditures (Capex) should be thoroughly reflected, prepared and decided. For instance, *Barkema et al.* identified that it is crucial to adapt management tools to the challenges of internationalization in order to create shareholder value via foreign direct investments.[20] Structured investment decision processes and sophisticated capital budgeting models are assumed to be capable of supporting these requirements. Thereby, MNCs have to balance the conflicting demands of **decision process speed** and **decision process comprehensiveness** to keep pace with the dynamic environment within the BRIC countries.

To sum up, only a few studies have been undertaken to understand unfolding foreign investment decision processes within MNCs, so that the present work intends to address this research gap. Due to the low state of exploratory research and the high practical relevance of emerging market investments, the **overall objective** is to investigate decision processes for cross-border investments into BRIC countries in its real-life context within MNCs. This general goal can be divided into three sub-goals:

- The **first sub-goal** is to describe the foreign investment decision process of multinational corporations. Therefore, a multiple case study design is applied to empirically investigate two company-specific foreign investment decision processes. A cross-company analysis intends to explain process-related similarities and differences. Subsequently, critical success factors for the design of investment decision processes are discussed against the theoretical foundation **(firm-level)**.
- The **second sub-goal** is to explore country-specific challenges related to Greenfield investment projects in BRIC countries. Based on the investigated BRIC investments within the two MNCs, country-specific challenges are described and compared by political-economic and socio-cultural aspects **(country-level)**.

18 Cf. *Haka* (2007), p. 705.
19 Cf. *Mittermüller/von Nitzsch* (2008), p. 779.
20 Cf. *Barkema et al.* (1997).

- The **third sub-goal** is to evaluate country-specific challenges along the investigated foreign investment decision processes by consolidating the firm-level and country-level results of the two preceding sub-goals. Thereby, the influence of the country-specific challenges on the identified critical success factors is discussed to draw analytical recommendations for the design of decision processes for investments in the BRIC countries **(cross-level)**.

To achieve these goals, foreign investment decision processes and their underlying success factors are empirically investigated in two German MNCs by applying a multiple case study design. Country-specific challenges for foreign MNCs are explored by focusing on interviews regarding investment projects targeting BRIC economies. This study aspires to reach **practical relevance** by identifying elements of the decision process that are critical for foreign investment strategies in BRIC countries. Country-specific challenges are evaluated according to their importance for the investment decision process.

The **theoretical relevance** arises due to the low state of research regarding foreign investment decision processes in MNCs. Furthermore, the future economic importance of the BRIC countries creates the necessity to deal with their country-specific challenges and related solutions to cope with them. Therefore, business administration – as an applied science – should deliver starting points for managers to overcome these country-specific challenges. Building on this, the **main contributions** of this study are threefold. First, this study contributes to a more **comprehensive understanding** of foreign investment decision processes in MNCs based on a broad interview database. Second, **BRIC country challenges** are explored for the first time taking a German MNCs perspective, so that results may differ compared to studies based on Anglo-American MNCs. Third, this investigation provides a **multi-perspective view** on foreign investment decision processes by analyzing interviews with managers, business developers and management accountants in order to consider the interdisciplinary character of the research object. Due to the practical barriers in business administration of gaining access to qualified interviewees, the broad and differentiated interview data base represents a strength of this study.

To sum up, this process-oriented study[21] contributes in gaining a better understanding of the dynamics in MNCs by observing sequences of events and their underlying generative mechanisms that are germane for foreign investments to be implemented in real-life contexts.[22]

---

21 A detailed description of the characteristics of process studies and theories can be found at *Mohr* (1982). One important aspect is to differentiate between a process theory and a variance theory. A process theory aims to explain how certain outcomes come about rather than to explain different variances in outcomes. Similarly, a process theory comprises a temporal order of states and phases rather than relations of dependent on independent variables without temporal structure, c.f. *van de Ven/Huber* (1990), p. 213.

22 Cf. *Tsoukas* (1989), p. 522.

1.1.2 Outline of the investigation

The outline of the investigation is depicted in Figure 1-1 showing that the present study consists of five chapters. Following the introductory elaborations on the research motivation and the underlying goals, **chapter one** continues with a presentation of the main scientific objectives and epistemological streams of business administration in order to position the present work. Subsequently, relevant terms and definitions for the further analysis are elaborated. A basic comprehension of investment decision processes within the context of shareholder-value oriented corporations is subsequently provided. Besides the illustration of a process understanding, this section serves to highlight the interdependent relationship between corporate objectives and investment decisions. The section closes with a brief description of decision parameters that have to be specifically considered within foreign investment decision processes. The investigation proceeds by explaining the background of the BRIC phenomenon and its growing importance for MNCs which represents the main selection criterion for the underlying study. Finally, a research gap is identified by reviewing prior research with respect to foreign investment decision processes.

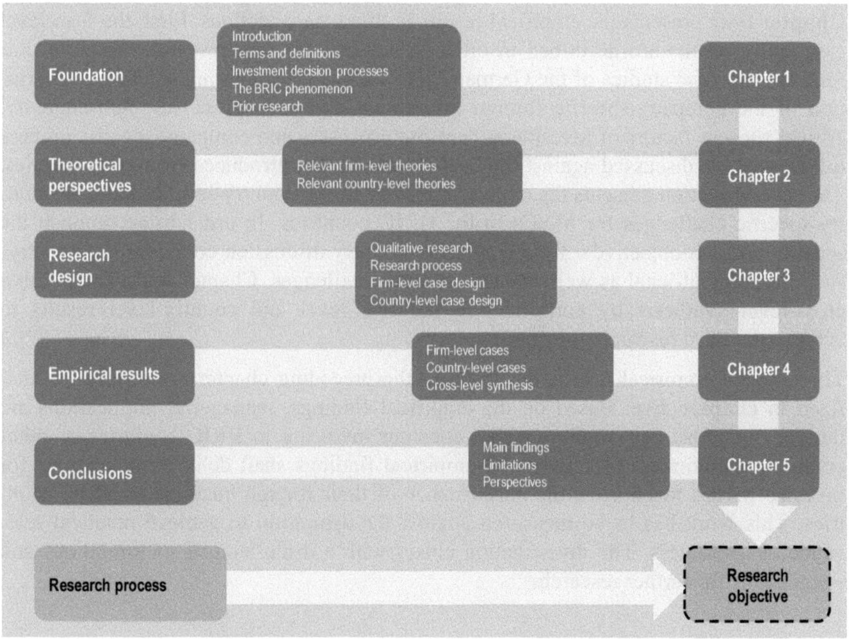

Figure 1-1: Outline of the investigation

Chapter two lays the theoretical foundation of this study. Firm-level theories in general and international firm-level theories are differentiated. The behavioral decision theory, agency theory and the promotor model have been selected as general firm-level theories. Subsequently, two international firm-level theories are introduced. The behavioral theory of *Aharoni* and the internationalization process model of the *Uppsala school* are explicitly concentrated on internationalization processes on the firm-level. This "analytical toolkit" or "theoretical lens" serves to analyze the empirical findings on the firm-level against this theoretical background. The next section presents relevant country-level theories which focus on explaining why and how country-specific challenges are related to foreign investments. Moreover, these concepts are introduced in order to highlight the influence of the internationality on the investment decision process and why country-specific challenges in the BRIC countries can be expected.

The research design of the present work is presented in **chapter three**, which is split into four major sections. In the first part, a brief overview of qualitative research and its underlying research principles is given. Characteristics of case study research are elaborated by illustrating alternative research design configurations. The selection rationale for the case study method in the present research context is disclosed thereinafter. Subsequently, the research process is revealed by describing the data collection and data analysis procedures. The specific firm-level and country-level case designs are elaborated in the last two main sections in chapter three.

Chapter four presents the empirical results in three main sections. First, the firm-level case study results are described in order to achieve the first research objective. For this, the two case studies of the German MNCs focus on delivering a detailed description of the company-specific foreign investment decisions processes. Subsequently, critical success factors of investment decision processes and company-specific process differences are discussed against the background of the introduced firm-level theories. The second section presents the empirical results on the country-level to indicate country-specific challenges for MNCs in the BRIC countries. In order to accomplish the second research objective a following cross-country discussion confronts the country-specific political-legal as well as socio-cultural challenges. Chapter four closes with a cross-level synthesis by consolidating the firm-level and country-level results to achieve the third research objective.

The detailed empirical results disclosed in the preceding chapter are briefly summarized in **chapter five**. Based on the empirical findings, managerial implications are derived for those corporations which consider investing in BRIC countries or other emerging economies. Moreover, the empirical findings shall deliver implications for invested MNCs to improve the performance of their foreign business in BRIC countries. This work has to be measured against the aspiration to achieve practical relevance or usefulness. The investigation closes with a discussion of its limitations and suggestions for further research.

1.1.3 Scientific positioning

This section serves to briefly introduce the philosophy of sciences and the underlying scientific position of the present study. Philosophy of sciences ("science of science") involves the question of *how* scientific progress can be achieved and new knowledge can be obtained. For this reason business administration as a centerpiece of economic sciences is subject to considerations of the philosophy of science.[23] Philosophy of science can be classified as a **meta-scientific discipline** to the individual sciences because it reflects what science is and what science could be. It articulates hypotheses about the science itself. In addition, the philosophy of science deals with the term, the classification, the principles of knowledge, the methods, the languages, the assumptions, the objectives and results of the single scientific disciplines.[24]

The discussion of objectives and basic procedures of science to generate knowledge are also parts of the philosophy of science. Science is not exercised as an end in itself, but to pursue designated objectives. For science in business management **four main objectives** prevail.[25]

(1) **Descriptive target of science**: A fundamental target of sciences in business management is the precise description of the subjects under consideration. In order to create a clear communication, terms, elements and features in business management must be defined.

(2) **Theoretical target of science**: The explanation and prediction of the subjects under consideration are elements of the theoretical target. For this reason, theoretical statements must be formulated as hypotheses ("cause-and-effect-relationships").

(3) **Pragmatic target of science**: If research in business management aims to provide decision support, a pragmatic target of science is followed. Through predictive abilities of a theory, recommendations for the composition of corporate structures can be derived. The former "cause-and-effect-relationships" are transformed into instructions for achieving practical objectives.

(4) **Normative target of science**: If science claims to articulate values how a corporation *should* act in specific contexts, an exchange between practice and theory is needed. These statements are usually not based on empirical data.

This work pursues an explorative descriptive target as corporate investment decision processes are reconstructed in their real-life context and country-specific challenges are presented. Furthermore, this study aims to provide recommendation with respect to efficient decision process designs. In order to highlight *how* these new insights can be gained, the **main epistemological schools** are presented hereinafter. Highly simplified, four epistemological basic positions are identified.[26] The four epistemological schools can be roughly displayed in a two-dimensional coordinate system. *Rationalism* and *empiricism* constitute the dichotomy regarding the importance of **experiences** on the horizontal axis; while *constructivism* and *realism* are the opposites concerning **reality construction** on the vertical axis.

The classical *rationalism* has its roots in the ancient science. Knowledge is based on understanding and logical reasoning, independently of experience. Consequently, the

23 Cf. *Fülbier* (2004), p. 271; or *Kornmeier* (2007), p. 3f.
24 Cf. *Fülbier* (2004), p. 266.
25 Cf. *Schweitzer* (1978), p. 2ff.
26 Cf. *Kornmeier* (2007), p. 29.

strict rationalism is dominated by **deductive reasoning** ("from the general to the specific"). In *empiricism*, the sensory perception or experience are considered as the main source of epistemological progress. In contrast to the rationalism, the empiricism is characterized by **inductive reasoning**. For instance, an explorative investigation of decision processes without a theoretical preconception would be characterized as a purely inductive study. According to the empiricism, theories or rules are derived from a limited number of individual cases (from the specific to the general). This work combines deductive and inductive elements by developing an investment decision process model prior to the empirical investigations which is further refined within the course of the explorative case studies.

Representatives of the *realism* assume that there is an **independent reality**. Through human perception or thinking substantial parts of the reality can be reconstructed. Hence, humans can perceive things, phenomena or events without distortion.[27] The *constructivism* takes the view that reality depends on the individual subject and is a construct of the human spirit. This obviously means that a **subjectively perceived reality** differs among individuals and is not objectively describable.[28] All knowledge is constructed in as much as it is contingent on convention, human perception, and social experience.[29] Constructivism proposes new definitions for knowledge and truth that form a new paradigm based on inter-subjectivity and viability instead of objectivity and truth. Since generation of knowledge is dependent on humans, a subject independent reality cannot be described. For this reason, the value or quality of a theory is measured by the adequacy for predictions and practical recommendations for action.

But the radical positions of rationalism, empiricism, realism and constructivism are more or less outdated and seldom applied in their strictest sense in business management research.[30] Moreover, modern business management research combines elements of the four concepts. Thereby, two **predominant research programs** have been evolved in business management research.[31] The concept of critical rationalism – advanced by *Popper* – and the constructivism of the *Erlangen school* – advanced by *Lorenzen* – are the prevailing research programs in business administration in recent years.[32]

Critical rationalists hold that scientific theories should be rationally criticized, and (if they have empirical content) must be tested to falsify them. The basic assumption is that human reason is fallible, why results of rationalistic argumentation are not irrefutable.[33] Hence, knowledge can never be proven as ultimately true. Instead, knowledge is only temporarily true until it is falsified. Hypotheses must be formulated in a way that they are consistent and falsifiable by empirical testing. Not falsifiable theories are

---

27 Cf. *Frank* (2007), sp. 2012.
28 Cf. *Jonassen* (1991), p. 9.
29 Cf. *Jonassen* (1991), p. 10.
30 Cf. *Kern* (1979), p. 16.
31 Cf. *Kornmeier* (2007), p. 39.
32 Cf. *Fülbier* (2004), p. 268.
33 Cf. *Fülbier* (2004), p. 269.

worthless or non-scientific because they cannot fail in reality.[34] Vice versa, hypotheses gain in scientific value if they provide greater opportunity for falsification, e.g. the hypothesis "*if company A invests ten percent of sales in R&D, it will be five percent more profitable than its competitors*" is easier to falsify than "*if company A invests ten percent of sales in R&D, it will be more profitable than its competitors*". Consequently, the first hypothesis has higher information content and is scientifically more meaningful than the second. Critical rationalists regard the falsification of theories and hypotheses as the main procedure for achieving scientific cognition. By advancing theories through permanently setting up, testing and rejecting hypotheses, truth is approximated.[35]

The **constructivism** of the *Erlangen school* should not be mistaken for the radical constructivism. The *Erlangen* version represents an epistemological position which criticizes philosophy of science and science in general.[36] The knowledge is the result of argumentation and discussion of experts in a special field of studies. On the basis of theoretical considerations conclusions are drawn by the help of deductive reasoning. Since in this approach the fallibility of human reasoning performance is recognized, these statements are not irrefutable. Opposite to the critical rationalism the constructivism postulates that methodologically sound decisions can be made.[37]

This work basically assumes that reality is rather socially constructed or perceived than objectively observable. As a consequence this work is more strongly influenced by the constructivist concept of reality. Based on this reality comprehension an open, communicative and context considering research design is necessary for empirical analyses.[38] This is consistent to the applied **case study design** in the present context. For instance, inter-personal misunderstandings can be clarified during the interview sessions. In contrast, common survey-designs assume an objective reality which can be mirrored and is independent of human experience and perception.

Furthermore, the present study uses an **empirical research strategy**[39] to achieve its scientific objectives because a multiple case study design has been adopted which is based on empirical interview data. Thereby, theoretical conceptions are tested, further refined or explored based on empirical data in real-life contexts of MNCs. The present work is of **qualitative-explorative** character. Thus, statistical generalization from the setting to a broader population is not intended. Moreover, the aim is to understand the

---

34 Cf. *Kornmeier* (2007), p. 41.

35 Cf. *Popper* (1994), p. XXV; or *Brühl* (2006), p. 594.

36 Cf. *Kornmeier* (2007), p. 40.

37 Cf. *Raffée/Abel* (1979), p. 6f.

38 Cf. *Wrona* (2005), p. 4.

39 Three basic research strategies can be differentiated: analytical, conceptual and empirical research strategies; cf. *Grochla* (1978), p. 79ff. The analytical research strategy seeks to simplify reality and specific problems in order to develop models which can be applied to solve these specific problems; cf. *Kaplan* (1986), p. 439. The conceptual research strategy intends to formulate interpretative-descriptive hypotheses related to a research problem. Hypotheses are not based on empirical but derived from argumentative reasoning and plausibility; cf. *Al-Laham* (1997), p. 10.

deeper structure and context of foreign investment decision processes. From an interpretative position the validity of a generalization from individual cases depends not on the representativeness of such cases in a statistical meaning.[40] Generalization validity is based on plausibility and cogency of the logical reasoning used in describing the results from cases and drawing conclusions from them.[41]

Apart from the consistent scientific positioning, the present work shares the general view of pragmatist researchers that the priority should be on answering the research questions, rather than selecting the "right" scientific method. *Tashakkori and Teddlie* (2007) describe the **pragmatic approach** as follows:

> *"Pragmatist researchers consider the research question to be more important than either the method they use or the paradigm that underlines the method. We refer to this as the 'dictatorship of the research question'."*[42]

1.2 Terms and definitions

1.2.1 Foreign investment projects

An investment is a commitment of resources in order to generate future cash flows and returns. Investment decisions belong to the tasks of strategic management to save, respectively enhance future performance potential.[43] The investment definition of this work is constricted to **strategic investments**. Strategic investments have a significant influence on the organization and its long term performance. Hence, investment decisions represent crucial management responsibilities. Managers can use investments as instruments to implement corporate strategies in order to sustain or expand competitive advantages.[44] Investments are future oriented. Hence, assumptions are required for the evaluation of projects. This means that the decision maker is confronted with **uncertainty** concerning the future external and internal conditions.[45] Predicting the events of the next twelve months is difficult enough, but looking five or ten years ahead is almost impossible due to the inability to foresee external changes in market conditions.[46]

---

40 Cf. *Yin* (2009), p. 38f.
41 Cf. *Eisenhardt/Graebner* (2007), p. 27.
42 *Tashakkori/Teddlie* (2003), p. 21.
43 Cf. *Haka* (2007), p. 698.
44 Cf. *Ott* (2000), p. 54.
45 Cf. *Haka* (2007), p. 699.
46 Cf. *Maritan* (2001), p. 515f.

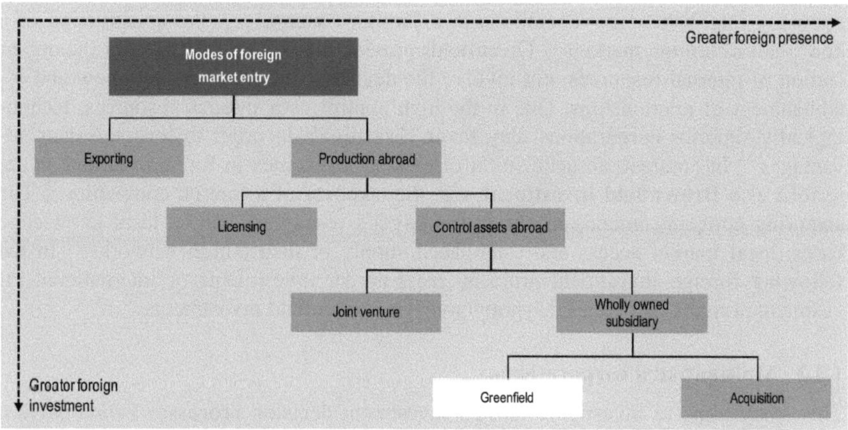

Figure 1-2: Foreign market entry modes
Adopted from *Eiteman et al.* (2010), p. 458.

Thereby, a central parameter within the foreign investment decision process is the **entry mode decision.**[47] Different criteria are germane to select an adequate market entry strategy, such as transaction costs, resource commitment, reversibility, flexibility or time-to-market.[48] As depicted in Figure 1-2 the two most challenging entry modes in terms of capital commitment and management requirements are Greenfield investments and cross-border acquisitions.[49] Partially, joint ventures could involve similar requirements due to the complexity arising from two or more joint venture partners with possible conflicting interests and high amounts of capital.[50] These three equity-based entry modes can be subsumed under the term **foreign direct investment (FDI).**[51] Thereby, the investor intends to hold a long-term interest and influence in the investment.[52] Investors who undertake FDI are usually MNCs or on the development path to become a MNC.[53] As opposed to FDI, **foreign portfolio investments** are characterized by a short- to medium-term horizon of the investor.[54]

The present work intends to investigate expansion investments in foreign countries or so called **Greenfield investments.**[55] Greenfield investments occur when an investing

---

47 Cf. *Erramilli* (1991), p. 482.

48 Cf. *Erramilli* (1991), p. 483.

49 Cf. *Johnson/Tellis* (2008), p. 2.

50 Cf. *Gilroy/Lukas* (2006), p. 448.

51 Cf. *Chang/Rosenzweig* (2001), p. 748.

52 Cf. *Shimizu et al.* (2004), p. 311.

53 Cf. *Fox* (1999), p. 48.

54 The Organization of Economic Cooperation and Development (OECD) and the International Monetary Fund (IMF) have defined an interest of more than ten percent of the stocks or voting power of a foreign company as a threshold level for long-term interests; cf. *Betschinger* (2010), p. 11.

55 Although the term *Greenfield* may also refer to domestic investments, this work uses the term exclusively in the context of foreign investment projects.

company establishes new operations in a foreign country, e.g. the construction of a new plant in foreign markets.[56] Greenfields provide the highest control over the organization of internal resources, but involve the development of local know-how and establishment of relationships. Due to the high control over internal resources, technologically superior corporations may favor Greenfields in order to leverage their advantages.[57] In contrast, an acquisition of existing capacities in foreign markets is described as a **Brownfield investment**, e.g. the takeover of a foreign competitor.[58] The acquiring company intends to obtain the target's resources such as local knowledge bases, local market access and established supply or distribution networks.[59] In the following foreign investment projects, cross-border investments or international investment projects will be used synonymously to Greenfield investments.

1.2.2 Multinational corporations

This study aims to investigate foreign investment decision processes *within* MNCs. Therefore, it is necessary to disclose a working definition for MNCs in order to define the organizational context for the following investigation of foreign investment decision processes. Nevertheless, the term "multinational corporation" is **not consistently defined** respectively understood in literature, which makes it necessary to provide a comprehension of MNCs. This section intends to give a brief overview of the tedious theoretical discussion related to the definition of MNCs. Subsequently, the working definition of multinational corporations for this investigation will be presented.

The following definitions of MNCs illustrate the diversity of this terminology.[60]

> *"Corporations [...] which have their home in one country but which operate and live under the laws and customs of other countries as well."*[61]
>
> *"A multinational firm is a firm owned by persons from many nations."*[62]
>
> *"The multinational enterprise is [...] a closely controlled single enterprise, located in markets separated by national boundaries, and operating under several governments. Its essential feature is 'unity in diversity'."*[63]
>
> *"An 'international company' may be defined as one with foreign content of 25 per cent or more; 'foreign content' defined as the proportion of sales, investment, production or employment abroad."*[64]

56 Cf. *Newburry/Zeira* (1997), p. 89.

57 Cf. *Hennart/Park* (1993), p. 1068.

58 Some authors only refer to the term Brownfield investment, when an acquired foreign target firm requires very deep restructuring; cf. *Meyer/Estrin* (2001), p. 575.

59 For a detailed meta-analysis of prior research regarding the influencing factors on foreign market entry mode decisions; cf. *Shimizu et al.* (2004).

60 For a detailed overview of different definitions for multinational corporations; cf. *Fischer* (2006), p. 15ff.

61 *Lilienthal* (1960), p. 119.

62 *Aharoni* (1971), p. 28.

63 *Behrmann* (1969), p. 62.

> *"A multinational company must possess the following five characteristics, (1) it must operate in many countries at different levels of economic development, (2) its local subsidiaries must be managed by nationals, (3) it must maintain complete industrial organizations, including research and development and manufacturing facilities, in several countries, (4) it must have a multinational central management, and (5) it must have multinational stock ownership."*[65]

> *"Transnational corporations are enterprises which own or control value-added activities in two or more countries. The usual mode of ownership and control is by foreign direct investment [...]."*[66]

A fundamental distinction between multinational and national corporations can be derived from the context and conditions in which they operate. Opposed to national enterprises, a multinational company operates in different social, political and economic conditions. Hence, MNCs are confronted with different socio-cultural norms and government regulations as well as with heterogeneous customer preferences. Therefore, the management across borders in MNCs is more **complex** and **diverse**, e.g. national corporations are concerned with the management and control of products and business functions, whereas the multinational management must also provide control over its **geographic diversity**.[67] Besides this additional global dimension, managers in MNCs are exposed to obstacles with respect to long geographic distances, time differences, language problems and national cultures.

This study uses the term multinational corporation for companies which have the two following main characteristics: (1) corporations must have **substantial foreign direct investments** in host countries, and (2) corporations must be engaged in the **active management** of these foreign assets opposed to passively managed portfolio investments.[68] The terms multinational corporation (MNC), multinational enterprise (MNE) and international corporation are interchangeably used for a corporation that conducts international business from a multitude of locations in different countries with employees from all over the world. Moreover, a significant characteristic of this understanding of MNCs is that the management disposes over a global mindset and outlook so that the operations of these corporations are not limited by national borders.[69]

1.2.3 Emerging markets

The focus of the present study is on investments in emerging economies – specifically the BRIC countries. Thus, a characterization of an emerging market country will be presented in the following. International institutions like *The World Bank, the Interna-*

---

64 *Rolfe* (1970), p. 17.

65 *Maisonrouge* (1974), p. 8.

66 *Dunning* (1993), p. 1.

67 Important strategic management decisions within international contexts will be presented in detail in section 1.3.3.

68 Cf. *Bartlett/Ghoshal* (2000), p. 2.

69 Cf. *Khambata/Ajami* (1992), p. 5.

tional Monetary Fund (IMF) or the United Nations (UN) provide different country classification schemes. Finally, the understanding of the current work is disclosed.

The World Bank defines developing countries according to the annual gross national income (GNI) per capita.[70] This classification distinguishes between low, middle and high income countries, whereas middle income countries are subdivided into lower and upper middle income countries.[71] In 2012, the annual GNI per capita thresholds were as follows: low income countries equal USD 1,025 income per capita or less; lower middle income countries between USD 1,026 and 4,035 per capita; upper middle income between USD 4,036 and USD 12,475 per capita; high income countries equal USD 12,476 per capita or higher. Developing countries are referred to low and middle income countries. The World Bank does not use the term emerging economy on purpose because their country categorization scheme aspires to be objective and does not allow a judgment about the development status on the GNI per capita ratio.[72]

Advanced and emerging/developing countries are forming the two main country categories under the **IMF** country classification. This division of the world in two groups is not based on strict criteria and takes different country aspects into account. The IMF's intention is to facilitate analysis with a meaningful method of organizing data within a wider scope.[73] Per capita income level, export diversification and integration into the global financial system are expected to have a significant influence on the classification as this data is disclosed within the *World Economic Outlook* reports. But the respective weights or the influence of other aspects are not made explicit. Although the classification criteria are not publicly available, the IMF classification criteria for developed/advanced economies are more demanding than those of the other international institutions. The IMF classification has regularly the fewest countries categorized as developed or advanced.[74]

The **United Nations** country classification is based on the Human Development Index published within the Human Development Report.[75] This approach intends to capture the multilayered nature of a country's development. The Human Development Index is a summary composite index which covers the three human development aspects of health (measured by life expectancy at birth), knowledge (measured by a combined measure of actual and expected years of schooling) and income (measured by GNI per

70 The main difference between GDP and GNI is that the latter comprises the market value of goods and services produced by state citizens and corporations regardless of their location, whereas GDP measures the market value of goods and services within a state; cf. *van den Bergh* (2009), p. 117.

71 Cf. *Gitlin/Fuentes* (2012), p. 298.

72 Cf. *The World Bank* (2012b).

73 Cf. *International Monetary Fund* (2012), p. 177.

74 One important reason for the fewer advanced economy classifications is obviously that export diversification is considered as a criterion. Oil-exporting countries such as Saudi Arabia and the United Arabic Emirates with very high GDP per capita are classified as emerging/developing country.

75 The Human Development Report is published since 1990 in order to create awareness for human development around the world. Opposed to other development reports, the well-being of people is placed within the center of this publication; cf. *The United Nations* (2012), p. 16.

capita) as an alternative to conventional measures of national development. The top quartile within the Human Development Index is classified as developed countries and those in the bottom three quartiles are rated as developing countries.

The definition of emerging markets is more focused for this study. A central characteristic is that these countries have experienced **superior economic performance** in the past and are expected to achieve **significant economic** and **political importance** in the global arena.[76] Thus, developing countries are not yet an advanced economy but are on the move to become a member of this category. These countries "emerge" from a less-developed country to an advanced industrialized nation.[77] This convergence is attributed to the high dynamics of economic growth.[78] In many cases, the development of political freedom, human rights or anti-corruption measures cannot keep up the pace with economic liberalization in emerging markets.[79] To sum up, these are the major reasons why investment projects targeting these markets are in the focus of many researchers or the business press because they provide huge potentials on the one side, but also entail significant risks due to institutional issues on the other side.[80]

For the purpose of the present work the terms emerging markets, emerging economies, developing countries or transition economies will be used synonymously. Investment projects in Brazil, Russia, India and China (BRIC) – representative for the emerging market economies – will be investigated in this context. These four countries are on the fast move to become developed/advanced or industrialized economies and received enormous attention since the publication of *Goldman Sachs* and its invention of the BRIC-concept.[81] A country-specific presentation and analysis with respect to foreign investment processes will be conducted in the course of the empirical results presentation within the country-level investigation of the present work in section 4.2. The country classification of these four emerging countries is presented below in Table 1-1.[82]

	The World Bank[83]	IMF[84]	United Nations
Brazil	Upper-middle income	Emerging/developing country	Developing economy
Russia	Upper-middle income	Emerging/developing country	Transition economy
India	Lower middle income	Emerging/developing country	Developing economy
China	Upper-middle income	Emerging/developing country	Developing economy

Table 1-1: BRIC country classification by major international institutions
Adopted from *Graser* (2011), p. 53.

76 Cf. *Dehnen* (2012), p. 16.
77 Cf. *Bekaert/Harvey* (2002), p. 429.
78 Cf. *Ernst et al.* (2012), p. 147.
79 Cf. *Meyer/Thu Tran* (2006), p. 179.
80 Cf. *Peng et al.* (2008), p. 924.
81 Cf. *Koubek* (2010), p. 324.
82 The BRIC phenomenon will be explained in section 1.4.
83 Cf. *The World Bank* (2012b).
84 Cf. *International Monetary Fund* (2012), p. 194f.

1.3 Investment decision processes

The objective of this section is to provide a comprehension of an ideal-typical investment decision process in an international investment context. This is necessary to develop a basic understanding of investment decision processes and to set a benchmark for the comparison with the empirically-grounded real-typical investment decision processes. Furthermore, a common investment decision process success definition is introduced.

1.3.1 Corporate context

This section intends to classify investments and their importance – either domestic or foreign – within the general corporate **goal system** as well as to highlight the crucial influence of corporate goals on investment decisions and the underlying processes. Furthermore, the connection between the overall corporate goals, management accounting, capital budgeting and investments will be disclosed. An introduction of corporate goal systems seems to be necessary at this point because investment targets should be incrementally derived from the overall corporate goals.[85]

After the general importance of goals and the basic targets of corporations have been introduced, the value based management approach will be presented which aspires to integrate the achievement of these basic corporate objectives. According to the development of the last two decades, **value based management** (shareholder value orientation) turned out as the prevailing performance management concept among capital market oriented MNCs.[86]

1.3.1.1 Corporate goals

One of the basic **management responsibilities** is to articulate corporate goals[87] in order to explicitly define the perceptions of the management about the future corporate position.[88] Additionally, the management has to decide about strategic programs or measures to achieve the desired positions. Thereby, investments are crucial instruments to shape the corporate future position and pursue formulated goals. Strategic objectives and corporate visions can serve as frame of reference for the subsequent management levels to reduce decision uncertainties about the future corporate position.[89] In the following, three basic corporate goals and the role of investment will be explained: **Performance potential**, **performance** and **liquidity**.[90] The long-term existence of corporations is predetermined by the corporate capabilities to create, maintain and leverage strategic performance potentials. Performance potentials are classi-

---

85 Cf. *Dahlhaus* (2009), p. 15.

86 Cf. *Kajüter* (2011), p. 29.

87 In the following the terms targets, objectives or aims will be used synonymously for corporate goals.

88 For an overview of different goal functions; cf. *Welge/Al-Laham* (2012), p. 201ff.

89 Cf. *Al-Laham* (1997), p. 91.

90 Cf. *Gälweiler* (2005), p. 163f.

fied according to the place of origin in external (e.g. market-driven) and internal (e.g. cost-driven) performance potentials.[91]

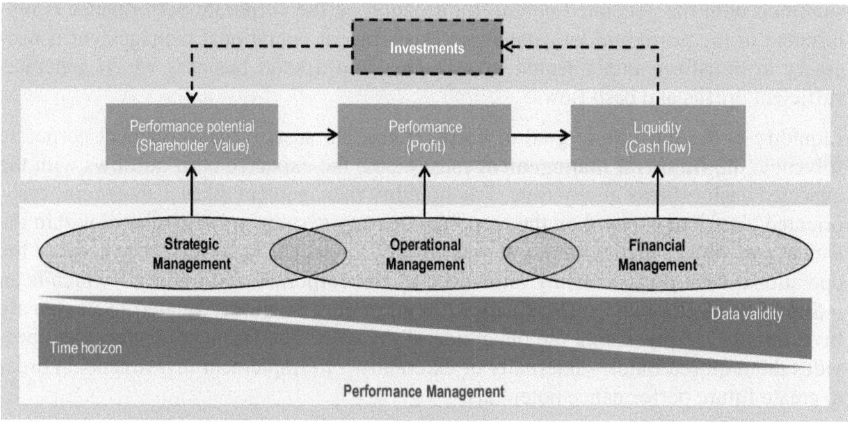

Figure 1-3: Corporate goal and management layers
Own illustration based on *Coenenberg/Günther* (2011), p. 7.

According to figure 1-3 these three layers of goals are managed by three different performance management subsystems. **Strategic management** sustains and creates future performance potentials of the corporation. For this work the creation and defense of competitive advantages in a complex environment is of significant importance because foreign investors in emerging economies are confronted with an extremely dynamic environment and high levels of uncertainty. Performance potentials are understood as a bundle of corporate competitive advantages, e.g. a superior product quality, cost advantages or special access to resources. Thus, the strategic management is also concerned with the analysis of developments within the external environment, like market or competitor screenings, in order to identify opportunities or threats.[92] **Corporate investments** are the main instrument to build up performance potentials, e.g. R&D[93] investments are required to design superior products, whereby foreign investments can serve to create a market-leading position in growth regions.

In contrast, performance potentials must be leveraged by an efficient **operational management** in order to generate a competitive advantage and thereby a constant stream of profits.[94] The operational management uses the existing corporate capacities and capabilities in the most efficient manner. Key performance indicators (KPIs) are

---

91 Cf. *Fischer* (1993), p. 13.

92 The SWOT-analysis (strengths, weaknesses, opportunities and threats) is a popular strategic planning method to evaluate the competitive position of a company; cf. *Piercy/Giles* (1989). Other strategic planning tools are for example Porter's five forces (cf. *Porter* (2007)), the BCG-matrix (cf. *Drews* (2008)), the life-cycle concept (cf. *Anderson/Zeithaml* (1984)), or the experience curve concept (cf. *Day/Montgomery* (1983)).

93 "R&D" means research and development.

94 Cf. *Welge/Al-Laham* (2012), p. 213.

usually calculated on a periodic basis, like annual net income or return on investment. Performance can be measured by different KPIs which compare the resource consumption with the generated output. Information on the corporate performance is represented in the profit and loss statement. An efficient operational management is necessary to transform implemented **investments** into a solid business which generates sufficient profits and cash flows.

Liquidity is the third basic goal of corporations. To sustain the permanent corporate solvency, the **financial management** must match the expected cash outflows with the expected cash inflows at any time. The liquidity management takes a short-term cash-oriented view that is based on the corporate treasury system and is disclosed within the annual cash flow statement. Liquidity is closely connected to performance because the operational cash flow is mainly influenced by the corporate profitability – which is an indicator of performance. The financial management is closely related to **corporate investments** – representing the other side of the coin. The financial management provides the required funds – internally or externally – to implement investments in order to create future performance potentials.

Liquidity, performance and performance potentials can develop in different directions, e.g. increasing liquidity may be related to decreasing performance potentials because investments have been neglected in the past. For this reason, an **integrated performance measurement** and **management** approach is necessary covering all three levels of goals. It is assumed that the shareholder value expresses the market expectations about the future opportunities and performance potentials of corporations.[95] Moreover, the **shareholder value concept** embraces the long-term performance potentials as well as the operationally-oriented targets of current performance and safeguarding liquidity. A shareholder value orientated perspective has been increasingly adopted among MNCs[96] because it covers – theoretically – the three central steering or management levels of corporations.[97]

On the one side investors look at the strategic position and invest in expectations about the future performance potential. On the other side they are also interested in continuous returns in terms of dividend payments – which are determined by the current performance and liquidity position. **Investments** play a central role in creating shareholder value. Future investment projects can be regarded as sources of long-term performance potentials. Also, the application of a value based management approach has important implications for the design of investment decision processes and underlying content-related activities. The next section presents the basic idea of value based management and the consequences on investment decision processes.

---

95 Cf. *Baum et al.* (2007), p. 284.

96 For the adoption of shareholder value orientation in Germany; cf. *Fiss/Zajac* (2004).

97 Cf. *Velthuis et al.* (2005), p. 2.

1.3.1.2 Value based management

At the beginning of the 1980s several publications by American business schools initiated the idea of value based management to integrate shareholder value elements within the goal systems of the management or executive board.[98] In the United States, the adoption of the shareholder value concept in corporate performance management systems has been further stimulated by consulting firms.[99] The implementation of shareholder value approaches has significant **implications for investment decisions** due to the core principle of value orientation. Thus, corporate decisions must be made in compliance with the creation of shareholder value, e.g. the management's performance evaluation and the related incentive systems must be tied to the interest of shareholders.[100]

For the present work it is crucial to present the main ideas and characteristics of a value based management system because the implemented performance management system influences the design of investment decision processes and decision criteria.[101] For instance, value-oriented performance indicators and related supportive measures must be integrated in the investment decision process, e.g. in terms of hurdle rates. The main investment selection criterion for decision-makers must be based on the key fact, whether the potential investment case creates additional shareholder value or not. In contrast, investment projects and new business opportunities are seen as the main source of long-term superior shareholder performance which highlights the reciprocal connection between the shareholder value concept and investments.[102]

The core idea of a value based management approach is that managerial decision-making should be directed towards **maximizing firm value**.[103] Unambiguously, the most essential assumption in value based management is that owners (only) seek to maximize the financial value of their firm.[104] Non-financial targets like social and ethical commitment are just considered as long as these non-financial objectives serve as means to increase shareholder value. Managerial decision-making and the corporate strategy is focused on satisfying the corporate shareholders. This implies that a corporation must earn its capital costs after all contractually fixed claims, e.g. those of creditors, employees or suppliers, have been served in order to provide an adequate return

98 Cf. *Fruhan* (1979), *Rappaport* (1986) or *Copeland et al.* (1990).

99 At the beginning of the 1990s consulting firms discovered the implementation of the shareholder value concept as a consultancy product, which has been promoted by several business publications. Almost every consulting firm developed its "own" value metric. New consultancy firms like *Stern Stewart & Co (Economic Value Added)* and *LEK/Alcar (Shareholder Value Added)* have been founded to implement value oriented financial metrics. Critics argue that existing concepts have been sold under a new name to corporations. For a detailed discussion related to the role of consulting firms in the adoption of value-oriented management systems; cf. *Froud et al.* (2000).

100 Cf. *Fiss/Zajac* (2004), p. 514.

101 Cf. *Schaefer* (2004), p. 38.

102 Cf. *Rappaport* (2006), p. 10.

103 Cf. *Velthuis et al.* (2005), p. 51.

104 Cf. *Rappaport* (2006), p. 2.

for shareholders.[105] Thus, the weighted average **cost of capital** (WACC)[106] plays a central role within a value based management system because it is defining the minimum rate of return respectively the hurdle rate for corporate decisions and actions to safeguard value-increasing managerial behavior.[107]

An important perspective of the shareholder value concept is focused on aligning corporate decisions and actions for increasing shareholder value, especially by making **value-adding investment decisions.**[108] For the purpose of the present work, the internal perspective of the shareholder value concept is of significant importance because investment decision processes must comply with the principles of shareholder value creation. Furthermore, the investment process design and underlying decision criteria have to be aligned to the VBM approach.

Corporations can be understood as a **network** of value-adding or value-destroying **investment projects**. For this reason, investment decisions have a direct impact on the market value development of corporations which creates the link to the value based management system. An implemented value based management approach is seen as the framework for the design of investment decision processes. Furthermore, the shareholder value concept itself is based on investment theory considerations which represent a further argument for the impact of this performance management approach on corporate investment decisions as a main source of value creation.

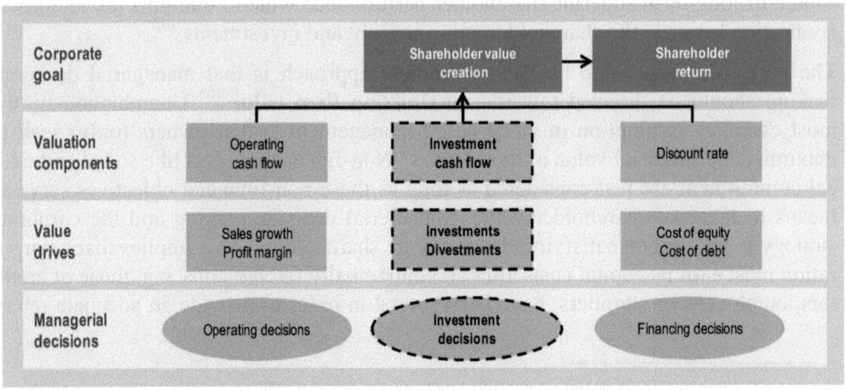

Figure 1-4: Shareholder value network and the influence of investments
Own illustration based on *Schierenbeck/Lister* (2002), p. 83.

As depicted in Figure 1-4 shareholder value creation is influenced by three different basic types of managerial decisions. The operating cash flow is mainly driven by sales growth and the profit margin which can be managed by **operating decisions** to leverage the existing capabilities of the firm, e.g. the profit margin can be increased by cost

105 Cf. *Kremin-Buch* (2007), p. 264.

106 For the WACC concept; cf. *Schierenbeck/Lister* (2002), p. 102ff.

107 Cf. *Henderson, JR.* (1979), p. 57.

108 Cf. *Pfaff/Bärtl* (1999), p. 87.

reductions or via raising prices. **Investment decisions** or divestment decisions for value destroying business segments specify the investment cash flow as the second component for the shareholder value calculation. Investment decisions can be characterized as strategic in the shareholder value network. At the beginning, investment decisions have a negative impact on the cash flow due to the required funds to implement and finance the investment projects. But after the new facilities become operational, they should have a positive impact on the shareholder value during their useful life through increasing the operating cash flow. In the following, international management philosophies are introduced. These management attitudes reflect the goals of the company regarding its international operations.[109]

1.3.1.3 International management philosophies

The overall international management philosophies of MNCs exert a significant influence on the investment decision process design. International management literature differentiates between four basic management philosophies of international operations.[110] They are briefly presented because they indicate the **degree of decision centralization** – which is an important determinant for investment decision processes.[111] These four international philosophies are ethnocentrism (home country orientation), polycentrism (host country orientation), regiocentricism (regional orientation) and geocentricism (world orientation).[112] A basic assumption of the EPRG[113] framework developed by *Perlmutter* is that these management attitudes to foreign investments and firm internationalization impact internationalization strategies and applied decision rules.[114]

Ethnocentric structures mean that the parent company in the home country is the decision-making centre. Foreign subsidiaries and their organizational structures, products and management styles are not adapted to specifics of foreign environments. All major competencies and decisions are controlled by the domestic headquarter. The corporation imposes its domestic culture on other foreign corporate entities abroad.[115] **Polycentric** orientation represents the opposite pole to ethnocentric structures. Besides operational responsibilities, strategic decision competencies are allocated to the foreign representation in polycentric oriented corporations. Furthermore, management styles

---

109 Cf. *Wind et al.* (1973), p. 14.

110 The initial framework was developed with the three basic attitudes of ethnocentric, polycentric and geocentric orientation; cf. *Perlmutter* (1969), p. 15. In 1973, the fourth attitude was added to explain firms which had moved beyond polycentrism but were not geocentric due to region-specific operations; cf. *Shoham et al.* (1995), p. 11.

111 Philosophy in this context means headquarters' orientations regarding the relation towards subsidiaries. The philosophies are expressed by the attitudes of executives regarding how to do business in the international arena; cf. *de Cieri et al.* (2007), p. 286.

112 Cf. *Perlmutter* (1969), p. 12 and *Wind et al.* (1973), p. 15.

113 EPRG means ethnocentric, polycentric, regiocentric, geocentric.

114 Cf. *Heenan/Perlmutter* (1979), p. 19.

115 Cf. *Perlmutter* (1971), p. 420.

as well as products and corporate processes are tailored to the host country environment.

A **geocentric** organization intends to establish a permanent exchange between the parent company and the foreign location in order to benefit from the gained experiences, values, developments and practices in the foreign market. The MNC organizes its activities on a worldwide basis, considering the entire world as a potential market isolated from national boundaries.[116] Key strategic decisions are made in cooperation between the parent company and the foreign location.[117] Different regional subcultures are evolving in **regiocentric** corporations. National boundaries are ignored and bundled to regional hubs, whereas corporate structures, products and policies are adapted to the specific regional requirements. So-called regional headquarters are taking a central position within the decision-making process.[118] A main difference to the geocentric philosophy is that regiocentric organizations divide the world market into different reasonable regions instead of considering it as a whole. Whereas managers in regiocentric organizations shall be rooted and prepared for a certain region, managers in geocentric corporations are trained for global assignments regardless their country of origin.[119]

Although these four basic corporate philosophies are simplified, it is necessary for the present work to distinguish between these types due to its assumed impact on the investment decision processes, management styles and the configuration of foreign investments. Particularly, it is expected that the corporate management philosophy has a major **influence on decision-making**, i.e. the regional allocation of decision authorities or target country selections.[120] Similarly, the four different management philosophies may have an influence on the foreign investment success, e.g. it could be expected that ethnocentric philosophies are doomed to failure for market-seeking investments in culturally-distant regions.

1.3.2 Single phases and decision process success

Successful corporations create shareholder wealth. Sustainable value creation is associated with the continuous search, identification and implementation of new accretive investments.[121] Thereby, every investment project initializes multi-layered planning-, implementation- and control-processes, which are usually spread over different corporate product departments and corporate functions.[122] It is a central management board responsibility to invest financial resources consistent with the corporate goals.[123] Therefore, complex MNCs need to dispose over effective investment decision pro-

---

116 Cf. *Wind et al.* (1973), p. 15.
117 Cf. *Lemak/Bracker* (2006), p. 522.
118 Cf. *Li et al.* (2010), p. 8.
119 Cf. *Ondrack* (1985), p. 8.
120 Cf. *Davidson* (1983), p. 440f.
121 Cf. *Shleifer/Vishny* (1989), p. 137.
122 Cf. *Mittermüller/von Nitzsch* (2008), p. 769.
123 Cf. *Myers/Majluf* (1984), p. 189.

cesses in order to select and implement accretive investments.[124] One purpose of this section is to present an ideal-typical model of an investment decision process, which comprises **four main stages**: Initialization, approval, implementation and start-up and control as depicted in Figure 1-5 and a common understanding of decision process success.

Furthermore, the responsibilities of management accounting are displayed within a support process below the key investment process. The four main process stages contain several phases, e.g. case description, search for alternatives, forecasts and case definition are phases during the initialization process.

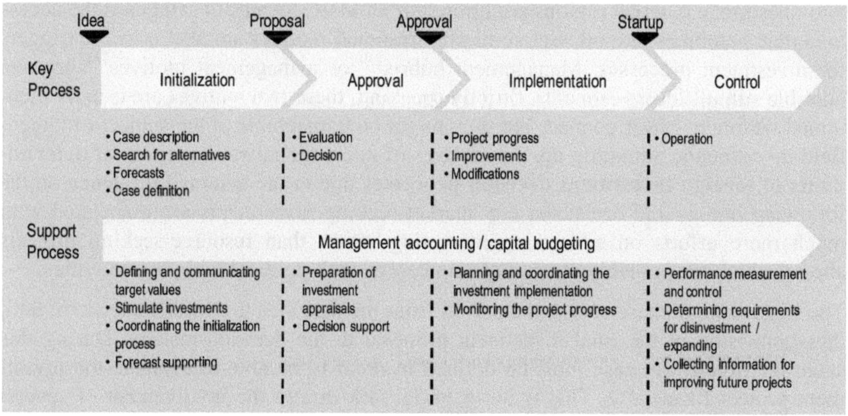

Figure 1-5: The investment process and related management accounting tasks
Cf. *Mittermüller/von Nitzsch* (2008), p. 769.

The following elaborations on the investment decision process are of **ideal-typical character**. Therefore, it is obvious that the process design varies in different corporate contexts, e.g. depending on the company size and its **organizational form**.[125] For instance, large MNCs often implement matrix organizations with product and regional units as the two main dimensions which involves balancing conflicting priorities.[126] A further example represents the **ownership structure**. When ownership and control are not separated like in large capital market oriented corporations, the main agency conflict within investment decision processes between the management and their shareholders is not existent.[127] For this reason, some control mechanisms within investment processes are not necessarily observable in owner-managed corporations, like supervisory board approvals or screenings.[128] Subsequently, the four single stages will be illustrated.

124 Cf. *Gaida et al.* (2008), p. 119.

125 Cf. *Küpper* (2008), p. 510.

126 Cf. *Doz/Prahalad* (1984), p. 71.

127 Cf. *Brunninge et al.* (2007), p. 296.

128 In Germany it is not unusual that strategic investments are subject to the supervisory board's approval in listed corporations; cf. *Dittmann et al.* (2010), p. 41.

1.3.2.1 Initialization

Corporate investments do not evolve within a vacuum. Moreover, investments are triggered by internal or external forces or events.[129] The initialization as the first stage within the investment process is often preceded by a **strategic need** or an upcoming business opportunity. A strategic need could arise if the strategic long-term goal cannot be achieved with the current corporate capacity. Thus, investments are possible measures to close these gaps by enlarging the corporate capacity. Cross-border investments can fundamentally intend **market-, resource- or efficiency-oriented motives**. Dependent on the pursued motives, different strategic investment options come into question, e.g. target regions are limited, if an MNC intends to safeguard the access to certain resources like oil. But similarly, irrational motives are also possible triggers for investment processes. Management hubris[130] or management motives[131] are two possible stimuli for investments. Strictly speaking, these two motives are usually mentioned within an M&A context, but they might be transferable to the subject of Greenfield investments. Summing up, the motives of internationalization represent **determinants of foreign investment decision processes** due to the assumed influence on the following phases and decisions, e.g. market-seeking investments are associated with much more efforts on addressing marketing issues than resource-seeking projects abroad which are probably much more concerned with political lobbying activities.

The initialization phase covers the period from the first idea to invest somewhere until the submission of the final investment proposal to the decision-makers. During this stage the investment case must be defined in order to be able to evaluate the investment project financially. This is not a trivial task due to the involvement of several different experts, like engineers, lawyers, sales people, production specialists or accountants.[132] Literature related to capital budgeting or investments often ignores the **investment case development**. Investment theory and capital budgeting literature assumes investment projects as given which must only be evaluated in order to make the best possible selection. The project development process is not considered.[133] This work intends to focus on this development process from the initial rough idea to the concrete investment case defined within the investment proposal.

129 Cf. *Sierke* (1989), p. 108.

130 Management hubris means that bidders in corporate takeovers pay too much for their targets due to the hubris of the decision-makers. They overestimate the business opportunities and their abilities to leverage the acquired corporate capacities, e.g. through the realization of synergies or efficiency gains; cf. *Roll* (1986), p. 201.

131 Opposed to the hubris theory, the free cash flow theory assumes that the management consciously acts against the interests of the shareholders. The corporate decision-makers try to invest more funds than rationally necessary in order to do not lose the control over these financial resources by dividend payments to the shareholders; cf. *Jensen* (1986), p. 328; or *Jensen* (1988), p. 29.

132 Cf. *Fahey* (1981), p. 55.

133 Cf. *Arbeitskreis Finanzierung der Schmalenbach-Gesellschaft Deutsche Gesellschaft für Betriebswirtschaftslehre e.V.* (1994), p. 901.

The **investment proposal** is a summarizing document which comprises descriptions and evaluations from all relevant business functions to the following topics: strategic evaluation, description of the technical concept, characteristics of the new facilities (e.g. volumes, size etc.), sales-side market evaluations, business planning with overall financial evaluation (e.g. calculation of key decision criteria like IRR or NPV), financing concept, description and evaluation of the legal and tax concept, country-specific descriptions and evaluations (e.g. infrastructure or access to employees), human resources concept (e.g. organization of know-transfer, role of expats etc.) and foreign sourcing concept (e.g. organization of supplier networks). This list of relevant topics for investment proposals does not raise the aspiration of completeness.

Similarly, it is often not explicitly articulated that besides the final management investment decision based on the investment proposal, a multitude of decisions is necessary to develop an investment proposal, e.g. the middle management, the project team or the business development has to decide between possible **alternative investment configurations**. The complexity of such decisions during the initialization is expected to be very high because decisions in different areas may influence each other, e.g. legal changes may have an impact on the tax concept or technical modifications are changing the NPV evaluation. Therefore, it is crucial to understand during this work-sharing process how local decisions affect areas of other experts working on the investment project. Managing these interdependencies requires an effective interface management and coordination.

One important influencing factor for the process efficiency during this stage is the **release of investment directives**. Investment directives structure and shape the process of undertaking these kinds of projects. Investment directives may have the potential to guide the applicants and reduce the perceived uncertainty. As prior research and literature assume investment projects as given, it is also interesting to investigate which organizational units push investment projects. This is also a part of this early stage of investment initialization in order to identify investment stimuli. Accounting literature often assumes that the management accounting functions, especially capital budgeting, plays an important role for stimulating new investment projects.[134] During this stage of the investment decision process management accountants are expected to focus on planning activities, like cash flow and cost estimates.

1.3.2.2 Approval

The approval phase comprises the period from the submission of the investment proposal to the decision-makers until the final investment decision has been made. During this stage it is assumed that the submitted investment proposal is reviewed by an independent screening committee or department. It could even be possible that the decision-makers, usually the executive board, review the investment proposals themselves, but it seems to be more realistic, e.g. due to time, cost and knowledge constraints, that the management mainly relies on a recommendation by specialized **screening com-**

---

134 Cf. *Dahlhaus* (2009), p. 24f.

mittees. But the management has to make the final investment decision and takes the responsibility for the success of the project.[135]

A determinant during the approval phase is the **distribution of decision authorities**. The distribution of decision authorities or the design of decision levels (e.g. in terms of investment volumes) is a central influencing factor for the investment decision process because it determines the decision responsibilities and the addressees of investment proposals. The design of authority levels determines the route of investment proposals through the organization. It is expected that the process range – in terms of involved departments and employees – increases with the strategic importance of investments.

But besides the aspect of personal decision authorities (who is able to make decisions?) the **investment decision criteria** (what is the basis for the decision?) are also important design parameters for the approval stage. For this reason, the application of capital budgeting methods plays an important role during this stage because these tools are dedicated to evaluate investment projects and deliver decision support.[136] Within the international context of the present work it is of special interest how the additional uncertainty sources, like different exchange rates or country risks, affect the application of capital budgeting tools.

Capital budgeting is necessary in order to evaluate the investment proposals against the background of the corporate goal system, e.g. the consequences on shareholder value creation.[137] The main tasks at this stage of the investment process are to collect the relevant information and to make plausible assumptions for the investment appraisal.[138] The **evaluation** of foreign investment projects involves a variety of issues seldom encountered in the domestic environment.[139] Differences in political and economic conditions, floating exchange rates, different inflation rates, cultures, tax and legal systems are factors which drive the complexity of such decisions.[140] These differences and sources of risk are expected to be even stronger for investment projects in emerging economies like the BRICs. Although capital budgeting researchers tried to develop modified evaluation tools for foreign projects, no approach has been really established in practice.[141]

A further main responsibility is to coordinate investment decisions.[142] Capital budgeting has to assure an **effective capital expenditure allocation** in order to create long-term shareholder value.[143] Due to the corporate interfaces, interdependencies and lim-

---

135 Cf. *Lorie/Savage* (1955), p. 229.

136 Cf. *Pinches* (1982), p. 7.

137 Cf. *Savvides* (1994), p. 4. An overview of capital budgeting concepts to evaluate investment opportunities can be found at *Reichmann* (2011), p. 227.

138 Cf. *Reichmann* (2011), p. 246.

139 Cf. *Mrotzek* (1989), p. 4.

140 Cf. *Shapiro* (1978), p. 7.

141 For conceptual literature on capital budgeting in an international context; cf. *Gaddis* (1966); *Lessard* (1985); *Giddy* (1981); *Mrotzek* (1989); or *Scholz* (1996).

142 Cf. *Dückert* (2009), p. 25.

143 The shareholder value approach and value based management will be explained in section 1.3.1.2.

ited investment budgets, capital expenditures must be distributed to investment projects that create the greatest value for the shareholders.[144] Coordinated investment decision-making is even more complicated in MNCs due to higher internal and external complexity.[145] For instance, different cultures, exchange rates, inflation rates, legal systems and tax regulations drive complexity.[146]

The formal modes of making investment decisions are also a constitutional aspect of the approval phase. Possible formal modes of investment decision are voting mechanisms within institutionalized investment committees, releases within management support systems or signatures on investment documents. These **formal modes** of making investment decisions are also an important determinant within the approval stages. If investment decisions are made within investment committees, the approval stages are expected to differ compared to investment decisions by signing investment documents, e.g. decision-making in committees requires spatial and temporal coordination of managers.

Management accountants are responsible for preparing or supporting the final management decision.[147] Therefore, it is intended to investigate if management accountants fulfill their assumed roles. The relationship between central management accounting and the decentralized management accounting within the business units which submitted investment proposals is also an interesting area to explore. It is of special interest to examine if decentralized management accountants are perceived as a partner to push investment proposals through the screening processes or more as an extended control authority of the central management accounting function.

1.3.2.3 Implementation

The implementation phase is assumed to be initialized after the final approval for the investment project has been received. This period during the investment process ends when the new location and its facilities are ready for operation. As opposed to the two preceding phases, this stage is characterized as an **execution level** and does not necessarily belong to the general planning process.[148] This phase is decisive for realizing the business case, which means that the investment proposal needs to be filled with life. The key task during the implementation of investments is coordinating resources and routines in order to transform the preceding investment decisions into concrete actions, such as a physical construction of new plants.[149]

For this reason, a detailed **project plan** including a temporal schedule with project milestones must be developed in order to create a framework for a successful project implementation. Successful means that investment projects are implemented on time within their budgets. It is assumed that separate project organizations are necessary to

144 Cf. *Schmidbauer* (1998), p. 182f.
145 Cf. *Ott* (2000), p. 31.
146 Cf. *Welge/Amshoff* (1998), p. 446.
147 Cf. *Baines/Langfield-Smith* (2003), p. 675.
148 Cf. *Dückert* (2009), p. 12.
149 Cf. *Hellgren/Stjernberg* (1995), p. 384.

implement investments.[150] Investment implementations are time-consuming and cannot be handled among the usual day-to-day-operations.[151] Setting-up a **project organization** is one of the first tasks which have to be fulfilled after the final management approval has been received to create an infrastructure for efficiently implementing the investment.

One critical task of the project management is breaking down the project into reasonable work packages in order to spread responsibilities and make the project manageable. Therefore, respective project teams with **different work streams** need to be established.[152] The formulation of respective targets for evaluating the progress of single work streams is a means of managing the investment project implementation, i.e. corrective measure can be introduced faster due to better project monitoring options. The **project monitoring and reporting** as well as the project decompositions are special areas of interest for the empirical investigation because they are important for timely problem escalations. Based on the project decomposition a project plan is developed in order to implement the investment project.[153]

As described above, investment project implementations are not occasionally confronted with problems, e.g. **cost overruns** or **significant delays**. Investment projects are always confronted with uncertainty because the investment planning involves predication, estimations and assumptions about future internal and external conditions.[154] Due to this associated uncertainty during the two prior phases of investment initialization and approval, it is often necessary to modify decisions taken earlier, e.g. due to unforeseeable events. These changes or modifications with hindsight to the final project approval are expected to be more common for foreign investments in emerging markets due to the lower market and country experiences. Similarly, the more volatile institutional environment may also represent a source of additional uncertainty during the project implementation as well as within the following start-up and control phase, e.g. regarding land acquisition or receiving permissions by local authorities.[155]

As opposed to the transition from the initialization to the approval phase, **investment project responsibilities** are subject to changes between the approval and the implementation phases. The project implementation requires physical work to a great extent, like constructions or civil works, which imposes different qualification requirements compared to the initial investment planning and approval activities. Thus, it is reasonable that approved investment projects are handed over to a more operational oriented project team to execute the agreed investment configuration within the proposal. This **interface** may be a potential area of agency conflicts, if there is a change of responsibilities between the development of investment projects and the following execution and implementation of the approved projects. Investment project developer may have

150 Cf. *Rösgen* (2000), p. 256.
151 Cf. *Sapper* (2007), p. 5.
152 Cf. *Clarke* (1999), p. 140.
153 Cf. *Rösgen* (2000), p. 252.
154 Cf. *Ferderer* (1993), p. 31.
155 Cf. *Luo* (2003a), p. 292.

incentives to push projects by too optimistic planning, when they are not in charge to fulfill the agreed business plans for the investment projects.[156]

The **role of management accountants** changes with the beginning of the project implementation. Whereas during the initialization and approval management accountants are mainly in charge of planning activities, the implementation as well as the start-up and control stages are characterized by **control and monitoring activities**. The initial planning documents, e.g. a project schedule, serve as the project benchmark for deviation analyses with the actual figures. As usual for managing projects, the three central dimensions of costs, time and quality are closely monitored by management accountants.[157]

1.3.2.4 Start-up and control

The start-up and control period starts after the implementation process is completed. This transition from the implementation stage until the full production capacities have been achieved is also labeled as the **ramp-up time.**[158] The comprehension of this work comprises the control process as well. **Control** means at this stage that the initial assumptions within the investment proposal are compared to the actual figures. Deviations to the investment proposal, e.g. regarding the Capex amount or the agreed project schedule, are analyzed in order to generate implications for improving future investment projects. An interesting aspect during this last stage is how corporations try to extract and absorb the **lessons-learned** within the investment process in order to improve, preserve and share the expertise on a corporate-wide level.

A central challenge within these final stages represents the **resource transfer process** because it is not assured that domestic strategic resources create the same advantages in a different environment. Thus, in foreign investment processes one key challenge is to transfer corporate resources into a new business environment, e.g. with different customer preferences, competitor behavior, climate conditions or institutional pressures. According to the resourced-based view[159] resources are defined as tangible and intangible firm-specific capabilities that enable competitive advantages.[160] A **strategic resource** ensures sustainable rents, if it is strategically valuable, rare and difficult to imitate and substitute.[161] **Complementary assets** are required to run the operations efficiently, but do not provide competitive advantages from a stand-alone perspective.[162] According to *Cuervo-Cazurra et al.* (2007) three categories of resource transfer

156 Cf. *Arbeitskreis Finanzierung der Schmalenbach-Gesellschaft Deutsche Gesellschaft für Betriebswirtschaftslehre e.V.* (1994), p. 904.

157 Cf. *Khang/Myint* (1999), p. 249.

158 Cf. *Carrillo/Franza* (2006), p. 537.

159 The resource based view is a strategic management concept. Its key message is that a bundle of valuable resources constitutes the basis for a sustainable competitive advantage; cf. *Wernerfelt* (1984), p. 172.

160 Cf. *Barney* (1991), p. 101.

161 Cf. *Peteraf* (1993), p. 180.

162 Cf. *Teece* (1986), p. 188ff.

problems may arise during the foreign investment process: Loss of an advantage (1), creation of a disadvantage (2) or lack of complementary resources (3).

(1) A **loss of an advantage** arises when strategic resources lose their ability to create competitive advantages when transferred to a new business environment. This can be the case when a certain strategic resource is rare in the home market, but common in the foreign country.[163] For domestic or familiar markets, MNCs still have strategies and resources to compete in a particular industry structure, but these have to be tailored to the new environment.[164] When strategic resources lose their advantageous character, the question can be raised whether the critical resource should be developed locally or centrally by the headquarters.[165]

(2) The **creation of a disadvantage** occurs when certain firm resources implemented in the new region destroy the created value of the transferred resource bundles. Due to the fact that strategic factor markets are incomplete and imperfect, most strategic assets or resources must be accumulated internally over time.[166] This implies that a company needs to build strategic resource bundles over time, which leads to a path dependency of strategic assets with tacit knowledge and implicit routines.[167] In particular path dependencies may also cause strategic inertia.[168] Thus, a further challenge in foreign investment decision processes is to maintain the ability and flexibility to tailor strategic asset bundles to the target environment. For instance, *Hastings* analyzed the resource transfer problems of an US-based electric company.[169] The management tried to impose the American incentive system to the German subsidiary without considering the specific working habits, e.g. like the important role of labor unions, which led to the closing of the German subsidiary in the end.[170]

(3) Transferring or creating **complementary resources** is crucial for the efficiency of foreign operations, e.g. employees with direct contact to local stakeholders must be able to speak the local language fluently to avoid misunderstandings. Adding new corporate capacity and transferring resources, especially to geographically distant countries, is associated with additional transportation, communication and coordination costs.[171] In contrast to domestic investments, for-

---

163 The case of Wal-Mart is an example in this respect. Wal-Mart dominated the home market with a low cost strategy based on economies of scale. This firm-specific advantage did not succeed in Germany due to well-established German competitors like Aldi or Lidl with similar strategic resources; cf. *Christopherson* (2007).

164 Cf. *Cuervo-Cazurra et al.* (2007), p. 11.

165 Cf. *Birkinshaw et al.* (1998), p. 223.

166 Cf. *Dierickx/Cool* (1989), p. 1509. For a model of strategic factor markets; cf. *Barney* (1986).

167 Cf. *Ray et al.* (2004), p. 26.

168 Cf. *Hutzschenreuter et al.* (2007), p. 1057f.

169 Cf. *Hastings* (1999), p. 174.

170 The case of *Opel* in Germany and the conflicts with the US headquarters of GM is a current practical example in this respect.

171 Cf. *Hitt et al.* (1997), p. 772.

eign projects demand more spare management capacity due to greater distances, language problems or different time zones.[172]

A further central aspect within this phase of the investment process is how the **HR management** is set up within foreign and culturally distant environments. In this context, HR management essentially means the acquisition, training and retention of qualified employees. A major challenge is expected to be the training of the new employees to meet the corporate standards. Different educational and cultural backgrounds may require adapting business processes to the foreign location specifics. During the start-up and control usually foreign investors try to introduce measures for enhancing the local embeddedness[173], e.g. through cooperation with universities or by supporting local non-profit organizations.[174] It is often highlighted that especially in culturally distant emerging markets the creation of local embeddedness is a critical success factor within these markets to achieve local responsiveness.[175]

It seems to be obvious that foreign production facilities may not be copied from the home country without adapting it to the foreign country specifics in order to be competitive within these markets. Therefore, corporations try to **adapt their business processes and transfer knowledge** to the host country. Similarly, it could be necessary to adapt the company's product portfolio to the foreign customer preferences and characteristics, if the investment motives are driven by market-seeking intentions.[176] Especially, emerging economies or customers based in emerging markets are more price sensitive compared to their counterparts in mature markets.[177] Thus, foreign investors may modify the product engineering in order to be able to offer products at competitive price levels.[178]

After the ramp-up or rather the full production capacity has been achieved, the initially assumed business plan has to be controlled. Like the project implementation the operational stage with first revenues has to undergo a **deviation analysis** in order to analyze whether the investment delivers the desired added value for the shareholders. After the main phases were introduced, a success definition is developed in the following.

1.3.2.5 Investment decision process success

In the present context, it is necessary to disclose a definition of success because two alternatives are possible: **investment success**[179] versus **investment decision process success**. Consistent with the prior sections, this study focuses on discussing critical

---

172 Cf. *Cuervo-Cazurra et al.* (2007), p. 10.

173 Local embeddedness means in this context the degree of which a foreign investor is socially tied, trusted and perceived to share common values; cf. *Dhanaraj et al.* (2004), p. 429.

174 Cf. *Birkinshaw/Hood* (2000), p. 145.

175 Cf. *Luo* (2001), p. 458.

176 Cf. *Lankes/Venables* (1996), p. 334.

177 Cf. *Meyer/Thu Tran* (2006), p. 180.

178 Cf. *Cooper/Kleinschmidt* (1985), p. 39.

179 Successful investments create additional shareholder value by earning their cost of capital, which is expressed by positive NPV, EVA or IRR above the cost of capital.

success factors for the investment decision process success. It is assumed that the efficiency[180] of investment decision processes represents an indicator of the investment decision process success which antecedes the overall investment project success as depicted in Figure 1-6.[181]

Thereby, a critical success factor determines a measure which is required for a company or an investment to be successful.[182] Critical success factors are often mixed up with performance measures.[183] For instance, if growth is the underlying corporate goal, a certain percentage of sales increase represents a performance measure, whereas improvement of customer services may serve as a critical success factor. A general assumption is that every investment of the investigated portfolio in the empirical study has the potential to be accretive. The efficiency of the accompanying investment decision processes and external environmental factors are assumed to determine to what extent value creation potentials of investment projects are exploited.[184] In this context, decision process efficiency serves as a performance indicator for the investment decision process success. For this reason, decision process efficiency has to be defined. Consistent with prior studies this work assumes that the decision process efficiency is determined by the **balance** between **decision process speed** and **decision process comprehensiveness**.[185]

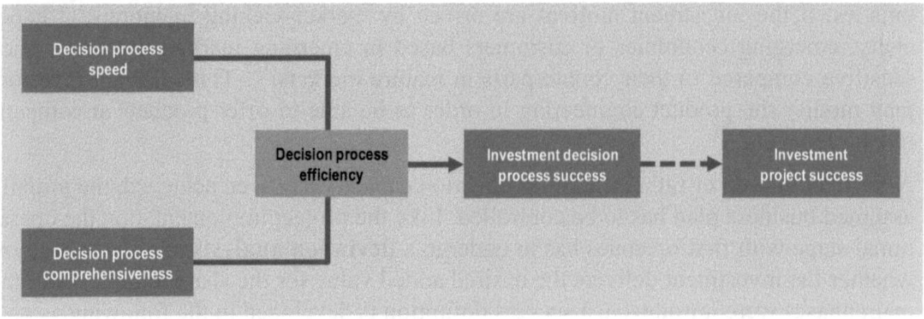

Figure 1-6: Success of investment decision processes

Decision comprehensiveness refers to the extent to which investment decisions have been prepared and analyzed. It can be understood as the degree of accuracy in terms of applied evaluation techniques, extent of information search or the consideration of investment alternatives.[186] Decision process comprehensiveness shall not indicate fundamentally good or bad managerial decisions in this context. In contrast, decision pro-

180 Achieving "efficiency" in decision processes is a core question of the strategy process research; cf. *Chakravarthy/Doz* (1992), p. 6.

181 Cf. *Dean* (1996), p. 389.

182 Cf. *Boynton/Zmund* (1984), p. 17.

183 Cf. *Freund* (1988), p. 21.

184 Cf. *Dean* (1996), p. 371.

185 Cf. *Talaulicar et al.* (2005), p. 521.

186 Cf. *Fredrickson* (1984), p. 445.

cess speed is defined as the pace of investment decision processes from the initial idea until the closing of the investment project at the end of the start-up and control phase.

Therefore, an efficient decision process design can be expressed in two ways. First, **efficient decision processes** generate accurate decisions of fixed (satisfying) comprehensiveness levels as fast as possible. Second, an efficient decision process design implies that the highest possible decision comprehensiveness is achieved within a given timeframe. These two forms of efficiency assume that decision process comprehensiveness and decision process speed are negatively related and need to be balanced – the faster the investment decision process, the lower is the decision process comprehensiveness all else being equal.[187]

Influences on decision process speed and decision process comprehensiveness at the cases companies are discussed along the four investment decision phases in the empirical part of this work. Thereby, decision process speed and decision process comprehensiveness are not solely focused on the final investment decision made by the respective decision authorities. Moreover, theses two determinants of decision process efficiency are illustrated within the light of the **full range of decisions** involved in foreign investments, like change management decisions during the investment implementation or configuration decisions at the investment project development stage. Although the final investment decision represents doubtlessly the central decision, it would not be consistent with the aspiration of this study to analyze only the final investment decision.

1.3.3 Specific foreign investment decisions

After the basic phases within investment decision processes have been presented, this section intends to describe central strategic decision parameters specifically for foreign investment projects. These decisions are defining basic alternative courses of strategic actions within the foreign investment process and the organization of international activities. This introduction seems to be necessary in order to identify the main configuration decisions within international investments. According to *Schmid,* the management has to make four main decisions to configure foreign investments.[188]

(1) In which foreign markets shall be invested? **(Target market decision)**

(2) What time-related aspects have to be considered for the investment? **(Timing decision)**

---

187 It is assumed that comprehensiveness and speed cannot be increased at the same time without the commitment of additional resources and efforts. For instance, increasing the comprehensiveness of an investment evaluation in a fixed timeframe can only be realized with additional work-forces.

188 Cf. *Schmid* (2013), p.13; or *Simon* (2007b), p. 25. The market entry mode selection is a further main decision. Due to the study's focus on the entry mode of Greenfield investments, this decision parameter will not be presented separately at this point; see section 1.2.1.

(3) How shall the corporation handle the conflicting forces of centralization and decentralization as well as the conflicting demands of global integration and local adaptation? **(Allocation decision)**

(4) How shall the corporation coordinate its new international operations with existing production facilities? **(Coordination decision)**

1.3.3.1 Target market decision

The selection of target markets to establish new foreign operations is a central decision within the foreign investment decision process.[189] International corporations need to continuously rethink where they want to be present considering external market or country conditions as well as internal strengths and weaknesses.[190] In the early stage of foreign investment decisions, the management has to define desired target markets to enter. This decision has to be coordinated with the market entry mode decision due to their interdependent relationship.[191] The selected target country may constrain the possible entry mode options due to political or legal coercions. Contrarily, the decision of entry modes cannot be made isolated to the target market decision. International management literature also highlights the importance of taking the geographic, cultural and psychic distance to the host country for selecting target countries into account.[192]

Reviewing the literature related to international market selection **three decision criteria** receive the greatest attention: (1) country market attractiveness, (2) country market risks and (3) country market entry barriers.[193]

(1) **Country market attractiveness** defines the country-specific benefit potential, which could be evaluated based on different foreign market characteristics such as market volume, market growth, competition, supplier presence or price and cost levels.[194]

(2) **Country market risks** are different to the risks related to transactions in the domestic arena. One possible reason is that these risks are not existent in the domestic market (e.g. exchange risks). Second, the probabilities of risk occurrences are higher in the foreign environment (e.g. expropriations). A third reason for the difference between risks in domestic and foreign markets is that risk evaluations (e.g. for market risks) in foreign countries are more challenging due to usually lower information levels.[195] Country-specific risk evaluations are provided by of-

189 Cf. *Weinstein* (2006), p. 126.
190 Cf. *Sirmon et al.* (2010), p. 1403.
191 Cf. *Brouthers/Hennart* (2007), p. 419.
192 Cf. *Brewer* (2001), p. 157ff.
193 Cf. *Papadopoulos et al.* (2002), p. 166ff.; or *Schmid* (2013), p. 19.
194 Cf. *Davidson* (1983), p. 440.
195 Cf. *Duncan* (1972), p. 33f.

ficial and private institutions, e.g. *rating agencies, the World Bank, the United Nations or Transparency International.*[196]

(3) **Country market entry barriers** have to be overcome by international investors if they intend to operate in a host country. These barriers could differ substantially between different geographic markets, which also influence the two other criteria of market attractiveness and country-specific risks.[197] Three different types of market entry barriers can be classified in the international context. *Institutional market entry barriers* are imposed by governmental authorities, e.g. local-content requirements for wholly-owned subsidiaries.[198] *External behavioral barriers* are attributable to a variety of causes, e.g. problematic customer or supplier access, discriminatory behaviors of public authorities or communication problems to name just a few.[199] *Internal behavioral barriers* arise due to biased information processing during the screening phase of specific countries. Thus, corporations construct their own cognitive or psychic barriers due to an overestimation of certain country-specific problems.[200]

Nevertheless, the market attractiveness, country-specific risks and country market entry barriers must always be assessed with regard to the company-specific competitive advantages, weaknesses and the underlying goals and surrounding value system.[201]

1.3.3.2 Timing decision

Furthermore, MNCs need to select a consistent timing strategy about when to embark a Greenfields. The management has to choose a promising point in time to invest overseas.[202] A thorough timing strategy can be critical to the overall investment success, e.g. first-mover-strategies[203] can be pursued to create market entry barriers for other foreign corporations in order to lower the competition and attain superior profits.[204] For the present investigation, the timing decision is a critical determinant because it is controversially discussed within the international management literature if an early- or late-entry strategy is more promising for investments in emerging economies.[205]

Authors for early-entry strategies in developing countries argue that investors may have preemptive opportunities and benefit from market, product and technological

---

196 For an overview of different country risk evaluation methods; cf. *Holtbrügge/Welge* (2010), p. 94ff.

197 Although market entry barriers could also be presented as a determinant of market attractiveness and country-specific risks, it seems to be adequate to present entry barriers as a separate criterion due to its special relevance for foreign investment decisions.

198 For an analysis of the impact of local content requirements on FDI; cf. *Qiu/Tao* (2001).

199 Cf. *Karakaya* (1993), p. 11.

200 Cf. *Andersen/Strandskov* (1997), p. 65f.

201 Cf. *Ekeledo/Sivakamur* (2004), p. 94.

202 Cf. *Kutschker/Schmid* (2011), p. 986.

203 For a detailed discussion of first-mover-strategies; cf. *Lieberman/Montgomery* (1988).

204 Cf. *Isobe et al.* (2000), p. 470.

205 Cf. *Luo* (1998), p. 394.

leadership.[206] Especially, when emerging economies are liberalizing foreign investment policies, early MNCs may benefit from developing their own market segments due to the limited capabilities of local firms to fully exploit market opportunities and the inertia of state-owned enterprises.[207] On the other side, late entrants face lower risks because early movers have made their mistakes, governments have learned to deal with foreign companies and early investments have enforced FDI legislations.[208] Thus, late investors may benefit from the pioneering work of early-movers especially from a more stabilized environment for foreign investors.[209]

Two different levels of timing decisions can be distinguished. First, decision-makers have to create strategies to select adequate investment timing for a single country-specific market. Second, MNCs entering into more than one foreign market have to coordinate timing decisions for a series of investment projects. For this reason, the management develops integrated transnational market entry timing strategies for a variety of target countries as depicted in Figure 1-7.

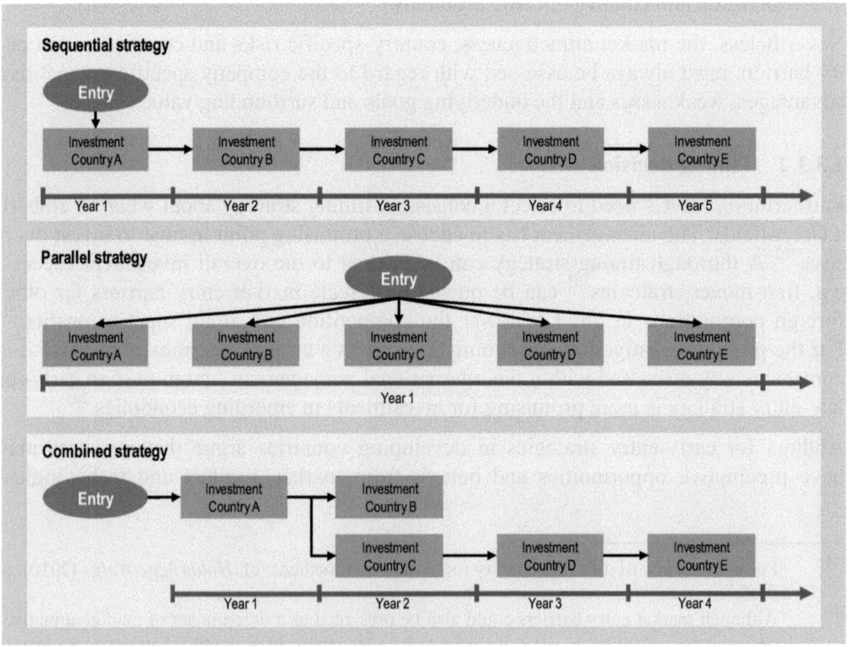

Figure 1-7: International investment timing strategies
Adopted from *Schmid* (2013), p. 22.

[206] Cf. *Luo* (1997), p. 649.
[207] Cf. *Luo* (1998), p. 394f.
[208] Cf. *Mitchell* (1989), p. 211.
[209] Cf. *Kvint* (1994), p. 70.

Three basic different international investment timing strategies can be differentiated.[210] An MNC applies a **sequential strategy** when foreign investments are undertaken successively – which tend to need a longer time frame than parallel strategies. Often corporations start to enter familiar markets. Culturally and geographically distant countries or regions are increasingly entered as international experiences increase.[211] Advantages of sequential strategies are lower risks of failures due to the slower and more cautious internationalization process. The demand for resources is distributed over a longer period of time, so that initial losses can be offset by profits in established markets.[212] In addition, generated knowledge from earlier market entries can be used to optimize later market entries.[213]

A parallel investment timing strategy is implemented by entering several or all desired target regions simultaneously or within a short period of time. MNCs consider a **parallel strategy** in order to achieve first-mover advantages by quick internationalization and to surprise competitors.[214] Similarly, this strategy facilitates the establishment of standards on a global scale. According to the wording, a **combined strategy** intends to combine the advantages of both strategies. MNC may focus on investing simultaneously in some regions or continents, while applying a sequential approach in others. Similarly, a combined investment timing strategy can be pursued due to financial and human bottlenecks.

1.3.3.3 Allocation decision

Two important areas of decision-making have to be distinguished regarding the allocation decision. First, a configuration decision with respect to the geographical dispersion of the value chain has to be made. Second, a reasonable balance between global product standardization and local product differentiation has to be found. In the course of the **configuration strategy**, MNCs have to decide on a configuration regarding the geographic dispersion or allocation of value-adding activities and the supply chain (centralization vs. decentralization). A centralization or concentration strategy is pursued if all value adding activities are focused in one country, usually the country of origin.[215] The opposite pole is represented by a decentralization strategy by conducting each activity within the value chain in every host country.

210 Cf. *Schmid* (2013), p. 20f.

211 Cf. *Benito/Gripsrud* (1992), p. 463.

212 Cf. *Zhang et al.* (2007), p. 754.

213 The sequential strategy can be explained by the Uppsala internationalization process model; cf. *Johanson/Wiedersheim-Paul* (1975); *Johanson/Vahlne* (1977); *Johanson/Vahlne* (2009).

214 Cf. *Forsgren* (2002), p. 271,

215 A pure centralization configuration can be excluded for MNCs by definition due to the geographic focus on a single country. Similarly, corporations pursuing a mere export strategy cannot be classified as MNCs in the sense of this work; see section 1.2.2.

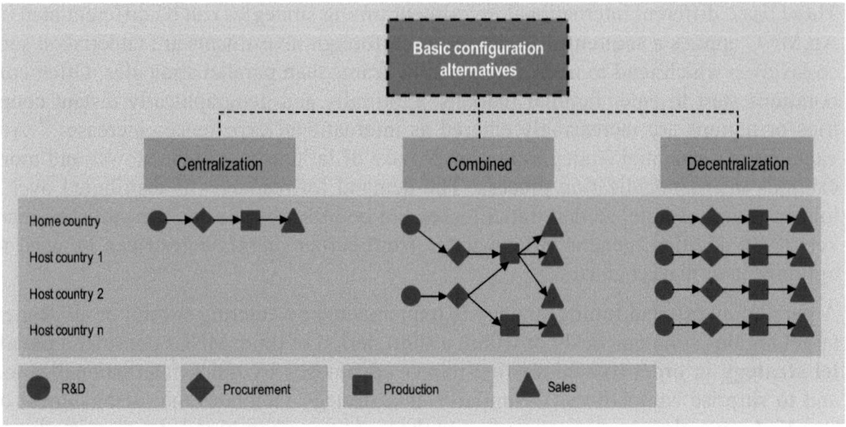

Figure 1-8: Geographic configuration alternatives
Adopted from *Kutschker/Schmid* (2011), p. 1001.

Pure **centralization** and **decentralization** decisions constitute both ends on the continuum of possible allocation configurations, whereas a wide range of combined strategies exist in between the poles as depicted in Figure 1-8. While the extreme forms of dispersion are relatively rare for MNCs, the **combined configurations** are more common in practice.[216] Corporations often perform value chain activities involving core competencies in the domestic country while other activities without the involvement of core-competencies are disaggregated and allocated within the foreign subsidiary network.[217] These separations of value chain activities across the world cause networks of interdependencies between headquarters and foreign subsidiaries which require coordination mechanisms – as explained in the next section.[218]

The **second allocation decision** is concerned with the global product and service design. Decision-makers must find a trade-off regarding the tensions between global **standardization** and local **differentiation** as the two extreme forms of product and service customization.[219] Products and services are globally standardized if those are provided identically across the globe in a uniform manner, like Apple's IPhone.[220] Differentiation takes place when products and services are tailored to the specific local requirements and conditions, like menus of fast food chains.[221] Just as for the configuration design, a variety of combined alternatives can be applied on the continuum in the sense of a partial differentiation or standardization.

MNCs need to define their combination on the continuum between global standardization and local differentiation which is one of the key decisions for achieving market

216 Cf. *Roth* (1992), p. 534f.
217 Cf. *Contractor et al.* (2010), p. 1421.
218 Cf. *Morrison/Roth* (1994), p. 799.
219 Cf. *Cavusgil et al.* (1993), p. 480.
220 Cf. *Kotler* (1986), p. 15.
221 Cf. *Calantone et al.* (2004), p. 186.

acceptance in the host countries.[222] Coordinating headquarter-subsidiary relationships involves balancing forces that call for international integration against forces for national responsiveness within the strategic decision-making process.[223] This is a main structural and textual difference between investment decisions in home and in foreign markets.[224] In every single decision during the investment process these conflicting forces have to be considered by the management.[225] From the parent perspective, MNCs need to integrate their operations in order to achieve global competitiveness (e.g. lower costs due to economies of scale and scope). In contrast to the parent viewpoint, MNCs are pushed to tailor their operations to the host country conditions for local responsiveness at the subsidiary level.[226] Local responsiveness requires a local modification strategy to adapt products and processes to local customer preferences, management styles or business ethics.[227]

1.3.3.4 Coordination decision

Decisions about coordination mechanisms represent a further dimension of strategic decisions in the international context. Especially the globally dispersed value activities in MNCs demand for coordination mechanisms in order to align the variety of corporate measures.[228] As described in the preceding sections, the interdependent relations between market entry mode, target market, timing and allocation decisions cause additional coordination necessities due to the international dimension.[229] While some resources and competencies are centralized in the domestic markets, others are located overseas or globally distributed. This complex configuration of assets and know-how with strong interdependencies amplifies the need for cross-border coordination.[230]

Coordination needs in organizations arise due to the division of labor[231] and specialization in general which lead to interdependencies and interfaces.[232] To align the corporate units to a common shared objective especially in geographically dispersed organizations, interfaces and interdependencies between these corporate units need to be managed and coordinated.[233] MNCs face intensified coordination problems due to greater geographic, psychic and cultural distances.[234] The higher environmental complexity due to various country-specific characteristics represents a driver of additional

222 Cf. *Xu/Shenkar* (2002), p. 609f.
223 Cf. *Porter* (1986), p. 25.
224 Cf. *Doz/Prahalad* (1984), p. 55.
225 Cf. *Doz/Prahalad* (1984), p. 56.
226 Cf. *Roth/Morrison* (1990), p. 541.
227 Cf. *Petersen/Pedersen* (2002), p. 343.
228 Cf. *Martinez/Jarillo* (1989), p. 490.
229 Cf. *Kutschker/Schmid* (2011), p. 1021.
230 Cf. *Bartlett/Ghoshal* (1999), p. 182.
231 When the entire value creation is generated by a single person, interpersonal coordination is not necessary due to the absence of interfaces or interdependencies with other persons.
232 Cf. *Cray* (1984), p. 85.
233 Cf. *Luo/Shenkar* (2006), p. 322.
234 Cf. *Egelhoff* (1984), p. 73.

coordination requirements.[235] MNCs need to differentiate their foreign presence in response to the diverse environments but without losing sight of coordinative and integrative needs.[236]

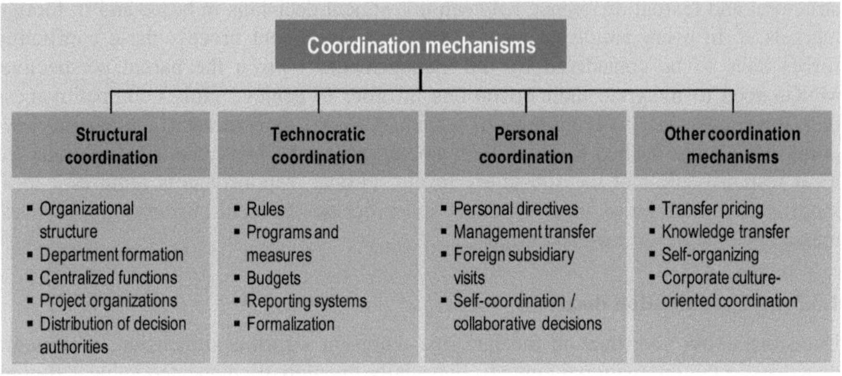

Figure 1-9: Coordination mechanism in MNCs
Modified and adopted from *Kutschker/Schmid* (2011), p. 1035.

MNCs can pursue two different approaches to manage their coordination needs. First, decision-makers can implement coordination mechanisms in order to manage interfaces and interdependencies. Second, coordination requirements can be reduced by reorganizing or restructuring the corporate operations. The most prominent classification of coordination instruments was developed by *Leavitt* distinguishing structural and procedural coordination, whereas procedural coordination is divided in technocratic and personal mechanisms.[237] Specific structural, technocratic, personal and other coordination instruments are differentiated as depicted above in Figure 1-9.[238] Relevant coordination mechanisms in the foreign investment context will be presented in the following.

Structural coordination includes all coordinative elements belonging to the MNC's formal organization. The organization design, e.g. functional, divisional or matrix structures, represents the overall framework for structural coordination mechanisms of a corporation.[239] On the one side, the organizational design is itself a coordinative mechanism on the highest level, but it determines the coordination requirements on the other side, e.g. switching a corporate structure from a functional to a divisional structure leads to different coordination requirements.[240] Departmentalization, project organizations, central functions as well as the distribution of decision authorities unfold coordinative effects. Similar tasks or jobs are placed together in organizational units, e.g. creating a regional headquarter intends to develop a foreign market and establish

235 Cf. *Epstein/Roy* (2007), p. 391.
236 Cf. *Mascarenhas* (1984), p. 92.
237 Cf. *Leavitt* (1964) in combination with *Macharzina/Wolf* (2010), p. 472.
238 Cf. *Khandwalla* (1972), p. 305; or *Welge* (1982), p. 23.
239 Cf. *Harris/Raviv* (2002), p. 854.
240 Cf. *Crowston* (1997), p. 159.

the company locally. In the context of foreign investment decision processes, the **distribution of decision authorities** between the headquarter and the new foreign subsidiary is of special interest.

Technocratic coordination mechanisms do not belong to the formal organization, but they complement structural coordination mechanisms.[241] These coordination mechanisms are dedicated to standardize repetitive problems and tasks with rules, programs and measures, plans, budgets, reporting systems and formalization in order to create corporate routines. Goal, plan, budget or rule pursuance implies coordinative behavior of organizational subunits.[242] Budgets may have a coordinative effect due to the strong influence on the flexibility of decision-making through the distribution of resources, e.g. tight investment budgets limit the alternatives of project managers during the implementation.[243] Reports serve to provide the basis for future corporate measures, e.g. performance reports may deliver starting points for portfolio decisions.[244] In this context, frequent progress reports may be sent to the headquarter to safeguard coordinated decision-making.

Personal coordination is assumed to be effective in complex MNCs due to its greater flexibility.[245] Personal directives are an example for vertical hierarchical coordination whereas self-coordination represents horizontal coordination.[246] Self coordination means that decision authorities are delegated to lower hierarchies in order to make collective decisions, e.g. consensus decision in committees or project teams.[247] For instance, expatriation is a personal coordination and control mechanism for internationally operating corporations. International management delegations intend to transfer knowledge, to develop the future management or to control the foreign operations.[248] For the present work in the context of foreign **investments in emerging countries**, expatriates may be used as an instrument to transfer technological knowledge as well as management capabilities in order to develop local employees and resources.[249]

Transfer pricing, knowledge transfer, self-organizing and corporate culture represent **other coordination mechanisms**. Transfer pricing is used to determine the value of intra-company transactions between subunits to create coordinative effects of internal markets.[250] A strong corporate culture based on a shared set of values, missions, creeds, norms and attitudes can hold geographically dispersed MNCs together. Enhanced coordination unfolds through a strong corporate culture when it leads to consistent behavior and decisions among organizational members.[251] For this study, **cor-**

---

241 Cf. *Reger* (2004), p. 56.
242 Cf. *Kutschker/Schmid* (2011), p. 1043.
243 Cf. *Hirst/Yetton* (1999), p. 214.
244 Cf. *Boddewyn* (1979), p. 23.
245 Cf. *Holtbrügge* (2005), p. 566.
246 Cf. *van de Ven et al.* (1976), p. 323.
247 Cf. *Grant* (1996), p. 115.
248 Cf. *Harzing* (2002), p. 367.
249 Cf. *Wang et al.* (2009), p. 1182.
250 Cf. *Burns* (1980), p. 23.
251 Cf. *Sörensen* (2002), p. 70.

porate cultures tend to be important for the foreign investment decision process. In particular emerging economies, like the BRICs, have different lower compliance and business ethics standards. A strong corporate culture may support to align the actions of local managers to the corporate standards. Self-organizing is not explained due to its assumed lower relevance for the investment decision process.[252]

To sum up, the prior sections served to introduce the main strategic decisions during foreign investment processes. The interplay or combinations of market entry mode, target market, timing, allocation as well as coordination decisions determine the international management philosophies of MNCs, e.g. whether an MNC pursues an ethnocentric, polycentric, regiocentric or geocentric approach.[253] This strategic orientation has significant **implications for the foreign investment decision process**, in particular the distribution of decision authorities between the home and the host country. Ethnocentric corporations tend to manage the entire foreign investment decision process with close headquarter control and a lower degree of decision decentralization. A relatively strong centralization of decision authorities is expected to result in lower coordinative efforts and a shorter approval mechanism. This example highlights the importance of the underlying international strategic decisions for the design of foreign investment decision processes.

1.4 The BRIC phenomenon

In this section the background of the acronym "BRIC countries" will be briefly introduced, focusing especially on the question why the four countries Brazil, Russia, India and China are subsumed under this analytical group of nations or economies. Furthermore, the rationales for selecting the BRIC economies as the desired Greenfield investment region to analyze will be explained. On the one side, the BRIC countries possess promising economic outlooks and **foreign direct investment potentials** which will shift the economic and political power from the matured to the emerging markets. On the other side, still weak institutional environments and distant cultures entail significant risks for foreign investments.[254]

The world's economic system is passing a stage of transformation due to the rise of several emerging market economies which have been the major sources of global growth during the last years.[255] Some authors have little doubt that the next decades will be marked by the **biggest economic changes** since the Industrial Revolution in the 19th century and the BRIC countries are expected to play a major role in this reorientation of economic **power from West to East and North to South**.[256] *Goldman Sachs* has invented the memorable acronym "BRIC countries" for Brazil, Russia, India and China as the largest emerging economies in 2001.[257] Since then, the economic and

252 For a description of self-organizing; cf. *Kutschker/Schmid* (2011), p. 1046ff.
253 See section 1.3.1.3.
254 Cf. *Khanna/Palepu* (2006), p. 67.
255 Cf. *The World Bank* (2011), p. 1.
256 Cf. *Sachs* (2008), p. 15.
257 Cf. *Wilson/Purushothaman* (2003), p. 16.

business press has dedicated enormous attention to these countries.[258] The key statement of Goldman Sachs' research paper is that the list of top ten economies will be subject to major changes until 2050 – with the BRIC countries as dominant players.[259] The dynamic developments of the BRIC countries and the related structural changes in the global economic landscape are expected to have crucial implications for MNCs.

At first glance, the four BRIC nations are different concerning culture, language or the structure of their economies. Although there are main differences[260] among the four geographically distant BRIC economies, these countries share a common denominator that justifies the BRIC concept as an analytical category of nations – apart from above average economic growth in recent years.[261] For this work, the most important common characteristic is that these nations are seen as the main **sources of future economic growth**.[262] Rising economic strengths, educational levels and population will create the potential for the emergence of new centers of political power.[263] Since 2009, the political decision-makers of the four countries meet on the annual **BRIC summit** which shows their aspiration to create a geopolitical alliance.[264] The growing importance for political actors as well as for decision-makers within MNCs is the main criterion for examining these four countries as an emerging collective.[265]

The focus of this study therefore is on foreign investment projects in BRIC countries. The relevance for decision-makers within MNCs will be illustrated by five aspects (1) economic prospects, (2) FDI prospects, (3) political power, (4) institutional environment and (5) emerging market multinationals.

1.4.1 Economic prospects

The World Bank suggests that by 2050 the current biggest seven emerging economies (China, India, Brazil, Russia, Indonesia, Mexico and Turkey) will be around 50% larger in terms of GDP than the current G7 states (USA, Japan, Germany, United Kingdom, France, Italy and Canada). According to forecasts published by *PricewaterhouseCoopers*, China will be the leading economic power in 2050 followed by the USA and India.[266] *Goldman Sachs* predicts similar results with China overtaking the United States in terms of GDP by 2041.[267] The *IMF* estimates that 31% of world GDP will be attributable to the BRICs in 2017, roughly the same like those of G7 countries as depicted in Figure 1-10.

258 Cf. *Armijo* (2007), p. 8.

259 Cf. *Wilson/Purushothaman* (2003), p. 17.

260 For a scientific discussion related to the BRIC concept as an analytical category of states; cf. *Armijo* (2007); or *Payne* (2008), p. 526f.

261 Cf. *Biggemann/Fam* (2011), p. 5.

262 Cf. *Alon et al.* (2010), p. 17.

263 Cf. *The World Bank* (2011), p. 78f.

264 Cf. *Roberts* (2010), p. 40.

265 Cf. *Bird/Cahoy* (2007), p. 424.

266 Cf. *PricewaterhouseCoopers* (2008), p. 25.

267 Cf. *O'Neill et al.* (2005), p. 3.

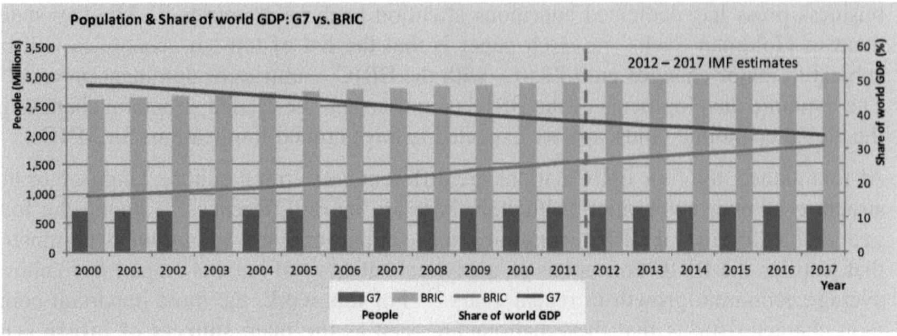

Figure 1-10: Population and share of world GDP of G7 and BRIC countries
Based on the *IMF* economic outlook database[268]

Furthermore, the BRIC population already accounted for 42% of the world population in 2011. Emerging middle classes are expected to be further on the rise. Therefore, consumer spending from BRIC countries is expected to quadruple G6 demand in 2050[269]. Thus, a strong market presence in these countries is expected to be a major condition for future growth. The BRIC nations as the world's engine of new demand growth and spending power can offset the impact of the demographic development and slower growth in the developed economies.[270] "Growth nations" provide investment opportunities for foreign investors, but they are still associated with weak corporate governance and different business ethics.[271] However, higher growth rates contain the potential to higher returns and increased demand for capital. Thus, the weight of the BRICs in the investment portfolios may sharply rise. Being invested and involved in the emerging markets will be an increasingly important strategic choice because of the expected declining importance of developed economies.[272]

1.4.2 FDI prospects

The fast economic development of the BRIC countries over the last years attracted huge amounts of foreign capital by foreign MNCs. In earlier years, these firms mainly intended to get access to resources and cheap labor. Due to the fast growing middle class and its purchasing power in the BRIC countries, nowadays market-seeking has increasingly become the most important motive for foreign investors.[273] In recent years, inward Greenfield investments to BRIC countries experienced stable growth as depicted in Figure 1-11.

---

268 Historical and expected GDP growth (based on constant prices) is published by the *IMF* twice a year. The world economic outlook database by the *IMF* is publicly available on their internet platform and contains selected macroeconomic and demographic data on a global scale (see www.imf.org).

269 Cf. *Wilson/Purushothaman* (2003), p. 5.

270 Cf. *Sachs* (2008), p. 15.

271 Cf. *Borodina/Shvyrkov* (2010), p. xiv.

272 Cf. *Wilson/Purushothaman* (2003), p. 2.

273 Cf. *Johnson/Tellis* (2008), p. 1.

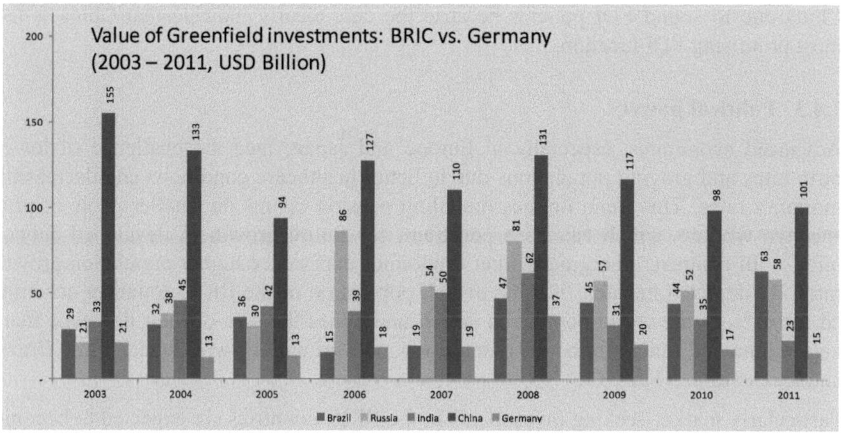

Figure 1-11: Inward Greenfield investment value: BRIC vs. Germany
Cf. *UNCTAD* (2012), p. 192ff.

Except 2006, the value of inward Greenfield investment flows to each of the four BRIC countries exceeded the value of investment flows to Germany between 2003 and 2011.[274] The trends indicate that the gap between the investment values to these four emerging countries and Germany will increase due to assumed high FDI potentials.

The United Nations Conference on Trade and Development (*UNCTAD*) has developed a so called **"inward FDI potential index"** which measures the attractiveness of countries for foreign investors. Countries are ranked based on four FDI determinants using a range of proxy indicators.[275] The determinants cover the three main motives of foreign investors by evaluating the market attractiveness (for market-seeking motives), availability of low-cost labor and skills (to capture efficiency-seeking FDI) and the existence of natural resources (for resource-seeking motives). A forth determinant is the presence of an FDI-enabling infrastructure because it provides the essential framework and services for economic activities. The overall FDI Potential Index rank is calculated by combining the score on all four determinants with equal weights.[276]

According to the UNCTAD inward FDI Potential Index three BRIC nations were ranked among the first six countries with the highest FDI attractiveness in 2012. China is ranked on the first place, India on the third place and Russia on the sixth. Even though Brazil is only on the 25th place the country is still among the first quartile of countries with the highest FDI potential. An interesting aspect is whether the Greenfield investment volumes are consistent to the investigated country-specific challenges within the firm-level cases. For instance, it can be expected that MNCs may focus on

274 In 2006, Brazil‘s inward Greenfield flows amounted to USD 15 billion US-Dollar compared to USD 18 billion for Germany. UNCTAD data for Greenfield investments in Germany are integrated in Figure 1-11 in order to set a benchmark.

275 For the single determinants of a country's FDI potential; cf. *UNCTAD* (2012), p. 30.

276 Cf. *UNCTAD* (2012), p. 30.

China due to sound FDI policies because the data clearly indicate that China is the most promising FDI location.

1.4.3 Political power

Advanced economies, especially in Europe and Japan, face the challenge of lower birth rates and graying populations due to better healthcare conditions and decreasing mortality rates. This trend implies mounting pension claims on smaller pools of prospective workers which can be a constraint for future growth in developed economies.[277] In contrast, emerging market economies experience higher population growth rates. As depicted in Table 1-2, the overall population of the BRIC countries accounted for 42% of the world population which underlines the size of their domestic markets. China and India are the most densely populated nations worldwide, while Brazil and Russia rank 5th and 7th.[278]

Particularly market-seeking investments in the BRIC countries are expected to become the most important motive for MNCs due to the sheer market size.[279] The combination of their large and young populations with rising educational and income level create the foundation for strong market growth rates.[280] As opposed to expected decreasing populations in Germany, Italy or Japan, the BRIC populations are predicted to further increase except for Russia.[281] The Composite Index of National Capabilities (CINC)[282] shows that the BRICs will be indisputable members of the top five to seven **major political powers**. Altogether the BRIC countries already accounted for 34% of worldwide national capabilities in 2007 compared to 28% of the G7 countries – which indicates the political power potential of these four countries.

277 Cf. *Eberstadt* (2010), p. 54.

278 Cf. *Danmarks Nationalbank* (2004), p. 50.

279 Cf. *Morschett et al.* (2010), p. 82.

280 Cf. *Wilson/Purushothaman* (2003), p. 13.

281 Cf. *Kedia et al.* (2006), p. 61f.

282 The Composite Index of National Capabilities (CINC) has been developed by the University of Michigan's Correlates of War in the 1970s. The index is calculated by the average share of the country in six different categories. Share of worldwide population, urban population, iron and steel production, energy consumption, military expenditures and military personnel. Taking the average of each country's share in the international system in every single category leads to the country's share of worldwide material capabilities called the Composite Index of National Capabilities. Although the CINC is just a rough indicator, it could deliver a first insight for a country's power potential. For further explanations see *Chan* (2005), p. 689ff.

	Composite Index of National Capabilities			Population 2007	
Country	1991	2001	2007	Total (millions)	% of World
Canada	1%	1%	1%	33	1%
France	2%	2%	2%	62	1%
Germany	3%	3%	2%	82	1%
Italy	2%	2%	2%	59	1%
Japan	6%	5%	4%	128	2%
United Kingdom	3%	2%	2%	61	1%
United States	14%	14%	14%	302	5%
G7	31%	29%	28%	727	11%
Brazil	2%	2%	2%	188	3%
China	11%	16%	20%	1,325	20%
India	6%	7%	7%	1,134	17%
Russia	10%	5%	4%	142	2%
BRIC	30%	30%	34%	2788	42%

Table 1-2: Composite Index of National Capabilities (percent of world total) and population Based on the correlates of war database (www.correlatesofwar.org).

The **large domestic markets** of these four countries are expected to grow rapidly as the evolvement of the middle class creates new consumers. Large emerging economies in terms of population, like the BRICs, are less exposed to certain risks – like economic shocks – than small emerging markets creating opportunities for foreign companies.[283] According to a study conducted by *A.T. Kearney*, the Chinese as well as the Indian middle class will account for 800 million people in 2030 or roughly ten times the entire German population.[284] This implies huge consumer markets, but foreign MNCs face the challenge to gain these focus groups as new customers. For instance, a questionnaire among executives concluded to build new R&D centers in emerging markets.[285] Product development should be conducted by local researchers due to their proximity and familiarity to the host market.[286]

1.4.4 Institutional environment

Institutional forces in foreign countries influence the organizations' processes and decisions, e.g. related to the legal form of a market entry.[287] Besides the growth opportunities, BRIC countries have also in common that they still do not have sound institutional environments.[288] Although business conditions and corporate governance are improving, the negotiation process works differently in these countries, mainly due to the lack of legal systems and contracts that can be trusted. Established MNC must re-

283 Cf. *Armijo* (2007), p. 11.
284 Cf. *A.T. Kearney* (2010), p. 2.
285 Cf. *Klesse et al.* (2012), p. 63f.
286 Cf. *Lewin et al.* (2009), p. 904.
287 Cf. *Hoskisson et al.* (2000), p. 252.
288 Cf. *Schuster* (2006), p. 418.

think and adapt their competitive behavior due to the absence of a stable and sound institutional environment.[289]

Main problems arise related to corruption and insecure legal systems. The Transparency International **Corruption Perceptions Index** (CPI) 2011, which scores 182 countries and territories from zero (highly corrupt) to ten (very clean), provides indications for high levels of corruption in BRIC countries. The index is based on factors such as enforcement of anti-corruption laws, access to information and conflicts of interest. According to the CPI 2011, Russia is ranked as 143rd (out of 182), India 95th, China 75th and Brazil 73rd.[290] Summing up, MNCs still have to face significant risks referring to the unstable institutional environments in these countries.[291] But the four BRICs are not homogenous due to different starting points on the way to establish sound institutional environments.[292]

The **national culture** is a main determinant of the informal institutional environment. National culture[293] needs to be considered because the individual and organizational decision-making processes are influenced by different layers of cultures.[294] Organizational behavior in culturally pervasive countries, such as India, is influenced by the national culture as companies or institutions are managed by people who are culturally rooted in the local environment.[295] The consideration of these cultural aspects is crucial for the success of FDI decisions, especially in culturally-distant regions, e.g. management styles must be adapted to the cultural specifics to gain the acceptance of the local stakeholders.[296]

The culturally-distant traditions, philosophies and religions of the BRIC countries result in different value systems and sets of business practices. Cultures tend to exhibit specific values, behaviors and beliefs which have an impact on the evaluation of situations and the related decision-making.[297] In culturally-distant regions, MNCs often fail to tailor the business processes and products to the local requirements, e.g. regarding consumer needs, disposable income or marketplace constraints.[298] But creating these products and services according to the local specifics is not sufficient for achieving success in these markets, if the company representatives do not know how to do business in BRIC countries. Finally, the company needs to learn how to adapt its behavior for successful negotiations in BRIC economies.[299] Developing a global mindset[300] is

---

289 Cf. *Hitt et al.* (2005), p. 354.

290 Cf. *Transparency International* (2011).

291 Cf. *Holtbrügge/Baron* (2011), p. 109.

292 Cf. *Hoskisson et al.* (2000), p. 259.

293 The term *culture* can be understood in different contexts or layers, e.g. national culture, family culture or organizational culture. These different forms or manifestations of culture have in common that a group of humans share the same values, beliefs and behaviors which have been evolved over a long period of time; cf. *Child* (1981), p. 303ff.

294 Cf. *Morschett et al.* (2010), p. 134.

295 Cf. *Tayeb* (1994), p. 429 or *Gupta et al.* (2011), p. 65.

296 Cf. *Macharzina/Wolf* (2010), p. 995.

297 Cf. *Gupta et al.* (2011), p. 65.

298 Cf. *Hitt et al.* (2005), p. 362.

299 Cf. *Schuster* (2006), p. 411.

one of the key sources of long-term competitive advantages in the global business, especially in the emerging markets.[301]

Business practices in emerging markets are dominated by informal rules compared to the more formal ones in advanced economies.[302] A common characteristic of BRIC countries is the relationship-oriented culture of "favors" which influences business practices in these countries. Maintaining relationships and building local networks to local stakeholders and government authorities is expected to be critical for success.[303] Government authorities can provide relevant information for doing business in the host markets, simplify regulatory decision processes and reduce political risks for the foreign investor.[304]

Blat[305] and **Guanxi**[306] are expressions for personal networks in Russia and China that have been critical for economic success or even survival in these countries.[307] Both terms express the drawing on personal connections to safeguard favors in personal relations.[308] Cross-cultural proficiency and the quality of **personal networks** is one of the main influencing factors for business success, e.g. related to dealings with national institutions or communication with customers and suppliers.[309] As described earlier, BRIC countries – especially the transition economies China and Russia – have in common that their unstable institutional environment makes personal networks and informal relationships even more important than in developed countries with sound legal systems.[310] This highlights the relevance to consider and understand their cultural background and their predominant worldview in order to be able to create personal networks which can be trusted.[311]

---

300 For a conceptualization and synthesis of current thinking about the *global mindset*, cf. *Levy et al.* (2007).

301 Cf. *Gupta/Govindarajan* (2002), p. 124.

302 Cf. *Rabbiosi et al.* (2012), p. 207.

303 Cf. *Luo/Peng* (1999), p. 118.

304 Cf. *Holtbrügge/Baron* (2011), p. 118.

305 Blat is a term which appeared in the former Soviet Union for denoting the use of personal networks and channels in order to satisfy the needs of personal consumption, e.g. during socialism in conditions of shortages Blat was used as an exchange mechanism for material welfare. For a more detailed description of Blat and its role in Russia's business environment; see section 4.2.2. or cf. *Ledeneva* (1998).

306 Similar to the Russian counterpart Guanxi is an expression for personal relationships with mutually agreed obligations in China. The term Guanxi refers to interpersonal relationships with socially binding reciprocal obligations for the exchange of favors. As well as Blat in Russia Guanxi is historically and culturally embedded in the Chinese society and hardly translatable into English. For a more detailed description of Guanxi and its role in China's business environment; see section 4.2.4; or cf. *Tsang* (1998); or *Luo* (2007).

307 Cf. *Michailova/Worm* (2003), p. 510.

308 Cf. *Michailova/Worm* (2003), p. 511.

309 Cf. *Morschett et al.* (2010), p. 136.

310 Cf. *Luk et al.* (2008), p. 592.

311 Cf. *Luo* (2003b), p. 1326.

1.4.5 Emerging market multinationals

After the growing importance of the BRICs on the country-level has been explained, this section intends to explain the rising competitive pressures from EMNCs. The dynamic economic development will inevitably create serious competitors who will seek to dominate their industries on a global scale.[312] EMNCs use the momentum from their home markets to strengthen their global presence.[313] Recent years showed that EMNCs entered into a **new phase of international expansion.**[314] Outward FDI flows from developing and emerging economies increased from USD 12 billion in 1990 to USD 340 billion in 2008.[315] Outward FDI flows attributable to BRIC countries experienced even higher growth rates. Between 2000 and 2008 outward FDI flows from India increased annually[316] by 176%, followed by China (165%), Russia (151%) and Brazil (151%).[317]

In particular during the last years of global economic slowdown, EMNCs took the opportunity to expand their global presences via foreign direct investments. These firms are combining **global reach** with significant lower costs than established MNCs due to their large footprint in low-cost countries.[318] The Indian industrial conglomerate *Tata Group* represents an example in this respect, which acquired the British traditional automotive company *Jaguar Land Rover* in 2008. Russian *Gazprom* continues to strengthen its strategic position in the European gas market with the Nord Stream gas pipeline.[319] The Chinese company *Lenovo* emerged as global leading computer hardware provider by acquiring *IBM's* personal computer division in 2005 and the German electronics manufacturer *Medion* in 2011.[320] If established MNCs from the developed world want to stay ahead in the worldwide competition, they must create strategies to compete in the huge emerging consumer markets by adapting local knowledge in order to reach the rising middle classes.[321] Otherwise, EMNCs can further pick up the momentum from their home markets to strengthen their international positions.

The *World Bank* 2011 report on emerging markets underlines that EMNCs are on the way towards dominating their industrial sectors worldwide. These companies are already competing with MNCs from advanced economies for natural resources, technology and international market shares.[322] The annual volume of cross-border M&A by emerging market corporations is expected to double by 2025, while the number of

---

312 Cf. *Ghauri/Santangelo* (2012), p. 146.

313 Cf. *Sauvant* (2006), p. 382.

314 Cf. *Kumar* (2009), p. 115f.

315 Developing and emerging economies include 113 countries which are classified as developing countries by UNCTAD plus Russia; cf. *Gammeltoft et al.* (2010), p. 255.

316 Compound annual growth rate (CAGR).

317 Cf. *Chen* (2012), p. 11.

318 Cf. *Ramamurti* (2012), p. 242.

319 For a detailed analysis of the impact of the north European Gas pipeline (*Nord Stream*) on Europe's energy security; cf. *Cohen* (2006); or *Stern* (2005).

320 Cf. *McManus et al.* (2012), p. 187.

321 Cf. *Khanna/Palepu* (2010), p. 89.

322 Cf. *The World Bank* (2011), p. 73.

cross-border M&A is projected to triple.[323] Greenfield investments attributable to emerging market companies amounted to USD 1.72 trillion, which is a further indicator for EMNCs to become global players.[324] Companies from BRIC countries have taken advantage of inward internationalization in their home markets via strategic cooperation and joint ventures with established MNCs. EMNCs use the accumulated organizational, managerial and technological capabilities for outward internationalization to compete with established global players on the world markets.[325]

A current practical example is the **German solar industry**. Former German world-leading solar corporations like *Solon* or *Solar Millennium* filed for bankruptcy, *Solar World* is fighting for survival and *Q-Cells* was taken over by its Asian rival *Hanergy Holdings*. Due to massive price erosions *Siemens* and *Bosch* also decided to cease their solar businesses.[326] In particular Chinese solar corporations, like *LDK Solar* or *Yingli Solar*, are globally integrated with financing from American stock exchanges, production in China and distribution networks in Europe.[327] Cost advantages between 30-40% compared to the German solar industry make it possible for the Chinese solar companies to offer their products significantly cheaper at the same quality. This development of the Chinese solar corporation led to the demise of almost an entire industry in Germany.[328] This example illustrates that Western MNCs need to anticipate the rising competition from EMNCs by rethinking established strategies.[329]

In this section the practical relevance of investment projects in BRIC countries has been presented, while the theoretical rationale for this study is illustrated by analyzing prior research in the next section.

1.5 Prior research

1.5.1 Research field characteristics

This section reviews prior research on foreign investment decision processes to gain a deeper understanding for unexplored areas and related **research gaps**. The literature review and underlying research provide starting points for the development of the research questions and objectives. At this point, it has to be pointed out again that besides the theoretical aspirations, the predominant emphasis of this work is to investigate research questions of **practical relevance** in order to meet the requirements of an applied science like business administration. In this respect, the development of the research objectives was more strongly driven by this practical aspiration – while the course of investigation is driven by theory.

323 Cf. *The World Bank* (2011), p. 5.
324 Cf. *The World Bank* (2011), p. 5.
325 Cf. *Luo/Tung* (2007), p. 481.
326 Cf. *Financial Times* (2013).
327 Cf. *Technische Universität München* (2012), p. 88ff.
328 Cf. *Klooß/Lirsch* (17.08.2011).
329 Cf. *Khanna et al.* (2005), p. 64.

This study aims to investigate foreign investment decision processes in MNCs. Due to the **multidisciplinary research field** empirical studies are attributable to three main research streams. It is a general feature of process-related investigations that relevant research areas are more difficult to demarcate due to their interdisciplinary, complex characteristics and holistic intentions.[330] For this reason, the research field is defined prior to the review of single empirical studies in the following two sections.

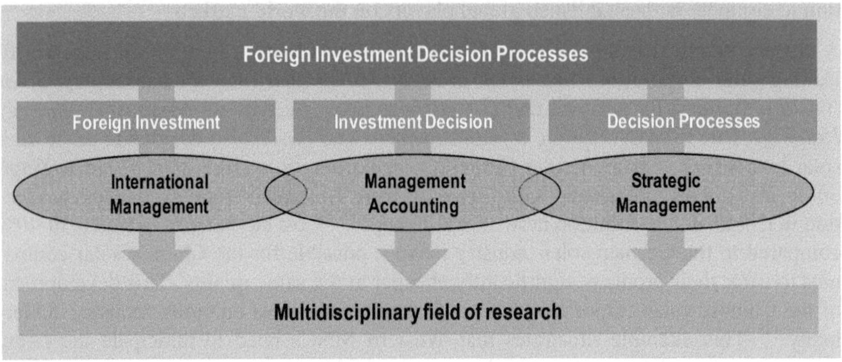

Figure 1-12: Research field characteristics

As depicted in Figure 1-12, the thesis topic has been decomposed in three parts – (1) foreign investment, (2) investment decision, (3) decision processes – in order to illustrate influencing research streams. This decomposition shows that the research topic of "foreign investment decision processes" is influenced by international management, management accounting and strategic management research. Furthermore, this separation of the research topic may provide a first indication that comparable studies have not been conducted. It can be suspected that only **limited empirical research** exists that covers the entire foreign investment decision process and provides a comprehensive view of the research object. But prior to the review of single empirical studies the general characteristics of international management, management accounting and strategic management research in this context are presented.

Research on foreign investments is mainly attributable to international management studies, investment decisions are primarily investigated by management accounting research and decision processes represent research objects of strategic management investigators.[331] In the following relevant aspects of these three research areas for the present study are briefly characterized.

A problem related to **international management** research is that there is no clear consensus about the conceptual domains.[332] In this respect, international management re-

330 Cf. *Chakravarthy/Doz* (1992), p. 6.

331 The allocation of the three study title components to different research streams, like foreign investments to international management studies, is a rough indication to gain a better overview of the research field.

332 Cf. *Toyne* (1989), p. 1.

search can be classified according to the specific foreign investment decisions as introduced in section 1.3.3, e.g. a lot of empirical investigations try to find relationships between certain target market decisions (see 1.3.3.1) and foreign investment performance.[333] A further prevailing feature of relevant international management studies is that empirical longitudinal investigations are relatively scarce compared to the flood of cross-sectional studies. Possible reasons for this underrepresentation may be the lower practicability of dynamic, longitudinal studies and the associated complexity of process investigations.[334] Therefore, this work intends to provide a more dynamic picture of foreign investments by taking a process perspective. *Aharoni* (1966) conducted one of the few studies which are explicitly concentrated on foreign investment decision processes.[335] To avoid redundancies his empirically grounded model will not be discussed at this point because it will be presented separately within section 2.1.2.

Management accounting research in the context of this work is mainly concerned with the evaluation and coordination of investment decisions. For this reason, the majority of empirical research is focused on the application or diffusion of capital budgeting tools. Studies on the diffusion rate of capital budgeting methods are mainly descriptive in order to identify, whether the theoretically sophisticated models are common practice in corporations.[336] Just a few exploratory studies investigated the relationship between firm performance and the implementation of sophisticated capital budgeting tools (see section 1.5.2.). Moreover, conceptual studies tried to develop theoretical capital budgeting models which can consider the additional risk associated with foreign investments.[337] Studies on investment decision processes are relatively rare compared to the investigations of the diffusion of capital budgeting tools.

Empirical studies on decision processes are usually attributable to the field of **strategic management**. Strategy-process and strategy-content research are the two centerpieces of strategic management research.[338] The former investigates how effective strategies are shaped within the corporations.[339] In contrast, strategy-content research focuses on corporate strategic positions that lead to maximum performance under varying environmental factors.[340] As opposed to the strategy-content stream, the process school does not necessarily assume rational decision-making which requires considering behavioral scientific disciplines, like sociology or psychology.[341] Results of the strategy-process research are considered for the firm-level case analysis because this research stream is also mainly focused on decision processes as the main unit of analysis. In this context of investment decision processes – which can be regarded as strategy processes – the empirically developed promotor model by *Witte* and related extensions

333 Cf. *Melin* (1992), p. 100.
334 Cf. *Simon* (2007b), p. 40f.
335 Cf. *Aharoni* (1966).
336 For an overview of prior research see Appendix A.
337 See for example *Kolbe* (1989); *Mrotzek* (1989); or *Scholz* (1996).
338 Cf. *Al-Laham* (1997), p. 23.
339 Cf. *Chakravarthy/Doz* (1992), p. 5.
340 Cf. *Huff/Reger* (1987), p. 211f.; or *Chakravarthy/Doz* (1992), p. 5.
341 Cf. *Eisenhardt* (1989a), p. 71.

made by *Chakrarbati* and *Hausschildt* are of special relevance for this research project.[342] Due to their focus on innovation processes, their studies are not separately discussed in this section. Moreover, the publications of *Witte* will be presented separately within the relevant firm-level theories in section 2.1.4.

After the germane research fields for this study have been reflected, **single studies** are discussed in the following. Due to the interdisciplinary and composed character of this research topic, comparable studies are almost non-existent. Although only limited investigations concerning foreign investment decision processes are available, investment-related prior research is reviewed to gain a distinct sense for research questions. Single studies are not always unambiguously attributable to one of the three research streams as indicated by the overlapping circles in Figure 1-13. Hence, prior research is separated in **investment decision** studies (section 1.5.2) and **investment decision process** inquiries (section 1.5.3.). Domestic and foreign investment decision studies as well as domestic and foreign investment decision process investigations can be differentiated within the two categories.

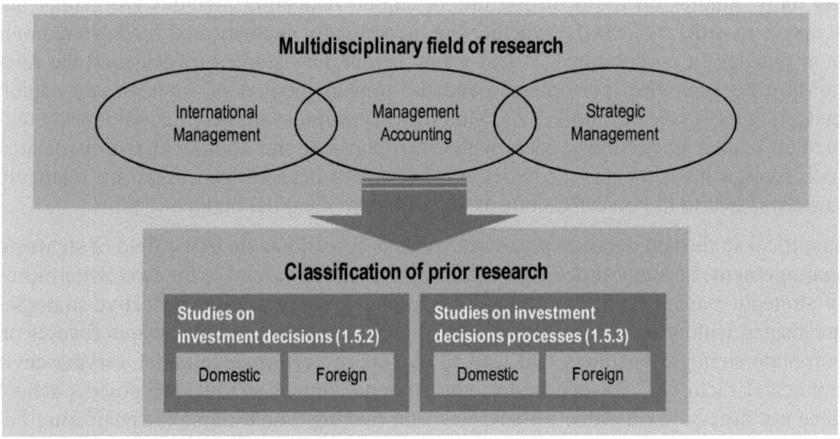

Figure 1-13: Classification of prior research

1.5.2 Investment decisions

First, studies are presented which are focused on domestic investment decision evaluations. Thereby, descriptive and explanatory investigations can be differentiated. Second, empirical studies are reviewed that are explicitly focused on foreign investment decision-making. Due to multitude of empirical investigations, conceptual studies are not considered here. Although the presented studies in this section are only focused on the investment decision evaluation at the approval stage, these investigations are discussed in order to gain a deeper understanding of interesting aspects at this critical stage within the investment decision process.

342 See section 2.1.4.

Domestic investments

A lot of survey-based analyses concerning the implemented capital budgeting methods were undertaken in the Anglo-American region by **descriptive investigations**. Most authors tried to ascertain whether the usage in practice is consistent to the preferred methods in theory. Subsequently, two exemplary studies will be presented which illustrate the continuously decreasing theory-practice-gap related to investment evaluation practices.[343] Earlier studies identified a significant gap between financial theory and capital budgeting methods used in practice.[344] Payback and accounting rate of return were preferred to time value of money concepts, like NPV or IRR, despite the theoretical superiority of the latter. *Brigham* (1975) observed that discounted cash flow methods are not consistently applied. For instance, many corporations used historical rate of returns for the discount rate.[345] A further interesting aspect is that for a long time IRR was more common in practice than NPV. The author explained this trend toward more sophisticated capital budgeting methods by the fast development of information technology and managerial education.

Pike (1996) criticizes that authors try to identify capital budgeting trends by means of comparison with earlier empirical studies.[346] He argues that dissimilar data samples do not permit comparisons. Moreover, mail surveys tend to overstate the degree of sophistication due to non-response biases. Therefore, *Pike* undertook a longitudinal study using the same samples and survey questions in order to identify reliable trends in capital budgeting adoption. The surveys were conducted at five-year intervals between 1975 and 1992. He observed that the gap between theory and practice is almost insignificant at the end of the investigation period. The greatest changes are explored in the areas of risk analysis, discounted cash flow methods and post-investment audits. These findings related to the diffusion of sophisticated investment decision evaluation practices are consistent with other investigations.[347] For this reason, additional studies are not discussed in further detail.

A special category in this research field represents **comparative management accounting** research. This research stream intends to identify and explain country-specific differences of implemented capital budgeting methods. *Carr and Tomkins* (1996) investigated the relation of capital budgeting methods and strategic management tools in order to analyze the interlock between strategy and investment projects.[348] Their work is based on 25 case studies in German and 24 case studies in British vehicle component companies. Thereby, the study does not explicitly differentiate between capital budgeting methods for domestic and foreign investment projects – the focus is country-specific differences. British companies tend to adopt tighter financial controls than Germans. Surprisingly, both countries place less value on DCF methods

343 For an overview of further investigations in this respect see Appendix A.

344 Cf. *Mao* (1970); *Klammer* (1972); *Gitman/Mercurio* (1982); or *Sangster* (1993).

345 Cf. *Brigham* (1975), p. 19.

346 Cf. *Pike* (1996), p. 80.

347 Cf. *Farragher/Kleiman* (1999); *Gitman/Vandenberg* (2000); or *Ryan/Ryan* (2002).

348 Cf. *Carr/Tomkins* (1996), p. 200.

within the context of strategic investments than for minor investment decisions. This implies that the usage of DCF methods is not just an issue of the relative financial sophistication of different companies. Moreover, companies question the appropriateness of DCF techniques on strategic investment decisions and prefer to apply them for minor investments with broader databases.[349]

Explanatory studies represent a further category which intends to discover significant relationships between dependent and independent variables. These studies differentiate in a simplified manner between sophisticated and not sophisticated capital budgeting methods or developed sophistication indices in order to identify influences on the overall firm performance.[350] Compared to the variety of descriptive studies on diffusion rates, just a few authors tried to investigate the relationship between capital budgeting sophistication and firm or investment performance. In the following, the three latest explanatory studies are discussed – further investigations are even older.[351]

Haka, Gordon and *Pinches* (1985) investigated the effect on firm market performance after switching from so called "naïve" capital budgeting techniques to sophisticated models.[352] Therefore, the authors used personal interviews to explore companies which switched from naïve to sophisticated capital budgeting tools and companies which did not. They analyzed the market performance of the two groups – 48 months before the switch and 48 months after the switch. The results of the study indicate no superior market performance of firms adopting sophisticated techniques compared to the firms without sophisticated capital budgeting techniques. Only positive short-term effects on market performance could be identified close to the switch from naïve to sophisticated techniques.[353] The main criticism is that capital budgeting sophistication is not further defined. Therefore, it is not assessable whether the authors appropriately differentiate between sophisticated and not sophisticated tools. A general question in this respect is if this strict distinction between the two groups is reasonable at all. Furthermore, the performance measure is based on stock returns – which may be impacted by external capital market influences.

In contrast, *Moore* and *Reichert* (1989) found a significant correlation between the use of sophisticated capital budgeting methods and superior firm performance. But opposed to other explanatory studies, they investigated a significant positive relation between firm performance and use of modern analytical tools in general.[354] Therefore, they surveyed the companies concerning the regular use of certain analytical techniques in the area of working capital management, capital budgeting and operations research. The authors used more indicators than just the employed method for the degree of capital budgeting or working capital management sophistication. Similarly,

---

349 Cf. *Carr/Tomkins* (1996), p. 204.

350 Sophisticated capital budgeting methods are concepts that incorporate the time value of money, like DCF or IRR. Static methods like payback or accounting rate of return are classified as not sophisticated.

351 Cf. *Christy* (1966); *Klammer* (1973); and *Kim* (1981).

352 Cf. *Haka et al.* (1985), p. 652.

353 Cf. *Haka et al.* (1985), p. 666f.

354 Cf. *Moore/Reichert* (1989), p. 86.

they collected data about the usage of modern computer technologies. To determine superior firm performance, they used the difference between the companies' and industries' return on investment.[355] This accounting-based performance measure is not consistent to the definition of capital budgeting sophistication or shareholder value creation. However, a main difference to other investigations is that the sophistication measure is not only focused on capital budgeting tools but moreover on sophisticated tools concerning working capital management and operational management. In this context, the results cannot be generalized that higher capital budgeting sophistication results in superior firm performance. For this reason, the authors concluded that higher firm performance is attributable to managerial sophistication in general which is represented by the adoption of sophisticated tools in all relevant corporate functions.[356]

Farragher, *Kleimann* and *Sahu* (2001) found no significant relation between the adoption of sophisticated capital budgeting methods and superior firm performance. Their study was an attempt to measure the relation between investment decision evaluation sophistication and firm performance.[357] Therefore, they developed a capital budgeting sophistication metric which is based on the answers concerning the importance of several capital budgeting activities, e.g. strategic analysis, risk analysis or forecasting of cost and returns. Based on the respondents' opinions on the importance of different capital budgeting activities they calculated a firm-specific sophistication metric. The sophistication metric includes equal aspects of the whole investment process, e.g. whether or not a company employs full-time capital investment staff or uses formal screening committees.[358] For the corporate performance the authors used industry-adjusted measures – defined as operating return relative to the operating return of the industry. Their investigation does not support their hypothesis that firms with superior performance can be associated with higher capital budgeting sophistication.[359] This may be explained by methodological weaknesses. Their capital budgeting sophistication can be regarded as relatively imprecise, e.g. respondents were asked to evaluate the importance of risk or strategic analysis without specifying it. Furthermore, CFOs responded to the surveys who are usually not the users of capital budgeting tools.

Foreign investments

Compared to the variety of empirical research on the implementation of capital budgeting methods in general, previous empirical research on **capital budgeting for foreign direct investments** is relatively rare. *Kelly* and *Philippatos* (1982) studied the foreign direct investment valuation practices of U.S. manufacturing MNCs. Their survey-based analysis – complemented by follow-up interviews – provides evidence that companies were more concerned with business risks than currency or political risks. All three types of risk were subjectively evaluated and assessed through adjustments in

355 Cf. *Moore/Reichert* (1989), p. 82.
356 Cf. *Moore/Reichert* (1989), p. 86.
357 Cf. *Farragher et al.* (2001), p. 300.
358 Cf. *Farragher et al.* (2001), p. 301.
359 Cf. *Farragher et al.* (2001), p. 306.

the discount rate.[360] Surprisingly, the authors found significant relationships between the target investment regions and related evaluation practices. Companies investing in Asia tended to take a strong parent company perspective compared to the European investments with a stronger subsidiary perspective. These results indicate that the companies adjust their evaluation technique with the associated risk of the investment region. Therefore, it may be interesting, whether the in-depth case analysis of this work identifies differences related to the application of analytical tools between the four BRIC countries.

Oblak and *Helm* (1980) investigated applied capital budgeting methods as well as underlying procedures to estimate project returns, risks and required rate of returns of U.S. MNCs.[361] The survey results indicate that MNCs have implemented more sophisticated capital budgeting tools compared to earlier investigations. Nonetheless, the specific project risks are subjectively calculated and incorporated as premiums on the discount rate.[362] *Wilson* (1993) concluded that only very few companies in the UK employ a conceptual framework of risk and return in which they can consider the project risk in the financial evaluation.[363] The author suggests that further research should aim to investigate investment decision processes in their organizational context in order to gain a deeper understanding of the underlying rationales of applied capital budgeting tools.[364]

The findings of *Block* (2000) demonstrate that the implemented concepts for FDI evaluation are not consistently used in practice. While half of the respondents used WACC as the appropriate discount rate, over 60% take foreign affiliate cash flows rather than the funds transferred to the investor in the home country.[365] The survey-based dissertation of *Fox* (1999) investigates the role of management accounting and the applied concepts in foreign direct investment processes. He surveyed German companies and came to the result that "rules of thumbs" dominate the assessment of risk in evaluating international investment projects.[366] These findings are consistent to the conclusions of an earlier investigation by *Scholz* (1996). He observed that risk assessments for the evaluation of foreign projects are challenging tasks for German companies. *Scholz* claims that theory should focus on developing comprehensive models that are capable to integrate the additional risks in the investment appraisals.[367]

Summary

The literature review with respect to investment decisions underlines that the adoption of sophisticated capital budgeting methods has increasingly become common practice. The gap between the postulated concepts by theory and the implemented tools con-

360 Cf. *Kelly/Philippatos* (1982), p. 24.
361 Cf. *Oblak/Helm* (1980), p. 37.
362 Cf. *Oblak/Helm* (1980), p. 39.
363 Cf. *Wilson* (1993), p. 30.
364 Cf. *Wilson* (1993), p. 31.
365 Cf. *Block* (2000), p. 320.
366 Cf. *Fox* (1999), p. 312.
367 Cf. *Scholz* (1996).

verged to insignificance. Thus, further research focusing solely on the investment decision evaluation sophistication and diffusion rates are of limited interest.

Explanatory research on investment decisions tried to identify significant relationships between superior firm performance and the usage of sophisticated capital budgeting tools. Most studies cannot discover significant relationships between superior performance and the implementation of sophisticated tools. Besides their methodological weaknesses, the results are not surprising. Although sophisticated capital budgeting tools are effective to plan, select and monitor investments, shareholder value or superior performance is mainly created through innovative ideas or accretive strategies. Sophisticated capital budgeting tools themselves are not able to actively manage or change the prospects of performance. Similarly, a multitude of other determinants affect the company performance – like the environmental context – wherein the capital budgeting sophistication is just a piece of the puzzle. Therefore, this work takes a holistic view on foreign investment projects in order to understand the processes from the initial idea until the first revenue recognition of the new facilities.

As opposed to the studies on domestic investment decision evaluation, the investigations related to foreign investment decision evaluations deliver heterogeneous results. Evaluation practices with respect to foreign investment decisions differ among corporations due to the difficult consideration of the additional risks, like exchange rate or political risks. Prior research indicates that evaluation techniques for foreign investment decisions are dominated by "rule of thumbs", but this is not surprising because the financial literature cannot provide standardized approaches to incorporate the additional risks. To the best of the author's knowledge explanatory studies – which investigate the relationship between foreign investment decision evaluation sophistication and investment or firm performance – have not been conducted.

1.5.3 Investment decision processes

Consistent to the prior section two types of studies are differentiated. First, investigations concentrated on domestic investment decision processes are discussed. Second, the research field explicitly focused on foreign investment decision processes is illustrated. A difference to the review of prior research related to investment decision is that conceptual studies are also considered at this point. This seems to be reasonable due to the very limited scope of empirical research related to investment decision processes. In the following, relevant studies are presented chronologically from the earliest to the most recent.

Domestic investments

Hill (1955) argues in his pioneering work that the investment proposal has to go through different preceding steps prior to its analytical evaluation by sophisticated methods. His conceptual work criticized the strong emphasis on analytical problems of appropriate project evaluation.[368] For this reason, he tried to develop an **idealized pro-**

368 Cf. *Hill, JR.* (1955), p. 285.

cess model in order to present the "life history" of an investment proposal from inception to its final disposition in order to address the administrative problems related to investment decisions. He developed fifteen ideal-typical stages to create investment proposals.[369] The conceptual work of *Hill* has not been empirically tested, but it is a first attempt to develop a comprehensive phase model. A main problem of his idealized model is that it does not consider internal and external context factors that may have an impact on the "life history" of investments. His phase model assumes that investment ideas are generated on the middle management level and does not consider that investment ideas could emerge on different management levels. As opposed to *Hill* the conceptual study of *Norton* (1955) identified only initiation, screening and approval as the three main stages of capital budgeting processes. *Norton's* work provides little new insights regarding the topic of capital budgeting processes because his phase model is too imprecise. Furthermore he excludes the project implementation in his approach.

Bower (1970) was one of the first authors who argues that capital budgeting is a **general management task** rather than financial specialists' exercise. Moreover, capital budgeting involves the coordination of the multi-personal investment processes in order to tie these processes to the corporate goals.[370] The general management must handle the diverse, and often conflicting, requirements of the employees, the corporate sub-units and the corporation in order to allocate resources in the most effective way. He analyzed four major investment projects in a diversified U.S. firm by documenting the organizational path of investments based on interviews with different management levels. *Bower* followed the investments from the beginning through rejection or approval in order to develop a descriptive model of the socio-political investment decision process. He provided evidence for the important role of human factors and organizational structures in investment decision processes.[371] *Bower* postulates that positive NPV projects are not necessarily implemented when the general management does not support the project.

Another author who considered the importance of organizational, environmental and human factors was *King* (1975). He also claimed that the focus of capital budgeting research on the evaluation stage is misplaced and should be **refocused on the project search and definition**. His hypotheses are based on two case studies of large capital investments in a British MNC. *King* attempted to develop a decision process model for large-scale investments in diversified companies which is adapted to the influence of human and organizational factors, like politics.[372] He postulates that top management should influence the search for ideas and project definition, so that the outcomes of these early stages are consistent to the corporate strategy. *King*'s point of view is that

369 Cf. *Hill, JR.* (1955), p. 285ff.
370 Cf. *Bower* (1970), p. 15.
371 Cf. *Bower* (1970), p. 279ff.
372 Cf. *King* (1975), p. 71ff.

the definition stage is an implicit evaluative process of balancing technical and economic characteristics to develop a promising business case.[373]

The following formal evaluation stage intends to develop an investment case which can be transmitted upwards through the organization in order to get political top management support. His opinion is that capital budgeting methods are not central to **optimal choice** due to the following reasons: First, projects are assumed to already exist for the evaluation. Second, the selection of defined projects is presumed to be sufficient to indentify the optimal allocation of capital. For this reason, the search and creation stages are more critical to the overall success of an investment project than the evaluation with more or less sophisticated tools.[374]

The empirical work of *Papadakis* (1998) is an explanatory study which pretends to investigate the relation between **investment decision processes and firm performance.**[375] Although the study's title indicates the focus on investment decision processes, the investigation is rather concentrated on strategic decision processes in general. *Papadakis* applied a mixed-method design[376] in order to investigate the relationship between the decision process design and organizational performance. His sample comprised 89 Greek manufacturing companies with more than 300 employees. A combined performance measure with subjectively perceived measures and objective financial reporting data has been used.[377] The independent strategic decision process variables were measured along nine process dimensions.[378]

Papadakis found only significant relations between process dimensions and single elements of the combined performance measure. Apart from the small sample size, the study does not disclose further sample company characteristics. This seems to be necessary in order to evaluate the appropriateness of the strategic decision process dimensions, e.g. a sample based on large MNCs requires a different process comprehension than SME samples. A further main limitation is that the environment or context, in which the decision process takes place, was not considered in the model. Finally, the study was conducted in a very specific setting of probably locally-oriented firms in Greece so that the transferability to other contexts is questionable at all.

Maritan (2001) used a case study approach in order to identify differences of investment processes within a single firm depending on the type of the investment. Her case study was conducted in a large *Fortune 500* U.S. pulp and paper firm based on 29 different investments.[379] Each investment constitutes a single case study. She concluded significant differences between decision processes for investments in "new" capabilities and investments in "existing" capabilities. An interesting aspect is that the **pro-**

373 Cf. *King* (1975), p. 77.
374 Cf. *King* (1975), p. 80.
375 Cf. *Papadakis* (1998), p. 115.
376 Mixed-method design means to combine quantitative and qualitative research designs; cf. *Teddlie/Tashakkori* (2003); or *Greene* (2008), p. 7ff.
377 Cf. *Papadakis* (1998), p. 121.
378 For the nine process dimensions; cf. *Papadakis* (1998), p. 123.
379 Cf. *Maritan* (2001), p. 515ff.

cesses were neither explicitly designed nor even recognized as existent by the companies. Based on her results she modified the standard process model to recognize the differences of investments in "new" capabilities. While the standard process model was consistent to the results of "maintain" or "add" investments, the decision process model differs for investments in "new" capabilities.

A key difference is that "new" investments involve more senior management activity. The results provided evidence that new investments were mostly originated at the senior division level rather than at the operating level. *Maritan* explains the different degrees of senior management involvement by the information requirements.[380] Operating-level managers are better able to identify opportunities to invest in existing capabilities due to their detailed local information of the operational management. This allows the senior management to devote attention to develop new capabilities. A senior management responsibility is to identify investment opportunities that are outside the current experience. Furthermore, investments in new capabilities are directly influenced by the senior and top management during the development of the investment proposal. This leads to a more **political decision process** with less procedural rationality.[381] She defines procedural rationality as the extent to which decision makers collect, analyze and rely upon relevant information. To sum up, it is not surprising that strategic investments in new capabilities require more **senior management involvement**. It should be one of the major top management tasks to force new investments that expand the company's opportunity set. Moreover, *Maritan's* study provided evidence – consistent to Bower's propositions – that investment decision processes are significantly influenced by internal political processes and not always driven by purely rational decision-making criteria.

Mittermüller and *von Nietzsch* (2008) conducted a study on large European corporations concerning critical success factors related to single stages in investment processes.[382] They criticized earlier studies because almost 90% just examined the evaluation phase or the post-audit control stage, although prior surveys indicated that the **implementation is the most critical part** for the process success.[383] They structured the investment process in four different stages and deductively defined critical success factors for each stage. Additionally, they incorporated context factors in their survey that were expected to influence the investment process success. Successful and less successful companies were classified by return on invested capital (ROIC). The main result of the study is that the overall investment performance does not solely depend on certain single stages. Moreover, the performance is based on the complementary interaction of all the elements involved in the investment process. The implemented capital budgeting tools tend to have a smaller impact on the success than assumed by the bulk of research on the diffusion of certain capital budgeting methods.[384] This

380 Cf. *Maritan* (2001), p. 527.
381 Cf. *Maritan* (2001), p. 523ff.
382 Cf. *Mittermüller/von Nitzsch* (2008).
383 Cf. *Mittermüller/von Nitzsch* (2008), p. 770.
384 Cf. *Mittermüller/von Nitzsch* (2008), p. 779.

practically-oriented investigation provided implications for further research projects covering the entire investment decision process.

Foreign investments

The review of literature related to the investment decision process for domestic projects shows a limited state of research, but relevant studies explicitly focusing on foreign investment decision processes are even scarcer. As stated earlier, *Aharoni's* pioneering work is certainly the most striking investigation related to foreign investment decision processes.[385] But surprisingly, only a few Finnish researchers tried to further refine *Aharoni's* results. *Boddewyn* already criticized in 1983 that *"The conditions, motivations, and evaluation practices bearing on the decision to invest abroad have also been studied extensively (...) This kind of analysis sheds relatively little light, however, on the foreign investment decision process itself."*[386]

The conceptual work of *Boddewyn* applied *Aharoni's* foreign investment decision process framework in order to develop a **divestment decision process model.**[387] He proposed a seven step divestment phase model and discussed differences between foreign and domestic divestment processes. A main argument is that foreign divestment decisions are easier to make due to the lower emotional involvement and the greater spatial distance of the domestic decision center.[388] Although this study used foreign investment decision processes as a starting point, the results are of limited relevance for this work due to the focus on divestment decisions. Thereupon, only one empirical investigation has been conducted which addresses this research gap and is worth mentioning.

Larimo (1995) is one of the few Finnish investigators who tried to explore firm-specific foreign investment decision processes. The main purpose of his study was to illustrate various **types of foreign investment decision processes** based on a case study approach in five Finnish firms.[389] *Larimo* applied the strategic decision process model by *Mintzberg, Raisinghani and Théorêt* (1976) as an underlying framework in order to investigate unstructured foreign investment decision processes.[390] The study results provided evidence that various factors influence the foreign investment decision processes, like firm size or firm-specific internationalization experiences. Furthermore, *Larimo* complements the results of *Aharoni* that the foreign investment decision process is a very complicated social process – but without further specifications. Although the study contributes to a more comprehensive description of foreign investment decision processes, the study is exposed to several limitations. A main criticism is that the five different foreign investment decision processes are each based on only one interview. Therefore, subjectivity and individual biases represent the main limitations. Similarly, the five different foreign investment decision processes are sim-

385 Cf. *Aharoni* (1966); or see section 2.1.2.
386 *Boddewyn* (1983), p. 23.
387 Cf. *Boddewyn* (1983), p. 26.
388 Cf. *Boddewyn* (1983), p. 30ff.
389 Cf. *Larimo* (1995), p. 26f.
390 For the strategic decision process model; cf. *Mintzberg et al.* (1976).

ple process descriptions without deeper theoretical analysis or comparison. Furthermore, the investigation does not cover the implementation and control phase after the final investment decision has been made. This is surprising because the initial aspiration of this study was to provide a comprehensive and differentiated view on the entire foreign investment decision process.

Summary

A common impetus of the presented process studies is the view that the strong focus on the evaluation stages within investment decision processes is misplaced. The unilateral focus on final investment decision evaluations isolates the underlying socio-political processes which may be crucial to understand corporate investment and related critical success factors. The present work takes the same view that the investment decision evaluation represents a formal technique to identify the consequences on the corporate performance. Additional value can only be generated via search for ideas, project development and at last the implementation of the defined project.

But the presented investment decision process studies in this section are also exposed to several limitations. Although the basic propositions may be still valid today, an obvious limitation is that the three studies[391] – which intend to develop decision process models –lack actuality because they have been conducted between 1955 and 1970. In the meantime business practices and internal processes changed significantly due to huge technological progress in recent years. Therefore, this study aims to investigate recent foreign investment decision process models in MNCs. A similar limitation in this respect is that these studies do not cover the entire foreign investment decision process until implementation and start-up of the new facilities. The empirical study of *Mittermüller* and *von Nietzsch* (2008) provided indications that the implementation phase is the most important stage for the investment performance.[392] For this reason, this work intends to explore the entire investment decision process.

The review of prior research explicitly investigating foreign investment decision processes shows that this research area is almost unexplored. Only one empirical study has been conducted since *Aharoni's* model was published in 1966. As this study is only based on a handful of interviews and has been conducted in a unique Finnish setting. It is questionable whether reliable conclusions can be drawn from this study.

1.5.4 Conclusions

The literature review shows that **research on the diffusion rates** of certain investment decision evaluations is quite well developed. In particular due the insignificant theory-practice-gap, there is limited need for further research. All studies specifically focused on capital budgeting tools for foreign projects are based on surveys addressed to MNCs. But responses to surveys do not always reflect the corporate-wide situation because individual respondents of large MNCs may not be informed about all parts of

391 Cf. *Hill, JR.* (1955); *Bower* (1970); and *King* (1975).

392 Cf. *Mittermüller/von Nitzsch* (2008), p. 770.

the corporation.[393] A closely-related critical aspect is that surveys are addressed to the headquarters. Thus, because of the complexity of large MNC, headquarters are more strongly focused on control aspects like the allocation of the capital during the annual budgeting process. For this reason, it can be expected that the knowledge of actual capital budgeting application is concentrated in the decentralized units or on project levels. A way to overcome this limitation of surveys in this respect may be the application of **explorative case studies within MNCs** to open the "black box."[394]

For instance, *Pike* (1996) postulates that further research should be focused on in-depth analysis through the case study method. Further survey-based analysis is expected to contribute little to the existing body of empirical knowledge.[395] One major advantage of in-depth analysis is that **different perspectives**, e.g. headquarters vs. subsidiary, can be integrated in these designs to gain a more comprehensive understanding of the research object.[396] To date theory fails to provide an integrated concept for evaluating foreign projects. Every attempt to develop an integrated "standard approach" to evaluate foreign investment opportunities has its limitations. Thereby, none of them is really established in practice and theory.[397] For this reason, there is a broad variety of implemented concepts and "rule of thumbs" in practice. Thereby, qualitative research designs are able to investigate the evaluation as part of the investment decision process from different perspectives and in a more detailed way which may be a major advantage. Reflecting the current state of research, it seems to be necessary to investigate foreign investment decision processes in their real-life contexts considering the variety of socio-political influences within MNCs.

Reviewing prior research provides evidence that the literature is very focused on the evaluation of already defined business cases. The search for ideas, project development or control phases are almost uncovered. Similarly, the interface between the corporate strategic planning processes and the investment planning has received very little attention in previous research projects.[398] This is very surprising because strategic management literature usually understands investments as a measure to implement a formulated strategy.[399] Thus, it is promising to gain a deeper understanding for the development and constitution of investment cases. In addition, the project definition is expected to be an implicit evaluation process, which is almost not considered in capital budgeting theory. Similarly, many other factors through the investment process influence the investment performance so that it seems to be inadequate to **solely focus on project evaluation**. The present work intends to close this gap and investigates the whole foreign investment decision process.

393 Cf. *Aggarwal* (1980), p. 31.
394 Cf. *Chakravarthy/Doz* (1992), p. 6.
395 Cf. *Pike* (1996), p. 90.
396 Cf. *Scapens* (1990), p. 160.
397 For attempts to develop an integrated model for evaluating foreign projects see *Pensel* (1977); *Kolbe* (1989); *Mrotzek* (1989); *Schäfer* (1995); or *Scholz* (1996).
398 Cf. *Pinches* (1982), p. 16.
399 Cf. *Welge/Al-Laham* (2012), p. 532.

Previous investigations on the **investment decision processes** are relatively rare compared to the studies related to the adoption of investment decision evaluations techniques. Most research focuses on investment decision processes in general, but only two empirical studies aim to investigate foreign investment decision processes. Significant differences compared to domestic investment decision processes are expected due to the higher uncertainty and complexity involved in these decision situations.[400] A further point of criticism – as of the studies on diffusion rates – is that no empirical study exists that inductively explores foreign investment decision processes in **German MNCs**. The study of *Mittermüller* and *von Nitzsch* is based on a pre-defined process model in order to identify critical success factors of investment processes imposing their comprehension on the respondents. Hence, this work intends to apply an open approach by using a phase model as a rough template that has to be adapted to the empirical results.

Other studies on investment decision processes are **solely based on Anglo-American MNCs**. Different results between German and Anglo-American companies can be expected due to the different corporate governance models. In Germany, the two-tier-system is common practice which implies the separation of the executive and the supervisory board. In Anglo-American corporations management and supervision are not institutionally separated; both functions are fulfilled by the board of directors in a one-tier-system. This traditional separation of power in Germany may also have an effect on the design of corporate-wide decision processes; e.g. more control-oriented processes or consensus decision-making may be expected for German MNCs as opposed to US MNCs.

To sum up, two main points of criticism can be identified to illustrate the theoretical contribution of the present work. The first point of criticism is focused on the **content of prior research**. A multitude of researchers focused on the diffusion of capital budgeting methods to evaluate investment decisions, whereas the state of investment decision process studies is very low. Only a small number of studies is explicitly concentrated on investment decision processes. The underlying decision processes related to foreign investments are virtually not reflected in prior research. Furthermore, this limited state of research is almost exclusively based on Anglo-American companies. A main limitation of the investment decision process studies is that they do not investigate the entire process. All studies assume a very narrow investment decision process definition so that the implementation and start-up phases are almost unexplored. This work aims to close this research gap by developing a comprehensive investment decision process model for foreign investment projects.

The second point of criticism is closely connected to the content-related criticism. Due to the concentration on the investment evaluation practices prior research shows unilateral **methodological characteristics** towards quantitative survey-based designs. Qualitative research projects are expected to be more effective to explore foreign investment decision processes.[401] Therefore, the low state of research with respect to

---

400 See section 2.2.

401 See section 3.1.3.

investment decision process studies can also be explained by practical considerations. Qualitative research requires a high commitment of research partners, like MNCs, to study investment processes in their real-life context. This is usually not easy to achieve because corporation and interviewees need to invest a lot of time. Thus, the very limited state of research related to foreign investment decision processes may be explained by the restricted access to internal process data. Furthermore, the foreign investments are based on **confidential strategic decision processes**. Thus, corporations are very cautious to grant access to these reliable in-depth data. This represents a central practical challenge to conduct investment decision process studies. But this study intends to overcome these practical challenges to contribute to the very limited state of research related to foreign investment decision processes.

After the foundation has been laid by defining the main terms, illustrating the practical relevance and reviewing prior research in the first chapter, the second chapter intends to introduce the theoretical perspectives for this study.

2 Theoretical perspectives

Developing a theoretical framework of what is being studied is a central aspect in case study research.[402] The important role of preceding theory development in designing case studies is a main difference compared to other methods in qualitative research, like ethnography or grounded theory.[403] As opposed to quantitative research, theory is **not used as a pre-defined model** of the investigated research object to derive hypotheses for testing by large-sample designs.[404] Instead, theories help to understand the investigated research object from a conceptual perspective. Furthermore, theoretical perspectives provide starting points for the data analysis in order to explain why identified processes are designed like the way they are. Furthermore, the underlying theories define the **theoretical comprehension** of the scientist on the topic which is being investigated in the case study.[405] For this study, theory is understood in a pragmatic way. For instance, the country-level approaches are rather collections of practical knowledge than scientific theories in their strictest sense.[406] In the following sections theoretical concepts are presented that can help to understand the research object on the firm- as well as on the country-level.

2.1 Relevant firm-level theories

Investigating or evaluating foreign investment decision processes on the firm-level requires introducing different theoretical perspectives to explain the design of decision processes. Therefore, theoretical perspectives have been selected that provide realistic assumptions and propositions with respect to decision processes in large organizations. In particular the cross-company case analysis in section 4.1.3 requires considering theoretical perspectives in order to explain company-specific similarities and differences.

The investment decision process and the related sub-processes in large MNC are expected to be highly affected by human, social and political factors. For this reason, it is appropriate to use **behavioral theories** to analyze investment processes in MNCs. The *homo oeconomicus* is assumed to have the relevant knowledge of his environment and stable preferences that enables him to make decisions which lead to the highest attainable point on his preference scale.[407] Due to the fact that case studies investigate phenomena in their real-life context, the adoption of behavioral and social approaches – which consider the decisions of individuals and groups in their cultural, social and political environment – are more appropriate in the present context. This study assumes a combined framework of the **behavioral decision theory**, **agency theory** and the **promotor model** of *Witte* (1973). Moreover, the behavioral theory of foreign investments by *Aharoni* is presented as an extension of the behavioral decision theory. The combination of multiple theoretical approaches is necessary due to the complexity of

402 Cf. *Humphrey/Scapens* (1996), p. 91.
403 See section 3.1.2.
404 Cf. *Flick* (2009), p. 202.
405 Cf. *Al-Laham* (1997), p. 21.
406 Cf. *Kieser/Walgenbach* (2010), p. 32.
407 Cf. *Simon* (1955), p. 99.

the research object. The means of theory triangulation is used to create different perspectives for the data analysis or approaching the raw data from different positions in order to generate differentiated results and explanations.[408]

2.1.1 Behavioral decision theory

This theoretical approach can be characterized as a decision theory because decision processes are the starting point for analyzing organizations.[409] According to *Simon* (1976) the aim of his research was to *"show how organizations can be understood in terms of their decisions processes"*. The main contributions to the behavioral decision theory are attributable to the studies of *Simon*, *March*, *Cyert*, *Aharoni* and *Bower* which intended to develop a theory on real-life decision behavior within organizations.[410] Their pioneering approach constitutes a renunciation of the neoclassical theory of the firm with its unrealistic assumptions of rational behavior under complete information. *Simon* postulates that if economists want to understand real decision behavior, research needs to concentrate on the perceptual, cognitive and learning factors that cause human decision behavior to be different from that predicted by the normative "economic man" model.[411] The limited computational capabilities of decision-makers interact with the complexity of the environment and the limited human capabilities to consider all possible decision alternatives to produce **bounded rationality**. The concept of bounded rationality is the core of behavioral decision research.[412] Although humans try to act and decide rational, they are not able to decide like the "economic man" due to the three following constraints:

1. Humans have **limited knowledge** about the conditions, which influence the consequences of the decision alternatives. They are not able to accurately evaluate decision alternatives like assumed in the neo-classical models.[413]
2. Even if the entire decision alternatives could be precisely predicted, humans are **not able to accurately evaluate** them.
3. In contrast to the assumption of the neo-classical economic man decision-makers are not able to consider **all possible decision alternatives**.

Given the limited computational abilities of humans, the **main question** of this research stream is how organizations ensure rational decisions. The representatives of the behavioral decision theory answer this question with formal organization structures. They argue that the **complexity** and **uncertainty** of decisions within formal organizations is lower due to several characteristics of organizations. For instance the *division of labor* decomposes complex corporate problems into better controllable subproblems. Different departments and members of the organization have to manage the

---

408 Cf. *Flick* (1992), p. 176.
409 Cf. *Kieser/Walgenbach* (2010), p. 37.
410 Cf. *Simon* (1955); *March/Simon* (1958); *Cyert/March* (1963); *Aharoni* (1966); or *Bower* (1970).
411 Cf. *Simon* (1955), p. 99.
412 Cf. *Kieser/Walgenbach* (2010), p. 38.
413 For the three constraints; cf. *Berger/Bernhard-Mehlich* (2006), p. 177ff.

different sub-problems which reduces the complexity and uncertainty of the single problem for the person in charge so that at least a "local rationality" can be accomplished.

The superior management has to coordinate the interdependencies between the different corporate divisions. **Standardized procedures** and **programs** determine how members of the organization have to proceed in regularly appearing situations and problems. In this case decision makers do not have to consider all alternatives and their consequences which facilitate their work.[414] **Hierarchy** is another organizational mechanism to reduce the complexity and uncertainty of decision situations. In a corporate hierarchy, the top management has the most power and authority. Following hierarchy levels have less decision authorities. Thereby, superior levels constrict the scope of decisions of the subordinated hierarchy levels which reduces the complexity and uncertainty of decisions.

Complexity and uncertainty can be absorbed through **communication.** Information is filtered and aggregated by formal communication channels for the individual decision problems to ensure that only selected relevant information has to be processed by the decision-maker. The danger is that definite inferences are wrongly drawn from ambiguous information. If these drawn conclusions are communicated through the organization, the following decisions are based on misinterpreted information.[415] **Indoctrination** means to create a corporate culture to navigate the behavior of the organization members in areas which are not covered by formal rules.[416] For instance, the behavioral decision theory assumes that holders of subordinated positions possess information monopolies because the superior level lacks detailed knowledge about the decision problem. For this reason it is essential that the superior level can trust that the subordinated level decides in the interest of the organization.[417] **Corporate cultures** can tie the employees to the organizational goals and principles.[418] Thus, elaborate organizations can be understood as *"machinery for coping with the limited man's abilities to comprehend and compute in the face of complexity and uncertainty."*[419]

In the context of **foreign investment decision processes** the behavioral decision theory can provide a theoretical basis for the firm-level case study analysis. One aim of this work is to empirically analyze foreign investment decision processes taking a behavioral decision theory perspective. The behavioral decision theory can serve as an overall framework in order to analyze and understand why certain structures and processes are implemented in the way they are. For this reason, the behavioral decision theory has the potential to explain elements of the firm-specific investment decision processes. Furthermore, the behavioral decision theory explicitly considers the cognitive influences on corporate decision processes which are of special relevance within the

414 Cf. *Simon* (1976), p. 102.
415 Cf. *March/Simon* (1958), p. 167.
416 Cf. *Kieser/Walgenbach* (2010), p. 39.
417 Cf. *Berger/Bernhard-Mehlich* (2006), p. 176.
418 See 1.3.3.4.
419 *Simon* (1979), p. 501.

context of investment decisions, e.g. for the search of investment alternatives. In the following, the behavioral theory of foreign investment is presented which picked up the main ideas of the behavioral decision theory in the investment context.

2.1.2 Behavioral theory of foreign investments

The behavioral theory is attributable to *Aharoni*, who explains firm internationalization from a behavioral decision theory perspective on the firm-level. The behavioral decision theory is concerned with decision processes within organizations and their implications for organizational structures.[420] *Aharoni* transferred this theoretical framework to the field of foreign investment decision processes. He aimed to explain *how* firms decide to consider investments in the international environment, rather than just answer why internationalization takes place. This behavioral approach formulates propositions with respect to (1) decision processes in general, (2) decision processes of single foreign investments and (3) decision processes within the overall firm internationalization.[421]

(1) Decision processes in general

Decision processes in organizations are assumed to be rarely rational which makes them hardly predictable.[422] Group members have own goals and relations to other individuals inside and outside the corporation, so that each decision must be analyzed at the background of the organizational members.[423] Instead of checking all possible investment alternatives, consequences and combinations, decisions are taken under **incomplete information**. Thereby, individuals and groups of individuals have limited information processing and computing capabilities – which causes **bounded problem solving abilities.**[424]

Assuming these characteristics of human decision-making capabilities, the majority of decisions is based on the **"principle of satisficing"**.[425] As long as individuals or groups are satisfied with their established decision rules and behaviors, they would not search for new procedures. To sum up, these decisions can be characterized as dynamic social processes of reciprocal forces amongst individuals grouped in subsystems.[426]

(2) Decision processes of single foreign investments

Based on case interviews within 38 US-based corporations, *Aharoni* identified four main phases of the foreign investment decision process.[427]

420 Cf. *Bäurle* (1996), p. 50; or see section 2.1.1.
421 Cf. *Kutschker/Schmid* (2011), p. 427.
422 Cf. *Vernon* (1966), p. 200.
423 Cf. *Welge/Holtbrügge* (1998), p. 68.
424 See section 2.1.1.
425 Cf. *Bäurle* (1996), p. 50f.
426 Cf. *Robson/Katsikeas* (2005), p. 401.
427 Cf. *Aharoni* (1966), p. 49.

The decision to look abroad (phase 1): It is assumed that a strong **internal** or external trigger is required to make the decision to consider the investment abroad.[428] Internal triggers arise due to a high interest of top management executives to invest in a specific region, e.g. based on personal preferences for the country. External pushes come from outside proposals, like strategic suppliers or distributors, to invest in a certain region. Furthermore, fear of losing market shares, bandwagon-effects[429], follow-the-leader pressures[430] or strong competition in the home market represent further external triggers to decide to look for foreign investments.[431] Thus, strong external or internal forces are necessary to trigger the process.[432]

The investigation process (phase 2): Due to high information costs, corporations are not able to evaluate multitudes of investment opportunities abroad. For this reason, the initial triggers are extremely important to determine which projects are further investigated.[433] Similarly, not every single aspect of the selected investments will be evaluated due to the constrained human information processing capabilities and information costs.[434] Moreover, the top management decides, respectively evaluates the selected opportunities on the basis of a few predefined criteria and decision rules.[435]

The decision to invest (phase 3): Eventually, the decision to invest is not necessarily the last one in a chain of decisions or the outcome of the investigation process. It is even possible that the decision is made before the investigation stage has begun. In such a case, the aim of the investigation is to find an optimal way for an investment configuration abroad. If the evaluation phase reveals that additional information or conditions inside or outside the organization have changed, feedback loops may arise and the initial decision is modified.[436]

Reviews and negotiations (phase 4): Only in rare cases the decision to invest can be declared as final because it must be asserted within the organization, e.g. in investment committees with the executive or supervisory board. Promoting the foreign investment opportunity through the organization is assumed to be highly influenced by social networks among individuals inside and outside the organization as well as by the initial triggering forces and political processes within the corporation. Some authors expect

428 Cf. *Bäurle* (1996), p. 52.

429 Horizontal and vertical bandwagon-effects can be distinguished. Horizontal means that a firm took notice of a successful foreign investment by its competitors and follows them into the foreign market. A vertical bandwagon-effect takes place when a certain corporation follows its customers or suppliers to a foreign environment; cf. *Müller/Kornmeier* (1997), p. 86.

430 Cf. *Morschett et al.* (2010), p. 81.

431 Cf. *Aharoni* (1999), p. 9.

432 Cf. *Aharoni* (1966), p. 49ff.

433 Cf. *Schoppe* (1998), p. 113.

434 Cf. *Aharoni* (1966), p. 78.

435 Cf. *Kutschker/Schmid* (2011), p. 429.

436 Cf. *Aharoni* (1999), p. 11.

that power and process promotors are even more important than know-how promotors.[437]

(3) Decision processes within the overall firm internationalization

As well as decision processes for a single foreign investment, *Aharoni* investigated the decision processes of the overall firm internationalization through time. According to the behavioral decision theory firms have **learning capabilities**, which influence the foreign investment decision behavior.[438] Information costs and associated risks decline with advancing internationalization, e.g. by implementing an international division in order to coordinate the international activities. In general, the organization gets more receptive to international investment opportunities and decision processes are accelerated.[439]

All in all, *Aharoni's* approach is the first attempt to consider the behavioral aspects of foreign direct investment decision processes. The behavioral theory of foreign investment decisions is able to explain why certain projects deliver suboptimal results or exhibiting irrational decision process elements.[440] Critics argue that *Aharoni's* approach is just a description of reality and an explanation how **suboptimal investment decisions** take place rather than a general theory of foreign direct investments.[441] Reflecting the objectives in science, this point of criticism is not appropriate. An objective of science in business administration is to deliver a proper description of reality which is a necessary requirement to deliver fruitful implications for improvement.[442] Commonly, unrealistic assumptions within theoretically elegant models are not capable to provide feasible opportunities and solutions to enhance structures in reality.[443]

A further point of criticism is that *Aharoni's* approach is of partial-analytical character, but he never raised the aspiration to deliver an integrated theory on firm internationalization.[444] Closely related to the explanation of the internationalization process of the firm is the subject of **organizational learning** which is addressed by *Aharoni's* work on foreign investment decisions.[445] It is one of his merits that he made the topic of organizational learning a subject of academic discussion. Considering all these innovative and at that time provocative ideas, *Aharoni* made a major contribution to broaden the perspectives on foreign investment decision processes.[446] In this context, the behavioral theory delivers a theoretical description of foreign investment decision pro-

437 For a description of the promotor model; cf. *Witte* (1999); *Gemünden/Walter* (1995); *Witte* (1977); *Wicher* (1995); see also section 2.1.4.

438 Cf. *Bäurle* (1996), p. 55.

439 Cf. *Aharoni* (1966), p. 180.

440 Cf. *Welge/Holtbrügge* (1998), p. 69.

441 Cf. *Jahrreiß* (1984), p. 254.

442 Cf. *Schweitzer* (1978), p. 3.

443 Cf. *Kutschker/Schmid* (2011), p. 432.

444 Cf. *Bäurle* (1996), p. 57.

445 Cf. *Kutschker/Schmid* (2011), p. 432f.

446 Cf. *Bäurle* (1996), p. 57.

cesses – which reflects the understanding of foreign investment decision processes of this study.

2.1.3 Agency theory

The principal-agent-theory belongs to the economic perspective of the **new institutional economics.**[447] In contrast to the broader approach of the behavioral decision theory, the principal agent approach focuses on interpersonal relationships of a principal who delegates decision competencies to an agent. The basic assumptions are (1) the existence of **asymmetric information** between the contract partners in favor of the agent and (2) that principals as well as agents are each **self-interested** with contrary utility functions.[448] The contract between principal and agent, used as a metaphor for the principal-agent-relationship, is the main unit of analysis.[449] It is assumed that the better informed agent acts opportunistically in order to maximize his own utility. This results in a divergence between the agent's decisions and those decisions which would maximize the welfare of the principal. The focus of this theory is on determining the most efficient contract design governing the relationship between principal and agent.

Information is seen like a commodity which can be purchased by different actions, like the implementation of **monitoring systems**, to reduce the extent of asymmetric information. A further option is to design the contract with **incentives** that align the interest of the agent to that of the principal, e.g. share-based payment for managers.[450] These two mechanisms represent two possible exemplary ways to reduce **agency costs**. *Jensen* defines agency costs as *"the sum of (1) the monitoring expenditures by the principal, (2) the bonding expenditures by the agent and (3) the residual loss."*[451] The residual loss constitutes the welfare loss that the first best solution cannot be reached due to the asymmetric information.

Agency problems related to investment decisions arise because in many decentralized companies owners delegate investment decisions to managers. Goal congruence becomes an important aspect because owners' and managers' interests can differ substantially.[452] It is reasonable to urge the adoption of an agency theory perspective in the present context due to the several existing principal-agent relationships in decision processes for international investments. The separation of ownership and control in MNCs causes the most striking agency-relationship between the **management** (agent) and its **shareholders** (principal), commonly represented by the supervisory board as depicted in Figure 2-1.[453]

---

447 Cf. *Ebers/Gotsch* (2006), p. 247.
448 Cf. *Kieser/Walgenbach* (2010), p. 46.
449 Cf. *Eisenhardt* (1989a), p. 58f.
450 Cf. *Tosi/Gomez-Mejia* (1989), p. 171.
451 *Jensen* (1976), p. 6f.
452 Cf. *Haka* (2007), p. 698.
453 Cf. *Jensen* (1976), p. 317.

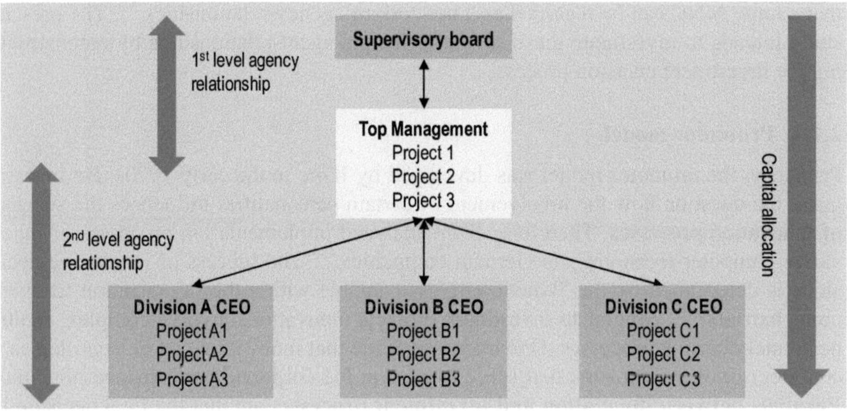

Figure 2-1: Main agency relationships in the capital allocation process

Foreign investment projects involve multi-personnel organizational processes with potentially deviating interests. Thus, in this context it is of great interest how **screening and approval processes** of proposed investment projects are designed. Inefficiencies might be occurring when too many financial resources are allocated to less promising investment projects.[454] Managers have incentives to withhold dividends for the shareholder in order to increase the resources under their control.[455] In contrast, capital rationing means an under-allocation of resources so that desirable investment cannot be undertaken. Both misallocations are producing inefficiencies.[456] Implemented **value based management** systems provide a solution to align the interests of managers and shareholders in order to reduce the incentives for opportunistic behavior.[457]

Multiple principal-agent relationships can be identified in the capital allocation process, e.g. the **top management** acts as a principal to distribute financial resources to the agents of the **second management level** (e.g. division CEOs) which want to acquire scarce financial budgets for new investment projects. Every division CEO has an incentive to receive the highest possible budget in order to enlarge his business division beyond the optimal size and strengthen his position in the overall company. This can be a major problem if the limited financial resources are not spent in the most valuable way. A third example for agency-relationships in the context of the present work is the delegation of decision competencies by the **parent company** (principal) to **subsidiaries** (agent) in foreign countries. In general, each corporate management or hierarchy level is connected via agency-relationships at least to the next superior level, so

454 In literature, this inefficient overinvestment behavior of self-interested managers is explained by the existence of organizational excess resources ("slack"); cf. *Tan/Peng* (2003), p. 1251; or *Bourgeois* (1981), p. 35.

455 Cf. *Harris/Raviv* (1996), p. 1140.

456 Cf. *Antle/Eppen* (1985), p. 163.

457 See section 1.3.1.2.

that a large MNC can be regarded as a network of agency-relationships.[458] The present study intends to investigate these several principal-agent-relationships by reconstructing the investment decision process.

2.1.4 Promotor model

Primarily, the promotor model was developed by *Witte* in the early 1970s. He investigated the question how the involvement of certain personalities influences the success of innovation processes. Therefore, *Witte* analyzed implementation processes of innovative computer technology in German companies.[459] The success of innovative decisions is determined by the "kinetic energy available within the organization to overcome barriers."[460] Similar to investment projects innovations involve complex, multipersonnel decision processes. One may also argue that innovation can be regarded as a subcategory of investments that serve to sustain the corporate performance potential. **Parallels between innovation and investment processes** are that the final decision is preceded by numerous activities like problem identification, problem solving, information search or evaluation of alternatives. Similarly, innovations and investments in the present context have in common that both are leading to an implementation of new resources. Due to the similar characteristics of innovations and investments, it seems to be appropriate to use the promotor model in the present context.

The basic assumptions of the promotor model are that neither the willingness to participate in the decision process nor the ability to provide problem-solving proposals is much diffused within organizations. *Witte* distinguishes two different kinds of barriers: **(1) Barriers of will**[461] and **(2) barriers of capabilities.**[462]

(1) **Barriers of will** are caused by the human tendency to maintain the status quo. Members of the organization are well-informed about the current situation in terms of predicting individual opportunities and risks. If innovations shall be implemented, members of the organization are concerned with the **uncertainty** regarding the future conditions. Consequently, persons do not advance innovative projects or even more fatal constrain innovations. *Witte* explains this human behavior by the inducements-contributions-approach[463] of the behavioral decision theory. He postulates that innovations disturb the relationship of inducements to contributions.[464] **Competing projects** may cause further barriers of will. If a certain innovation will be authorized by the top management, it is possible that another plan of a different division must be refused. These people of competing innovations could equally oppose the innovation. A parallel to international in-

---

458 Cf. *O'Donnell* (2000), p. 526.
459 Cf. *Witte* (1999), p. 21.
460 *Witte* (1977), p. 47.
461 Cf. *Witte* (1973), p. 6ff.
462 Cf. *Witte* (1973), p. 8f.
463 For the inducements-contributions approach; cf. *Berger/Bernhard-Mehlich* (2006), p. 172.
464 Cf. *Witte* (1973), p. 7.

vestment projects is that employees in the domestic market are concerned to lose their jobs, e.g. caused by investments in low-wage countries.

(2) **Barriers of capabilities** are explained by the nature of innovations. Not solely the innovative technical object is unknown; equally the work processes for the effective and efficient usage of the innovation must be newly defined. The extent of capability barriers increases with the complexity of the innovation and the related interdependencies to other problem areas. The only way to overcome this barrier is expert qualification. The barriers of capabilities can be transferred to the context of cross-border investments. Foreign markets, cultures and politics can be seen as the innovative technical object which must be effectively implemented in the firm. For instance, it is necessary to reengineer the distribution and production processes. In the context of international investments expert knowledge can be acquired through the employment of local experts.

Given the two main assumptions as described above innovations fail because people do not want them to happen or they are not able to implement them. Efforts are required to overcome these barriers – **promotors** can solve these problems. According to *Witte* promotors are people who actively support innovation processes and invest their energy to push the innovation through the organization until the final decision is made.[465] *Witte* differentiates **promotors by power** and **promotors by know-how**. A promotor by power actively supports an innovation through hierarchical power. The promotor by power is able to order sanctions against opponents and protects the advocates of the innovation. He determines budgets and enforces the innovation.[466] A promotor by know-how ("inventor") can advance an innovation through special expert knowledge, while his hierarchical position does not matter. For instance, he might become aware of the potential innovation through weaknesses in his daily work routine. *The main hypothesis is if a closely cooperating team of a promotor by power and a promotor by know-how can be found in an organization, innovations are more efficiently implemented and the degree of innovative change increases significantly.*[467] An empirical investigation provides evidence that a promotor structure is superior to other constellations in innovation processes.[468]

Hauschildt and *Chakrabarti* expanded the initial model of *Witte* by introducing a **process promotor**.[469] The process promotor acts as a communicator between the promotor by power and the promotor by know-how and has detailed knowledge about the organization.[470] Furthermore he is able to translate the technical language of the promotor by know-how into a language which is understood by the promotor by power (management).[471] A crucial aspect is that the process promotor must be able to evaluate the strategic fit in his decision whether a certain innovative idea will be presented

465 Cf. *Witte* (1973), p. 15.
466 Cf. *Hauschildt* (2001), p. 332.
467 Cf. *Witte* (1973), p. 22.
468 For the empirical investigation of the promotor model; cf. *Witte* (1977), p. 58.
469 Cf. *Hauschildt/Chakrabarti* (1999), p. 161ff.
470 Cf. *Hauschildt/Kirchmann* (2002), p. 44.
471 Cf. *Hauschildt/Chakrabarti* (1999), p. 78.

to a promotor by power. The coordination of the innovation process is the main responsibility of the process promotor.[472] He decomposes problems into sub-problems and delegates them to the promotor by know-how.

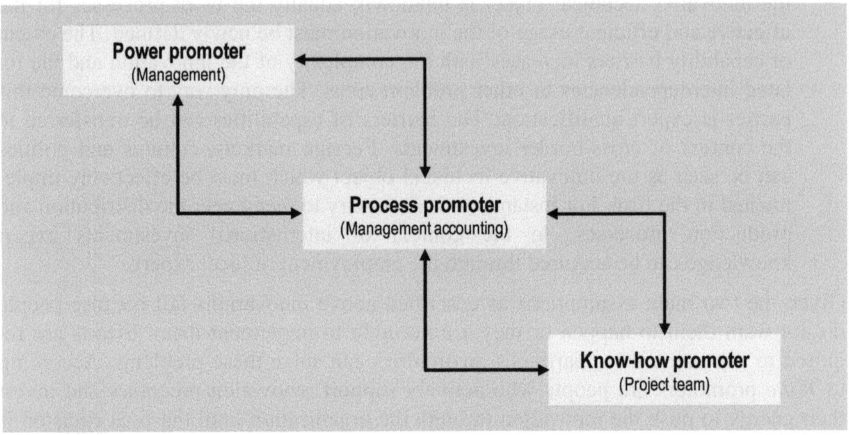

Figure 2-2: The promotor model in the context of foreign investments

Similarly, the process promotor coordinates the sub-solutions and puts them together to an overall solution which must be supported by the promotor by power.[473] *Hauschildt* postulates that a **troika of power, process and know-how promotors** is superior to other forms of promotor models or personal unions, so that this form of division of labor has a positive impact on innovation processes.[474]

The three-part promotor model seems to be appropriate for the present context (see Figure 2-2). Management accounting can play the role the process promotor, whereby the role of the power promotor is assumed by the corporate management – usually the executive board in the context of foreign investments. A project team – which creates the business case and the physical investment configuration – may serve as a technology promotor.

Due to the present definition of **cross-border investments**, it is expected that the initial investment stimuli arise on strategic management levels (top-down). This may lead to a main distinction between the promotor model for innovations and for top-down initialized foreign investments. The initial investment ideas are generated and articulated by the power promotor or the process promotor, whereas innovations are assumed to be generated by know-how promotors on lower hierarchical levels.[475] This seems to be plausible due to the assumption that – technological – innovations require detailed expert knowledge which is concentrated on the operational levels. For the pre-

472 Cf. *Hauschildt/Kirchmann* (1999), p. 93.
473 Cf. *Hauschildt/Chakrabarti* (1999), p. 81.
474 Cf. *Hauschildt* (2001), p. 337.
475 Cf. *Hauschildt* (2004), p. 200.

sent investigation the know-how promotor may be represented by a project team which is solely established for the operational realization of the cross-border investment. Possible team members are people with detailed knowledge about the target country, like local experts. The management accounting may serve as a mediator between the project team and the management in order to streamline the process and to safeguard the strategic fit.

2.1.5 Summary

A consolidation of different theoretical perspectives is necessary because no integrated approach exists which is able to explain decision processes for cross-border investments. It has been described in the three prior sections how the different theoretical concepts can be applied to the topic of foreign investment decision processes. At this point the interplay of the behavioral decision theory, the agency theory and the promotor model are explained to set up the theoretical firm-level framework as depicted in Figure 2-3.

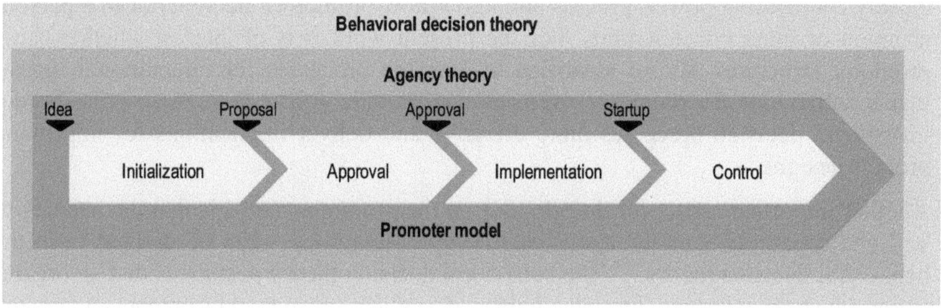

Figure 2-3: Theoretical firm-level framework

The **behavioral decision theory** serves as the overall theoretical concept for the present work. This theoretical approach is able to explain structures within and at the border of the organization. Furthermore, the agency theory is based on the concept of bounded rationality which was introduced by the authors of the behavioral decision theory, so that the two theoretical concepts are consistent to each other. The agency theory is more focused on the optimal contract design between principals and agents, whereas the behavioral decision theory represents a broader – and more abstract – approach. A very important aspect is that the behavioral decision theory is based on human decision behavior instead of rational decision logic. As strategic investment decisions are often affected by political and social factors, it seems to be appropriate to adopt the behavioral decision theory. This concept is applied in order to analyze the organizational structures surrounding the foreign investment decision process. The behavioral decision theory provides the organizational perspective to analyze the design of investment decision processes.

Cross-border investment decision processes in MNCs are influenced by several hierarchical levels, corporate departments and different corporate locations, so that a lot of different people – with heterogeneous and conflicting interests – are involved. Multiple principal-agent-relationships are attributable to these multi-personnel and work-sharing processes. The **agency theory** is able to analyze the agency-relationships and process structures on a more detailed level than the behavioral decision theory. Similarly, the agency theory should be used to investigate agency-relationships which take place at the border and in the context of the investment process, e.g. the principal-agent-relationship between the management board and the representatives of the shareholders. Apart from the description of structures in agency-relationships, the agency theory can explain that principal-agent-relationships can cause organizational inefficiencies.

The **promotor model** has been introduced to analyze foreign investment decisions from a process perspective. This theoretical concept was primarily developed for innovation processes, but for this work it is transferred to the context of investment decision processes. The similarities of innovations and investment processes have been described above, so that the application of the promotor model in this respect seems to be reasonable. Previous empirical investigation provided evidence that structures of closely cooperating power, process and know-how promotors are superior to a personal union or other constellations. For the present work it is of interest whether these promotor structures can be identified in decision processes for international investments. Otherwise the promotor approach can provide guidance to make cross-border investment decision processes more effective and deliver implications for improving process designs.

Another important aspect for the adoption of the promotor model is that the barriers of will and capability – as the main underlying assumptions – can be derived from the behavioral decision theory.[476] The behavioral decision theory postulates that an organization saves its existence through a balanced relation between inducements and contributions.[477] Investments are associated with uncertainty, especially investments in low-wage countries, which could disturb the equilibrium of inducements and contributions.[478] The result is that barriers against the planned investment could evolve. The role of the process promotor can be taken by management accountants. To sum up, the **three theoretical approaches are consistent** with each other without main contradictions. Every introduced theoretical approach seems to be necessary to capture the research topic as completely as possible from a theoretical perspective.

2.2 Relevant country-level theories

This section has been labeled "country-level" theories because these concepts constitute the theoretical foundation for the **country-level analysis**. Thereby, country-level theories are not understood as theoretical constructs that explain why single countries are targeted by MNCs. This section rather provides explanations why foreign MNCs are exposed to disadvantages and country-specific challenges. Moreover, country-level

476 Cf. *Witte* (1977), p. 50.
477 Cf. *Berger/Bernhard-Mehlich* (2006), p. 172.
478 Cf. *Simon* (1979), p. 502.

theories provide starting points to explain country-specific influences on investment decision processes on the firm-level.

2.2.1 Cost of doing business abroad and liability of foreignness

The **psychic distance**, which is defined as the sum of factors preventing the flow of information between the home and the host market, is a plausible explanation of country-specific challenges related to foreign investment projects. [479] Psychic distance causes difficulties of collecting and interpreting information properly.[480] Possible influencing factors on psychic distance are differences in languages, education, business practices, industrial development or culture.[481] The concept of psychic distance appeared first within the pioneering work on internationalization processes at the Uppsala University.[482]

The **core idea** of psychic distance is that any corporation faces differences between certain countries with respect to the generation of relevant market knowledge and capabilities. Therefore, some countries are easier to enter for foreign investors depending on the degree of psychic distance. All else being equal, countries with lower psychic distance to the home country of MNCs are more likely to be targeted.[483] The implicit assumption that similarity is better manageable than dissimilarity can be a point of criticism. But not considering and preparing for differences in obviously psychically close countries can be an argument why MNCs are not succeeding these countries.[484] In prior research, the concept of psychic distance was broadly used in a simplistic manner as an indicator for the perceived differences between countries that affect the flow of information between MNCs and the host market.[485] *Hofstede's* empirically based systematic **classification of culture** – which is as a subset of the psychic distance concept –found broad acceptance in academia.[486] Other potential influences than cultural factors were not systematically formalized in a widely accepted manner.[487]

The **institutional distance** is a broader concept than psychic distance and considers politics, ideology, law, culture and other societal factors. *Kostova & Zaheer* take the view that the consideration of institutional distance in transferring practices to the MNC's foreign subsidiary should be a key determinant of FDI decisions in order to achieve local legitimacy.[488] Institutional distance can be decomposed into three pillars – regulatory, normative and cognitive distances.[489] The **regulatory** institutional dis-

---

479 Cf. *Johanson/Vahlne* (1990), p. 13.

480 Cf. *Eriksson et al.* (1997), p. 341.

481 Cf. *Johanson/Vahlne* (1977), p. 24.

482 For the Uppsala internationalization process model; cf. *Johanson/Wiedersheim-Paul* (1975); *Johanson/Vahlne* (1977); *Johanson/Vahlne* (2009).

483 Cf. *Brewer* (2007), p. 45.

484 Cf. *O'Grady/Lane* (1996), p. 310.

485 Cf. *Johanson/Wiedersheim-Paul* (1975), p. 307f.

486 For the concept of cultural distance; cf. *Hofstede* (1983).

487 For an attempt to measure psychic distance; cf. *Brewer* (2007).

488 Cf. *Kostova/Zaheer* (1999), p. 72.

489 Cf. *Kostova* (1999), p. 313.

tance represents existing laws and rules in a certain national environment which support particular types of behaviors while sanctioning others. The regulatory dimension prescribes and proscribes certain kinds of behaviors. It defines "may" or "may not" behaviors. For MNCs, the regulatory distance is the easiest observable dimension because rules and laws are explicitly codified and formalized.[490]

Social norms, values, beliefs and assumptions about human nature and behavior that are shared by the local society constitute the **normative** pillar. The normative dimension defines how things "should" or "should not" be done according to values and norms of a certain society. This dimension of institutional distance is more difficult to observe for MNC due to the culturally driven and tacit understandings which are often inscrutable and not traceable for outsiders.[491] The **cognitive** institutional pillar influences the way people select and interpret information. *How* people notice and evaluate stimuli from the environment is affected by cognitive institutions. Practices or routines to solve problems are influenced by the cognitive pillar, e.g. emerging market managers tend to rely more on informal mechanism to solve problems.[492] The cognitive pillar comprises what "can" or "cannot" be done.[493] A high cognitive distance between home and host environment implies for the FDI decision a strong pressure for local responsiveness to act consistent to host country practices.[494]

MNCs are asymmetrically rooted in their host and home environments. For this reason, it is crucial to create capabilities to bridge the institutional distances in order to be competitive.[495] The **costs of doing business abroad** and the **liability of foreignness** concepts address country-specific challenges. Both approaches explain obstacles of foreign firms in cross-border investments as opposed to local corporations.[496] While the initial CBDA approach is focused on market-driven economic costs, the LOF concept takes the social cost of access and acceptance into account.[497] As illustrated in Figure 2-4, geographic and institutional distance – surrounded by high complexity and uncertainty – are the main determinants for CBDA and LoF. Geographic distance refers to the spatial distance between the MNC's home county and the foreign subsidiary country. As geographic distance increases economic costs are expected to be higher due to increasing traveling expenses, communication and coordination efforts.[498] Furthermore, it is more likely that geographically distant countries show more distinct unfamiliarity, relational and discrimination hazards.[499]

490 Cf. *Gaur/Lu* (2007), p. 87.
491 Cf. *Kostova/Zaheer* (1999), p. 69.
492 Cf. *McCarthy et al.* (2012), p. 27.
493 Cf. *Ionascu et al.* (2004), p. 4.
494 Cf. *Scott* (2003), p. 881.
495 Cf. *Xu/Shenkar* (2002), p. 615.
496 Cf. *Kaiser/Sofka* (2006), p. 2.
497 Cf. *Zaheer* (2002), p. 352.
498 Cf. *Boeh/Beamish* (2012), p. 26.
499 Cf. *Håkanson/Ambos* (2010), p. 207f.

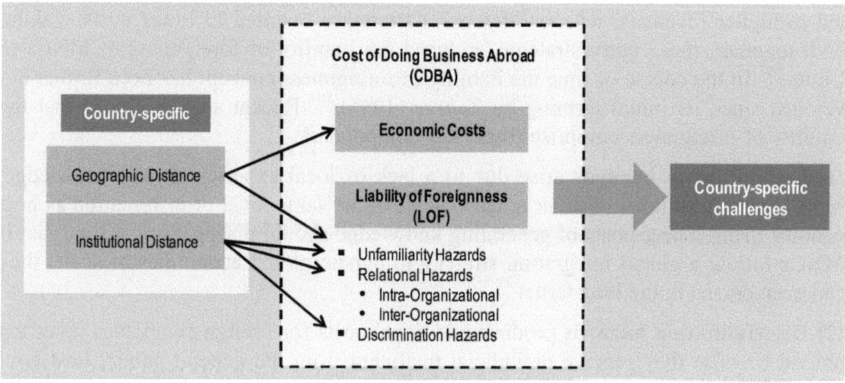

Figure 2-4: Liability of foreignness and cost of doing business abroad approach

Hymer was the first author who theorized that MNCs face disadvantages of foreignness arising from the unfamiliarity of the environment, from cultural, political and economic differences.[500] He identified **four main areas**, in which national companies have advantages compared to their foreign competitors. First, national firms have more detailed information about their country and its socio-economic environment, so that MNCs need to acquire additional knowledge in order to reduce the information backlog. Second, foreign investors have to handle discriminatory treatments of host country government, suppliers and customers. Third, MNCs can face differentiated treatment by their home governments, e.g. in order to preserve domestic firms. Lastly, foreign firms are exposed to foreign exchange risks due to cash inflows and cash outflows in different currencies.[501]

MNCs are exposed to a lot of uncertainties and specifics in foreign investment decisions due to the **lack of regional information** and the **higher environmental complexity** in foreign investment projects. Assuming that an MNC moves into a new foreign market implies that the level of regional-specific information is lower than for domestic investment decisions. This lack of socio-economic knowledge compared to local companies results in a so called **liability of foreignness**, which means that foreign companies have to face barriers and higher risks as opposed to local firms. Therefore, MNCs must learn from the environment in the foreign country to achieve local responsiveness.

Overcoming the liability of foreignness can be characterized as **a socio-economic process** that requires the simultaneous use of offensive strategies like local networking, input localization or resource commitment and defensive actions such as contractual designs, parental control or output standardization.[502] *Luo et al.* (2002) investigated financial performance and entry strategies of MNCs in China. Offensive strategies

500 Cf. *Zaheer* (1995), p. 341.
501 Cf. *Eden/Miller* (2004), p. 189f.
502 Cf. *Luo/Mezias* (2002), p. 219.

led to higher revenues, whereas defensive strategies resulted in lower costs. Taking both together, these entry strategies reduced the liability of foreignness of MNCs in China.[503] In the course of time the liability of foreignness concept has been further developed since its initial terming by *Zaheer* (1995).[504] Recent studies agreed that the liability of foreignness comprises three key components:

(1) Unfamiliarity hazards arise due to a lack of local experiences and knowledge. MNCs incur additional costs in order to achieve the same level of information as host country firms. These costs of generating knowledge should disappear over time, but if MNCs follow a global integration strategy to pursue global economies of scale, they can even persist in the long term.[505]

(2) Discrimination hazards produce additional costs for foreign companies investing abroad because they receive prejudicial treatment from the general public, host governments or customers in contrast to their local competitors. MNCs face political hazards[506] and customer ethnocentricity[507], so that costs are imposed on foreign companies in order to achieve external legitimacy. MNCs may be formally treated like national companies, but informal discriminatory treatment can emerge, when foreign firms are perceived as "strangers" by the general public and the environment.[508]

(3) Relational hazards imply higher internal and external organization costs for MNCs compared to local competitors. Firms operating in foreign countries have to handle greater internal and external uncertainties. Coordinating employees from different cultures and managing resources from a distance create higher internal uncertainty, whereas the unpredictability of foreign environments is responsible for higher external uncertainty.[509]

Depending on the source of uncertainty (internal vs. external), **intra-organizational** relational hazards and **inter-organizational** relational hazards can be differentiated.[510] From the intra-organizational perspective, additional governance costs arise due to the higher probability of opportunistic behavior as geographic distance increases as well as the associated management challenges to handle these agency relations.[511] Cultural distance causes further internal governance costs because managerial goals and motivations vary across cultures and parent headquarters may have tacit or implicit components of managerial behavior which are hardly transferable to the foreign subsidiary.[512] Inter-organizational hazards are the risk of opportunistic behavior of a business partner, e.g. in a strategic alliance.[513] The existence of inter-organizational hazards leads to

503 Cf. *Luo et al.* (2002), p. 298.
504 Cf. *Zaheer* (1995), p. 341.
505 Cf. *Petersen/Pedersen* (2002), p. 350.
506 Cf. *Henisz/Williamson* (1999), p. 267.
507 Cf. *Balabanis et al.* (2001), p. 159.
508 Cf. *Kostova/Zaheer* (1999), p. 68.
509 Cf. *Anderson/Gatignon* (1986), p. 7.
510 Cf. *Eden/Miller* (2004), p. 199f.
511 Cf. *Hennart* (2003), p. 134f.
512 Cf. *Kostova* (1999), p. 310f.
513 Cf. *Eden/Miller* (2004), p. 199f.

costs of trust building. Trust within the MNC's buyer-supplier network is a critical determinant to reduce transaction costs in uncertain business environments, wherein the foreign investor is exposed to inter-organizational hazards.[514]

In the present context of **foreign investments in BRIC countries**, both concepts are expected to be relevant for German firms. The BRIC countries are relatively distant to Germany – in geographical as well as in institutional terms – which explains the relevance in this context. But besides the sheer existence of country-specific challenges for German MNCs in BRIC countries, it is crucial to explore how these firms overcome or cope with the CDBA/LOF.

2.2.2 Liability of outsidership

Additional arguments and explanations for the specifics of foreign investment decision processes arise from business network research.[515] Foreign markets can be characterized as complex networks of partly invisible relationships. One further critical success factor of internationalization is to reach acceptance as a foreign investor by the local network members. If MNCs invest in foreign markets without a relevant business network, they need to handle a **liability of outsidership**.[516] While a lack of institutional market-knowledge – caused by the degree of institutional distance – leads to a liability of foreignness, a lack of business market knowledge constitutes a liability of outsidership. Business market knowledge is related to the firm's business environment which comprises networks of companies and local stakeholders that are germane for MNCs to do business.

From this viewpoint, foreign market entries can be characterized as decisions in the context of a **position-building process** in a foreign market network.[517] Therefore, foreign investors need to understand how the relevant market actors like customers, suppliers or competitors are connected to each other. A main difficulty is that the members of the targeted foreign market network are connected in a complex and invisible way, so that the entering firms must experience a market-specific learning process to overcome the liability of outsidership. Managing the liability of outsidership means to set up relationships to the relevant business partners in the target markets, which is a time-consuming process of trust and commitment building. Therefore, the **company-specific capabilities of trust-building** represent critical success factors in the early stages of developing a position within a foreign business network.[518] In contrast to domestic projects, it can be necessary to acquire local experts or agents as communicators just to achieve responsiveness in the targeted networks. Therefore, internationalization and foreign investment processes are associated with costly and time-consuming procedures to become a member within the targeted business networks.[519]

---

514 Cf. *Doney et al.* (1998), p. 601f.

515 For a brief overview of business network research; cf. *Anderson et al.* (1994), p. 1.

516 Cf. *Johanson/Vahlne* (2009), p. 1411.

517 Cf. *Johanson/Vahlne* (2009), p. 1415.

518 Cf. *Madhok* (2006b), p. 32.

519 Cf. *Madhok* (2006a), p. 7.

According to business network research foreign investment processes are more a matter of **relationship- and network-specificity** than one of country- and region-specificity.[520] But the two concepts of liability of outsidership and liability of foreignness can be seen as interdependent to each other. The network-building process itself is influenced by geographic distance and national frontiers. Although modern communication systems and mobility developed fast during the last decades, it is assumed that the origin of the network members and cultural backgrounds still play an important role in the network-and trust-building process.[521]

2.2.3 Disadvantage of foreignness

One can distinguish between government-based and consumer-based disadvantage of foreignness, when either the government or the consumers discriminate against a company's country of origin. These possible discriminations by the two parties represent further differences compared to domestic investment projects. Therefore, government-based disadvantages as well as consumer-based disadvantages have to be assessed within the initialization and approval stages of the foreign investment decision process by evaluating the relationships and attitudes to the MNC's country of origin.

Possible **government-based disadvantages** – synonymously political risks[522] – may have a negative influence on revenues due to limitations concerning the operations of foreign investors or may result in higher costs compared to their local competitors. Examples for negative interference of political actors are expropriations, discriminatory taxation or limited transferability of profits.[523] Because of this risk of adverse political decisions against the MNC in the foreign country, political lobbying is expected to be a more critical aspect in the foreign investment decision process opposed to domestic investments.[524] The case of *British Petroleum (BP)* in Russia is a prime example for immense negative impact of Russian political decision-makers on the value of foreign investments.[525] In 2008, *BP* was forced to sell their majority of a joint venture company – called *TNK-BP* – to *Gazprom* at a discount due to a tightened Russian energy strategy. Otherwise, *BP* would have lost their license to produce gas from the *Siberian Kovykta* gas field.[526]

A **consumer-based disadvantage** of foreignness arises when the consumers in the host country have negative associations with the firm's country of origin.[527] Thus, consumers may reject the MNC's product portfolio due to the national background which

520 Cf. *Johanson/Vahlne* (2009), p. 1426.

521 Cf. *Doney et al.* (1998), p. 602f.

522 For the purpose of the present work, political risk is defined as the risk of negative consequences arising from changes in the political environment; cf. *Butler/Joaquin* (1998), p. 599. For a literature review on the conceptualization of political risk; cf. *Fitzpatrick* (1983).

523 Cf. *Kobrin* (1979), p. 67.

524 For the importance of political lobbying in the international arena; cf. *Henisz/Zelner* (2003), p. 452ff.

525 Cf. *Betts/Hill* (2010).

526 Cf. *Financial Times* (2008).

527 Cf. *Al Sulaiti/Baker* (1998), p. 150.

ends up in lower revenues compared to local companies or companies with roots in other regions.[528] Possible reasons for disadvantages are that customers perceive poor quality with a certain country or they prefer domestically produced products for nationalistic reasons. Sometimes current events may have an influence on the consumer's attitude concerning certain nations. For example, at the beginning of the Iraq war in 2003 when Germany did not supported the US-troops, American consumer associations made an appeal to boycott German cars.[529] Even though it could be possible that MNCs take advantage from country-of-origin (COO) effect, for instance many companies from Germany benefit from the "made in Germany" label due to the worldwide reputation that German products are of high quality.[530] No matter if a foreign investor faces an advantage or a disadvantage due to his country of origin, international business, consumer behavior and marketing research provided evidence that the country of origin has an influence on buyers' perceptions.[531]

2.2.4 Summary

To sum up, the four theoretical concepts – cost of doing business abroad, liability of foreignesss, liability of outsidership and disadvantage of foreigness – intend to explain why country-specific challenges may arise during foreign investment decision processes. Furthermore, the country-level theories suggest why foreign investment decision processes are exposed to additional obstacles compared to domestic investment projects. Specifics of foreign investment decision processes are attributable to the requirements to cope with upcoming country-specific challenges, e.g. like culturally-driven product adaptation processes. Due to the heterogeneous character of the four BRIC countries it is expected that a multitude of country-specific challenges can be explored. Moreover, the emerging market status of these countries is usually associated with weaker formal institutional environments and higher reliance on informal networks as explained in section 1.4.4. For this reason, the liability of outsidership seems to be of special relevance for investment projects within the BRIC countries.

528 Cf. *Agrawal/Kamakura* (1999), p. 256ff.

529 Cf. *manager magazin* (2003).

530 For empirical investigations concerning perceived quality of German products in foreign countries; cf. *Han/Terpstra* (1988) p. 248; *Elliott/Cameron* (1994), p. 57; or *Johansson et al.* (1994), p. 166.

531 Cf. *Peterson/Jolibert* (1995), p. 884.

3 Research design

This chapter illustrates the research design of this study. The basic principles of qualitative research and case studies are elaborated in order to create a methodological understanding. This is required due to heterogeneous comprehension of case studies in the methodological literature.[532] In the first section 3.1, qualitative research and specifically the case study approach are introduced. Additionally, the selection of a qualitative research strategy for the present investigation and the case study approach in particular are justified. In section 3.2, the case study designs of this study are presented. Finally, the data collection and data analysis procedures are described within the context of the research process (section 3.3) in order to meet the demand of more transparency in qualitative research projects.[533]

3.1 Qualitative research

3.1.1 Overview

In the 1960s and 1970s, organizational research was dominated by quantitative research designs which have been adopted from natural sciences. The dissatisfaction of many researchers – due to the unilateral oriented research approaches – provoked a growing interest to qualitative research methods in organizational studies.[534] Although qualitative research methods can be traced back to the early 1900s, these methods have been more or less **postmarked as not sophisticated** enough for scientific purposes.[535] Initially, qualitative research designs have been established as an empirical research approach in the late 1980s, especially due to much conceptual groundwork.[536]

Prior to the presentation of basic principles of qualitative research designs the basic differences between qualitative and quantitative designs are pointed out (see Table 3-1). The main distinction criterion between qualitative and quantitative research designs is the **degree of standardization**. While quantitative investigations use standardized data collection methods, like surveys, data analysis tools and standardized predeveloped models of research objects, qualitative designs in their strictest sense represent the opposite extremes. The appropriateness is always contingent on the underlying research questions and objectives.[537] For this reason, it is not possible to indicate a general superiority of one approach because it is always context dependent.[538]

The role of **theory** in qualitative and quantitative research differs significantly. While qualitative research is more focused on developing theory, quantitative research intends to test theories with statistical methods. Due to this basic difference, qualitative

532 Cf. *Flyvbjerg* (2006), p. 221.

533 For further readings related to the requirements of more transparency; cf. *Andersen/Skaates* (2004); or *Zalan/Lewis* (2004).

534 Cf. *Morgan/Smircich* (1980), p. 491.

535 Cf. *Wrona* (2005), p. 10.

536 Cf. *Erickson* (2011), p. 44ff.

537 Cf. *Morgan/Smircich* (1980), p. 499.

538 Cf. *Howe* (1988), p. 14.

designs select cases on purpose based on theoretical considerations. The **sample selection** in quantitative designs is driven by statistical representativeness and random sample selection.

Criterion	Qualitative research	Quantitative research
Theory	End point, shall be developed	Starting point, shall be tested
Sampling	targeted case selection, theoretical sample selection	statistical representativeness, random sample selection
Data collection	open	standardized
Data analysis	interpreting	statistical
Generalization	theoretical generalization	statistical generalization

Table 3-1: Differences between qualitative and quantitative research
Cf. *Flick* (2009), p. 26.

Consistent with the sampling approach, qualitative research intends to make inferences by means of theoretical **generalization**. Thereby, it is important to differentiate theoretical from statistical generalization. The latter tries to infer from a representative sample to the entire population based on quantitative analyzes with statistical models.[539] Qualitative designs interpret qualitative data, like interviews, to draw general propositions in a theoretical sense.[540] After the main differences between qualitative and quantitative designs were described, the principles of qualitative research are elaborated in the following.

Principles of qualitative research

Despite the variety of different qualitative research designs, six main principles of qualitative research have evolved over the last three decades. In the following these main principles will be described in order to characterize qualitative research projects and their basic settings. The six basic principles of qualitative research are depicted in Table 3-2. **Openness** is the central principle in qualitative research designs. In the context of the theoretical and methodological foundation openness means that descriptions and explanations are not solely based on deducted research hypotheses. Moreover, a theoretical preconception is developed in order to refine it by considering explored aspects.[541]

Research as communications refers to the data collection methods. Interviews are the main data collection method in qualitative research. Therefore, qualitative designs are characterized by more intensive interaction between research subject and object. The **process character** of qualitative investigations is closely related to the previous principle. Collecting interview data can be seen as a communication process between the interviewer and interviewees. The attempt to gain participants is also a kind of com-

539 Cf. *Denzin/Lincoln* (2011), p. 8ff.
540 Cf. *Teddlie/Tashakkori* (2011), p. 288f.
541 Cf. *Mayring* (2002), p. 24ff.

munication process to convince potential interview partners. **Reflexivity** refers to the non-linear procedure of qualitative investigations, e.g. data collection and data analysis procedures are characterized by several feedback loops between the researcher and the interviewees. **Explication** is an important principle of qualitative studies in order to create inter-subjective traceability of interpretations. For instance, direct interview quotes can be used to show the line of argumentation. **Flexibility** refers to data collection process and methodological approaches in qualitative studies. Adopting flexible qualitative design is required in order to complement the prevailing principle of openness. For instance, interviews are flexible methods of data collection due to the possibility to adjust questions within the interview.

Principle	Description
Openness	Conceptual openness Methodological openness
Research as communication	Interaction between research subject and object Constitutional part of the research process
Process character	Research process as a communication process Process character of research objects in its real-life contexts Researcher involvement as a constitutional part of the research process and research results
Reflexivity	Non-linear process of data collection and analysis Variability of the research design and reflexivity of the researcher
Explication	Traceability of interpretations
Flexibility	Flexible data collection Flexible methodological approach – adaption to the research object

Table 3-2: Principles of qualitative research
Cf. *Lamnek* (2010), p. 20ff.

As opposed to quantitative designs the research subject is more actively involved in the data collection process. The six depicted principles show that qualitative research designs are characterized by openness and flexibility in particular. This creates great opportunities to explore complex research topics in their real-life context. But one major point of criticism related to openness and flexibility is that qualitative research projects and the research results are exposed to subjectivity due to the higher influence of the experiences and the horizons of the responsible researchers. Therefore, the consideration of quality criteria or standards is required in order to limit the **criticisms of arbitrariness**.

Quality factors for qualitative studies

Besides the requirement of content-related contribution, usefulness or practical relevance of empirical studies, the methodological and formal procedures of empirical investigations have to undergo an evaluation by **quality factors** or standards.[542] Qualitative research projects should fulfill defined quality factors in order to meet the re-

542 Cf. *Flick* (2009), p. 261.

quirements for an accepted research approach.[543] As opposed to quantitative research with established quality factors, like objectivity, reliability and validity, the qualitative research communities as well as their critics are still discussing adequate quality factors for qualitative research approaches.[544] Since the 1980s, controversial discussions exist concerning the standards of qualitative research.[545] Three main basic streams can be identified within the discussion about quality factors for qualitative research designs:

(1) **Postmodern rejection of quality factors**: Pursuer of this basic position argue from a postmodern and socio-constructivist view that the evaluation of qualitative research projects by adequate quality factors is not possible at all.[546]

(2) **Quantitative quality factors for qualitative research**: Advocates of this basic attitude take the view that traditional quality factors for quantitative designs like objectivity, reliability and validity should be modified for evaluating qualitative research designs.[547]

(3) **Own criteria for qualitative research**: Supporters of the third basic position question or doubt the transferability of quality factors for quantitative research projects to evaluate the qualitative research approaches. For this reason, this stream argues that qualitative research must develop separate quality factors which are considering the specific scientific position and methodological approach of qualitative research designs.[548]

The first basic opinion of strict rejection of quality factors is not shared because qualitative research projects would be exposed to arbitrariness and empirical results would be incomprehensible for third parties. Moreover, constructivist approaches provide implications for the development of a consistent methodological and scientific positioned blueprint that delivers starting points to design quality factors for qualitative research.[549] The second basic idea is to apply traditional quality standards of quantitative designs for qualitative approaches. The criteria of reliability, validity and objectivity are applicable to quantitative research designs due to the standardized research process which contradicts the open and flexible character of qualitative methods.[550]

This work takes the view to apply **own criteria** to evaluate qualitative research designs in order to find an adequate balance between strict rejection of any quality fac-

543 Cf. *Mayring* (2010), p. 116.

544 Cf. *Lincoln* (1995), p. 275; or *Flick* (2009), p. 262.

545 A detailed overview with respect to the discussion of quality factors for qualitative research can be found at *Steinke* (1999); or *Flick* (2010), p. 487ff.

546 For the postmodern rejection of quality factors in qualitative research; cf. *Smith* (1974); *Denzin* (1990), p. 231; or *Shotter* (1990), p. 69.

547 Quantitative quality factors for qualitative research design propose for example *Lincoln/Guba* (1990); or *Lincoln* (1995), p. 277.

548 Own or adapted quality factors according to the characteristics of qualitative research are pursued for example by *Steinke* (2008), p. 321ff.; or *Flick* (2010), p. 500ff.

549 Cf. *Steinke* (2008), p. 322.

550 Cf. *Hartleb* (2009), p. 98.

tors and mere usage of quality standards for quantitative investigations.[551] Six of the most prominent quality standards for qualitative research projects are presented in Table 3-3. In section 3.3.3 the research process of this investigation will be evaluated against the background of the following quality factors for qualitative research designs.

Quality factor	Description
Complete documentation of the research process	Data collection procedures and context Transcription rules Data description Description of data analysis methods Sources of information Decisions and problems Usage of QDA- Software
Applications of codified methods	*For example* Qualitative content analysis Grounded theory Structuring-thematic coding
Triangulation	Data triangulation Researcher triangulation Theory triangulation Method triangulation
Argumentative validation	Argumentation and interpretation as an instrument for the validation process
Communicative validation	Feedback-loops with interviewees
Multi-personal discourse	Data interpretation and results discussion with additional people

Table 3-3: Quality factors for qualitative research designs
Adopted from *Steinke* (2008), p. 324ff.

The quality factor of **complete documentation of research procedures** is associated with creating transparency and thus a better traceability for third parties. Specifically, this criterion means to disclose the data collection process, like the interview process, the applied interview guidelines or the adopted transcription rules.[552] Furthermore, the data analysis methods should be explained in order to understand the bridging process between the raw data and the research results. Similarly, problems and related decisions to solve these problems during the data analysis should be presented to the scientific community.[553] The use of qualitative data analysis (QDA) software is a further important aspect to improve the documentation of the research process.[554]

Adopting a **codified data analysis approach** is also important to achieve better intersubjective traceability. For example, structuring-thematic coding, grounded theory or qualitative content analyses are established qualitative approaches to conduct qualitative investigations. **Triangulation** is a further criterion to evaluate the quality of quali-

551 Cf. *Kuckartz* (2012), p. 166.
552 Cf. *Flick* (2010), p. 491.
553 Cf. *Kuckartz* (2012), p. 168.
554 Cf. *Kuckartz* (2010), p. 20.

tative research designs. Triangulated research designs can reduce biases and enhance the trustworthiness through different solution strategies, e.g. by multiple data sources, theories or analysis methods.[555] For example, the trustworthiness – which is often used as an expression for validity in qualitative research designs – can be improved by data triangulation when interview statements are supplemented by company documentations that support the interview evidence. Multiple sources of evidence can lead to convergent lines of enquiry and established chains of evidence which shall enhance construct validity or overall trustworthiness.[556]

The quality factor of **argumentative validation** is related to the applied methods for data analysis as well as to the interpretation of findings. A significant quality factor for the results of qualitative investigations is that the argumentation process follows pre-defined rules and systematic procedures in order to guarantee traceability and inter-subjectivity.[557] Rules and steps of argumentations shall be made transparent to the audience. **Communicative validation** means that the implications of the qualitative investigation should be shared and discussed with the interviewees. The research results of qualitative investigations can be further improved by **multi-personal discourses**.[558]

As opposed to quality criteria for quantitative designs, quality factors for qualitative studies must be adapted to the specific settings of single research projects, e.g. a case study design for investigations in MNCs requires rather different quality factors than archival research about a certain phenomenon.[559] In the following the case study method as the most common qualitative research design in business administration is presented.[560]

3.1.2 Case study research

Yin defines case studies for research purposes in the following way:

> *"A case study is an empirical inquiry that investigates a contemporary phenomenon in depth and within its real-life context, especially when the boundaries between phenomenon and context are not clearly evident."*[561]

Thus, the case study is an instrument to understand a real-life phenomenon in depth by explicitly recognizing the pertinent context of the phenomenon. A unique characteristic of the case study method is that the context is not divorced from the phenomenon.[562] An experiment, for instance, isolates the phenomenon from its context or is reduced to a few variables. The second part of the definition deals with the common characteristic that the phenomenon and the context are not always distinguishable in

555 Cf. *Flick* (1992), p. 178.

556 Cf. *Lamnek* (2010), p. 250.

557 Cf. *Corbin/Strauss* (2008), p. 299.

558 Cf. *Lamnek* (2010), p. 131ff.

559 Cf. *Corbin/Strauss* (2008), p. 309.

560 For an overview of different qualitative research designs; cf. *Morgan/Smircich* (1980); *Creswell et al.* (2007); or *Flick* (2008a).

561 *Yin* (2009), p. 18.

562 Cf. *Riege* (2004), p. 287.

real-life situations.[563] Technical characteristics such as data collection and analysis are subjects to the second part of the definition:

> *"The case study inquiry copes with the technically distinctive situation in which there will be many more variables of interests than data points, and as one result relies on multiple sources of evidence, with data needing to converge in a triangulating fashion, and as another result benefits from the prior development of theoretical propositions to guide data collection and analysis."*[564]

The two-fold definition of case studies encompasses the data collection strategies and specific approaches to data analysis in order to show that the case study method is an independent research approach. Other authors like *Schäfer/Brettel* and *Eisenhardt* see the main advantage of case studies in explorative research due to its open approach to new insights.[565] *Schäfer/Brettel* claim that the potential of case studies in conducting explorative research in German management accounting research is not exploited and stipulate more case study research in Germany.[566]

Basic case study designs

Four different basic case study designs can be identified as depicted in Figure 3-1. First, it can be differentiated between single and multiple case study designs. Second, multiple or single case studies can be holistic or embedded.[567]

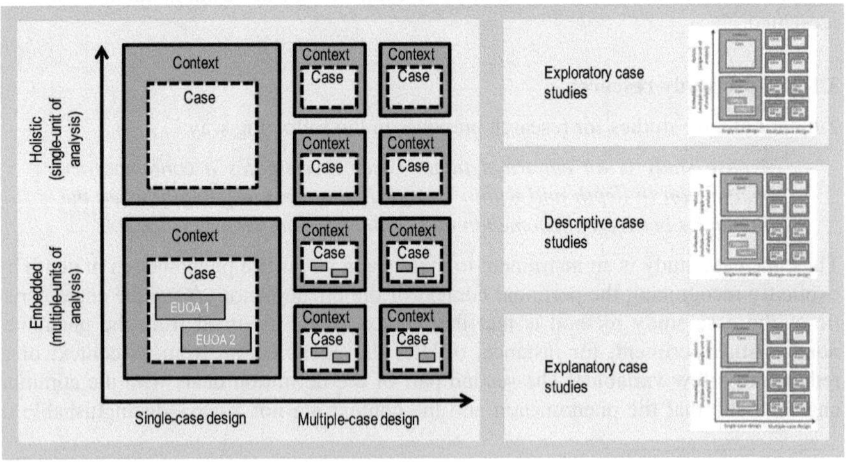

Figure 3-1: Basic types of case study research designs
Cf. *Yin* (2009), p. 46ff.

563 Cf. *Eisenhardt/Graebner* (2007), p. 25.
564 *Yin* (2009), p. 18.
565 Cf. *Eisenhardt* (1989b), p. 532; *Schäffer/Brettel* (2005), p. 44.
566 Cf. *Schäffer/Brettel* (2005), p. 46.
567 Cf. *Yin* (2009), p. 46.

Every type of the four basic case study designs has in common that contextual conditions are analyzed in relation to the case. It is usual that the boundaries between the context and the case are not sharply defined as illustrated by the dotted lines.[568]

When a single case can represent the **critical test** of an established theory, a single case may be preferred to a multiple case study design. Such an investigation can contribute to theory building and can deliver insights to refocus further work.[569] A second rationale for a single case design is where the case represents an **extreme** or **unique case**. In contrast to the first two circumstances for a single-case design, the third setting could be the representative or **typical case**. A **revelatory case** can be a further rationale for practicing single-case designs, for instance when the researcher has the opportunity to enter a previously inaccessible field – which also plays a main role for this work.[570]

Multiple-case study designs comprise more than a single case within the same study. While some authors consider multiple- and single-case studies as different methodologies, the present work takes the view of *Yin* who understands both types as variants within the same methodological framework.[571] Compared to single-case designs the evidence from multiple-case designs is regarded as more robust.[572]. Multiple-case studies require a replication design which is comparable with the replication logic of experiments as opposed to a random sampling approach. The selected cases shall either predict similar results **(literal replication)** or contrasting results **(theoretical replication)**. If all cases deliver the expected findings, the overall case analysis provides support for the initial set of propositions. Both, single- and multiple-case study designs, have the potential to derive valid empirical results, but if the possibility exists to prepare a multiple case, it should be preferred over single designs. Analytic conclusion arising from at least two cases will be more convincing than those derived from a single case.[573]

Furthermore a single as well as a multiple-case design can be either holistic or embedded. Whereas the **holistic** approach contains only one unit of analysis, the **embedded** design investigates two or more units of analysis. The unit of analysis determines the case and defines "what is being studied", for instance a "case" may be an individual in the classic case study. Clinical patients, exemplary students or business leaders can serve as a unit of analysis for conducting a case study on a single individual.[574] Groups, organizations, communities, relationships, projects or decisions are some more or less concrete illustrative units of analysis for case studies.[575]

568 Cf. *Yin* (2009), p. 46.
569 Cf. *Flyvbjerg* (2006), p. 229f.
570 See section 3.3.
571 Cf. *Yin* (2009), p. 60.
572 *Yin* (2009), p. 61.
573 Cf. *Yin* (2009), p. 60f.
574 Cf. *Yin* (2008), p. 11.
575 Cf. *Schnell et al.* (2011), p. 241ff.

Moreover, the four basic case study designs can be of exploratory, descriptive or explanatory nature.[576] An **exploratory** case study aims to discover questions and hypotheses for subsequent investigations, which not necessarily have to be conducted in form of a further case study. A complete description of a phenomenon with its real life context is presented by a **descriptive** case study design. An **explanatory** case design should be selected in order to examine cause-effect relationships to explain how events happened.

Role of theory and generalization

The first step in designing the study is to develop a theoretical preconception of what is being studied to follow the view of *Yin*. The comprehension of case studies according to *Yin* is not always shared in academic literature.[577] *Stake* takes up the position that case study research has to be conducted without predefined theoretical considerations.[578] For this study the position of *Yin* is preferred. Although his comprehension is more strongly oriented on theoretical preconception, Yin's case study method is still of open and flexible character to pursue explorative research objectives. Thereby, this work uses a pragmatic understanding of theory of *Sutton:*

> *"A theory is a hypothetical story about why acts, events, structure, and thoughts occur".*[579]

Furthermore, the theoretical framework predicts the conditions under which a certain phenomenon is likely to be found as well as the condition where it is not likely to be found. *Yin* (2009) describes the **role of theory** as *"the vehicle for generalization".*[580] If some of the investigated cases do not support the predictions of the theory, modification has to be made to the previously developed theory. In contrast, when a predefined theory gets support from two or more cases and an equally plausible rival theory does not, the empirical results become more robust or potent.[581]

A main criticism of the case study method is that the findings cannot be declared as representative for a larger population.[582] Case study researchers do not intend to generalize their findings by means of statistical generalization because the selected cases are not representative sampling units of a broader population, like in survey-based research. More-over, the cases are deliberately chosen to attend to the research objective ("theoretical sampling"). Therefore, **analytical generalization** is the mode of generalizing, in which the empirical case study findings are compared with a previously designed theory.[583] Theories serve as a template to design the data collection process and the presentation of the case study results. Thereby, it is essential to distinguish be-

576 Cf. *Yin* (2008), p. 5.
577 Cf. *Borchardt/Göthlich* (2009), p. 34.
578 Cf. *Stake* (1995), p. 12. For the method of the grounded theory cf. *Glaser/Strauss* (1967).
579 *Sutton/Staw* (1995), p. 378.
580 Cf. *Yin* (2009), p. 54.
581 Cf. *Yin* (2009), p. 38f.
582 Cf. *Hodkinson/Hodkinson* (2001), p. 10.
583 Cf. *Lamnek* (2010), p. 313.

tween analytical and statistical generalization when the empirical findings are interpreted.

3.1.3 Selection rationale

The research questions of this study can be mainly classified as "how" questions which are designated to be answered by a qualitative research approach. Due to the unexplored field of a precise conception of foreign investment decision processes in MNCs a case study design is the most adequate research method to achieve the research objectives of this study. In general, the complex research objects of foreign investment decision processes require an open and flexible approach to gain new insights.[584] For instance, "how much" questions, such as the volume or flows of foreign direct investments can be answered by using statistical analyses with large data sets, but the underlying decision processes of foreign investment projects can be more effectively investigated by applying a case study design.[585] This study intends to gain an understanding "**why**" things are done and further insights on "**how**" things are done, e.g. how foreign direct investments are implemented by MNCs in BRIC countries.

The main purpose of the study is to **explore** new interrelations, organizational processes and structures, rather than to test or falsify already existing ones – which is the main argument for adopting a case study design.[586] The decisive advantage of case studies is that the researcher can develop an understanding for the horizon and the perceived reality of the interview partner via direct communication. A survey based analysis assumes that the researcher and the practitioners act on the same mental horizon by offering limited multiple choice questions. This may lead to biased results when complex questions are analyzed.

Foreign investment decision processes in MNCs are multi-personal and work-sharing processes which involve the coordination of different stakeholders in the organization. For this reason, different parties, like the headquarter or the foreign subsidiary, have a different view on the foreign investment decision process. In this respect, the case study method is capable to capture a **multi-perspective view** on the research object by interviewing people from different corporate units. This represents a main advantage compared to quantitative large sample design.

Additionally, the **context** is crucial because it influences the research phenomena. For instance, the second sub-goal of this work aims to explore country-specific challenges for investment decisions in BRIC countries.[587] Thus, the context of decision processes is explicitly analyzed. In this respect, a case study has the advantage that the context is not assumed as given. The context is rather analyzed explicitly from different perspec-

584 Cf. *Newman et al.* (2003), p. 185f.
585 Cf. *Pratt* (2009), p. 856.
586 Cf. *Flick* (2010), p. 26.
587 See section 1.1.1.

tives to appreciate values and interests that affect the context itself.[588] For this reason, the case study seems to be an effective method.

Nevertheless, every research method has its strengths and weaknesses. Three main points of criticism are presented in order to show that the current work reflects the problems associated with case study research.

(1) **Generalization**: Case study results cannot be generalized through statistical generalization. Case study results can only be extrapolated to other cases via analytical generalization of plausible reasoning. It must be questioned to what extent the case study results are applicable to other corporations.[589]

(2) **Reliability and validity**: A common problem is that the case study results can be biased by subjective influences. On the one hand, the quality of case results depends on the ability of the researcher to interpret the findings, on the other hand the case study data can be biased through not objectively answering interview partners.[590]

(3) **Access to information**: A major practical problem in conducting case studies is the access to the required information. Case studies are more time-consuming for the investigated corporations than any other research method. One of the most difficult challenges is to convince corporations to support the research project.[591]

Apart from these main criticisms the case study as a qualitative empirical approach seems to be the most adequate method to achieve the pursued research objectives. A case study design has advantages in raising questions, highlighting issues, developing theory, and providing guidance in solving practical problems.[592] In some research projects the strengths and weaknesses of the particular methods may overlap so that the author must weigh which arguments predominate for his purposes or may combine the advantages within a mixed-method design.[593] But in this empirical study the arguments for a qualitative case study design are prevailing.

3.2 Case study design

Based on the introduced basic case study design in section 3.1.2, the firm-level and country-level case designs of this study are specified in the following. Due to the research objective of the present work, it was necessary to develop two different case study designs. Firm-level and country-level cases require different chronological orders of analytical dimensions and categorization of data. After the BRIC country focus was already justified in section 1.4, the case company selection process is explained first – prior to the illustration of the specific case study designs.

---

588 Cf. *Cooper/Morgan* (2008), p. 160.
589 Cf. *Al-Laham* (1997), p. 43.
590 Cf. *Lamnek* (2010), p. 44ff.
591 Cf. *Schuh* (2009), p. 1008ff.
592 Cf. *Cooper/Morgan* (2008), p. 161.
593 Cf. *Lieberman* (2005), p. 435.

3.2.1 Case company selection

The overall objective of the present study is to understand how foreign investment decision processes unfold in MNCs. Thus, this work required to find MNCs as research partners to investigate their foreign investment decision processes. As illustrated in section 1.4 the BRIC countries were selected as target investment countries due to their increasing practical relevance in the future. The investment **country focus** limits the population of eligible MNCs. A further practical sample selection criterion is that MNCs must have undertaken investments to BRIC countries in recent years in order to find involved interviewees within the corporations. When investments are already implemented since many years, involved interviewees may be hard to identify.

GasCo and **TechCo** were gained as research partners for the present work. Both corporations have substantial investments in each of the four BRIC countries. Furthermore, GasCo as well as TechCo are ranked among the top five internationalized German MNCs in terms of foreign assets, employees in foreign countries and foreign sales.[594] Therefore, the two corporations possess a significant international experience and capabilities concerning investments in foreign environments. Furthermore, both corporations have explicitly formulated that the establishment of market-leading positions is one of the centerpieces of their corporate strategies. Hence, growth markets, like the BRICs, are of the first priority for the strategic positioning of GasCo and TechCo. These considerations illustrate that GasCo and TechCo are promising case companies for this study. Certainly, other German MNCs would also fit to the explained selection criteria, but a further aspect of qualitative investigations is the **access to the research field.**

Due to the necessary high involvement of the investigated corporations the main practical challenge in this study was to receive the commitment of MNCs to participate in this research project. In an early stage, the commitment of GasCo and TechCo has been granted to investigate investments in the BRIC countries. This was a crucial milestone to assure the feasibility of this study. A key person who had first and second level executive positions in both companies served as a **gatekeeper and promotor** for the data collection process. This gatekeeper arranged the first contacts with both companies and positioned this research project within the organizations. Therefore, the unique possibility to explore foreign investment decision processes in their real-life contexts was also an important reason for selecting this research design.[595]

Foreign investment decision processes at GasCo and TechCo are analyzed based on **single investment projects** in BRIC countries. An overall objective was to discuss at least one investment in each of the four BRIC countries with GasCo and TechCo in order to make comparisons between the country cases across companies. Thus, the investment selection was dominated by pragmatic considerations. The initial inter-

594 Cf. *UNCTAD* (2013).

595 This rationale for selecting a case study design is quite common. In the literature the exclusive access to a specific research field is labeled as the "revelatory case", cf. *Yin* (2009), p. 49.

views at the corporate headquarters served to identify **recent investment projects**[596] in the BRIC countries. Therefore, the population of potential investment projects was significantly reduced. Additionally, involved key employees, like the head of business development at GasCo, had to be still employed by the corporation to participate in this study. Finally, twelve investments – three per country – were discussed within the data collection process. Hence, the minimum of required investment projects was achieved to draw comparisons among the cases. GasCo and TechCo as well as the twelve single investment projects are introduced in more detail at beginning of the firm-level cases in section 4.1.

3.2.2 Firm-level case design

The firm-level cases represent the first part of this qualitative investigation. This part intends to explore two firm-specific foreign investment decision processes in a first step and to analyze similarities as well as differences in a second step. Critical success factors are developed in the cross-company comparison by applying the introduced firm-level theories.[597] **GasCo** and **TechCo** are invented pseudonyms for the two case firms (see Figure 3-2) in order to comply with the confidentiality agreements. Similarly, the three dimensions of the cuboid show the different opportunities for analysis.

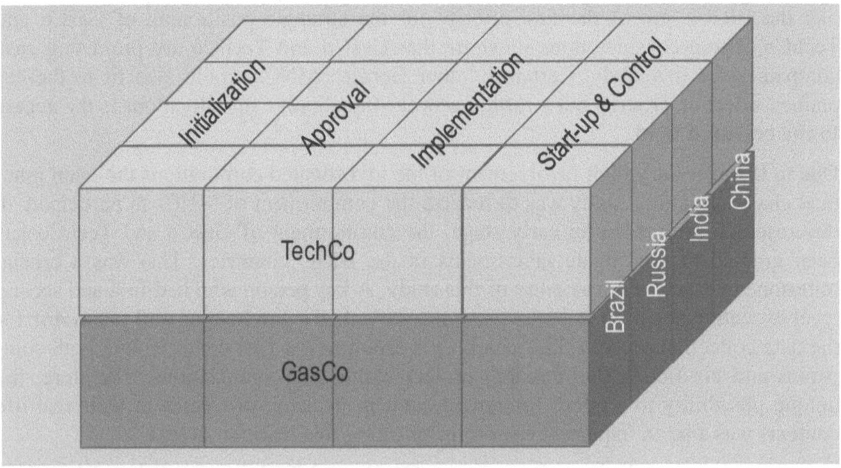

Figure 3-2: Visualization of firm-level analysis dimensions

Firm-, process-, and country-level analyses are possible top layers of the investigation. In the first part, the two companies represent the highest level of analysis focusing on the firm-specific investment decision processes. The sixteen cubes within each of two

596 Recent investment projects must be selected in order to find people who were involved in the investment decision process. Otherwise, the investigation would fail because of the limited availability of interview partners.

597 See section 2.1.

cuboids constitute units of analysis, e.g. the upper front cube on the right sight represents the start-up and control phase at TechCo in Brazil.

It is common in qualitative research that the exact definition of the "case" or the "cases" is not a trivial exercise.[598] Unfortunately, many qualitative publications pretend to adopt the case study method but without disclosing a clear case definition.[599] As depicted in Figure 3-3, the present investigation uses an embedded multiple-case study design. The first part of the empirical study is structured according to the two case companies GasCo and TechCo. Interview data and documents were sorted by the respective two companies and then by the four underlying investment countries.[600]

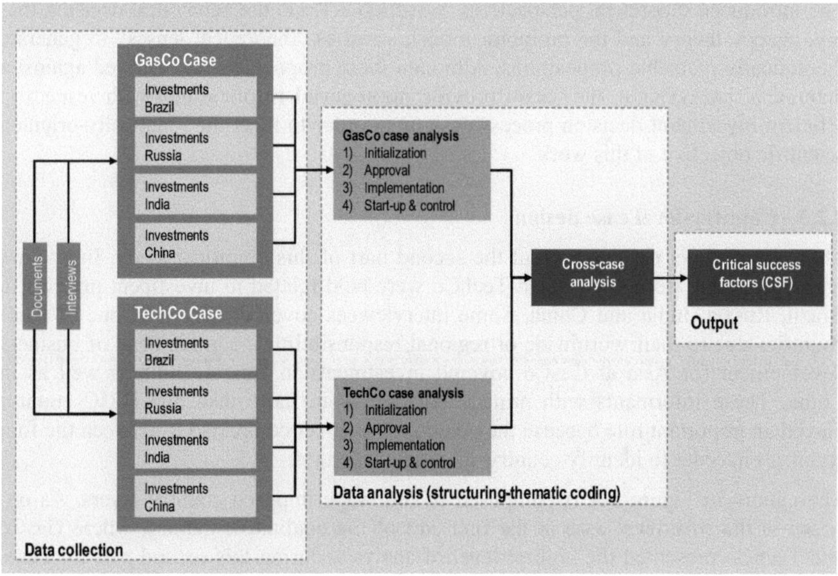

Figure 3-3: Firm-level case study design

The firm-level case study design can be characterized as "multiple" because the two corporations – **GasCo and TechCo** – represent the **two cases** during this part of the study. Embedded design means that the GasCo as well as the TechCo case contains multiple units of analysis – represented by the investigated investments.[601] At each company interviews have been conducted related to investment projects in the BRIC countries – supplemented by internal company documents, like presentations or directives. The data for each corporation has been analyzed in order to develop company-specific foreign investment decision process comprehension.

598 Cf. *Yin* (2009), p. 32.

599 Cf. *Gerring* (2004), p. 352; or *Al Qur'an* (2012), p. 160.

600 The interview data statistic by company will be presented in the next section 3.3.1.1.

601 Cf. *Creswell* (1994), p. 160.

Subsequently, a **cross-case comparison** reveals similarities and differences in order to deliver explanations for different process designs and related influences based on the introduced theoretical perspectives in section 2.1. Moreover, this cross-company comparison serves to generate more general propositions regarding the design of foreign investment decision processes – whereby these explanations and propositions have to be understood in a theoretical-analytical and not in a statistical sense.[602]

Subsequent to the cross-case analysis, **critical success factors** regarding an effective design of foreign investment decision processes are derived. Success factors are deduced from theoretical considerations supplemented by the collected empirical data. The introduced theoretical perspectives in section 2.1, i.e. the behavioral decision theory, agency theory and the promotor model, serve as "theoretical lenses" to generate theoretically plausible propositions. Although these propositions are derived against a theoretical background, they shall provide **managerial implications** with respect to efficient investment decision process designs in order to meet the practically-oriented scientific objective of this work.

3.2.3 Country-level case design

The country-level cases represent the second part of this empirical study. Interviews with employees from GasCo and TechCo were held related to investment projects in Brazil, Russia, India and China. Some interviewees covered more than one of these countries due to their worldwide or regional responsibilities, e.g. the head of business development for Asia at GasCo covered investments in Russia, India as well as in China. These informants with project experiences in more than one BRIC country played an important role because they could draw direct comparisons between the four countries in order to identify country-specific challenges.

The cuboid in Figure 3-4 is composed of four superimposed country layers. As opposed to the firm-level case in the first part of the qualitative inquiry, where GasCo and TechCo presented the highest level of analysis, during this second part the cases are categorized by the four BRIC countries **Brazil**, **Russia**, **India** and **China** on the top level. Inductive thematic categories based on interview evidence will be further supplemented or validated with related country-specific publications, like OECD country reports. Strengthening interview statements with additional data represents a means of data triangulation in this second part of the study.

602 Cf. *Verschuren* (2003), p. 134.

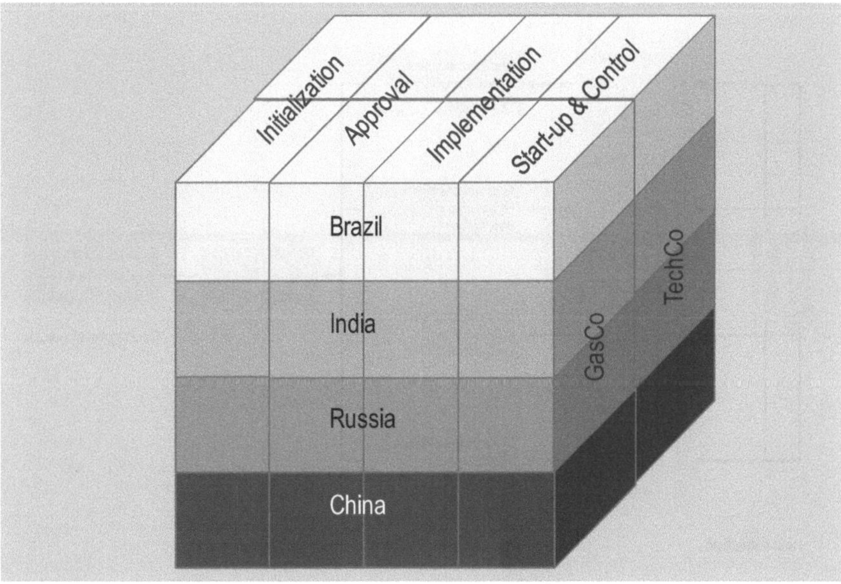

Figure 3-4: Visualization of country-level analysis dimensions

All investigated investment projects and conducted interviews at GasCo and TechCo are classified by the investment countries. Hence, each of the four BRIC countries represents a single case in this second part. Interview data was first sorted by the investment countries and then by the interviewees' corporations.

Just as on the firm-level, an embedded multiple-case study design has been applied to identify country-specific challenges to achieve the second research objective. The **four cases** of Brazil, Russia, India and China are depicted in Figure 3-5. Each country case will be analyzed according to the local specific investment challenges which are classified into the process-related context. A cross-country comparison delivers implications for common challenges of MNCs or other foreign investors in emerging markets to overcome. The country-specific challenges have been generated by ordering the collected data according to the four investment countries.

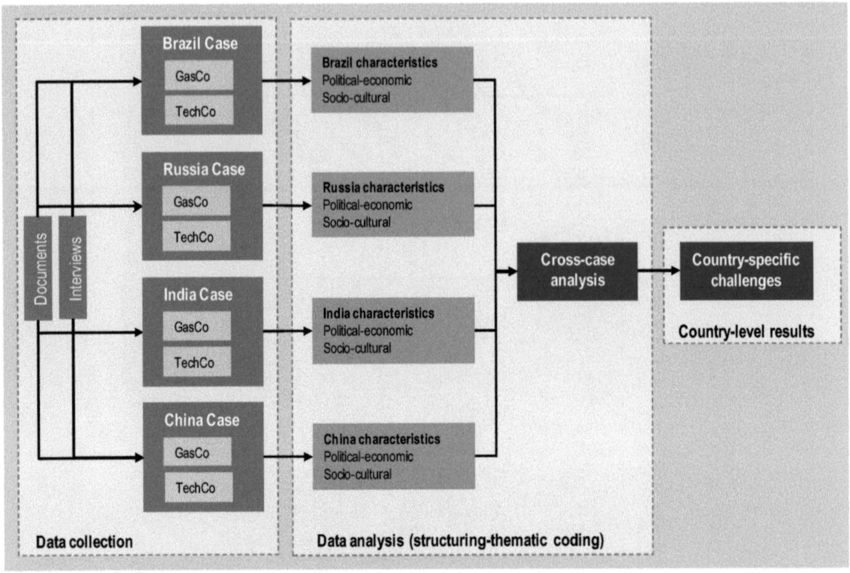

Figure 3-5: Country-level case study design

In a second step, an aggregated PESTEL framework was applied in order to systematically identify phase-specific investment challenges. The PESTEL framework is a systematic external analysis – often performed in the course of a SWOT analysis – incorporating political, economic, social, technological, environmental and legislative dimensions.[603] This work does not consider the technological dimension due to industry-specifics. Legal aspects are covered within the political-economic characteristics.[604] After the case study designs were elaborated, the research process is disclosed in the next section.

3.3 Research process

The presentation of the research process is of special relevance for qualitative investigations. As opposed to quantitative research designs, in interview studies the researcher is a constitutive part of the research process and thus constitutive for the research results as well.[605] The following statement of *Corbin* and *Strauss* emphasizes the importance to present the research process in qualitative studies:

> *"In judging the "credibility" of research, both the "doer" and the "reviewer" of research should be able to make judgments about some components of the research process. Even in a monograph [...] if there are no indica-*

603 Cf. *Bivolaru et al.* (2009), p. 105.

604 "Aggregated" means in this context that the six PESTEL dimensions are aggregated to political-economic and socio-cultural dimensions; cf. *Welge/Al-Laham* (2012), p. 292.

605 Cf. *Lamnek* (2010), p. 349.

> *tions of the research process, there is no way that readers can accurately judge how the data were collected or the analysis was carried out. [...] The detail need not be great, even in a monograph, but sufficient to give some reasonable grounds for judging the adequacy of the research process as such."*[606]

A challenging task of qualitative investigations is to present the evidence of dynamic, iterative and **cyclic research processes** within the linear confines of a study.[607] For this reason, the presentation of the research process at this place seems to be necessary in order to help the audience to understand the background of the research results and their development context. Furthermore, the introduced formal quality factors require disclosing the reasoning process.[608] Therefore, the research process is presented in the following three sections to meet the quality standards for this investigation.

3.3.1 Data collection

The use of interview data is common for **international business studies** in the cross-cultural context.[609] The interviews were either held in German or English. The interview transcription followed the original **interview language**. Thus, direct quotations based on German interviews were translated for the use in this study. Especially for studies with respect to different cultural backgrounds, interviews are capable to increase the reliability of answers because the posed questions can be verbally explained to the respondents.[610] Similarly, the interviewer and the informant can modify their questions or answers in order to prevent misinterpretations during the following data analysis.[611] The direct communication in interviews is especially valuable in explorative research projects due to the possibility that new topics of the research object arise during the conversation with the interviewees.[612] Therefore, the present work followed the approach to pose mainly open-ended questions, e.g. "why- and how-questions", in order to leave enough room for the respondents to articulate new topics, perspectives or aspects related to foreign investment projects.

A further advantage of interviews is that besides the formal answers on questions, the investigator can gather informal information through casual comments, tone of voice or physical gestures. Because this informal information can be very valuable for the data analysis and interpretation, the interviewer must always stay receptive and should follow up these signs in an appropriate way.[613] Within the context of the present work these **advantages of interview techniques** are important because investment decisions are managed within socio-economic processes with several agency-relations. For instance, casual comments of a foreign regional manager related to the investment

---

606 *Corbin/Strauss* (2008), p. 307.
607 Cf. *Bringer et al.* (2004), p. 254.
608 See section 3.1.1.
609 Cf. *Marschan-Piekkari/Welch* (2004), p. 13.
610 Cf. *Ghauri* (2004), p. 111.
611 Cf. *Hopf* (2008), p. 350.
612 Cf. *Peterson* (2004), p. 34.
613 Cf. *Scapens* (1990), p. 274.

screening department in the headquarters can deliver valuable insights to the agency-relationship between the headquarters and the foreign subsidiary.[614]

Apart from the interview data, publicly available information, like annual reports, analyst reports, press articles, management presentations or company websites have been studied prior to the first interviews and during the whole interviewing process[615] in order to gain an enhanced general understanding of the corporations and their business models. Furthermore, at the end of each interview, the interviewees have been asked to provide some internal documentation or presentations related to the prior discussed topics. The rationale behind this procedure was to use **multiple data sources** to prevent misinterpretations by cross-checks based on data triangulation.[616] Although, the provision of additional information was not possible for every interview, this procedure was very helpful to gain a deeper understanding of the discussed topics for the analysis of the interview data.

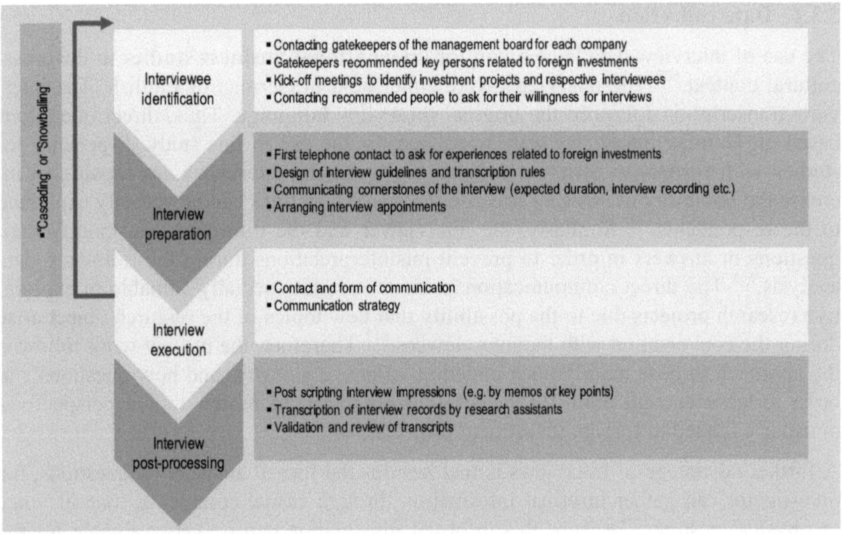

Figure 3-6: Interview process

As depicted in Figure 3-6, four stages of the interviewing process can be differentiated that are presented subsequently. This disclosure is crucial to enhance the procedural reliability of this investigation.[617]

---

614 For a detailed discussion of the strengths and weaknesses of interview techniques for data collection; cf. *Marshall/Rossman* (1989), p. 102ff.

615 Interview process at this point means the timeframe between July and December 2012, where the interviews have been conducted with the companies.

616 Cf. *Scapens* (1990), p. 275.

617 Cf. *Agndal/Nilsson* (2010), p. 154.

Interviewee identification

The interviewee identification proceeded mainly as presented in Figure 3-7. The gatekeeper for this research project established the first contact with the CFOs of the corporations due to their responsibilities related to investment projects. First telephone calls have been setup in order to explain the purposes and objectives of this investigation. In addition, the second main aspect was to explain the expected role of the companies and necessary contributions to this research project. After these two main points were clarified kick-off meetings with the CFOs were arranged in the headquarters.

The kick-off meetings served to establish a personal contact and relationship to key persons in the company in order to create a stronger commitment for the research project. Moreover, these introductory interviews intended to gain a better understanding of the respective company and its organizational structures and processes related to investment decisions.[618]

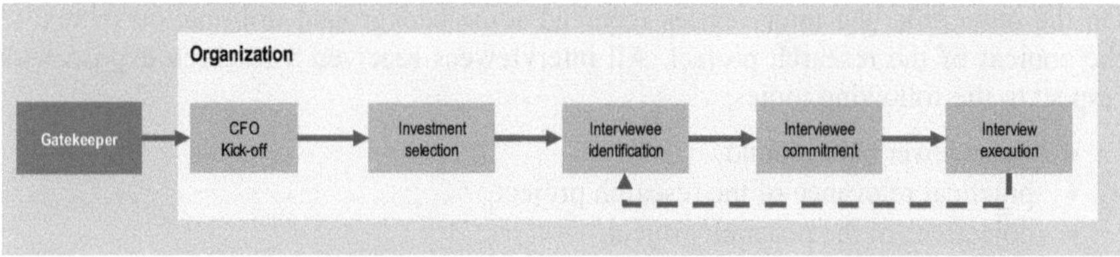

Figure 3-7: Interviewee identification process

Also a main purpose of these preliminary conversations was to **select specific Greenfield investments** to be analyzed and to identify involved people who are willing to participate in this research project.[619] After investment projects in BRIC countries were selected the responsible employees, usually the business development manager or project execution manager, were contacted by the CFO in order to request support for this research project. After the commitment for the interviews was confirmed, the specific interview preparation was initialized.

The dashed arrow in Figure 3-7 illustrates that subsequent to the interviews, the interviewed people were asked to recommend further people who were involved in the respective investment projects. This information identification procedure is referred to as "snowball" sampling. A **"snowball" sampling** tactic means that the investigator acquires new informants through recommendations by prior informants.[620] These repetitive processes lead to a "snowball effect" that describes the accumulative nature of this interview sampling strategy. The main rationale for applying the snowball strategy is that this approach was the most effective way to get access to new qualified informants.[621] Similarly, it is almost not possible for an outsider to identify the relevant persons in charge of single investment projects. It is common in qualitative studies to

618 For the kick-off interview guideline see Appendix B.

619 The investment project selection is presented in section 3.2.1.

620 Cf. *Noy* (2008), p. 330.

621 Cf. *Meuser/Nagel* (2010), p. 464.

adopt a "snowball" approach due to this problem of "hidden populations", like finding informants for specific foreign investment projects in this context.[622]

Interview preparation

Once the potential informant had confirmed his participation, the interview preparation was initialized. A common procedure was that **prior telephone calls** were arranged in order to gain a better understanding of the interviewee's professional background and experience related to foreign investments in general and the specific projects. Furthermore, the informants were asked for their country-specific experience and knowledge related to investments in BRIC economies. Finally, appointments were fixed for the ultimate interviews and informants were asked for the permission to record the interviews. All interviewees agreed to record the conversation which was important for reliability of the following interview analysis.[623]

On the other side, the interviewees received some background information related to the context of the research project. All interviewees received a research exposé with respect to the following topics:

- Interviewer background,
- practical relevance of the research project,
- objectives of the research project,
- expected interview duration,
- benefits for the interviewee,
- confidentiality agreement,
- reasons for being selected as an interview partner for this research project.[624]

Against the background of the interviewee's positions and experience regarding the selected investment project **a tailored interview guideline** was prepared for the upcoming interview. The interview questions were selected from a pre-developed pool of interview questions[625] which was developed on the basis of the theoretical foundation of this work. Main implications of the relevant sections for the development of interview questions are depicted in Figure 3-8.

622 Cf. *Atkinson/Flint* (2001), p. 4.

623 Cf. *Witzel* (2000), p. 4.

624 Other authors also recommend to give this introductory information prior to the interviews; cf. *Kurz et al.* (2004), p. 469.

625 For the pool of kick-off interview questions see Appendix B.

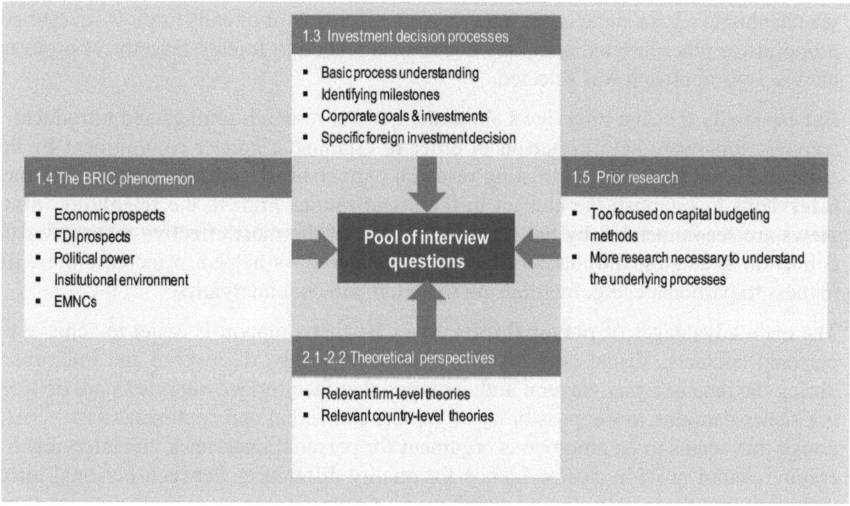

Figure 3-8: Development of the pool of interview questions

The basic structure of the interview guidelines was attributable to the ideal-typical process model (see section 1.3). Hence, the interview guideline comprised four main blocks of questions: **(1) initialization, (2) approval, (3) implementation, (4) start-up and control**. The investment decision process was not specified in further detail due to the underlying **inductive approach** of this study. Informants were not influenced with too detailed pre-conceptions of foreign investment decision processes. Thus, to stay receptive and open for new aspects was one of the most significant aspects in this explorative research design. To sum up, **openness** and **flexibility** to gain new insights were the two main principles underlying the data collection process and the interview guideline development. In particular, expert interviews have to be handled open and flexible in order to activate their specific expert knowledge.[626] Subsequent to the interview guideline preparation, the relevant persons received their interview guidelines according to their professional background.

Interview execution

After interview appointments had been fixed in prior calls and interview guidelines had been sent to the informants, interviews were conducted via telephone or personally at the companies' locations. A major determinant for either conducting personal or telephone interviews was the factor of **research efficiency**. Especially within the context of investment projects in BRIC countries, it was not possible to visit all informants at their foreign locations. Therefore, telephone interviews were usually preferred over personal interviews due to practical reasons of research efficiency. But when personal interviews can add obvious value and enrich the data which cannot be realized

626 Cf. *Meuser/Nagel* (2010), p. 465.

via telephone, e.g. in some cases interviewees offered in prior calls to show investment proposals or other internal company documents related to foreign investment projects, the vis-à-vis approach was selected.

But especially the first interviews about the general research settings and introductory conversations were held in person in order to establish a greater commitment by the companies and to develop a trusting research partnership.[627] Introductory **face-to-face interviews** to establish the contact to the organizations prior to the **telephone interviews** are recommended by the literature as one of the most effective interview data collection strategies. Introductory face-to-face interviews helped to increase the willingness to participate, e.g. by referring to earlier personal interviews.[628]

The main advantages of **personal interviews** are that a rapport is easier to achieve by personal contacts. Visual cues of the respondents can be discovered and interpreted during the data analysis. Several authors argue that face-to-face interviews are delivering richer data due to the possibility to capture nonverbal and contextual data.[629] Although this seems to be an obvious argument for personal interviews, the interview literature cannot provide clear evidence for quality differences between personal interview data and those collected by telephone.[630] Other authors argue that contextual settings may even have a biased influence on the interpretation process that undermines the quality of findings.[631] In the context of the present work, the advantages of personal interviews are not as material as in other research contexts, e.g. in biography investigations, where the interviewees themselves are the research objects to explore.

In recent years, the acceptance of **telephone interviews**[632] has significantly increased in qualitative research designs due to advancements in telecommunication and the grown familiarity with modern communication techniques.[633] The lower costs and the faster results of telephone interviews compared to personal interviews – especially within an international study with geographically dispersed respondents, like in this work – provide greater research efficiency.[634] However, lower expenditures cannot be used as a general justification of telephone interviews. This interview mode can only be justified when the collected data is of sufficient quality for the research questions.[635] Apart from these practical considerations, telephone interviews have some **methodological advantages**, like reduced interviewer effects[636] which can increase

627 Cf. *Marschan-Piekkari/Reis* (2004), p. 225.
628 Cf. *Carr/Worth* (2001), p. 513.
629 Cf. *Burnard* (1994), p. 68.
630 Cf. *Sturges/Hanrahan* (2004), p. 110.
631 Cf. *Burnard* (1994), p. 68.
632 In the 1970s and 1980s researchers were concerned with the use of telephone communication for scientific purposes due to the low telephone ownership and lack of familiarity with this medium; cf. *Victor* (1988), p. 164.
633 Cf. *Carr/Worth* (2001), p. 512.
634 Cf. *Marcus/Crane* (1986), p. 98.
635 Cf. *Sturges/Hanrahan* (2004), p. 110.
636 Interviewer effect means that the researcher consciously or unconsciously influences the respondent through non-verbal communication; cf. *Carr/Worth* (2001), p. 513ff.

the validity of empirical results.[637] A better possibility for quality control and comparability is a further rationale for selecting telephone interviews. In telephone interviews, the researcher is not that concerned to respond to the personal appearance of informants which decreases social pressure and facilitates a more consistent interview style as opposed to face-to-face conversations.[638]

Regardless whether telephone or personal interviews are conducted, it is important to distinguish two different **communication strategies**. On the one side, communication strategies can generate story-telling and on the other side communication strategies can be used to generate comprehension. These two different communication strategies are not exclusive and can be applied together in interviews, which reflects the interplay between existing knowledge and knowledge to explore.[639] At the beginning of each interview it was intended to start with open-ended questions that should incite the informants to story-telling and generate substance for induction. Thus, the first questions in the interviews were always the same:

> *"Can you please describe or explain the process for the "[Brazil, Russia, India, China] investment" from the initial idea until the final investment approval?"*

So, this introductory question allowed the interviewee to speak about the first process stage without confining or directing him or her with more detailed pre-conceptions.[640] This opening question was also posed at the beginning of the three other blocks of questions related to the approval, implementation and the start-up and control phase.

Subsequent to these opening questions, interviewees were asked more specifically for single aspects within these four stages, e.g. concerning the investment proposal development. These specific questions related to single aspects of the decision process are based on the previously acquired knowledge by the researcher. Previous knowledge was either accumulated within the interview or through other interviews or by literature research. This communication strategy to generate comprehension represents the deductive part of the data collection process and supplements the inductive part based on the uninfluenced informant's responses and perspectives.[641] As well as during the data collection the inductive-deductive approach was also applied during the stage of data analysis – especially for the category and code development – which will be explained in section 3.3.2.

Interview post-processing

After the interviews two central types of documents were prepared for the data analysis: the postscript and the transcript. The postscript comprises all relevant information

---

637 Cf. *Tucker* (1983), p. 85.
638 Cf. *Novick* (2008), p. 392.
639 Cf. *Witzel* (1982), p. 92.
640 Cf. *Gläser/Laudel* (2010), p. 131.
641 Cf. *Witzel* (2000), p. 6.

surrounding the interview that cannot be covered by the interview recording. Mainly, the **interview postscripts** provided information related to the following topics:

(1) Details related to the communication and events *prior* to the interview, e.g. some interviewees wrote emails prior to the interview session which provided some background or contextual information to specific investment projects;
(2) situational and non-verbal aspects *during* the interview, thematic conspicuities like a change of capital budgeting methods, or spontaneous interpretation ideas;
(3) details related to the communication and events *after* the interview, agreements for follow-up interviews or recommendations for further informants.

Complete **interview transcripts** are necessary before the data analysis can be initialized. Compared to the interview itself and the interview preparation, the interview transcription was the most time-consuming part of the data collection process.[642] Interview transcripts must be **verbatim accounts** of the discussed interview topics. This is a fundamental component of **rigor in qualitative research** projects.[643] In this context, the transcription was executed in two steps. First, student research assistants conducted the interview transcription. Second, these transcripts were reviewed during the data upload into the qualitative data analysis (QDA) software MAXQDA.[644] Due to the involvement of several student research assistants, the development of a transcription guideline was indispensable in order to guarantee consistent transcription procedures. The transcription rules[645] were developed in accordance to *Kuckartz* and are presented in the following:[646]

- Audiotapes were transcribed verbatim (exactly as said),
- non-verbal sounds were typed in parentheses (e.g. laugh),
- accents or dialects were cleaned up (e.g. Bavarian dialect was translated into standard German),
- interviews were transcribed in the original interview language (either English or German),
- spoken language was marginally smoothed,
- filler words such as "*hm*" or "*yeah*" were not considered in the transcript,
- words or phrases which are difficult to understand were highlighted in red,
- each interview speaker and their contributions were marked with initials in separate paragraphs.[647]

A greater transcription consistency was achieved by reviewing the interview transcripts prior to the upload into the QDA software. This was an obligatory step because all interviews were conducted by the author, so that this review process prevented

642 It is assumed that the time for transcription is the six folds of the interview time; cf. *Gläser/Laudel* (2010), p. 193.
643 Cf. *Poland* (1995), p. 306.
644 This transcription procedure is also proposed by *Kuckartz* (2012), p. 133.
645 For the different transcriptions approaches and its research contexts see *Oliver et al.* (2005).
646 Cf. *Kuckartz* (2012), p. 136.
647 For a detailed overview of possible specific transcription rules see *Seale/Silverman* (1997).

misunderstandings and improved the transcription quality.[648] A valuable side-effect of this procedure was to get **"closer to the data"** and receive a more detailed assessment of the collected data potential which delivered the first ideas and options for the following analysis and case interpretation.

After the overall data collection procedure has been explained, in the following sections the collected interview data is presented taking a firm- and country-level perspective. Disclosing the database is important to enhance the external reliability of the research project, but also to present the large database – which can be regarded as a strength of this investigation.

3.3.1.1 Firm-level data

As described earlier in section 3.3.1 the following case study findings are mainly rooted in interview data derived by key informants working for GasCo or TechCo. Data triangulation was applied by including supplementary data sources. This additional data consists of internal company documents as well as of publicly available data.[649] The interviews were conducted in a six-month period between **July and December 2012**. Altogether, interviews with **52 different people** were acquired for this research project representing approximately **57 hours of interview data**. Interviews ranged from 25 minutes to almost three hours. Prior to the interviews all informants agreed to record and transcribe the conversations under the condition to guarantee confidentiality and anonymity.[650]

For the purpose of the first part of the empirical investigations it was important to get a relatively equally balanced database between the two corporations.[651] Figure 3-9 shows that 25 interviews accounting for 28 interview hours were held at GasCo compared to 27 interviews of 29 interview hours with informants from TechCo. The almost equally weighted database between GasCo and TechCo leads to comparable evidences or implications due to the assumed similar empirical breadth and depth.[652] In contrast, extremely heterogeneous databases, e.g. when interview data from one company is significantly overrepresented, cross-company comparisons should be treated with caution due to the different sizes of the databases and the related empirical anchorage of the results within the data.[653]

---

648 Cf. *Gläser/Laudel* (2010), p. 194.

649 Business press articles, annual reports, analyst presentations or uploaded press conferences on company websites are some examples for publicly available data which has been used to support the analytical process.

650 For the complete list of interviews see Appendix C.

651 As opposed to quantitative research designs, qualitative projects cannot use power analyses to determine a minimum sample size. Qualitative researchers cannot apply standard procedures. More-over, the sample size must be evaluated against the purpose of the study ("purposeful sampling"). The researcher must reflect if the collected data is sufficient to deliver an information-rich case which involves the subjective judgment of the researcher; cf. *Sandelowski* (1995), p. 179f.

652 Cf. *Brod et al.* (2009), p. 1267.

653 Cf. *Oswald* (2010), p. 190.

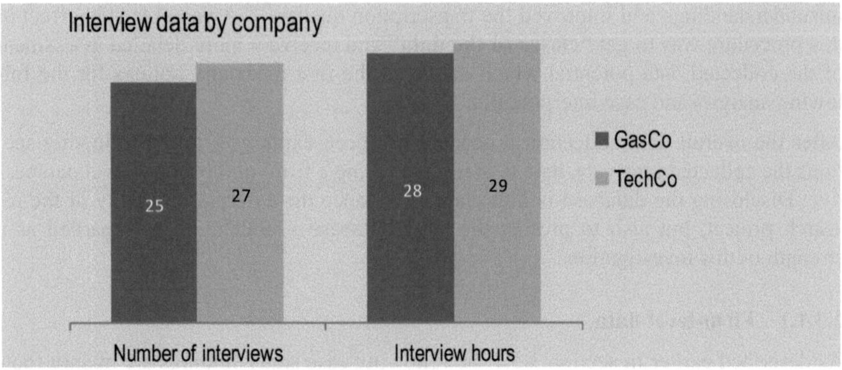

Figure 3-9: Interview data sorted by company

Interview data by informants' position

Revealing the job positions of interviewees plays an important role to convey an idea about the informants' abilities to deliver valuable insights for the purpose of the present work. Due to the fact that all informants were able to answer to the interview questions, it could be assumed that they possess the minimum qualification to talk about foreign Greenfield investments. Similarly, nobody rejected the participation in this research project after receiving the interview guideline. Of course, some interviewees were not prepared and did not screen the questions prior to the interview, but the impression is that this was not the typical case. In order to find a reasonable classification of interviews three different professional backgrounds were differentiated: Management, Business Development and Management Accounting.

Interviewees were classified as members of the **Management**, if they were authorized or obliged to participate in investment decisions by approving or rejecting investment proposals. Due to the matrix organizations of GasCo and TechCo, two types of management interviewees can be further differentiated. Interviews were held with managers belonging to the global product business as well as with members of regional management teams. People from **Business Development** were responsible for initializing, preparing and executing investment projects. These people are not authorized to participate in final investment decisions themselves, but business developers make a multitude of decisions regarding the investment configurations and project development. **Management Accounting** prepares investment decisions for the management. Thereby, two types of management accountants can be differentiated. First, centralized management accounting – for both companies located in Germany – is responsible for reviewing the submitted investment proposals mainly with respect to the financial evaluation. Furthermore, central management accounting has to coordinate the review process between the investment applicant and the reviewers and decision-makers. Second, decentralized management accounting actively supports the investment evaluation process to develop the financial model and the underlying business case.

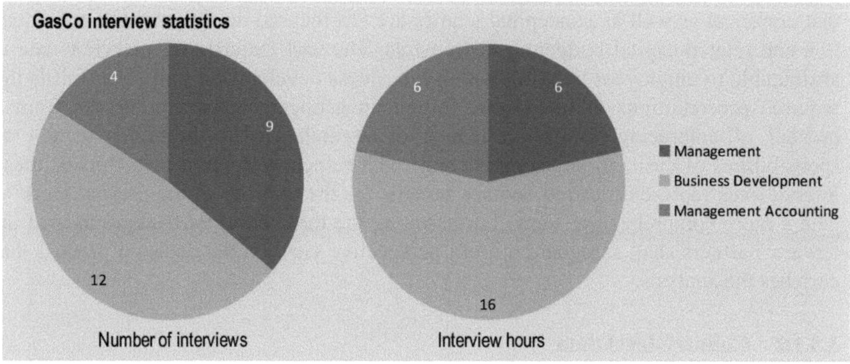

Figure 3-10: GasCo interview statistic by informants' position

GasCo's interview statistics show that almost 50% of the interviews were held with business development managers (Figure 3-10). As measured by interview hours, interviews with business developers even accounted for almost 60%. Nine management interviews (36%) represent the second largest part of interviews. Although only four management accountants were interviewed, management accounting interviews also amounted to six hours – approximately the same duration like the management interviews.

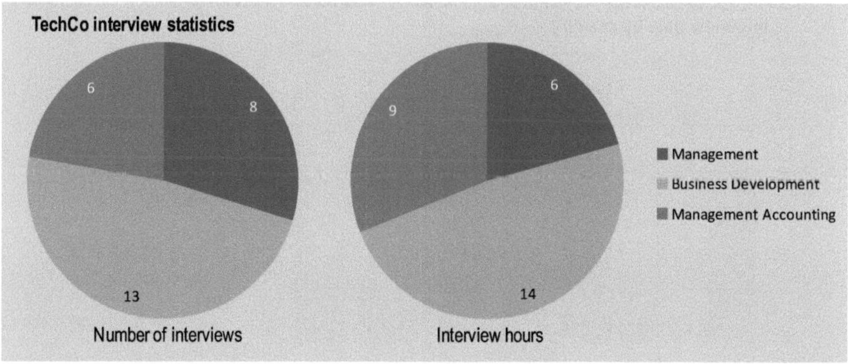

Figure 3-11: TechCo interview statistic by informants' position

Similar to GasCo, most interviews were held with business development managers at TechCo accounting for approximately 50% (Figure 3-11). The second largest part in terms of interview number is represented by managers (30%). Although only six interviews (22%) with management accountants were held, the interview duration exceed the management interviews by three hours.

The distribution of interviews between these three different types of professional background is **consistent to the motivation of this work** to cover the entire foreign investment process. One central implication based on the review of prior research was that empirical as well as conceptual studies are too focused on the investment evaluation and related capital budgeting instruments. The vast majority of interview data is attributable to employees working within a business development unit. This fulfils the required preconditions to investigate foreign investment decision processes from a broader, all-embracing perspective than prior research. Due to the multi-facetted responsibilities of business development staff with respect to foreign investments, these interviewees represent desired contact persons for the purpose of the present work to gain a more comprehensive view. Furthermore, the three different backgrounds of interview partners shall safeguard a multi-perspective view on the decision process that enriches the analysis.

3.3.1.2 Country-level data

As opposed to the description of the interview data by the informants' professional background at the firm-level cases, the interview categorization by investment countries is not that clearly distinguishable. Especially, interviews with management accountants and members of the management were often focused on more than one country. In these cases, interviews were classified under that country which accounted for the greatest part of the interview. Although one interview with the global head of business development covered all of the four countries – the mapping of business development interviews to investment countries was usually unambiguously.

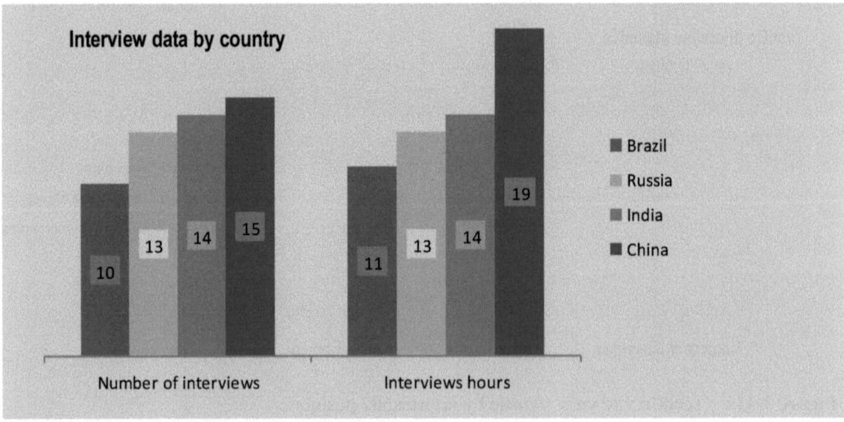

Figure 3-12: Interview data sorted by country

The broadest interview data in terms of interview number and hours of interviews are concerned with investment projects in **China** as depicted in Figure 3-12. Overall, 15 interviews for China account for approximately 19 interview hours. Greenfield investments in **India** received the second highest interview coverage both in terms of interview numbers and duration with 14 interviews and 14 hours. **Russia** achieved almost the same coverage as foreign investments in India with 13 interviews of 13 hours altogether. The fewest interview data relate to Greenfields in **Brazil** – ten interviews were conducted accounting for eleven hours of interview material.

The ranking of interview data quantity by country almost reflects the internal strategic importance of these four countries at GasCo and TechCo. China and India receive the highest attention by the management and are in the focus of their worldwide strategies as illustrated by the two following statements:

> *"China and India are in the absolute focus of our global strategy. These two future markets are on our priority lists since several years. We try to continuously strengthen our position in these markets."*[654]

> *"We are since many years established in China and India. We dispose over strong local organizations. But China and India stay on top positions of our agenda to anticipate and participate in the local developments."*[655]

For investments in Brazil or Russia, it was more difficult to identify and acquire qualified people to participate in this research project. This was mainly due to the present lower importance and weaker market positions in Brazil and Russia.

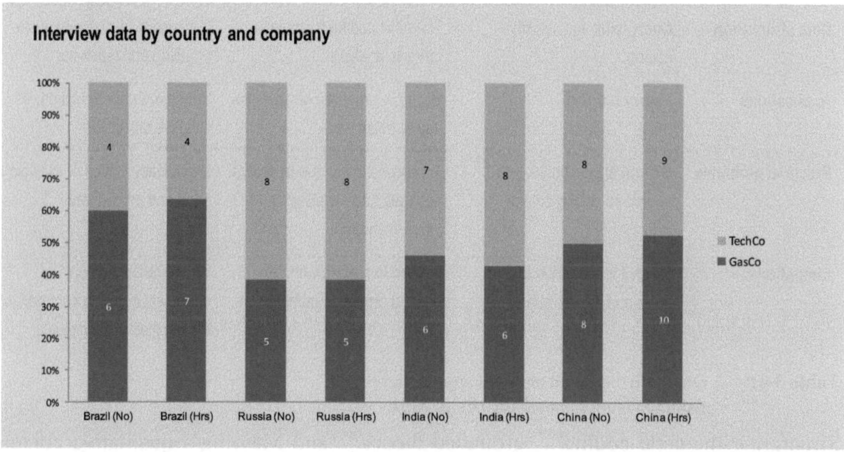

Figure 3-13: Interview data by country and company

According to Figure 3-13, interview evidence for China is almost equally balanced between TechCo and GasCo, while Russia and India are better covered by informants from TechCo. But for Brazil almost sixty percent of interview data – number of interviews as well as interview hours – is attributed to GasCo employees. Although not all four BRIC countries are equally covered by the two companies, the database classified by targeted investment countries can be described as relatively balanced. After the data characteristics were presented on the firm- and country-level in this section, the data analysis approach is explained in the next section.

---

654 Interview 29, GasCo, Management.

655 Interview 2, TechCo, Management.

3.3.2 Data analysis

Data analysis can be regarded as the step to raise the raw data to a more conceptual or abstract level.[656] Qualitative data analysis is associated with the term **coding** which means that codes – the names given to concepts – are assigned to the raw qualitative data sets. Selecting the adequate data analysis strategy is one of the most challenging tasks due to the potpourri of different data analysis techniques and their inconsistent and often imprecise description in qualitative research literature.[657] Additionally, the application of a codified data analysis procedure is an important quality factor of qualitative research projects in order to generate inter-subjective traceable[658] methods of reasoning.[659]

	Qualitative content analysis approaches		
Criteria	Grounded theory	Structuring-thematic coding	Qualitative content analysis
Data openness	Open coding; mainly driven by induction	Focused on cases or processes; interplay between induction and deduction	Focused on pre-defined contents, deductive and inductive category building
Data structuring	Open, axial and selective coding	Thematic coding for case or process analysis	Subsuming, structuring, para-phrasing and removing
Applications	Theory building	Group or process comparisons; theory extension	Structured data reduction; de-scriptive objectives
Practical problems	Difficult application due to imprecise coding criteria	Time-consuming due to several separate case analyses and interpretations	Difficult application of too rigid rules and procedures
Limitations	Difficult to learn due to the open and flexible character	Limited to studies with pre-defined groups of comparison	Strong orientation on quantitative criteria contradicts the qualitative principles

Table 3-4: Qualitative content analysis approaches
Adopted from *Lamnek* (2010), p. 514f.

Structuring-thematic coding[660], grounded theory[661] and Mayring's qualitative content analysis[662] are three of the most frequently applied data analysis approaches for quali-

656 Cf. *Corbin/Strauss* (2008), p. 66.

657 Cf. *Steinke* (2008), p. 319.

658 At this point, it is important to differentiate between traceability and verifiability. As opposed to qualitative studies, quantitative designs aime to create inter-subjective verifiability. Inter-subjective verifiability aspires that a third independent audience could replicate the investigation with identical results and implications. Identical replications of research projects in qualitative research are neither possible nor desirable due to the flexible and open character of these research methods; cf. *Krefting* (1991), p. 216.

659 Cf. *Steinke* (2008), p. 326.

660 For a detailed description related to the "structuring-thematic analysis" see *Flick* (2010), p. 402ff.; *Kuckartz* (2010), p. 84ff.; or *Kuckartz* (2012), p. 77ff.

tative research projects.[663] All three approaches share the characteristic that they are **codified, rule-guided procedures** in order to systematically categorize and analyze the informational content of textual data.[664] General differences can be obtained with respect to the underlying openness and flexibility of the three approaches as presented in Table 3-4.

Grounded theory can be seen as the most open and flexible approach of the three content analysis techniques, whereas **Mayring's qualitative content analysis** represents the opposite pole of the continuum. Structuring-thematic coding approaches can be classified in between the two other methods, whereas the distance on the continuum to the other approaches depends on the specific application of the single methods. The three approaches also differ with respect to the interplay between the category development and its application to the textual data. Mayring's qualitative content analysis combines induction and deduction[665], opposed to grounded theory which postulates a purely inductive approach in its strictest application supported by *Glaser*.[666] Structuring-thematic coding is also a hybrid method due to deductive thematic analysis and data-driven inductive elements.[667]

For this study, **grounded theory** is too imprecise for the aspiration to create intersubjective traceability. Central terms like category, code or dimension are not sufficiently defined to differentiate between them. The application of grounded theory is also difficult to grasp due to the overall idea that theory must be discovered or grounded within the data.[668] For this reason grounded theory is often described as a kind of art sciences.[669] The following statement by *Glaser* himself highlights the absence of

661 For a detailed overview of "grounded theory"; see *Glaser/Strauss* (1967); *Strübing* (2004); or *Corbin/Strauss* (2008).

662 For a detailed explanation of the "qualitative content analysis" of Mayring; cf. *Lamnek* (2010), p. 517ff.; *Mayring* (2010); or *Kuckartz* (2010), p. 92ff.

663 For the frequent application of structuring-thematic coding approaches; cf. *Kuckartz* (2012), p. 72. Grounded theory approaches and Mayring's qualitative content analysis are represented in almost every methodological textbook; cf. *Flick* (2010); *Miles/Hubermann* (1986); *Lamnek* (2010); *Hülst* (2010); or *Flick et al.* (2012).

664 Cf. *Forman/Damschroder* (2008), p. 39.

665 The initial ideas of qualitative content analysis were mainly driven by deductive category building, but inductive elements have become more important due to the aspiration of qualitative research to stay receptive for new aspects; cf. *Mayring* (2008a), p. 11. *Mayring* developed three versions of qualitative content analysis with different emphases of induction and deduction; cf. *Mayring* (2010), p. 66.

666 The strictest form of grounded theory was represented by *Glaser* who takes the view that theory should be discovered within the data without any theoretical preconception, research questions or research objectivities; cf. *Strübing* (2004), p. 68. The method of grounded theory was initially developed by *Glaser* and *Strauss* in the mid 1960s. In 1978, after a long dispute between the two founders on how to apply the method, Strauss published a new version of grounded theory with *Corbin*; cf. *Strauss/Corbin* (1990). Since then, two different versions of grounded theory can be differentiated.

667 Cf. *Fereday/Muir-Cochrane* (2008), p. 82f.

668 Cf. *Kuckartz* (2010), p. 82.

669 Cf. *Strübing* (2002), p. 332.

procedural instructions which is often misused as a justification for unstructured or not traceable qualitative investigations:[670]

> *„How are you doing? I'm doing. Just do it. Let's do it. Do it because it is meant to be. Do it because it is there to be done. Do it because it works. Grounded theory works and many people do it."*[671]

Although grounded theory is doubtless more than a justification or excuse for inexperienced authors who do not disclose or illuminate their applied methods, this **methodological openness contradicts** the aspiration of this study. In contrast, **Mayring's qualitative content analysis** represents the opposite extreme due the pre-defined procedures to consider during the data analysis.[672] These strict rules are constraining or **limiting the explorative potential** of the present work.[673] Furthermore, the strong orientation towards quantitative methods contradicts the underlying principles of openness and flexibility of this qualitative research design. Therefore, this work adopts a structuring-thematic coding approach in order to balance the trade-off between strict rigidity and total methodological openness. The structuring-thematic coding approach is briefly described in the following.

Structuring-thematic coding

For a long time the structuring-thematic coding was rather common-sense for analyzing qualitative data than an explicitly formulated method.[674] This approach was intuitively adopted by the majority of qualitative researchers, but without reflecting or discussing the method of structuring-thematic coding itself. Therefore, the approach of structuring-thematic coding was not covered in methodological literature until *Hopf*[675] published a series of qualitative studies with detailed information regarding the method of structuring-thematic coding since the mid 1980s.[676]

Opposed to the grounded theory, the data collection process is more strongly influenced by theoretical preconceptions and **deductive development of thematic categories**. A critical aspect to consider is that a theoretically-driven procedure is indeed intended but explicitly without constraining or framing the informants during the interviews.[677] Categories reprent themes in terms of headlines that are further differentiated during the coding process.

---

670 Cf. *Suddaby* (2006), p. 633 or *Strübing* (2002), p. 318.

671 *Glaser* (1998), p. 1.

672 Cf. *Flick* (2010), p. 416.

673 Cf. *Mayring* (2008b), p. 474.

674 Cf. *Kuckartz* (2010), p. 84.

675 *Hopf* and *Flick* can be regarded as the most actively promoting qualitative researchers who drive the development of qualitative methods in Germany; cf. *Reichertz* (2007), p. 1.

676 Cf. *Hopf et al.* (1985); *Hopf* (1995); *Hopf/Hopf* (1997); or *Hopf/Hartwig* (2001).

677 Cf. *Kuckartz* (2010), p. 86.

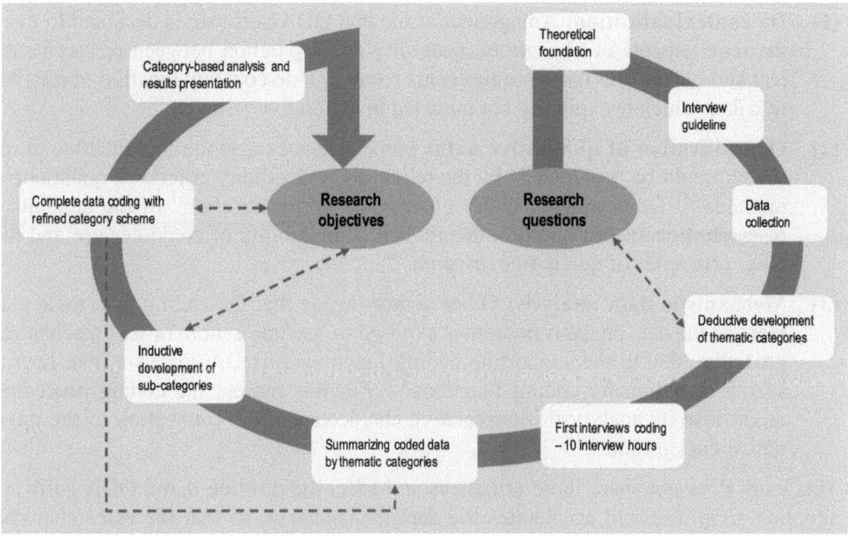

Figure 3-14: Schematic illustration of the data analysis process
Own illustration adopted from *Kuckartz* (2012), p. 78.

As depicted in Figure 3-14, the data collection is mainly determined by the interview guideline which is rooted within the theoretical foundation. The interview guideline was of similar importance for the deductive development of initial thematic categories. It served as a blueprint for the first thematic category system development against the background of the three-folded research questions. Thereafter, the category system was tested by coding approximately ten hours of interview data. Subsequently, the category system was refined and further differentiated by inductive development of subcategories. Like in many qualitative investigations, the data analysis process of this research project can be characterized through the interplay of deductive and inductive reasoning.[678] Thereby, QDA-software was crucial to enhance the practical efficiency of the data analysis process.

Role of QDA-software

The use of computer-assisted tools is seen as critical for **creating transparency** of the research process.[679] Although many qualitative researchers were very skeptical concerning the added-value of computer-assisted technology for their investigations, the usage of QDA-software has become state-of-the-art or common for qualitative research projects in recent years. The most frequent critics of the opponents of QDA-software adoption in qualitative research are:

678 Cf. *Walsh/Bartunek* (2011), p. 1021.
679 Cf. *Sinkovics et al.* (2008), p. 709.

(1) De-contextualization: Antagonists argue that QDA-software is designed to meet the requirements of objectivity, neutrality and separation between research subject and object. But these requirements result in a de-contextualization of qualitative data which is explicitly not intended in qualitative research.[680]

(2) Quantification of qualitative data: Some critics exaggerate that qualitative research might be "colonized" by the reliability and validity criteria of quantitative methods.[681] Other authors worry about the "industrialization" of the qualitative research process and question the general compatibility of computer use and the basic principles of qualitative research.[682]

(3) Mechanistic data analysis: Other authors argue that the coding as a main element of the data analysis process is exposed to become a more or less mechanical procedure due to the supporting coding functions of QDA-software, like lexical search or automatic coding functions.[683] For this reason, the coding procedure might lose its analytical-interpretative character and the connection to the theoretical background.[684]

This work does not share these criticisms and takes the position that a QDA-software adoption simplifies and accelerates the data management, so that the researcher can dedicate more time to the analytical and interpretative part of the research process. Apart from the more efficient data management, computer-assisted tools provide more **sophisticated data structuring** and **ordering mechanisms** that enable qualitative researchers to "play" with the data. These features create new room for creativity and may lead to new insights or interpretation options due to the **multi-perspective view on the data**.[685] These new possibilities through the adoption of QDA-software support a more differentiated view on the raw data which may also have an impact on the quality of the empirical findings.[686]

Similarly, the use of QDA-software provides standardized means of conducting qualitative research projects which increases the **transparency and traceability** of qualitative research procedures.[687] Standardized should be understood within the context of operational fieldwork, like data structuring and storing or filing and indexing data in order to encourage a systematic approach. Standardization should not be associated with the content-related analytical work or the underlying research approach. The QDA-software can only be understood as a helpful tool to support or enable the data collection and analysis – not as a mechanism or method for data analysis itself.[688]

---

680 Cf. *Atherton/Elsmore* (2007), p. 69.
681 Cf. *Webb* (1999), p. 324.
682 Cf. *Roberts/Wilson* (2002), paragraph 21.
683 Cf. *Webb* (1999), p. 325.
684 Cf. *Gilbert* (2002), p. 219.
685 Cf. *Kelle* (2008), p. 500.
686 Cf. *Sinkovics et al.* (2008), p. 695.
687 Cf. *Atherton/Elsmore* (2007), p. 62.
688 Cf. *Rettie et al.* (2008), p. 85.

Moreover, **methodological rigor** can be enhanced through the use of QDA-software by formalizing the manner in which qualitative researcher look at the raw data.[689]

A further central advantage of QDA-software use in qualitative research projects is the ability to **handle huge databases** in one all-embracing program which increases the efficiency of the data analysis process. Although the software cannot replace the intellectual interpretative work, it can provide critical support for the actual analysis.[690] Furthermore, the usage of QDA-software provides new research opportunities that cannot be realized or managed with earlier paper-and-pencil techniques, e.g. larger interview samples become manageable. Similarly, the application of computer-assisted analysis techniques provides new opportunities for results presentation, e.g. through visual tools like code-matrices or code-diagrams in MAXQDA.[691]

Finally, the adoption of QDA-software in qualitative investigations improves transparency, documentation and trustworthiness. Transparency is enhanced by more easily observable applied analytical procedures and techniques. Coding procedures are almost not comprehensible, if the coding process is solely documented on printed transcripts and not with computer-assisted tools. Similarly, software support makes qualitative analysis more systematic. Therefore, the QDA-software adoption increases the internal validity, whereas increased internal validity implies improved **trustworthiness** of qualitative research itself.[692] Summing up, the application of QDA-software in the current research context is critical regarding the two points of guaranteeing transparency and safeguarding research efficiency. For this reason, the reflection of the role of QDA-software seems to be appropriate in order to explain the importance for this research process and explicate the viewpoint regarding the role of computer-assisted tools in the present research setting. The present qualitative investigation was conducted with **MAXQDA**. Besides formal reasons for selecting MAXQDA, content-related aspects concerning the data analysis approach were decisive. *Kuckartz* shows opportunities how to conduct a structuring-thematic coding approach with MAXQDA.[693]

3.3.3 Review of the research process

Based on the detailed description of the research design and the underlying research process, the selected research approach will be reviewed in this section according to quality factors introduced in section 3.1.1. Some criteria are addressed at the research design stage while others are applied for the research process (data collection and analysis).[694] These evaluation criteria are specifically adapted to the characteristics of qualitative research designs.[695] This work shares the view of many qualitative re-

689 Cf. *Sinkovics et al.* (2008), p. 695.
690 Cf. *Kuckartz* (2010), p. 12.
691 Cf. *Kuckartz* (2010), p. 14.
692 Cf. *Kelle/Laurie* (1995), p. 19.
693 Cf. *Kuckartz* (2012), p. 132ff.
694 Cf. *Krefting* (1991), p. 217.
695 Quality in qualitative research is controversially discussed since more than thirty years, but without establishing a consensus within the methodological literature. Some authors argue that the aim to develop a consensual encompassing set of quality factors for the full-range of quali-

searchers that modified evaluation criteria for quantitative studies are not transferable to qualitative research projects due to the different underlying basic scientific and ontological positions.[696] The research design and process will be critically reflected against the background of the six previously introduced quality factors:

(1) Complete documentation of the research process,

(2) application of codified methods,

(3) triangulation,

(4) argumentative validation,

(5) communicative validation,

(6) multi-personal discourse.

(1) The **documentation of the research process** is the central quality criterion for creating inter-subjective traceability. A detailed documentation is necessary to make the underlying research process assessable. The present work addressed this requirement by disclosing the data collection process, especially the interview guideline, the sampling approach of interview partners and the overall context of the data collection process. The data structure, e.g. number of informants, interview hours, interviewee's position etc, and the interview transcription rules have also been disclosed.

The functionality of the **structuring-thematic coding** approach as the data analysis technique for the present work has been explained in the previous section. Furthermore, the detailed step-by-step procedure during the data analysis was unfolded in order to create a clearer comprehension for the "bridge" between the raw interview data and the empirical findings. Thereby, the use of MAXQDA for the data management and analysis was a further means of creating greater transparency and traceability.[697] An important positive side-effect regarding the documentation of the research process is that independent audiences are able to make their own judgments in the light of their quality factors or standards.[698]

Enhanced transparency is also achieved by supporting argumentations and interpretation with direct quotations **("power quotes")** based on the interview data. This seems to be a central quality factor for creating comprehensibility regarding the chain of interpretation. Besides the fact that direct quotations make the empirical findings more vivid they improve the trustworthiness of the study by disclosing the interpretations and their rootedness within the empirical data.

(2) Although the standardization of qualitative investigations is neither desirable nor feasible, the **application of codified methods** is a further means of creating greater inter-subjective traceability for the addressees. When codified procedures are adopted,

tative research is dedicated to fail due to the multitude of different qualitative research designs; cf. *Rolfe* (2006), p. 309. For an approach to translate quality criteria for quantitative research to qualitative settings see *Anfara et al.* (2002), p. 30; or *Krefting* (1991), p. 217.

696 Cf. *Steinke* (2008), p. 320.

697 Cf. *Erzberger* (1998), p. 65.

698 Cf. *Steinke* (2008), p. 324.

the audience has the possibility to verify the application against the background of the relevant methodological literature. Therefore, the present study applied the structuring-thematic coding approach as a codified and broadly-accepted qualitative method.[699] The structuring-thematic coding approach itself, the main analytical steps and the selection criteria were explained in the previous section to highlight the application of a codified method.

(3) **Triangulation** means investigating a research object from at least two different perspectives, whereas perspective can be understood in different ways.[700] Different perspectives may result from data, researcher, theory, within-method or between-method triangulation. For example, researcher triangulation can be used for collecting and especially interpreting and coding the data.[701] Each case was constructed on data gathered from interview transcripts and from additional external and internal company documents as mentioned earlier. Triangulation of these two basic data sources enabled richer and more reliable case descriptions. Thereby, **data triangulation** is a means of improving construct validity.[702] Instead of the quantitatively shaped criterion of validity, qualitative researchers prefer to speak of credibility or trustworthiness.[703]

Researcher triangulation was only conducted to a limited extent. Partially, further research assistants helped to analyze the interview data in order to get a more differentiated view.[704] Additionally, **theory triangulation** was used to broaden the horizon to generate a more differentiated view on the research phenomenon. The restriction to a single theory may constrain the thinking and prevent a more detailed apprehension of the research topic.[705] Therefore, this work introduced firm-level theories to derive a greater variety of explanations and interpretations on the firm-level cases. Furthermore, relevant country-level approaches were introduced to explain the existence of country-specific challenges and to enrich the following country-level analysis.

(4) As explained earlier, disclosing the line of interpretation with direct quotations and anchoring the empirical findings within the empirical data was necessary to make the **argumentative validation** understandable for the reader. Direct quotations were used for the description of the firm-specific investment decision processes and country-specific challenges.

(5) **Communicative validation** was important in order to check whether the interviewed persons were understood in the right way. On the interview data level, the informants received the interview transcripts to give them the opportunity to control their statements and to check whether the interviews were correctly transcribed. This feedback loop improved the quality of the transcribed data and safeguarded that no material misunderstandings distort the empirical results. In a second feedback loop, the

---

699 Cf. *Kuckartz* (2010), p. 84.
700 Cf. *Flick* (2008b), p. 309.
701 Cf. *Johnson* (1997), p. 283.
702 Cf. *Mathison* (1988), p. 13.
703 Cf. *Koch* (2006), p. 92.
704 Cf. *Shih* (1998), p. 635.
705 Cf. *Bennett* (1997), p. 97.

extracts of empirical results were validated with company representatives. On the one side, this review process was obligatory in order to get the commitment to participate in this investigation. But on the other side, this was also valuable for enhancing the quality of the results by preventing serious misconceptions.

(6) The last quality factor of **multi-personal discourse** was only feasible to a limited degree. Nevertheless, the empirical results and the underlying research design were frequently discussed with the doctorial supervisor and research colleagues, who delivered valuable feedback for the research design and different ways of analysis and interpretation. Furthermore, the progress of this research project was presented and discussed within several doctorial colloquiums.

4 Empirical results

4.1 Firm-level cases

4.1.1 GasCo Case

4.1.1.1 Company profile

GasCo is a world-leading gas supplier and engineering corporation. GasCo's business is reported along the three strategic segments gases, engineering and logistics. The second dimension of GasCo's matrix organization is represented by the three regional hubs of EMEA, America and Asia/Pacific. The company produces different industrial gases and provides facilities for gas applications. GasCo employs approximately 50,000 people in 100 different countries. In terms of foreign sales and employees GasCo is highly internationalized. In fiscal year 2011, revenues amounted to € 14 billion thereof 90% due to customers in foreign countries. About 43,000 employees work in foreign locations outside Germany. These numbers reflect the high degree of international experience which is an important factor for selecting GasCo's investments as research objects.

The strategic focus of GasCo is aligned to the three global trends energy & environment, healthcare and growth markets. GasCo's management intends to gain market leading positions in growth markets, whereby growth markets mean emerging markets like BRIC countries. Already in 2011, GasCo invested more in growth markets than in mature markets. GasCo's main strategic segment – the gases division – has a diversified customer base which supplies end-customers in chemistry, energy, manufacturing, metallurgy, glass, retail, electronic and food industries. The subsequent investment projects have been undertaken by GasCo's gases division. GasCo's engineering division delivered the core technology for the new plants.

In the past, GasCo used a few large cross-border acquisitions to create a strong regional platform rapidly, which has been successively expanded with Greenfield investments. The acquired regional network provided the required corporate infrastructure to implement further Greenfield investments and manage the relations to local stakeholders. As introduced in section 1.3.3.2, this timing decision at GasCo can be regarded as a combination of sequential and parallel strategies. In 2006, GasCo made a significant acquisition that served to open the entire Asian market due to the target's strong market positions in Southeast Asia, especially in China and India.

4.1.1.2 Investment profiles

In summary, **six** different foreign investment projects were discussed at GasCo. This portfolio consists of two investments in Brazil and China compared to one investment project in Russia and India. The total Capex of the six investments amounts to approximately € 400 million.

In **Brazil**, GasCo invested approximately € 50 million in a chemical plant to produce oxygen, nitrogen and argon for an industrial complex in the northeastern part at the Atlantic coast. A second Brazilian investment discussed was completed at the beginning of 2011. GasCo invested € 52 million for an on-site supply contract with a steel manufacturer in the southeast of Brazil. **Russia** was covered with one € 37 million investment project which was completed at the end of 2011. The new production unit is located close to Moscow to supply a main steel customer and the area's surrounding heavy industry with industrial gases.

The investment in **India** is based on a long-term on-site gases supply contract with an Indian steel producer. GasCo will invest approximately € 90 million once the new production units are going on-stream in 2014. The agreement with the customer was signed in 2012. In **China** two investment projects have been discussed amounting to € 120 million and € 45 million. Both investment projects have been approved by the board in 2011 and are expected to be completed at the end of 2013. The € 120 million investment was based on a long-term contract to supply a regional steel cluster in the north of China. The smaller investment is based on a contract to supply hydrogen to a petrochemical client located in the northeast of China.

All investment projects described above share a common characteristic. Each of these projects is strongly **customer-driven** within the four countries. The basis for the investment decisions is a long-term supply contract with either a single customer or a cluster of a few customers. Subsequent to the contract agreement, GasCo usually requires to invest close to the customer production facilities because the gas supply or chemical products are not efficiently transportable over longer distances. To fulfill the contractual obligations GasCo initializes its investment process. Generally the new production facilities are oversized to serve the regional merchant market ("merchant piggyback") which comprises smaller clients with industrial gases and chemical products. These by-products are usually distributed via cylinders on trucks instead of direct pipelines to the customer. Due to this specific business model, GasCo has a relatively constant flow of investment projects.

GasCo's investment motives in these six specific cases can be unambiguously classified as **market-seeking** and **follow-the-customer**. Cost-seeking or efficiency-seeking motives can be excluded because the produced gases and chemical products are not exportable to distant countries or regions. As explained above, GasCo's investment projects are strongly driven by the customers who create more or less a certain pressure to invest. In the following sections the GasCo's foreign investment decision process will be presented which has been derived from the interview data.

The **entry mode decision** is to a considerable extent predetermined by the customer due to regional limitations for the new production units. In most cases, there is simply no other choice than delivering the agreed gas volume with the implementation of a Greenfield investment. Especially within the four geographically huge BRIC countries and still underdeveloped areas there is no other option than to undertake a Greenfield project. Apart from the availability of other entry mode choices, GasCo prefers to undertake Greenfield projects due to its broad project experience. Usually GasCo uses

M&A transactions to acquire a competitor's worldwide operations – mainly in order to catch up quickly in certain regions where GasCo was rather underrepresented or virtually non-existent.

4.1.1.3 Foreign investment decision process

4.1.1.3.1 Initialization

As depicted in Figure 4-1 GasCo's investment decision process is strongly driven by its customers. The internal and external initialization process can be regarded as process-specific at GasCo. Market development and business development are the two organizational units which drive the initialization phase at GasCo.

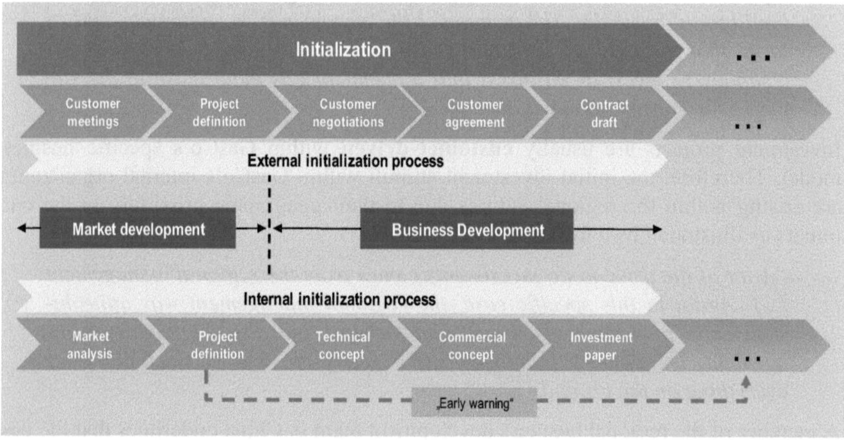

Figure 4-1: Initialization phase at GasCo

Investment stimuli

GasCo has mainly two channels for new investment projects. The first channel is managed by the **global market development**, whereas the second channel is represented by the **customer account management**. Global market development is systematically screening industry-trends in order to identify upcoming investment opportunities. This department is spread around the globe in growth regions upstream of business development which enters the process when ideas and visions are getting more concrete (project definition). Global market developers dispose over a strong industry-specific expertise, in industries such as oil and gas, petrol chemistry or steel business. A business developer describes that the initialization phase generally needs up to six months lead time:

> *"You can say that three to six months are between market development advises that an opportunity is becoming a prospect and the submission of the proposal by the business development."*[706]

Since the necessary supply volumes are fixed with the market development, the business development takes the full responsibility to create a technical and commercial solution in close coordination with the customer. If projects are arising through the customer account management, the process proceeds in the same manner. The initialization stage of GasCo is significantly influenced by its **industry characteristics** and the requirements for its business model and those of the customers. A GasCo manager describes the stimuli of investments as follows:

> *"It is this business unit or this business model we call on-site customer supply, where GasCo will not supply cylinders or gas by cylinder or gas by liquid form, basically. The demand of the customer is so continuous and so large that the only efficient and reasonable way to supply is for the gas company to invest or co-invest into a chemical gas plant close to the site where the consumption will take place."*[707]

Investment projects are usually **customer-driven** within GasCo's specific business model. Therefore, the initial investment stimuli within GasCo's internal organization are arising within the regional entities due to their geographic proximity to the customers as illustrated by a manager:

> *"A lot of the drive to do investments comes from the regional management [...]. Again in this specific case, the regional management was quite instrumental in pushing the investment forward, but also the country management. The country [management] is really the one who actually does everything on the ground."*[708]

A member of the regional business development team in China underlines that the customers may exert a significant influence on the foreign investment decision process at GasCo:

> *"Since we need to match our investments with customer projects, we cannot afford a long decision-making process, we are forced externally to have a rapid decision-making process."*[709]

This statement points out that the internal investment decision process of GasCo is strongly affected by customer requirements, e.g. in terms of project deadlines or plant capacities. The interviews indicate that investment processes at GasCo usually face the greatest time pressure and coordination necessities until the board approval has been received due to the coordination of customer preferences with GasCo's internal organizational processes as explained below.

706 Interview 42, GasCo, Business Development.
707 Interview 32, GasCo, Management.
708 Interview 36, GasCo, Management.
709 Interview 46, GasCo, Business Development.

Project development

During the above mentioned early stages of investment processes GasCo has to coordinate two aspects. First, the consideration of the **customer perspective** in terms of their requirements, decision procedures and their expectations is crucial to win a project. But agreements with customers also have to be coordinated within GasCo's **internal organization**, e.g. a business developer cannot agree to deliver a fixed volume of oxygen at a certain deadline, if it is not approved by the project execution organization which is responsible for the construction of the production facilities. A business developer at GasCo explains:

> *"Prior to the final investment decision you must be aware of the two different sides you need to consider. Two main things that we have to follow are what we have to do with the customers and on the other side we need to comply with our internal organization and processes. Promises to customers have to be internally agreed."*[710]

But before capital budgeting methods can be applied, a reliable technical solution for the customer requirements has to be developed by the **conceptual engineering**. The cust-omer's demand profile is the key information requirement for the development of a technical concept by the Engineering division. Technical and engineering experts design technically feasible facilities in close coordination with GasCo's project execution unit which is responsible for the implementation and construction of the investment.

Capital budgeting

GasCo's investment projects have to meet adjusted **hurdle rates**, resulting in minimum internal rates of return. Hurdle rates are defined by the central Finance & Controlling (FiCo) in the German headquarter. Thereby, the weighted average cost of capital (WACC) is adapted to the specific project and customer risks. In GasCo's business model the customer's creditworthiness and overall reliability plays a central role because single customers generate up to 80% of the future revenues. This creates a strong dependence between the investment performance and the solvency and willingness to pay of single customers.

NPV and IRR are calculated to determine the potential influence of new investments on the shareholder value. Capital budgeting tools are also necessary to indicate the key contract parameters like product price development for the long-term supply of the client. A manager explains:

> *"Our business model has a few parameters which could be negotiated with our clients. Price negotiations are usually based on investment appraisals. We are calculating our IRR, NPV or whatever to show that the project*

710 Interview 43, GasCo, Business Development.

makes sense in economic terms. But more important is to determine our margin for price negotiations."[711]

Furthermore, capital budgeting tools are tied to the value based management system of GasCo which means that investment projects need to earn the risk adjusted cost of capital. NPV is calculated by discounting the expected project cash flows with the **project-specific cost of capital.** Investment appraisals are necessary to determine whether new investment projects are expected to add value to the company. A manager explains that the IRR should align investment decisions with GasCo's **shareholder value** orientation:

"When we look at the investment essentially the main tool we use is a discounted cash flow analysis. For India it was a twenty year contract and we did a twenty year DCF. Normally when we look at this, the ratio, probably the one number that gets the most attention is the IRR for the investment on a post-tax basis to earn the required capital costs for our shareholders."[712]

The interviewee underlines that the **IRR** is GasCo's key figure for investment decisions. The interview evidence indicated that the IRR concept is very intuitive and relatively easy to communicate within the company. Prior research projects identified the same ten-dency, i.e. that IRR is probably the most important capital budgeting tool within the corporate practice despite of some methodological weaknesses.[713] A management accountant from central FiCo mentions these methodological weaknesses, but he explains that the advantages of the IRR prevail:

"Probably the academic's hair would stand on end, but we are focusing on an intuitive solution. For us the IRR is the KPI for investments. I know that the IRR could give inconsistent recommendations between alternatives, but we are in the comfortable position that usually we do not have to select between two or more investments. We are just looking if the project creates value for our shareholders."[714]

GasCo's FiCo department also calculates **NPV** but the interview data showed that decision criteria have to be intuitive and easy to communicate. NPV faces the problem that absolute measures are difficult to assess on a stand-alone view, e.g. it is easier to evaluate the return profile of a single project based on a given IRR of 20% than on a given NPV of € 100 million. A second simple key decision criterion is the **payback period.** Especially for investments in emerging markets the payback period delivers an intuitive impression for the riskiness and involved uncertainty of a project.

Sensitivity analyses are also obligatory in GasCo's specific business model because the supply conditions are relatively rigid for a period over 15 to 20 years. The management needs to get a deep understanding for the critical assumptions before draft contracts are handed to the customers as underlined by a business developer:

711 Interview 33, GasCo, Management.
712 Interview 36, GasCo, Management.
713 Cf. *Ernst/Häcker* (2012), p. 105.
714 Interview 39, GasCo, Management Accounting.

"The sensitivity of financial criteria is extremely important for us to understand the critical issues because our customer contract keeps the prices and the relationship with the customer in a very fixed manner, e.g. we could not simply absorb input cost increases with higher prices on the output side to reach our bottom line."[715]

A management accountant highlights that risk analyses are crucial to understand how different parameter variations or constellations may affect the business case because reliable forecasts are becoming more difficult in volatile environments:

"When you invest money today, you need to make assumptions to predict the world in 15 years which is quite challenging – or moreover impossible to do in this volatile environment. Who knows how prices will be in ten years? So you need to conduct a sensitivity study or other risk analyses, just to get a feeling for the riskiness of critical values, like break even volumes. You need to know how your return could be affected by adverse circumstances."[716]

Contract negotiation

After the customer has decided to choose GasCo as a supplier the detailed contract negotiations are following. The contract negotiations can be split in three phases. First **customer negotiations** focus on finding a technical concept which is capable to deliver the supply volumes. After a **customer agreement** has been achieved, a commercial concept has to be designed – putting emphasis on price development over the contract period. Both, the technical and the commercial concepts are the blueprint for the **draft contract**. The external initialization phase is finished by providing a first draft contract to the customer which has been discussed in several negotiation rounds. During these development processes from the technical concept to a contract draft, business development is responsible to coordinate the customer requirements and negotiations as well as the content-related work to create a desirable solution for the customer and for GasCo. The length of this negotiation period can vary substantially as explained by a business developer:

"Sometimes, I have joined up to thirty meetings with customers to discuss the overall project and the contract details – prior to the board decision! This stage can last anything from four weeks to two years. It involves a lot of work – especially in India, Russia and China you need to be very patient in some cases. But in China we have also seen the opposite that projects are fixed very quickly."[717]

After GasCo and the customer have agreed on the key contract conditions the business development initializes the internal approval process as soon as possible to receive the

715 Interview 43, GasCo, Business Development.
716 Interview 43, GasCo, Business Development.
717 Interview 47, GasCo, Business Development.

authorization to sign the customer contract. Therefore, it is necessary to prepare an investment paper[718] for the final decision by the investment committee (IC).

Investment paper preparation

The investment paper contains approximately 30 pages and a presentable version of 20 slides which are consistent with the draft contract provided to the customer. Each investment paper begins with a project description and a presentation of the customer. Subsequently, the strategic rationale behind the project has to be illustrated in order to guarantee that the investment fits to the corporate and the regional strategy. Potential projects must deliver answers to **three strategic core questions** as underlined by a manager:

> *"You have to provide answers to three strategic questions: First, why is the investment in that region important? Second, why is it important for us to have an agreement with this specific customer? Third, why is it important for us to prevent that a competitor will make it?"*[719]

These three strategic core questions have to be supplemented with **external market analyses**. Market share analyses are based on market volume and market growth estimate. A customer analysis shall deliver a more precise risk profile of the investment because GasCo's investment return generally depends on single customers, e.g. business development often uses external rating agencies to evaluate the customer-specific risks. The strategic section closes with a competitor analysis, which contains a list of main competitors in the target markets, threats of new local competitors and regional competition trends and behaviors.

At GasCo, the investment paper preparation is coordinated by the business development team which is organized in several regional hubs, e.g. the Southeast Asia hub in Singapore is responsible for the Indian market. One core element of the investment paper is the **business plan** and the **financial model**. The business plan preparation is a work-sharing process, which involves engineering and project implementation experts (Capex estimation), operations management (Opex estimation), legal, finance as well as tax specialists and the management of the local organization as described by a business developer:

> *"So there are probably five or six different functions that are involved in putting [data] into the paper but the business development team is the one who is responsible for compiling the whole thing [the financial model] and actually submitting it [the investment paper] to the investment committee."*[720]

The initial investment value is mainly estimated by the project execution[721] team which is responsible for the physical implementation of the investment. This **Capex**

718 "Investment paper" is GasCo's internal expression for investment proposals.

719 Interview 29, GasCo, Management.

720 Interview 41, GasCo, Business Development.

721 Project execution at GasCo will be presented in section 4.1.1.3.3.

prediction is supported by the engineering division which develops and delivers the core technology for the new plant. The project execution team is responsible for the actual Capex estimation as it has a comprehensive project and investment implementation experience. The revenues are estimated according to the contract draft. The future operational plant management is in charge of calculating the **Opex** for the business case. Price developments for input factors are delivered by regional FiCo. The overall business case and plan is created in close cooperation between business development and the regional FiCo team. As opposed to the central FiCo department, the local FiCo teams actively support and optimize the investment's business plan.

> *"Our regional FiCo colleagues are a part of the team from the first moment the customer selected us. They check all the assumptions on growth, costs or discount rates, transfer prices etc. Regional FiCo safeguards that the financial model fulfills the corporate-wide standards."*[722]

Apart from the strategic rationale and the project and customer description, the investment paper contains further qualitative sections to explain the legal, technical, operation and tax concepts as well as the implementation process for the business case. Each of these functional sections has to be coordinated with global team heads, e.g. the legal side has to be aligned with GasCo's global legal head. Furthermore, the business development has to define a list of critical success factors, significant risks and potential **risk mitigation procedures**. After the investment paper has been finalized the initialization phase closes and the approval process starts with the investment paper submission to the headquarter.

4.1.1.3.2 Approval

Prior to the final investment decision in the IC, the investment paper has to be released by the regional management and the global business unit management which is one level below the executive board. GasCo's investment decision process during the approval stages is centralized in the headquarter in Germany (see Figure 4–2).

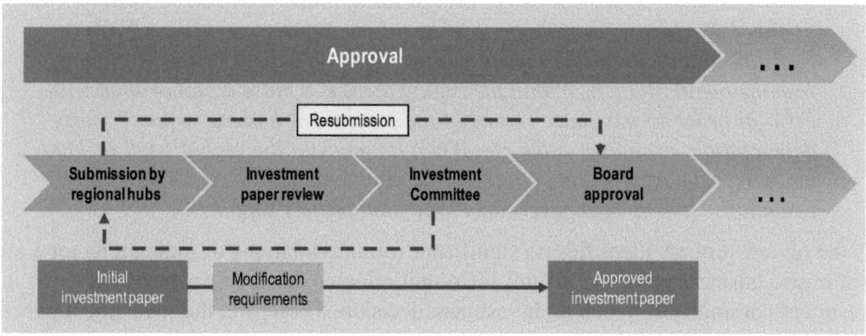

Figure 4-2: Approval phase at GasCo

[722] Interview 43, GasCo, Business Development.

Investment paper review

Prior to the discussion of potential projects within the IC, the respective investment papers have to be submitted to the central FiCo department in the headquarter. The investment papers are reviewed by the central FiCo department – which usually takes up to three weeks for large investment projects with volumes above € 100 million. This review process is necessary in order to receive the release for the IC. This review process shall safeguard that the investment papers fulfill the defined internal standards and formal procedures.

A business developer points out that the internal investment evaluation standards have been changed by FiCo in the past which created problems due to relatively high investment return requirements:

> *"There were some painful terms and conditions which we had to negotiate and re-negotiate. Finally, in the end of September, we had reached a closure of the contract negotiations and in October we went to the IC. What had happened: [...] FiCo used to work on a new template for analyzing business cases, and earlier everything was done on a world-wide standard rate. There was not such a hurdle-rate-concept. We really needed to optimize the case to achieve the required return – I am not sure if this is the right approach."*[723]

The interview data showed that GasCo's investment evaluations were changed from a standard corporate-wide cost of capital approach to a **project-specific hurdle rate** concept to adequately consider the individual risk profiles. Furthermore, central FiCo evaluates the plausibility of assumptions with respect to growth rates, price and cost developments. Internal benchmarking techniques are used to support the review process. Central FiCo disposes over a broad project database of prior investments because every investment proposal has to be released by this department for the IC since 1998.

Thereby, central and regional FiCo take different roles within the investment decision process as illustrated by a manager:

> *"Yeah, I would say, it probably breaks into two parts: we have a FiCo organization that sits in the region and we also have a FiCo that is globally responsible in Munich. Within the region there is a close collaboration with FiCo in order to maximize return of the investment looking at taxes, costs, depreciation, exchange rates etc. When it comes to the global level in Munich, it's primarily around checking the numbers and the underlying model essentially. It is more a governance role than project support."*[724]

If the review process identifies no significant formal violations or indications for a too optimistic business case, the central FiCo unit releases the investment paper to the investment committee to reach an investment decision. Therefore, the investment papers

723 Interview 49, GasCo, Business Development.

724 Interview 36, GasCo, Management.

are distributed to the executive board members – at least one week before the investment committee meets.

Investment committee

All investment projects over € 5 million (Capex) have to be decided within the monthly investment committee. The investment committee consists of the executive board and two representatives of the central FiCo department – which is responsible for the global investment process. Prior to the investment committee the executive board members are briefed about critical aspects within the investment papers by the head of central FiCo. A business developer describes that this review process is challenging for regional units:

> *"When we are moving forward with an investment proposal the strongest linkages are within the region and we do sometimes have to push quite hard to get support of the Munich organization. But having said that, I can't think of any case, where they haven't provided the support when requested. So at the end of the day, it does work out, but it can be a little bit painful in the process."*[725]

GasCo has an internal mechanism to accelerate the investment decision process called **early warning**. The early warning mechanism is used to receive the early attention of the executive board for investments which may have some critical features in terms of special customer risks, unusual business models or country specifics. The early board involvement ensures that the market and business development team is not moving in the wrong direction and too much work is invested in projects that are not desired in principle as emphasized by a manager:

> *"Let me just say that even early on before the final investment approval, we have sometimes an early warning. If we think there is something that smells of a project. Maybe a country that – you know – has some special risks to it, or a special customer that has some risk to it and we anticipate that the business model is not normal, something bad requires us to go and give an early warning so that we are not going down the wrong path."*[726]

The interview data indicated that the early warning mechanism is often used for projects in emerging markets because customer decision processes are often more difficult to assess. A manager clarifies that the early warning mechanism has been proved as useful for investments in emerging markets:

> *"So, the early warning is a process just to raise a flag that there is a probability that in a few weeks or months a rough project idea will become a firm investment. Sometimes we use the early warning to accelerate decision processes or to sign a letter of intent. Personally, I think this early warning is important for dealing with customers in emerging markets, because in*

[725] Interview 41, GasCo, Business Development.
[726] Interview 35, GasCo, Management.

some cases – when decision authorities are centralized – things are going very quickly and your internal procedures need to keep the pace."[727]

Approximately one day is typically scheduled for the monthly investment committee. The lead business developer or the regional management for larger investments above € 100 million presents the investment paper within the IC. The project-specific IRR is the key figure for the approval of investment projects but the investment presentation mainly serves to show the main value drivers of the project and potential risks which could threaten the business case. The executive board poses questions and approvals are frequently subject to additional requirements, such as contract modifications.

A manager explains that achieving the required hurdle rate is one of the main decision criteria, but exceptions could be made when strategic reasons are outweighing the financial evaluations:

"Probably, almost the single point of discussion was the return profile for the investment. We had a strategic customer and a desired country to invest. Globally we have a hurdle rate of 11.5% on a post-tax basis. When the project went into the investment committee the investment was at 10.8%. This was back in October 2009, when we were still in the midst of the financial crisis. There was a lot of pressure not to proceed with sub-hurdle rate investments. So as it turned out, we had our engineering, agreed to give a € 3 million discount to secure the project. That brought the return up to 11.5% and that was essentially to be able to move forward."[728]

These statements illustrate how external economic conditions may influence investment decisions of the executive board. In this specific case, there was huge pressure to show an 11.5% IRR on the investment being applied by the German workers counsel. Sub-hurdle-rate investments in India should be prevented when the management was considering layoffs in Germany due to the explosive political nature. In some cases, GasCo's management board approves investment projects below hurdle rates when these projects are of a specific strategic relevance, e.g. to establish relations to a strategic customer.

Investment portfolio coordination

The corporate-wide investment portfolio coordination proceeds in two steps. Prior to single investment decisions within the operational units the executive board has to receive the approval from the supervisory board for an annual investment budget. During the last years, GasCo's management disposed over an **annual investment budget** of € 2 billion to allocate among its divisions within the monthly ICs. M&A transactions are not included within the investment budget and need to be approved separately by the supervisory board. In general, the annual investment budget is approved in November before the financial year starts in January.

727 Interview 29, GasCo, Management.
728 Interview 36, GasCo, Management.

GasCo's investments are mainly-driven by the regional hubs due to its closer connections to the customers. Therefore, an investment portfolio coordination mechanism is necessary to avoid systematic misallocations of funds. GasCo uses **Capex-corridors** to tie the worldwide investment activities to the corporate strategy. Due to the matrix organization the annual strategic planning process is two-folded at GasCo. After the executive board has formulated the overall strategic goals, the global product business units and the regional hubs have to align their plans as exemplified by a manager:

> *"We have a two-step strategic dialogue within the group after the board has defined the broad strategy. In the April timeframe, the global business units fix their global strategies. The results are distributed to the regional executives to initiate an alignment process until the results are presented in July."*[729]

Capex-corridors are deducted from the strategic planning process as explained by a manager:

> *"We have a five-year strategic plan – which serves as the blueprint for defining Capex-corridors. The investment funds are allocated by the Capex-corridors, as a percentage of current revenues."*[730]

The FiCo department in Munich can be seen as an agent of the executive board to coordinate the international strategic decisions. Every investment paper has to be submitted in the headquarter which allows the FiCo department to evaluate single investment projects within the global investment portfolio. GasCo has introduced a **portfolio management** based on Capex-corridors for regions and business segments which is connected to the strategic planning process.

> *"We are using a modified BCG-matrix to manage our investment portfolio by defining target Capex-corridors. Based on the corridors we can monitor if we are investing according to our underlying strategy. For sure, we are focused on the BRIC and other growth countries. Single investments could be seen as elements or steps to create our desired overall strategic positions in these countries."*[731]

The strategic planning process defines GasCo's focus markets which are visualized within a **regions-/products-matrix**. Investment necessities are deducted from the corporate strategy by determining to what extent the current production capacities could achieve the planned strategic objectives. The gap between the maximum potential of the existing corporate capacity and the desired goals defines the approximate investment requirements by regions and product area. GasCo has developed a growth strategy program for each of the BRIC countries, derived from the desired market share. The target market share in combination with the predicted market potential determines the expected revenues within these markets. Furthermore, the portfolio management serves to identify critical investment levels in certain countries or regions. GasCo has

729 Interview 35, GasCo, Management.

730 Interview 36, GasCo, Management.

731 Interview 39, GasCo, Management Accounting.

defined risk management procedures to follow if **country-specific investment limits** are exceeded, e.g. to conclude hedging contracts or insurance covers.

After the investment paper has been approved in the German headquarter, the investment decision process shifts back to the regional organizations where the project has been initiated. The first milestone is that the regional management and the business development are signing the supply contract with the customer. Subsequently, the implementation process starts.

4.1.1.3.3 Implementation

GasCo's implementation process for cross-border projects consists of three main phases. Thereby, the investment transition as well as the project kick-off phase serves to implement an efficient project infrastructure and appoint responsible key persons as depicted in Figure 4-3.

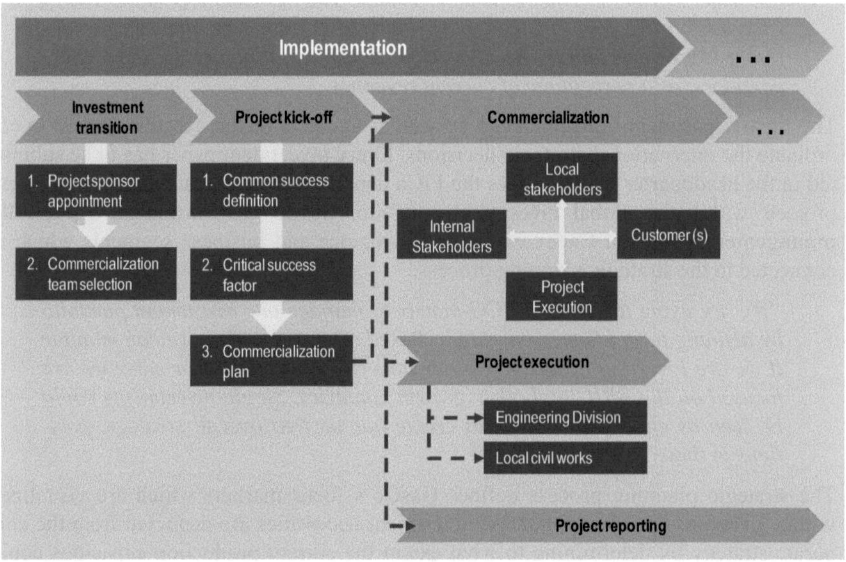

Figure 4-3: Implementation phase at GasCo

Investment transition

GasCo has a worldwide standardized process to implement investments – internally called **commercialization process**. The investment project is transferred from the business development team to a commercialization team – the latter can be regarded as the project management. The overall goal of this team is to convert a technical solution and the underlying contract into an operating business that will deliver returns as agreed within the investment case. A so called **project execution** team is a substantial part of the commercialization process which is responsible for the physical construction of the new production units. The business development team – being the process coordinator until the investment is transferred to the investment committee – delivers the investment case to the commercialization team and its project execution members as described by a business developer:

> *"We are still involved but as I mentioned it goes from nearly 100% of our time to about 5% of our time. A lot is about briefing the country organization, the people who we're doing the investment for, what are the terms we have agreed, letting the people know the critical success factors and deliver the investment. We try to transfer the business case as smoothly as possible to the project execution and commercialization colleagues."*[732]

This point represents a central interface within the investment decision process at GasCo due to the **changing process ownership**. Process responsibilities are shifted from the business development to the commercialization and project execution team. Although the project execution and commercialization has to support the business developers during the submission of investment papers, a close coordination between these three different teams is necessary. Until this stage business development was responsible to push the investment through the process, so that the business development is in charge to provide the required information for the commercialization and project execution team to implement the investment as agreed within the investment committee. Thus, one member of the business development stays involved as an advising body in the commercialization team.

Project Sponsors

The project sponsor team consists of two senior executives, e.g. the regional business unit head or the regional business development head. Due to their great internal influence and power within GasCo, the sponsors ensure that the agreed resources are provided from the respective organizations and support functions. The project sponsors ensure that the investments receive the **political support** within the organization. The first responsibility of the project sponsors is to appoint a commercialization team as illustrated by a manager:

> *"Personally, I act in several investments as a project sponsor. Usually, the regional manager, e.g. for Southeast Asia, has an entire portfolio of investments. First we are appointing the commercialization team – which is able to deliver the performance. Our part is to act as a kind of sparring partner in essential decisions for the commercialization team and escalate problems to the top management."*[733]

After the project kick-off meeting of the commercialization team the project sponsors have to approve the critical success factors and endorse the commercialization plan. The sponsors support the commercialization team to reach a decision when disagreements, tensions or conflicts arise during the commercialization process. High-level

732 Interview 36, GasCo, Management.
733 Interview 28, GasCo, Management.

customer interactions of sponsors shall align the project interests in order to prevent misunderstandings. Furthermore, the development of the previously defined success factors has to be assessed by the project sponsors. The project sponsor team reports directly to the responsible executive board member.

Project kick-off

When the commercialization team members have been appointed by the project sponsors, a kick-off meeting serves to gain a common understanding of the business case and its success. **Critical success factors** shall clearly define the financial, operational and customer management sub-goals (deliverables) along the implementation process in order to guarantee the overall success of the investment. The second purpose of this meeting is the development of a **commercialization plan** which prescribes the path to achieve the promised goals within the investment committee.

After this transition process has been finished, the practical implementation process starts. The implementation process is two-folded at GasCo: First, the commercialization team has the overall mission to "deliver the business case" which will be explained in the following. Second, project execution is responsible for constructing the physical facilities, properties and setting up the technical concept. One of the first steps is to fix the internal supply contract between the Gases and the Engineering division to define the scope of work between the two main organizational units. GasCo's Engineering division usually delivers the technical concepts, core technologies and components for the new production units.

Commercialization

Commercialization is an internal expression of GasCo and refers to the all-embracing process and activities from the contract closing with the client to the on-stream date when the first revenues are generated. As mentioned earlier, the commercialization process serves to **transform the investment case into a sustainable business**. GasCo's central concern is that a technically sophisticated and reliable solution must also be able to earn its cost of capital. Therefore, the commercialization process shall align the economic and engineering perspective of the investment. The commercialization team is empowered to make all project decisions – except concerning change management measure related to budget overruns exceeding 10% of initial Capex. Consequently, the foreign investment decision process is more or less concentrated within the local commercialization team during the implementation process.

Hierarchically, the project commercialization is superordinate to the project execution team. The commercialization team consists of persons with key functions within the regional business unit management and acts as the **owner of the project**. It is intended that members of the regional management team, the customer account manager, the operations management, the project execution manager and one of the lead business developers are involved within the commercialization team. A manager explains that business development should stay involved in order to prevent a total cut of responsibilities within the investment process:

"When the commercialization process kicks off, the responsibilities for the investment case are changing. Business development changes from the driver seat to an escorting role. We try that the business development stays involved because they were instrumental in designing the case – so they must also take a shared responsibility for executing projects."[734]

Furthermore, the commercialization team serves as an **advising body** for the project execution, decides on major project changes and raises critical issues to the project sponsors. But the overall responsibility of the commercialization team is to ensure that the investment project is able to fulfill the business plan as explained by a manager:

"The commercialization team has the responsibility to make the first year performance of the business case. The business cases that we normally do would be based on a fifteen or twenty year P&L projection. The commercialization team is responsible for essentially delivering the first year of that and after that it just goes on to our ongoing business – which should be able to deliver the rest of the investment."[735]

The commercialization team can be regarded as a process coordinator between the operational project implementation by project execution, the project sponsors and the customer. A business developer underlines the importance of managing customer relationships during investment implementations:

"The commercialization team coordinates the interfaces between the global organization, project execution, the clients and other external stakeholders. They are managing the interfaces during the construction of the new facilities. For example managing customer relationships during the life of a project is crucial to mitigate contractual risks. Sometimes investment implementations need to be coordinated with the customer because the new facilities are set up on customer sites."[736]

Specific-cases of GasCo investments are co-investments on customer sites, because the project execution is interdependent to the progress of the investment implementation of the customer. In some cases, GasCo needed to stop the implementation process because the customer could not achieve the agreed schedule as exemplified by a manager:

"In these projects we often face execution problems because the customer does not deliver the utilities on time. Customers agreed to do the civil works, provide water for our cooling systems or just energy supply. But also some clients still want changes after the contract has been signed or new legislations are requiring changes. These things can impact the IRR."[737]

Therefore, the customer account manager is a key member of the commercialization team to reduce these risks as highlighted within the statement above. The interview

734 Interview 30, GasCo, Management.
735 Interview 36, GasCo, Management.
736 Interview 45, GasCo, Business Development.
737 Interview 33, GasCo, Management.

data indicates that investment implementations are often exposed to changes in emerging markets because discussion with the customers continue during the entire "lifetime" of a project. This may be also the case for customers in developed countries, but they tend to rely on agreed contracts. In emerging markets the signed agreements are frequently seen as starting points for renegotiations.

Project execution

Similar to the business development, GasCo has a global project execution organization which is organized along different regional hubs in order to bundle the local project implementation experiences. Project execution is an organizational unit which exclusively provides the necessary operational project management capabilities as well as local project know-how to implement investment projects. This centralization within one corporate unit has the advantage that investments are implemented by specialists who dispose over a broad local project experience as emphasized by a manager:

> *"We always had a full investment pipeline – so that it makes sense for us to have specialized units which accumulate the project know-how. It is also important to have people which have local project implementation experience. You cannot compare investment implementation between the United States and India."*[738]

GasCo intends to handle investment implementations as a part of its core business in order to gain greater control over these processes, realize learning curves and reduce the risks of mismanagement. The conservation of local project implementation capabilities was also an important rationale to create the global project execution organization due to the variety of different local regulations. The project execution team has operational responsibility for the new facilities until the plant is accepted and handed-over to the operations management.

GasCo's approach is to source as much as possible of the required resources and supplies locally as particularly investment projects in China and India are exposed to high cost pressures, mainly due to high competition in China (see section 4.2.4) and high price sensitivities and cost awareness in India (see section 4.2.3). A business developer describes a project implementation in India as follows:

> *"Almost the entire implementation was done by our Indian project execution team or subcontracted to local firms. Our project execution team has an established local approach because it would not be viable if everything is coming from Europe. As soon as local products and services of a particular standard are available you need to make use of it. So a substantial chunk of the entire Capex was sourced from India and from Indian companies."*[739]

As mentioned above GasCo's project execution organization is centralized to establish broad project implementation know-how. The regional project execution hubs serve to

738 Interview 3, GasCo, Management.

739 Interview 49, GasCo, Business Development.

anticipate country-specific challenges in order to implement investment projects in the most efficient manner. In each foreign country GasCo's project execution appoints a **local project coordinator** who is responsible to assist the project execution process in all issues which require deeper knowledge of the local conditions, legislation and country cultures:

> *"We have one person called local project coordinator. Usually this person is a young local engineer with a high potential for a managerial career. He manages all country-specifics with local bodies."*[740]

Project reporting

GasCo has defined different reporting requirements depending on the progress within the investment process. As the project commission[741] deadline comes closer, the reporting requirements increase. The project progress is reported regularly on a monthly basis. A standardized traffic-light system provides a quick overview. Thereby, GasCo differentiates between the two reporting units project execution and commercialization concerning investment implementations. Project execution reports are standardized within the corporate intranet:

> *"Project execution has a cost-spending plan which has to be frequently reported to the central FiCo department via intranet. If you see red traffic lights, you have a problem which will be escalated upwards within GasCo's organization – in the worst case to the board. If certain critical values are exceeded you need a new board approval."*[742]

The progress of the investments' commercialization process is also reported to the regional management which takes the role of a project sponsor as illustrated by a manager:

> *"We essentially produce monthly project reports that would essentially say where we are on the schedule against what we have given to the investment committee. A spending curve is also analyzed compared to what was agreed in the investment committee. Major milestones of the commercialization process are also discussed in our monthly reporting."*[743]

In some investment projects, business development considers contingencies from five to ten percent of Capex in order to anticipate unexpected losses or delays due to external influences. This risk coverage should anticipate experiences from earlier investment projects. But a business developer highlights that the internal communication of contingencies has to be well-considered:

---

740 Interview 44, GasCo, Business Development.

741 Project commission means the acceptance process by the new operational management plant management. The new plant management is in charge to supply the agreed gas volumes to the customers.

742 Interview 47, GasCo, Business Development.

743 Interview 36, GasCo, Management.

> *"If we have a contingency within investment projects, you must be aware that you cannot tell everybody that we have a buffer of XY percent for this project. People are tending to spend it very quickly because they are choosing the simple way which could be more expensive for the project."*[744]

As the implementation process strides ahead both the internal reporting needs as well as the external reporting requirements to the customers increase. One year prior to the start-up quarterly **customer meetings** serve to coordinate the customer requirements with the investment ramp-up. Customers have to be kept informed in order to ensure the alignment of their interests with the project specifications. Weekly **management updates** begin four months prior to the start-up. The global business unit management and the regional management receive weekly reports to provide a quick snapshot of the project progress and potential upcoming project issues. After the physical construction and engineering work has been finished the new facilities have to undergo some performance tests prior to the commissioning for the commercial operation.

4.1.1.3.4 Start-up and control

Apart from the operational plant management, the country management is usually responsible for the new production unit. The commercialization team manages the hand-over process to the new operational management. Understanding the contract is the first important step during the transition as illustrated in Figure 4-4.

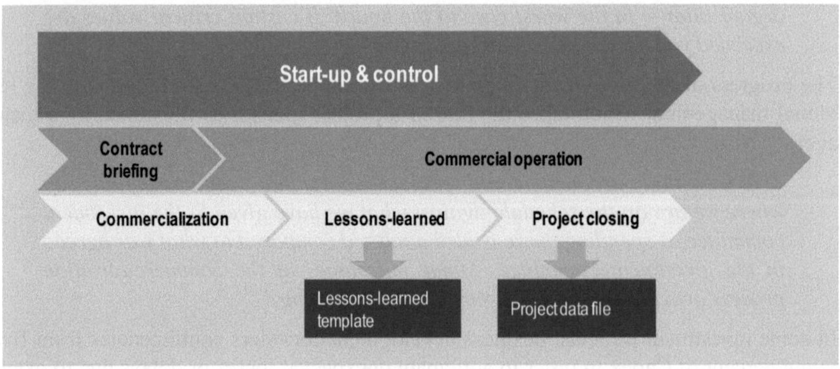

Figure 4-4: Start-up & control phase at GasCo

Contract briefing

During the last stage of the investment process the operations management receives the required contract information from the commercialization team. In the early stages, mainly business development and the account management designed and negotiated the long-term supply contract with the customer. The customer supply contract is the core element or determinant for the investment profitability because it generally deliv-

[744] Interview 50, GasCo, Business Development.

ers the majority of revenues for new projects and safeguards the necessary plant utilization. For this reason, the new plant management has to understand the contract in detail as emphasized by a business developer:

> *"The people who are operating the plant must also understand the customer contract and the related obligations. Therefore, business development and the accountant manager need to brief the operational management, e.g. by translating the legal contract into slides or more simple words."*[745]

This statement highlights that the new operational management has to understand the contract and the related contractual obligations in order to achieve the business case. Therefore, the commercialization team and the new operational management develop a **risk mitigation matrix** during a one-day workshop. This matrix contains and evaluates potential risks which can impact the IRR of the investments during the plant operation. In a second step, countermeasures or change management procedures are defined to mitigate these risks. A main purpose is that the operational management understands the risks due to the customer, the contract or local regulatory changes.

Commercial operation

At GasCo, the investment process is finished after the first year of successful plant operation (commercial operation). Thereby, 'successful' operation means that the investment faces no significant operational issues and develops in line with the business plan as agreed within the investment paper. Thereupon, the account manager is fully responsible to deliver the agreed contractual volumes to the customer. As a consequence, the account management depends on the operations management as pointed out by a business developer:

> *"After one year of commercial operation the commercialization team hands the project over to the operations management which runs the new business whereas the account manager represents GasCo at the clients and has to deliver the supplies. This is the 'official' closing of the investment process. Usually, the investment delivered the first results and should not require additional attention by our commercialization teams."*[746]

Furthermore, new employees have to be recruited in order to handle the plant's commercial operations. GasCo's approach is to employ local people to operate new facilities in emerging markets. As opposed to other industries in emerging markets, the recruiting of local people for the new production facility operations does not actually represent a challenge due to the limited manpower requirements, e.g. the € 50 million project in Brazil requires only 15 full time employees to manage the new location. For GasCo, the access to qualified employees is more restricted for the regional business development and project execution teams who are driving the investment process in the earlier phases due to the higher qualification requirements.

---

745 Interview 45, GasCo, Business Development.

746 Interview 49, GasCo, Business Development.

Lessons-learned

Three to six months after the on-stream date of the investment, key members of the commercialization team have to complete a lessons-learned template which will be consolidated by the local FiCo department and submitted to a global commercialization database. Moreover, the consolidated template serves as the basis for discussion during a joint-debriefing.

> *"We don't have a very rigorous process for capturing lessons-learned. There was a session after the project was completed where people got together to say what happened and what were some of the learning. But it did not become organizational knowledge because it has not been documented sufficiently. So, I would say we don't have a very good process for creating or maintaining organizational knowledge."*[747]

This statement underlines the general impression that GasCo does not, in fact, have a systematic approach to conserve the experienced-based knowledge. The frequent flow of new investment projects may be a reason for the insufficient documentation of lessons-learned and prior experiences since the priorities shift to new projects in order to meet the agreed project deadlines. Theoretically, GasCo has defined a lessons-learned process but it has not been observed within the discussed investment cases. According to the internal standards, the commercialization team has to prepare and facilitate a lessons-learned session with the project sponsors, the regional business unit and the involved corporate functions. The project learning should be documented within a globally standardized lessons-learned template and communicated to the relevant stakeholders to consider this knowledge in future projects.

Nevertheless, the entire investment process is documented within a global database. The close-out activities require to safe all project-related data – mainly the investment paper, the commercialization plan, the financial model, formal plant performance reports and main contracts – within a consolidated project file. The central FiCo department maintains the entire project file database. As mentioned during the approval stage, the database of earlier investment cases is used for **benchmarking purposes** in order to validate the plausibility of assumptions in future investment papers.

Furthermore, these documents are the basis for post-investment reviews. The central FiCo department performs **post-investment reviews** in specific cases when indications arise that the investment project will not meet the approved business case as described by a manger:

> *"We have a post-investment review, not so much on the technical part but on the business development and economic or commercial element. But it is done selectively, if some investments are struggling with the business plan. Central FiCo comes from Munich to investigate how we built the cases."*[748]

---

747 Interview 42, GasCo, Business Development.

748 Interview 35, GasCo, Management.

In fact, the interview data shows that post-investment reviews are seldom performed. The general approach is to solve arising problems with tighter controls by the regional management and frequent updates for the global business unit. Non-performing projects are focused more strongly by the different management levels – in the worst case upwards to the executive board. In earlier investment cases[749] responsible executive board members showed frequent presence on-site to demonstrate the seriousness of the situations but also to motivate the involved people.

Summarizing, the investment process at GasCo is globally standardized with clear definitions of responsibilities during the different process stages. A main influencing determinant is the **specific business model** of GasCo. The majority of GasCo's new business is based on long-term customer contracts to provide a certain volume of industrial gases or other chemicals for a period of at least ten years. New businesses require investments in new production plants situated close to the location of the customer. Therefore, Greenfield investments can be regarded as an integral part of GasCo's core business. For this reason, GasCo has two **specialized teams** which are focused on realizing investment projects. The project execution and business development organizations of GasCo provide the relevant process experience and specialized knowledge.

The matrix organization with regional hubs provides the required local market knowledge. Similar to the organization of the worldwide business, the functional business development and project execution teams are also distributed in regional hubs, in order to connect the specialized investment process experience with regional and local market knowledge to sufficiently consider country- and region-specifics. The capability to consider local country-specifics will be further investigated within the country-level cases in section 4.2. The investment decision process at TechCo is presented in the following prior to the cross-case analysis.

4.1.2 TechCo Case

4.1.2.1 Company profile

TechCo is a **diversified technology corporation** which is mainly engaged in electronics and electrical engineering. In 2011, 360,000 employees in over 140 countries around the world generated revenues of € 74 billion (thereof € 54 billion were made by foreign locations). Revenues generated by foreign customers accounted for € 63 billion or 85% of total revenues. TechCo is a globally operating corporation with 244,000 people working outside Germany. The company's product by region matrix organization is divided into four strategic product sectors and three regional cluster organizations.

The product portfolio as the first matrix dimension is organized within the **four strategic sectors** energy, industry, healthcare and infrastructure & cities. Below the four strategic sectors the business is managed along 19 divisions. The second matrix di-

[749] These investments were not part of the projects presented in section 4.1.1.2.

mension is represented by **three regional clusters**: 1. America, 2. Asia & Australia, 3. Europe, C.I.S.[750], Africa & Middle East. TechCo developed the main regional hubs in the BRIC countries organically over a long time period. The internationalization patterns are not clearly observable. No major cross-border acquisitions – relatively for TechCo's size – have been made in recent years.

Cross-sector activities comprise financial services (TFS) and real estate (TRE). TFS is the central project financing service for the four strategic sectors and provides financial consulting in the area of risk evaluation, equity and debt financing as well as financial engineering for foreign investments and the worldwide project business. TRE bundles the global corporate real estate activities mainly to optimize the utilization of space and coordinate the global business infrastructure.

This matrix organization reflects the corporate strategy by addressing the **four global megatrends** demographic change, urbanization, climate change and globalization. Therefore, TechCo's vision is to be the innovative leader in energy efficiency, industrial productivity, innovative healthcare systems and infrastructure solutions. One major direction of TechCo's global strategy is to grow the business in emerging markets in order to increase the overall share of revenues from emerging economies.

4.1.2.2 Investment profiles

In total, **six** different foreign investment projects were discussed at TechCo. This portfolio consists of two investments in both Russia and India compared to one investment project in Brazil and China. The interview data categorized by countries will be further discussed in the country-level analysis in section 4.2.

In **Brazil**, TechCo decided to invest € 40 million to build a plant for small to medium power transformers. The investment is located in the south of Brazil and was completed in 2011. A further transformer plant investment of approximately € 120 million has been implemented in the vicinity of Moscow, **Russia**. The plant was completed in the mid of 2012. A second investment in Russia of € 60 million was discussed with TechCo employees. The new plant manufactures compressors for the oil and gas industry since the beginning of 2012.

Two investment projects implemented in **India** were investigated at TechCo. The first project contained the development of a new turbine plant with a total Capex volume of € 75 million which has been completed in 2011.The second TechCo investment in India has been undertaken to create a new transformer plant close to Mumbai. The € 50 million project has achieved its full ramp-up in 2011. **China** was covered with an investment in a new compressor and turbine plant amounting to € 90 million. The new production unit became operational in 2010.

The investments are mainly driven by **market-seeking motives**. TechCo's corporate strategy explicitly articulates to develop a strong presence in the emerging markets. Thereby, the BRIC countries represent a centerpiece in the globalization strategy.

750 Commonwealth of Independent States.

Hence, an important investment rationale is to serve the growing local markets. Particularly, the energy and industry sectors benefit from the increasing infrastructural requirements in fast-growing economies. But the investigated investment projects were also driven by **efficiency-seeking motives** by leveraging local cost advantages. TechCo's approach in BRIC countries is to localize the complete value chain to be able to provide products at competitive price levels for the local market and generate higher margins for exported products.

The **entry mode decision** of TechCo's foreign investments is mainly determined by product and production process requirements. The investigated projects are technology-intensive manufacturing investments. Greenfields are preferred for technologically sophisticated and demanding product or production procedures. Acquisitions are often exposed to high modification efforts. Joint ventures with local companies are especially avoided in China and Russia if technologically sophisticated products or production techniques are involved. A business developer explains that intellectual property rights and intercultural risks are decisive for the selection of entry modes:

> *"When the product is technically not very demanding, you can buy a local company. But for our complex products that require sophisticated technologies, we prefer Greenfield investments – joint ventures create problems because you cannot really protect your technology and your know-how. And of course, you have always the intercultural risks in joint ventures."*[751]

TechCo's foreign investment decision process will be presented in the following, which has been extracted from the interview data.

4.1.2.3 Foreign investment decision process

4.1.2.3.1 Initialization

The initialization phase at TechCo is two-folded as depicted in Figure 4-5. A project profile serves to deliver a brief summary of the intended investment project. Subsequently, a detailed project definition has to be developed which represents the basis for the final investment decision during the following approval stages. A central requirement for Greenfield investments at TechCo is that new investment projects must be able to generate re-venues of at least € 40 million which represents the minimum size of a new factory.

---

751 Interview 27, TechCo, Business Development.

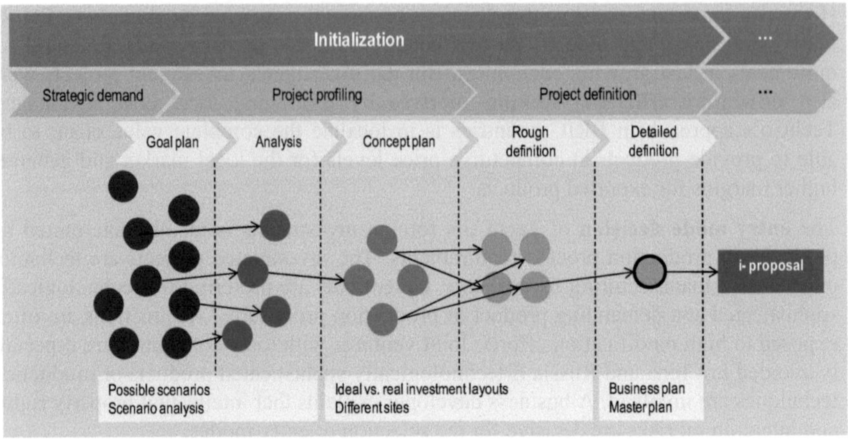

Figure 4-5: Initialization phase at TechCo

Investment stimuli

TechCo's investment stimuli are driven by strategic requirements to achieve a certain position in desired markets. The **strategic demand** as illustrated in Figure 4-5 may arise due to not promising performances in target markets, e.g. if the local market or the local competitors experienced higher revenue or profit growth rates. Therefore, the division or business unit management may consider undertaking new investment projects in order to meet the strategic goals. If the division or business unit management has decided to pursue the strategic plan by a new investment, the project profiling starts. A business developer explains:

> *"The first impulse came from our strategic analysis. We determined that we are losing market shares in China and we saw that our competitors grew faster. So we flagged these developments at the management. They decided that we only could catch up with new investments – from thereupon we received the responsibility to develop a project and the internal process starts."*[752]

Investment requirements are derived from the given strategic long-term goals based on the corporate-wide strategic planning process. Strategic analysis may come to the conclusion that **strategic gaps** can only be closed by new investment projects as pointed out by a manager:

> *"In the course of the strategic planning process, you see your actual position and your desired position. Thereupon, you realize that you still have gaps in certain markets. Based on these gaps, we define an action field in order to evaluate the options to achieve our desired strategic positions. The*

[752] Interview 17, TechCo, Business Development.

strategy process creates the necessary transparency to see the need for action."[753]

Strategic gaps are generally based on desired market shares or revenue objectives which initialize **market-seeking** investments as options to close the gaps. Nevertheless, the empirical evidence indicates that TechCo **efficiency-seeking** considerations also play an important role within the investment decision process. TechCo operates with globally dispersed supply chains to leverage local cost and efficiency advantages. The global value chain increases the complexity of the entire investment decision process due to the necessary coordination of interfaces and interdependencies within the global work-sharing processes.

The **entry mode decision** is often significantly influenced by external country-specific foreign investment policies. Particularly in BRIC countries, TechCo is obliged to invest locally due to high import tariffs. These protective measures prevent to serve the local market with exports at acceptable costs. A business developer explains the influence of protectionism to push the local economies:

"All BRIC countries have a reputation for high import duties. Especially Brazil and India have tremendous import duties – up to 20 percent in certain areas. If you want to participate you have no other choice than to invest. But once you make the decision to invest, you can also benefit from political support measures."[754]

After the general investment requirements have been identified – generally on the business unit level the investment project profiling and definition process starts. The following steps involve a considerable amount of engineering-related work in close coordination with management accountants to create a value-adding business case.

Project profiling

The starting point for every project development is the **demand clarification** in order to determine the required production capacities for the new facilities and to indicate the overall investment volume. A business developer explains this approach to estimate the necessary capacities:

"First, we define our market, product-wise and region-wise. Second, we estimate the rough market volume and expected growth. Based on this data, we set our market shares in close coordination with our strategic plans. Finally, you can deduct your required production capacities to achieve the desired market share."[755]

Based on the demand clarification the Capex and project timeline can be roughly estimated. After this basic investment features were estimated the formal investment decision process is initialized. As mentioned above, TechCo has implemented a two-step approach. First, a so-called **project proposal** (p-proposal) template has to be prepared

753 Interview 2, TechCo, Management.
754 Interview 25, TechCo, Business Development.
755 Interview 18, TechCo, Business Development.

which contains the core investment ideas, the strategic rationale and some background information about the expected key data, such as Capex or schedules to create a project profile. Second, a detailed investment plan has to be developed within an investment proposal (i-proposal). A member of the business development unit explains:

> *"The project proposal is more a rough project draft which contains answers to the questions: What are we trying to do? What is the underlying strategic rationale? How much do we need to invest? The proposal serves to flag that we have an idea and we need capital. We need to make sure that we are moving in the right direction because the i-proposal is a very expensive document – requires a lot of work and coordination among different parties."*[756]

The p-proposal has to be approved prior to the preparation of an investment proposal. It serves to ascertain that the project receives the general support of the corporation before more work is allocated to prepare a detailed investment proposal. The approval process for the p-proposal proceeds relatively fast because the decision-makers only agree that the applicant moves forward to concretize the investment idea with the preparation of the i-proposal. For investment projects below € 10 million Capex the preparation of p-proposal can be waived.

TechCo's project profiling process is very complex. The single circles in Figure 4-5 represent different investment configuration alternatives under varying scenarios in different locations. Demand uncertainties and related capacity configurations as well as the higher product distribution flexibility, e.g. products can be efficiently exported over longer distances, cause a multi-dimensional decision situation. Therefore, TechCo considers a variety of different investment configurations.

Project definition

After the p-proposal has been accepted, the **investment proposal** has to be prepared by selecting the most promising investment configuration. The i-proposal is an investment plan which presents the investment project in much greater detail than the p-proposal. The i-proposal is usually created on the business unit level by a specially established project team with people from different functional areas. TechCo does not dispose over a specialized corporate function which is exclusively responsible for investment processes and the related preparation of i-proposals. A manager illustrates that the i-proposal is the key document for managing the entire investment decision process:

> *"Our global investment decision process is documented within the i-proposal. It serves to consistently define the project ideas, to document the investment approvals and set the blueprint for the investment execution. Even the capital efficiency audits are based on this document to see what has been promised."*[757]

---

756 Interview 24, TechCo, Business Development.

757 Interview 3, TechCo, Management.

The i-proposal accompanies the entire investment decision process and contains and coordinates inputs from different internal stakeholders and support functions. Although the strategic fit has already been presented within the p-proposal, the i-proposal requires a detailed strategic analysis and fit which is the necessary basis for an investment project as highlighted by a manager:

> *"First of all, an investment has to fit to our strategy. Otherwise the project would not make sense at all. The investment proposal really needs to point out why a certain investment is strategically necessary."*[758]

Besides the underlying strategic analysis, a detailed investment configuration or **plant layout** has to be presented. These layouts contain an overview of major machines, equipment, workplaces, transportation ways and logistic areas. The production layout depicts the arrangement of functional areas and material flows between work stations while considering given restrictions (e.g. due to site limitations, government regulations etc.). The plant layout only shows the inner life of new production facilities since the construction-related work is centralized within TechCo's corporate-wide real estate unit.

Theoretically, TechCo follows the principle to entrust people with a high potential for a management career to take the operational responsibility for new investment projects – no matter if the person has a technical or financial background. It is intended that the coordinator of the i-proposal should be placed in a key position within the project organization during the following investment implementation, ideally as the project manager. But this is more or less an idealized view as indicated by a manager:

> *"We try to minimize interfaces. For investment processes, the preparation of i-proposals and the investment project implementation is driven by a single key person. But this is de facto not the case. Investment processes take a long time – in the meantime people change positions, projects are on-hold and so on."*[759]

Business planning

The business units have to coordinate investment projects with the corporate-wide **real estate unit**. Real estate is responsible for the site-selection process, land acquisition, property development, building construction and acceptance. Apart from these project-specific responsibilities, the real estate unit has to manage the entire TechCo real estate portfolio to leverage possible synergies. Afterwards, the investing business unit rents the new properties from the real estate unit which is managed as a profit center. Therefore, TechCo's i-proposal has two separate sections which increases the coordination needs as stated by a manager:

---

758 Interview 8, TechCo, Management.

759 Interview 1, TechCo, Management.

"A problem we face is that this document contains two separate sections – one from the business side and a second part for real estate – an independent unit at TechCo. Sometimes, the coordination could be improved."[760]

But besides the required coordination of the i-proposal, the negotiation process between the business unit and the real estate unit may lead to internal conflicts. Due to the profit responsibility of the real estate unit the negotiation processes about monthly rents and Capex requirements can be difficult. Therefore, the preparation process can face delays due to internal coordination problems. Subsequently, real estate delivers the agreed data for the real estate part, like property Capex, monthly rents or maintenance costs, whereas the business unit provides the information for the rest of the business case within the i-proposal. Based on this information the overall business case is assembled.

Further coordination is required between the engineering-related tasks and the financial evaluation of i-proposals. Until the final production layout has been determined, the conceptual engineering works in close coordination with management accounting in order to develop a solution which makes economically sense. Prior to the final preparation of the i-proposal, the engineering employees and management accountants have to pass a negotiation process as explained by a business developer:

"Usually, the engineer wants to develop the ideal production plants – the prettiest and best you can image – and then we start calculating this initial project draft. Often you have to admit that the project is going to be very expensive. Then a negotiation process kicks-off and we start to challenge the different items. This could be characterized as an iterative process which goes back and forth between the technicians and the accountants."[761]

This interview statement underlines the importance to balance technical idealism with economic criteria. After engineering and management accounting have come to a common solution, the business plan is fixed based on the agreed investment configuration.

Capital budgeting

Subsequently, capital budgeting tools can be applied in order to calculate the **project-specific EVAs**. A manager explains the connection to TechCo's value based management system:

"The project economic value added is the core criterion for investment decisions. This is derived from our value based management approach because our overall KPI is the economic value added. For this reason, every investment decision needs to contribute to this measure. Otherwise it would not support our corporate-wide goal achievement."[762]

---

760 Interview 1, TechCo, Management.

761 Interview 17, TechCo, Business Development.

762 Interview 8, TechCo, Management.

A central challenge for a targeted project-specific EVA calculation is the **cost of capital** determination. Country-specific risks are covered with country-spreads which are considered as premium on the corporate-wide WACC. TechCo's centralized corporate finance functions TFS defines country-spreads once a year. If significant events happen during the year, the country-spreads are adapted to the new circumstances. Similarly, the sophistication of applied capital budgeting methods varies with size and strategic relevance of investment projects. A business developer explains that projects with higher strategic importance and financing volumes are evaluated in greater detail with more complex capital budgeting tools:

> *"The sophistication of evaluation techniques also depends on the Capex and the strategic relevance, especially related to the extent in which we are conducting risk analyses. Sometimes we calculate probability distributions of NPVs in different scenarios."*[763]

Due to the highly diversified industry portfolio, TechCo does not use a corporate-wide template to setup a business case. A formal requirement is to calculate three different business case scenarios in order to identify the downside risk as well as the upside potential of the project. However, project-specific EVAs as the main financial decision criterion have to be calculated for every investment case. After the i-proposal preparation has been completed, the formal approval process begins by submitting the proposal to the next higher management level, generally the division management.

4.1.2.3.2 Approval

The approval process at TechCo consists of several approval cycles. The number of approval cycles depends on the hierarchical level on which the investment projects have been initiated. The lower the hierarchical level, the higher the number of approval cycles. Thereby, the i-proposal is subject to several modification requirements as a consequence of several approval cycles between different hierarchical levels.

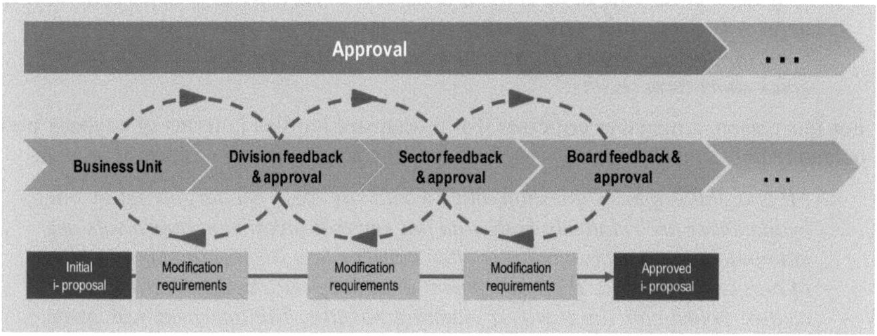

Figure 4-6: Approval phase at TechCo

763 Interview 17, TechCo, Business Development.

Approval cycles

In most cases, investment decision processes at TechCo involve **three approval cycles** as illustrated in Figure 4-6 because investment stimuli arise bottom-up within the business units. P- and i-proposal have to be released and cross-checked by management accountants on four different hierarchical levels: business unit, division, sector and executive board. Finally, the proposals are reviewed on the corporate level by a central function which monitors the compliance with formal corporate-wide standards.

The investment project is formally approved when the investment proposal is signed by the parties involved. The investment decisions as such are reached by consensus in different management meetings from the business unit level upwards to board meetings as explained by a business developer:

> *"The business unit presents it to the division, the division presents it to the sector and the sector presents it to the board. For investments, we have a bottom-up process and the projects are screened in detail on every level. Some project may make sense on the division level but not from the sector perspective."*[764]

Investment hurdles

TechCo uses different capital budgeting models to determine the added value of investment projects. Besides **EVA**, as the **central KPI**, payback period and ROCE represent two additional important decision criteria for investment approvals by the different management levels. In general, new investment projects have to be accretive on a stand-alone-basis, but frequently synergies are necessary to be considered. Otherwise investment projects cannot meet the required return to earn the cost of capital. A business developer argues that investment proposals are often too optimistic due to demanding approval requirements:

> *"Business cases tend to be more optimistic than realistic to get the required approvals. You could never design a business plan for your investment with a lot of start-up losses. In my opinion, sometimes we are too focused on quick short-term results."*[765]

For this reason, a manager criticizes that investment hurdles in terms of payback period and required return are relatively high and challenging to get projects approved:

> *"It is a philosophical question, but I would say 'yes', the targets set by our headquarter are relatively high. I do not say that investment appraisals are manipulated on purpose but it is often more or less wishful-thinking or kind of best case scenario. If an investment does not perform, afterwards the executive board can say it was a planning mistake. The approval was given under other circumstances."*[766]

---

764 Interview 18, TechCo, Business Development.

765 Interview 24, TechCo, Business Development.

766 Interview 3, TechCo, Management.

Besides the perceived high investment hurdles, the formal approval process itself represents a challenge due to the involved **administrative workload**. Some interviewees stimulate to streamline the approval phase in order to reduce the formal approval requirements:

> *"The problem was only internally driven. We are too bureaucratic. I will provide an example: for a new engine factory in Brazil, until today we have 39 signatures – I repeat 39 signatures and some people still have to sign. There are too many people who have to sign although they have no power or decision authorities. I have no idea why these people must sign the investment proposal."*[767]

> *"It gets escalated higher and higher. This is definitely one of the things where we are not so fast. You could end up having thirty signatures on the document – which is too much."*[768]

Up to this point the investment decision process at TechCo can be described as a highly work-sharing procedure. TechCo's **internal complexity** due to its sheer size and the multitude of specialist departments can be seen as a reason for the variety of involved departments, people, working groups or committees within the investment decision process. A business developer argues that the company's interests are often not aligned, especially between the headquarter, the product lines or divisions and the regional organizations. The organizational complexity at TechCo represents a challenge to align the business activities on a global scale:

> *"I have to admit that we are not always speaking with one voice – Munich, the global product division or business units and the regional organization have their own incentives which make coordinated decisions difficult. I remember an example with a joint venture partner in China – the Chinese were totally confused due to our conflicting behaviors."*[769]

A business developer explains how the steep hierarchy at TechCo influences the information level of decision-makers. He argues that the reliability of employees on the middle management level is important to ensure right investment decision ex-ante:

> *"Traditionally, TechCo is quite cautious, but on the other hand it's really based on what people know. The higher you actually go in our business, the less people know about the specifics of the business case that they are approving for. It's really reliant on the people on the ground level giving the right information and being open and honest with what the ranges of possibilities are."*[770]

The statement above highlights possible **agency-conflicts** within investment decision processes in large globally diversified corporations. TechCo's has a steep hierarchy so that the value creating operational activities are organized within the business units.

767 Interview 4, TechCo, Management.
768 Interview 15, TechCo Business Development.
769 Interview 24, TechCo, Business Development.
770 Interview 15, TechCo, Business Development.

From the business unit upwards the information level is systematically decreasing which requires that decision-makers on the upper management levels (principals) need to trust the lower management levels (agents).

Investment portfolio coordination

The annual investment budget is based on the **target investment rate** between 95% and 115%, e.g. an investment rate of 100% implies that investments equal depreciations in a financial year. Investments between € 100 million and € 600 million Euros have to be approved within the finance and investment committee of the supervisory board. Investments exceeding € 600 million have to be approved by the entire supervisory board.

Based on the annual strategy planning process and growth expectations, the investment rates are cascaded to the four strategic sectors. Thereupon, the sector management defines Capex limits to manage their investment budgets and to provide orientations for the operational levels. The expected depreciation amount serves as a benchmark level as emphasized by a manager:

> *"In stable business units with moderate or slightly negative growth expectation you are usually not allowed to invest above your depreciations. Growth areas or trends are able to get a Capex budget twice the depreciation. But of course, there may be exceptions, e.g. when we are going into new industries, but this is the usual mechanism."*[771]

Investment projects which involve new production capacities exceeding € 5 million Capex have to be approved by the executive board. This decision level appears to be as relatively low for one of the largest German industrial conglomerates, but a manager explains the importance of the portfolio view:

> *"For sure, some business units are generating several billion Euros of revenues. But our company is so large and diversified, that you can easily lose your focus. Imagine if hundred managers want to invest five or ten million – you quickly end up in billions. It is also a measure to coordinate the global investment activities. Maybe our industry colleagues want to invest in China as well as one from the energy division. It could make sense to invest in the same location to realize synergies."*[772]

4.1.2.3.3 Implementation

TechCo's investment implementation process is split in two processes as depicted in Figure 4-7. The main process is managed by the investing business unit or division to plan and implement a plant layout. The business unit or division, respectively, is responsible for the design and implementation of the value chain at the new facilities, whereas real estate is in charge of the entire construction-related aspects.

771 Interview 3, TechCo, Management.
772 Interview 2, TechCo, Management.

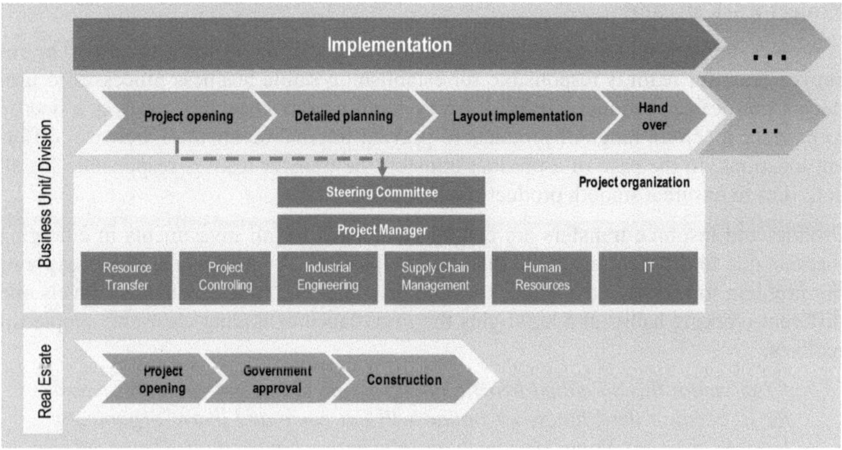

Figure 4-7: Implementation phase at TechCo

Project opening

The investment implementation starts with the determination of a project team after the required approvals have been granted. A project management is appointed by a **steering committee** which mainly consists of different members of the management from the business unit or division level supported by management accountants and representatives of the regional organization. The steering committee supports the project by providing political and organizational commitment. On the project level the steering committee approves milestones and scope changes, reviews the progress and resolves escalated issues.

Consistent to the preparation of the i-proposal the management of the implementation process is also split in two streams: the **project manager** acts as an internal entrepreneur in the matter of the respective project and has the overall responsibility except real estate related aspects. The project manager is officially appointed by the steering committee with a letter of empowerment. Furthermore, the project manager is responsible for the communication with the steering committee to escalate critical aspects. Ideally, the project manager was also responsible for the preparation of the i-proposal.

A **real estate project manager** is responsible of all construction work related issues from land acquisitions to the building acceptance. The necessary building and site requirements are deducted from the detailed plant layout which has been developed by the industrial engineering unit. Real estate is also responsible to coordinate the site selection process which has to consider the required infrastructure connections, like rail or port connections.

Project work streams

A project implementation team usually consists of six different work streams. The **resource transfer** team is responsible for establishing stable business processes to produce a pre-defined product portfolio. Every foreign production unit receives a license to produce a certain range of products to prevent internal competition between different locations. In the case of a product transfer, the transfer team is responsible for all activities to ensure a smooth product transfer.

Product and resource transfers are central challenges for all investments in emerging markets due to different access to qualified employees. A business developer explains the problem to transfer advantages to India or China due to low education levels and different working habits and highlights the importance of issuing clear and simple directives:

> *"You've got this so-called benefit sitting in one place, but you can't transfer it, because the Chinese or Indian will not come and learn, organically learn by working alongside somebody who knows how to do it. They need to see how it is done with a clear set of instructions. Then they need somebody to go and hold their hand and watch them do it and tick off that they are following the instructions. It is their culture. They are not used to have the freedom to make their own decisions to achieve a certain target."*[773]

A core task is to setup an employee training concept for the new production units including a full documentation of key processes and qualification profiles. A proven approach of TechCo is to define an established partner plant so that new employees are dispatched for training purposes to these locations. A business developer emphasizes the central role of human capital for transferring resources to foreign environments:

> *"Resource-transfer is mainly a human topic. You need employees who are controlling the technology and have the competence to make it work in different conditions. But it is a very clearly defined process with respect to what could be transferred and what not."*[774]

TechCo has organized a specialist unit called "**Global Footprint**" which supports the localization process of value chains in foreign environments. This team shall prevent to create local optimums without considering the global perspective, e.g. from a global view it could be favorable to split value chain activities. However, in BRIC countries the local value creation has to be increased in order to comply with local content agreements and to achieve competitive cost levels. The Global Footprint team works closely together with the resource transfer and supply chain management work streams in order to optimize local value creation and create local capabilities. The Global Footprint is still involved during the start-up and control stage in order to supplement the localization as well as product adaptation process.

---

773 Interview 15, TechCo, Business Development.

774 Interview 17, TechCo, Business Development.

The **project controlling** supplements the implementation process by monitoring the project budget and cost-spending plan. Similarly, the project controlling manages the business plan and is in charge of calculating updated scenarios. The foreign value chain and value drivers have to be defined in order to manage the interface between the new business and the value based management approach of TechCo. Taxes and customs optimizations are also within the responsibilities of the project controlling. Furthermore, the project controller supports the project manager to develop a detailed project time schedule and monitor the project progress.

Industrial engineering is already involved during the preparation of the i-proposal by developing the plant layout and specification. This work stream is responsible to coordinate the implementation of the entire production equipment. Based on the capacity requirements, the production equipment is specified and ordered in cooperation with the purchasing department. Thereby, the industrial engineering has to match the deliveries with the real estate timetable.

All necessary logistic processes have to be defined by the **supply chain management (SCM)** work stream. This includes the determination of in- and outbound logistic processes, required means of transportation within and outside the new plant. Furthermore, SCM is in charge to setup the inventory management by indicating required stock levels and warehouse sizes. The on-site logistic requirements have to be coordinated with the real estate implementation process.

At the end of the implementation process, the **human resources (HR)** work stream has to initialize recruiting processes based on the delivered staff requirements of the other work streams. TechCo chooses a practical recruiting approach and tries to entice employees from competitors to safeguard a minimum base of qualified production staff as explained by a business developer:

> *"The most important point is to have a solid competence base. Therefore, you need at the very beginning employees who are experienced in our business. The fastest way is to get the people from competitors. In the long-term you can develop your own employees, but at the ramp-up you do not have the time."*[775]

Furthermore, HR is responsible to familiarize with the local work regulations, such as working times, employment protections or other legal aspects. Thereby, HR starts to develop training concepts for new employees. The **IT** work stream implements the hardware and software infrastructure. SAP systems and other business-specific programs are implemented in order to connect the new facilities to the worldwide TechCo infrastructure, e.g. the performance evaluation is standardized globally via SAP.

The described work streams are constituted of employees from specialized business functions. Greenfield investments are not part of their usual job. Except for the industrial engineering which is mainly concerned with the design of new plant layouts, the members of the other work streams are often involved in implementation processes of Greenfield investments for the first time. In general, these people are delegated from

[775] Interview 27, TechCo, Business Development.

superiors to join the project. **Job rotations** and the heavy workload can be regarded as two reasons why know-how in investment implementation is difficult to conserve. In particular, Greenfield investments require experience-based know-how for an efficient project execution. TechCo uses job-rotations as a core measure to prepare high potentials for global management careers. The required high personal involvement in Greenfield investment projects can be regarded as another reason why people participate in investment implementations only for a limited period of time or just once in their career as described by a member of the business development team:

> *"It is hard to keep the people with that expertise willing to do it again and again, because it's a hell of a personal investment as well. Most people have to be away from their families for a long period of time on a regular basis. You do it one time, super, but if you do it over and over again than it is really a lifestyle choice."*[776]

Thus, foreign investment implementations demand a considerable personal commitment from an expatriate's perspective. Furthermore, in the early stages technologically sophisticated production processes and products still require the **support of expatriates** in emerging markets investments. But the next section delivers implications that TechCo increasingly tries to develop local talents who are able to take over the responsibilities from expats.

The implementation progress has to be reported frequently – generally monthly – to the steering committee by the project manager. During these meetings major milestones, the budget and the schedule are discussed along the different work streams. When the investment project shows more than 10% cost overrun compared to the i-proposal the entire approval process starts again. A manager describes that this is one of the worst cases which could happen during the implementation phase:

> *"It is a very painful process. In my opinion, the initial approval for investments still takes too much time, but in the implementation phase it [approval process] is even worse, you need to set everything on hold."*[777]

Once the investment implementation is completed, the acceptance and ramp-up stage starts. At this point the real estate team should have completed its property-related responsibilities. The project team gradually accepts the buildings and production facilities during the layout implementation.

4.1.2.3.4 Start-up and control

The last investment phase mainly serves to transition the implemented investment from the project organization to the future "owner" of the new business. Due to the matrix organization this can be either the global product line or the regional organization within the foreign country. TechCo's ideal approach is to appoint the project manager for the new management of the production units which allows a smooth transi-

776 Interview 15, TechCo, Business Development.
777 Interview 1, TechCo, Management.

tion. However, this approach is not always realizable, e.g. none of the investigated investments was taken under control by the respective project manager.

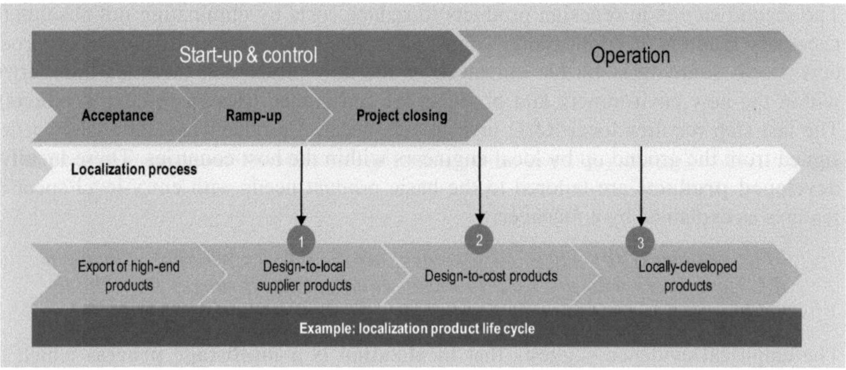

Figure 4-8: Start-up & control phase at TechCo

As depicted in Figure 4-8 the start-up & control phase is initialized with the beginning of the acceptance process which mainly contains the preparation of a snag list. But in many cases the acceptance starts during the ramp-up process because some deficiencies or planning errors can only be discovered during the plant operation. Prior to the acceptance of the new "business owner" the finalization of the implementation has to be approved by the steering committee.

Localization process

TechCo has introduced a new product adaption approach to fully exploit all market segments within emerging economies and realize cost saving potentials. The so-called SMART[778] concept is TechCo's solution to address price sensitivities and local product requirements in emerging markets as explained by a business developer:

> *"We have introduced new product concepts called 'SMART' to reach the bottom of the pyramid to protect the top. Customers in emerging markets look at quality products but with basic minimum features and affordable prices."*[779]

Three main steps are necessary to follow within the localization product life cycle. Prior to the investment implementation the usual starting point is that high-end products are exported from developed countries – which are not competitive due to diverging price expectations and import barriers in emerging countries. For this reason, the first step is to start a local production within the host country. During the layout implementation the SCM work stream is responsible to make use of local suppliers to benefit from price advantages. It is intended to create long-term supply partnerships. TechCo delivers the necessary support to develop local suppliers to make sure that the

778 SMART means simple, maintenance-friendly, affordable, reliable, timely-to-market.

779 Interview 27, TechCo, Business Development.

intermediate products are fulfilling the necessary standards for locally produced mid-range products (**design-to-local supplier products**).

The second step is to redesign products to reduce costs by eliminating not absolutely necessary features or applications – internally called de-featuring of mid-range products. Local sourcing is further enhanced as the new production facilities familiarize within the new environment and products are redesigned **(design-to-cost products)**. The last step requires local R&D investments because products are completely redesigned from the ground up by local engineers within the host countries. These **locally-developed products** are tailored to the basic product needs with entry-level specific features as explained by a manager:

> *"The customers are local, so are their needs. We are working with local R&D engineers who are used to these requirements. It ranges from the local handling to the language of manuals."*[780]

The empirical evidence suggests that **localization is a multistage process** which is organized along three product localization stages. Within the context of the investment decision process, the design-to-local supplier products are generally introduced with the ramp-up of the new manufacturing facilities. The next two localization steps are taken when the foreign investment decision process is completed and the new business is managed under the day-to-day operations. China and India represent the first two SMART product markets where the development process has been completed as illustrated by a business developer:

> *"Through a localized value chain and features fulfilling local requirements our SMART products are meeting local price levels, thereby ensuring profitable business. China and India are our trailblazers to push our SMART strategy because not every country is already equipped to do that in terms of having adequate local suppliers and engineering expertise."*[781]

These locally designed products do not only experience high demand within emerging markets, but also, being entry-level products, provide solid profit margins due to cost management measures. The final localization stage of locally-developed products is managed with a **target costing approach**. Local R&D engineers are obliged to align the product development process to the allowed target costs. This localization model has to be coordinated with the recruiting concept in order to attract R&D engineers with the necessary local experience and technical knowledge.

Recruiting approach

In the early stages – when the investment becomes a business – TechCo mainly appoints expatriates for key positions, particularly for those which require an engineering background, e.g. like manufacturing managers. These people are crucial to transfer know-how and resources to the host countries by training the local workforce as explained by a business developer:

---

780 Interview 2, TechCo, Management.

781 Interview 22, TechCo, Business Development.

"We send a long-term delegation of expatriates for two to three years to the new locations in order to train the local staff. Usually, these are people from our head office who had a key function in the project team during the implementation. If specialists are required we send them in the course of business trips for three to six weeks to the new facilities."[782]

The empirical evidence shows that TechCo currently adapts its recruiting approach to the relatively new SMART concept. Furthermore, TechCo increasingly attempts to train local high potentials for **global management careers** in order to reduce the number of German expatriates. A business developer argues that local talents are cheaper and also generate more satisfying results:

"We have systematically developed local people in BRIC countries. For instance China, we already have a lot of Chinese people who are very familiar with TechCo's worldwide operations. These people are employed in Shanghai or Beijing. We could send them to the rural areas to manage the localization process which is more efficient than sending people from Europe because these people are more efficient. They do not have language problems or cultural barriers. They know how TechCo works; they know how China works and they know how TechCo's business in China should work [laughter]."[783]

TechCo has difficulties to find people with the required experience who are willing to take up these vacancies, especially in BRIC countries with high regional differences of living standards. Therefore, the development of local people who are used to the local conditions seems to be a logical consequence. But the interviews also show that the recruiting processes for these development programs are far from easy. It is critical to acquire trustful people in order to reduce the risks of intellectual property rights violations which are not unusual in BRIC countries. However, TechCo's localization concept requires implementing local R&D centers with local engineers to be able to develop tailored entry-level products locally for emerging markets.

Performance evaluation

An important decision is the designation of the new investment to a reporting unit. A TechCo management accountant explains that the driving forces of investment projects are not always the same due to the matrix organization which has implications for the entire investment decision process. When the regional organization, e.g. TechCo India, initializes a new investment, this organization has a different involvement compared to a project stimulated from the headquarter in Germany. He explains that the influence of the new investment on the **performance reporting** also plays a critical role for people commitment:

"At TechCo we have a matrix organization – which means you have to differentiate between the local or regional perspectives and the global product

---

782 Interview 24, TechCo, Business Development.

783 Interview 22, TechCo, Business Development.

perspective, like gas turbines in our case. It is always a question about who takes care of the new business and which P&L is affected."[784]

Organizational units tend to be more strongly committed when the project has a direct impact on the performance, or gets integrated in their reporting unit respectively. The designation to the reporting unit is usually determined by the target markets. Manufacturing locations serving exclusively the local market are under the management of the regional organization (**local for local**). If Greenfields intend to export a certain degree of the output to neighboring countries or other regions, the responsibility for investments shifts gradually to the global product division based in Germany (**local for global**) as elaborated by a business developer:

"Investments just serving the local market are under full control of the regional organization. But we have also investments which serve outside markets. Sometimes, it is a significant portion of the business, then the power and direction comes more from the headquarter. It can be a little confusing who has the right of way."[785]

TechCo has adopted a balanced scorecard to manage the performance of new running factories. Balanced scorecard indicators are adapted to the development stage of foreign locations. In the early stages more attention is placed on security and production-related indicators. Financial figures are secondary during the ramp-up of production facilities. It has been argued that operational efficiency- and safety-oriented measures are the essential drivers of financial figures. In annual meetings, new indicators and target levels are negotiated mainly based on internal benchmarking data. In cases of significant adverse deviations, internal audit teams conduct so called "capital investment efficiency audits".

Post-investment review

TechCo uses **capital investment efficiency audits** in order to monitor if the approved business plan and investment appraisals have been fulfilled as agreed after two years of the start-up or even during the implementation if an investment faces significant negative deviations in terms of cost or schedule as illustrated by a manager:

"At the moment we have a capital investment efficiency audit in India. These guys from Munich are going to the details to determine the causes. We started to implement the Greenfield four years ago and we faced some internal problems, but for sure the global crisis put a lot of pressure on the project. The business case was created based on pre-crisis conditions – which are not realizable anymore."[786]

Although the capital investment efficiency is internally seen as a very inconvenient matter, personal consequences are often not associated with these internal investigations:

---

784 Interview 13, TechCo, Management Accounting.

785 Interview 15, TechCo, Business Development.

786 Interview 1, TechCo, Management.

> *"But we do not have these 1-1 mechanisms, which mean that if an investment does not perform, it is not so easy to make people responsible for it. Especially related to investment appraisals which are containing a variety of assumptions, it is difficult to say you are guilty because you made a wrong prediction five or seven years ago."*[787]

The control stage is characterized by shared responsibilities. In this context, 1-1 mechanism means to distribute success or failure to single managers – who take the responsibilities. At TechCo it also seems to be very difficult to find people who assume full responsibilities – not due to personal characteristics – but because the entire process and the project are influenced by a variety of different internal stakeholders.

After the within cases analysis provided a detailed description of the two company's investment decision processes, the cross-case analysis begins in the next section.

4.1.3 Cross-company analysis

In this section phase-specific investment decision process differences between GasCo and TechCo are analyzed in order to gain a deeper understanding of the influences on the critical success factors. Thereupon, it is discussed how the two critical success factors decision process speed and decision process comprehensiveness can be positively influenced – illustrated by the cases of GasCo and TechCo. A final conclusion serves to propose a context-dependent decision process model which may have the potential to improve the success of foreign investment decision processes.[788]

4.1.3.1 Phase-specific analysis

In the following sections the two company-specific investment decision processes are compared with each other. Thereby, cross-company differences between investment decision processes of TechCo and GasCo are explained by theoretical considerations. The cross-company process comparison serves to understand the reasons and determinants of investment decision process differences. Moreover, the analysis of cross-company difference provides starting points to discuss the two critical success factors of decision process speed and comprehensiveness.

In contrast to the prior sections, process phase characteristics are analyzed on a more abstract level by using the three behavioral firm-level theories. Behavioral means that the behavioral decision theory, agency theory and the promotor model consider the human characteristics of decision-makers in organizational contexts.[789] Based on the empirically explored decision processes, related differences between the two processes of GasCo and TechCo are illustrated at the beginning of each process phase. These basic process differences are discussed against the background of the introduced firm-level theories.

---

787 Interview 14, TechCo, Management Accounting.

788 For a comprehension of investment decision process success see section 1.3.2.5.

789 Cf. *Glaum et al.* (2009), p. 150.

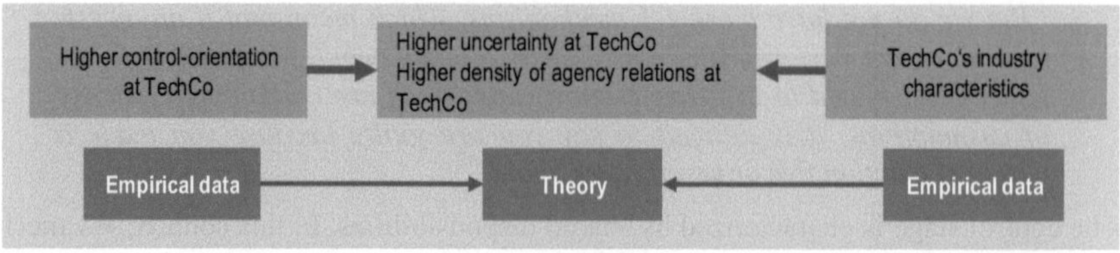

Figure 4-9: Example explanation for process-related differences between GasCo and TechCo

An example explanation for cross-company differences is depicted in Figure 4-9. For instance, the behavioral decision theory explains a more control-oriented initialization process at TechCo by a higher degree of involved uncertainty. According to the agency theory, a higher control-orientation at TechCo is associated with a higher density of agency relations in the decision process. Based on these theoretical considerations the empirical evidence shall deliver arguments for higher uncertainty levels at TechCo compared to GasCo. For instance, TechCo's industry characteristics can deliver explanations for higher involved uncertainty compared to GasCo. Hereinafter, the four main phases of foreign investment decision processes are compared between the two corporations.

4.1.3.1.1 Initialization

Comparing the two initialization processes, differences regarding the decision process speed and the decision process comprehensiveness are observable. GasCo's decision-making process in the initialization phase is faster due to more strongly standardized processes and fewer control cycles. TechCo's initialization process tends to be slower due to the prevailing focus on decision process comprehensiveness, more administrative barriers and control activities. The different decision process speed and decision process comprehensiveness are influenced by the company-specific investment stimuli, investment motives, internal investment drivers and investment project flow (see Table 4-1). These initialization process determinants and their influence on the decision process speed and comprehensiveness of GasCo and TechCo are discussed in the following.

Initialization	GasCo	TechCo
Investment stimuli	"Pulled" by the customer	"Pushed"; result of strategic planning process
Investment motives	Market-seeking	Market-seeking/efficiency-seeking
Internal investment drivers	Regional/country management	Global product line
Investment project flow	Frequent/part of the core business	One-off character

Table 4-1: Initialization process influences of GasCo and TechCo

Investment stimuli

Important determinants for the structure of investment decision processes are the underlying driving forces of new investment projects. Comparing the stimuli or the initial triggers of investments, a basic difference between TechCo and GasCo can be observed, which influences the entire course of the foreign investment decision process. While TechCo invests in a certain **product/regional market**, GasCo's approach is to invest in single customers. As described in the previous sections, TechCo's investments are deducted from strategic planning processes. The five year strategic plans are the outcome of a top down strategic planning process, whereas the business unit represents the smallest planning entity. Thereupon, the business unit management is responsible for defining an action plan to close its strategic gaps, e.g. by initializing new investment projects. Thereby, investments are **pushed** into strategic markets.

As opposed to TechCo, GasCo's investments are driven by single **strategic customers** who are interested in gaining GasCo as a long-term supplier for a predefined product volume at a specific location over a certain period of time. Investments can be regarded as **pulled** by the customer. This investment process characteristic of GasCo is consistent with the behavioral theory of *Aharoni*, who argued that an **external trigger** is required for the initialization of foreign investment projects. In *Aharoni's* theory the required external trigger is regarded as a main reason why foreign investment decision processes are not necessarily driven by rational considerations. As opposed to the theory of *Aharoni*, the external triggers of GasCo's investments are central determinants of lower decision complexity and uncertainty – which drive the investment decision process speed.

Due to the more or less specified customer preferences, the complexity and involved uncertainty of the investment configuration decision is reduced. The investment configuration and the investment schedule are more or less predetermined by the customer requirements. In contrast, TechCo is confronted with a variety of feasible investment configurations. Therefore, TechCo's **search process** for the most satisfying investment configuration is more time-consuming due to the required definition of different alternatives as explained during the prior sections. Only the necessary coordination between customer requirements and GasCo's internal decision processes during the entire investment decision process creates an additional interface which is not relevant for TechCo's processes.

Moreover, the investment configuration at TechCo – in particular the production capacity – is associated with a higher uncertainty due to a more **fragmented customer market**. The demand behavior of more fragmentized, anonymous markets is more difficult to evaluate which increases the involved uncertainty to determine an adequate plant size – which is a main determinant of the necessary Capex volume. For instance, investment projects cannot create the estimated shareholder value when production facilities have lower utilization rates due to an overestimation of demand. The plant size determination at GasCo is exposed to a lower degree of uncertainty. In contrast to TechCo, GasCo negotiates supply contracts with customers in the early stage in order to fix a minimum purchase volume, e.g. by take-or-pay contracts. Therefore, GasCo's planning certainty is significantly higher than TechCo's because the majority of required revenues are contractually guaranteed or legally enforceable.

The different investment stimuli lead to a higher uncertainty at TechCo, which induces slower decision processes in the initialization phase and greater attention on decision process comprehensiveness. Furthermore, the entire investment decision situation at TechCo is more complex than GasCo's due to the multitude of conceivable investment alternatives. GasCo's investment decision process complexity is limited by the demand profiles of customers and their geographic location of production facilities.

Investment motives

Although TechCo's investments have been characterized as market-driven, the underlying motive profile also contains **efficiency-seeking** considerations. TechCo undertakes Greenfield investments to leverage local cost advantages. An important motive is to use local resource in order to produce products for an entire continent or even for the world market ("local for global"), whereby the value chain is globally dispersed. Compared to GasCo, TechCo's investments are not that strongly motivated by the local demand conditions and sales potentials. In some locations, TechCo solely assembles components which have been shipped through the entire world. Due to these multi-dimensional investment motives and globally dispersed value chains, TechCo's decision process is exposed to more **decision alternatives** and interdependencies to other operating units. As a consequence, TechCo is obliged to evaluate more decision alternatives and to analyze interfaces within the global supply chain. Thus, TechCo's initialization process needs higher decision process comprehensiveness by means of search for information and applied evaluation techniques. In particular, the behavioral decision theory predicts that decision-makers are not able to assess all possible alternatives rather they are overstrained in decision situations with too many alternatives which may reduce the investment decision process speed.

GasCo's investments are to a great extent driven by the demand of single customers or industrial clusters to supply a limited local geographical area ("local for local"). The investigated foreign investment projects at GasCo are completely motivated by **market-seeking motives** – which means that investments are solely focused on generating new sales potentials. These new locations are designed to produce the output for the regional areas independently which reduces the required interface management to other production locations.

Therefore, the target market decision is driven by different motives. These different motives influence the **freedom of choice** and the **decision uncertainty** itself. Whereas the target market decision at TechCo involves more internal coordination in order to prevent competition with other locations, GasCo's target market is more or less predetermined by its customers. Competition with other locations of GasCo's new plants is not really relevant because the product characteristics do not allow efficient supply chains over longer distances. Hence, GasCo's business model and underlying motives reduce the possible decision alternatives which may increase the confidence to decide.

Thus, the decision process speed at GasCo is higher due to lower internal and external decision complexity and uncertainty.

Internal investment drivers

A further difference between the two initialization decision process speeds is closely related to the investment stimuli. The **point of investment origins** within the matrix organization represents a determinant for the length and duration of the following decision process. Whereas GasCo's initialization process is driven by the regional or the country management, TechCo's investments are typically driven by the global business unit (product line) – internally called verticals – from Germany (see Figure 4-10).

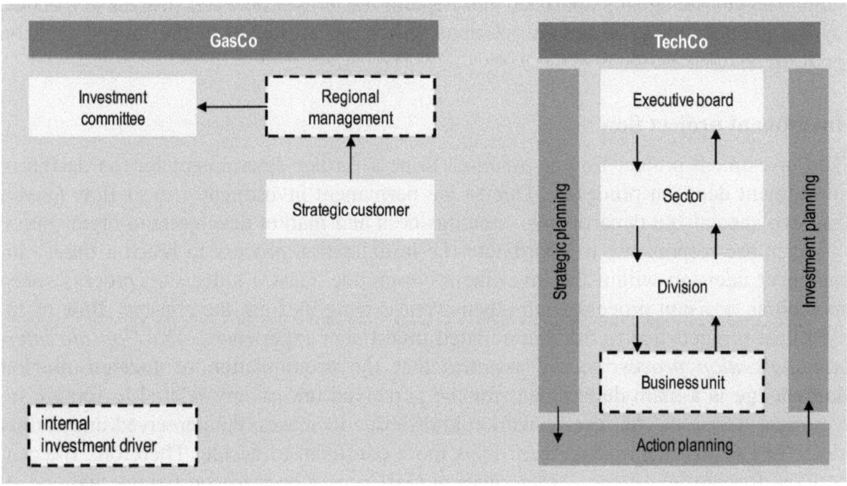

Figure 4-10: Internal investment drivers GasCo and TechCo

Due to the strong influence of customers on the initialization of investment projects, it is reasonable that the regional matrix dimension internally drives the investment process because GasCo's regional management is closer to the foreign customers. At TechCo, the strategic planning process – as a main influencing factor for new investment projects – is centralized in Germany. The business unit management, which is usually also located in Germany, proposes investment projects as core instruments of action plans which serve to achieve the top down defined strategic objectives.

The regional matrix dimension as the usual point of investment origins in combination with GasCo's flatter hierarchy already leads to a **shorter decision path** in the early stage. Only the regional business development team coordinates the preparation of the investment paper, which is directly submitted to the investment committee in the headquarter. TechCo's steeper hierarchy causes multiple approval cycles between hierarchical levels. As explained above new investment ideas are usually driven by the business units or business segments[790], so that the investment has to be approved by the division and the sector prior to the positioning within the executive board. The division and the sector do not have sufficient decision authorities to approve investments above € 5 million, but each of these management levels has to be involved in the decision process. The interview evidence indicated that these control cycles are taken seriously which leads to relatively **long decision processes** due to the multitude of feedback loops between hierarchical levels.

The different length of the two initialization processes further implies a different extent of agency relations. More agency relationships at TechCo imply higher coordination requirements and monitoring processes among hierarchical levels or functional units. Hence, the agency approach can explain the slower decision process at TechCo by the greater extent of agency relations which are attributed to the longer decision process.

Investment project flow

The investment project flow is assumed to be a further determinant for the design of investment decision processes. Due to the permanent investment project flow GasCo has two specialized departments – the business and market development organization – which are responsible to coordinate the initialization process to reach a timely investment decision within the investment committee. GasCo's decision process speed as well as decision process comprehensiveness benefits from the constant flow of investment projects due to the accumulated investment experiences. The *Uppsala internationalization process model* assumes that the accumulation of **foreign market knowledge** is a main determinant for the perceived uncertainty related to foreign investment decisions. As foreign market knowledge increases, the perceived uncertainty decreases so that the management feels more confident to decide. Therefore, the centralized foreign investment experiences at GasCo may be a reason for the fast investment decision process at GasCo.

TechCo does not dispose over an institutionalized corporate unit which is focused on initializing new investment projects. Moreover, investments are treated as temporary project teams with members from different functional areas, whereas formal rules for the project team composition during the initialization phase have not been defined. In contrast, the initialization process at GasCo proceeds internally in a standardized manner, while this phase can be shaped differently at TechCo.

A further important industry-specific of GasCo is that Greenfield investments are more or less a significant part of the core business. Typically, GasCo's tender based business model requires new investments if new customer contracts have been closed. Therefore, GasCo has a comprehensive **investment experience**. The investment decision process is one of GasCo's core processes. In contrast, Greenfield investments are not that regularly on the agenda at TechCo. These different flows of investment pro-

---

790 At TechCo, a business unit consists of two business segments. The business unit is the fourth management level; see 4.1.2.1.

jects and associated project know-how can be regarded as an additional driver for a lower perceived uncertainty at GasCo and associated higher decision process speed. The organizational learning approach of the behavioral decision theory can provide further implications. Corporations are assumed to be of **adaptive rational nature** – which means that higher investment experience is associated with higher decision process speed as well as higher decision process comprehensiveness and overall increased decision process efficiency.

Furthermore, the investment experience also influences the promotor role typologies. Al-though a clear troika constellation cannot be observed in the initialization phase, higher decision process speed at GasCo can be indicated by relatively **strong process promotors**. At GasCo, the business development team can be regarded as the process promotor due to the responsibility to prepare the investment paper in order to position the investment project within the investment committee as the main decision authority. Technology promotors are involved during the investment paper preparation because the leading business developer receives evaluations from different corporate functions, like legal, tax or engineering, which are consolidated within the investment paper.

The initialization process at TechCo is more difficult to access from a promotor perspective due to the lower degree of standardization. Certainly, technology promotors are involved in order to develop an investment configuration and the underlying business case. As opposed to GasCo, the responsibilities for the preparation of the i-proposal are not so clearly defined – which makes it difficult to identify a process promotor. Therefore, the lower decision speed may also be attributed to the **absence of a clear role allocation** at TechCo. GasCo's business development has a broad investment and process experience to assume the responsibilities of a process promotor to overcome organizational barriers – which may also cause faster decision-making. Nevertheless, power promotors – who have the capability to accelerate decision processes – cannot be clearly observed in both initialization processes.

4.1.3.1.2 Approval

Company-specific determinants which imply higher control activities and slower approval processes at TechCo are presented in Table 4-2.

Approval	GasCo	TechCo
Main approval cycles	One	Three
Company size	50,000 employees	360,000 employees
Corporate strategy	Concentrated on core competencies	Diversification strategy
Political support	Informal early warning mechanism	Formal approval of p-proposal
Decision authorities	Executive board/investment committee	Executive board
Decision criteria	Practicable decision criteria	Theoretically sophisticated decision criteria

Table 4-2: Approval process influences of GasCo and TechCo

Main approval cycles

A substantial difference between GasCo's and TechCo's approval processes is the number of formal approval cycles and the extent of **control activities**. GasCo has a monthly institutionalized investment committee as the main investment decision authority. At TechCo, the bottom-up approval process proceeds gradually from the business unit management upwards to the executive board. This approval process involves three main formal approval and feedback cycles, whereas formal means that i-proposals need to be reviewed and released by management accountants and signed by the respective management for the next higher level. Therefore, the decision process speed in the approval phase is significantly lower than GasCo's due to the multiple agency relations and related coordination requirements.

Additionally, management approvals often require further modifications of i-proposals. In these cases, additional coordination is necessary because the business unit management or the main project coordinators are not part of management meetings on the sector or executive board level. As discussed in the prior section, TechCo's investment decision process can be characterized as control-oriented – especially the comparison between the two company-specific **approval cycles** demonstrates this process characteristic of TechCo. GasCo's investigated investments were approved via one main feedback-loop within the IC, whereas TechCo's projects usually had to undergo three approval stages as depicted in Figure 4-11.

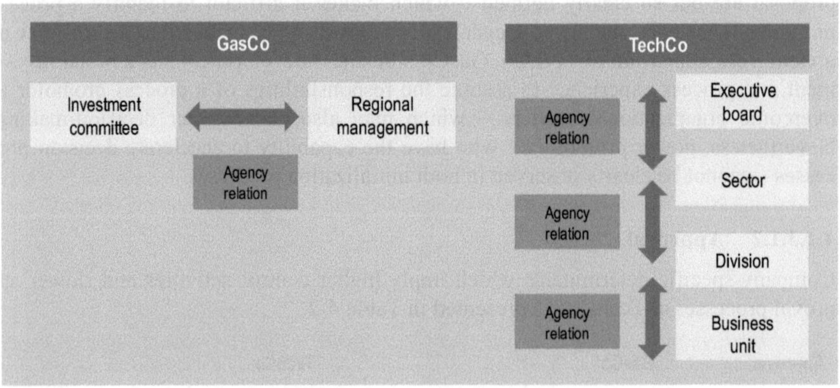

Figure 4-11: Approval processes and agency relations

The **agency theory** delivers indications to explain these different process characteristics by the extent of information asymmetries. Control activities increase with the variety of agency relationships and the degree of information asymmetry.[791] The **behavioral decision theory** also provides starting points to explain more strongly control-oriented investment decision processes. Thereby, control activities are a consequence of hierarchical leadership, delegation and division of labor. Therefore, agency theory

[791] See section 2.1.3.

and the behavioral decision theory provide complementary explanations, e.g. leadership and work delegations entail the emergence of agency relations.

A further explanation for more strongly control-oriented processes can be derived by behavioral **characteristics of decision-makers**. Looking from the behavioral decision theory, control activities and cross-checking are attributed to the bounded rationality of managers. For instance, managers do not feel confident to decide due to the uncertain and complex investment decision settings.[792]

Company size and corporate strategy

TechCo is characterized by a higher density of agency relationships and degree of information asymmetry compared to GasCo. The different **company sizes** and underlying corporate strategies can explain the different density of agency relations and degree of information asymmetry. TechCo with 360,000 employees is a much larger company than GasCo with a workforce of 50,000 people – which can be assumed as a main determinant for the higher density of agency relations at TechCo. The behavioral decision theory addresses this issue of leadership between different hierarchical levels because the lower management levels dispose over an information monopoly due to its direct connection to the day-to-day operations. Furthermore, company size is surrogate of organizational complexity and related organizational practices as empirically determined in a multitude of studies.[793]

Moreover, TechCo manages a **diversified portfolio** of products, whereas GasCo is strictly focused on its core competencies. A diversified product portfolio drives internal complexity, e.g. due to different production processes or an increasing variety of input products.[794] Furthermore, the information asymmetries within a diversified corporation are assumed to be higher than in companies adopting a core competence strategy, e.g. decisions about investments in the energy sector have to also be approved by the responsible healthcare executive board member at TechCo – who has lower industry-specific expertise and evaluation capabilities. Similarly, the steep hierarchy at TechCo enforces information asymmetries because the operational, industry-specific expertise is mainly concentrated on the fourth management level within the business units, while decision authorities are centralized within the executive board. For this reason, the higher organizational complexity of TechCo can be a driver of slower decision process speed.

Political support

Both corporations have a mechanism to receive the required commitment of higher management levels. From a theoretical point of view, these organizational mechanisms serve to gain **power promotors** for the investment decision process. GasCo's early warning mechanism and TechCo's preparation of p-proposals basically pursue the

792 See section 2.1.1.
793 Cf. *Baum/Wally* (2003), p. 1118.
794 Cf. *Fredrickson* (1986), p. 284.

same purpose to receive the necessary political project support of higher management levels from early on. But the organizational mechanisms to obtain the required political or top management support between the two companies show substantial differences, especially in terms of the degree of formalization and the related decision process speed.

GasCo uses an informal early warning mechanism, which means that the responsible executive board member is informed about potential investment projects coming up by the business development or regional management team. The executive board member grants the permit to move forward with the project development. During the project development in close customer coordination, the executive board member receives frequent updates of significant decisions or changes.

In contrast, TechCo applies a more formal mechanism which is more or less identical to the actual i-proposal approval process. The single difference is that the p-proposal shows the investment case in lower detail in a premature stage. Due to the two significant **differences of formal requirements**, GasCo uses a lean informal process to receive early top management support, whereas TechCo sets almost the same formal requirements like for final investment decisions. Although both mechanisms intend to introduce power promotors to the investment decision process in order to accelerate decision-making, TechCo's organizational mechanism itself requires significantly more time and coordination than GasCo's.

Investment decision authorities

GasCo and TechCo have defined the same approval levels in absolute terms. Investment projects exceeding € 5 million have to be finally approved by the executive board/ investment committee. But compared to the two different company sizes – TechCo generates roughly five times the revenues of GasCo – the **decision levels** at TechCo appear to be as relatively low. For instance, the largest business units generate more than € 3 billion of revenues, but the management is not authorized to make investment decisions exceeding € 5 million of Capex. The relatively low investment decision authorities of the business unit and division management require that every Greenfield project has to be approved by the executive board.

Although nearly every GasCo Greenfield investment requires board approval too, the main difference is the **length of the decision processes**. Investment papers can be more or less directly submitted to the investment committee without passing several feedback loops and approval cycles. The shorter decision process improves the speed of decision-making at GasCo and reduces the problem of outdated assumptions. Furthermore, GasCo is externally forced by the customer to reach a fast investment decision as explained in the prior sections. Informants emphasized that GasCo cannot afford slow decision-making processes. Otherwise supply contracts would be signed with competitors.

Decision criteria

Both corporations have adopted a **value based management** system in order to align the management decisions with the interests of the shareholders. Therefore, investment decisions in both companies are based on value oriented KPIs. GasCo's key decision criterion is the IRR – which has to exceed the project-specific cost of capital – whereas TechCo's management uses an EVA approach with country-specific cost of capital. An emerging market specific in both companies is that the expected payback period receives a greater attention compared to investments targeting mature markets. Due to the more volatile environment in developing countries, the expected payback period delivers an intuitive indication for the involved investment uncertainty.

Setting key investment decision criteria involves a balancing act between **theoretical sophistication** and **practicability**. Although GasCo and TechCo also calculate NPVs, different scenarios and sensitivities, the interviews indicate that TechCo is much more concerned with applying theoretically sophisticated models. GasCo's approach appears to be more practically oriented focusing on intuitive decision criteria to facilitate internal communication processes. Management accounting at GasCo is aware of the methodological weaknesses of the IRR concept, but the advantages of the simplicity are prevailing, especially in meetings with people of different educational backgrounds. TechCo's EVA approach can be regarded as theoretically superior, but periodic EVAs in absolute terms are difficult to assess especially in comparison with other investment projects.

The different design of decision criteria and application of capital budgeting models is consistent with the general impression of the prior process characteristics. GasCo is focused on **satisfying** and especially timely investment decisions, whereas TechCo tends to be more focused or aspired to find theoretically **optimal solutions** – that relates to the engineering as well as to the financial or accounting aspects within decision processes. These content-related process differences are assumed to be a further reason for the different pace of decision-making.

To sum up, many control activities, intensive cross-checking and validating lead to a slower approval process at TechCo. The greater external uncertainty for investments at TechCo is reflected within the investment decision process. The interview data indicated that TechCo needs to find a better balance between **decision process speed** and **comprehensiveness**. TechCo's current approach is more focused on developing an optimal solution which is often the main reason for slower approval processes.[795]

The interview evidence suggests that TechCo's investment decisions often take too long. Due to the several layers and work streams, informants emphasized to **shorten approval cycles** and reduce process complexities. From a technological or functional view, the delivered solutions are often perceived as sophisticated. Especially, the case study at TechCo illustrated a reciprocal relation between decision comprehensiveness and decision-making speed. In contrast, prior research projects are filled with contro-

795 Cf. *Eisenhardt* (1989c), p. 545.

versy regarding the relationship between decision process comprehensiveness and decision process speed.[796]

A further consequence of slow decision-making processes is that once the investment is finally approved the initial assumptions of the business cases may be subject to significant changes. But often the investment applicant – who has passed a long and expensive investment approval process – is satisfied that the investment implementation can be initialized. Therefore, in most cases an updated financial evaluation is usually not distributed to the decision-makers. In the past, this procedure led to significant deviations between the approved business case and the actual performance of the investment. This problem of **outdated assumptions** can only be solved by accelerating the decision processes.

4.1.3.1.3 Implementation

As opposed to the two prior phases, differences concerning the underlying decision process speed and decision process comprehensiveness are more difficult to assess in the implementation phase. Nonetheless, three main implementation process characteristics (see Table 4-3) and their expected influence on the decision process speed and decision process comprehensiveness are discussed subsequently.

Implementation	GasCo	TechCo
Political support	Project sponsor (2nd management level)	Steering committee (4th management level)
Project organization	Institutionalized	One-off character; six work streams
Value chain dispersion	Locally-concentrated	Globally-dispersed

Table 4-3: Implementation process influences of GasCo and TechCo

Political support

Similar to the approval phase, the two company-specific implementation phases contain mechanisms to gain **power promotors** for the following decision processes. The establishment of committees which provide the necessary political support within the internal organization can be interpreted as an attempt to implement promotor structures. According to the theory, a key characteristic of the power promotor is to dispose over the necessary hierarchical power to overcome barriers of will.[797] GasCo's project management is supported by the projects sponsors, whereas the steering committee provides the political support at TechCo. From a functional point of view, these two bodies fulfill the same functions to guarantee the internal political support, the availability of resources and the general **organizational commitment** for the investment implementation.

---

796 For empirical investigations of the relationship between decision speed and decision comprehensiveness see for example *Mintzberg* (1973); *Fredrickson/Mitchell* (1984); *Schweiger et al.* (1986); or *Eisenhardt* (1989c).

797 See section 2.1.4.

Although the functions of theses bodies are almost identical, the compositions show differences related to the political power of their members. Due to underlying purposes of the steering committee (TechCo) and the project sponsors (GasCo) to provide the required political support, these bodies must have the **necessary political power** to assume their roles of power promotors. In this respect, GasCo's project sponsors tend to be located on a higher hierarchical level than the steering committee members at TechCo. In some investment cases, the project sponsors are on the second management level which provides a direct communication to the executive board – the investment decision authority. TechCo's steering committees usually consist of the business unit management – including management accountants – who do not possess the same organizational power than GasCo's project sponsors. Based on these characteristics it can be questioned that the steering committee at TechCo possess the required internal political power to efficiently fulfill the functions of a power promotor compared to the project sponsors at GasCo.

Similar to the initialization and approval phases, this constellation is a further driver for a lower decision process speed at TechCo. Nonetheless, a central difference compared to the two prior phases is that lower decision process speed is solely associated with **change management** measures. When investment projects are implemented according to the approved i-proposals, the lower hierarchical power of the steering committee of TechCo does not affect the overall decision process speed in this phase. But in the worst case, critical issues like cost overruns or additional resource requirements have to be escalated in several steps to the executive board instead of addressing them directly at the authorized decision-makers.

Project organization

Comparing the two implementation processes, TechCo and GasCo pursue a different **project management** approach. Whereas GasCo uses a (commercialization) team for the overarching project management, TechCo officially appoints a single project manager. The commercialization team and the project manager perform similar functions, like the development of a project schedule, the coordination of work streams, acting as a communicator between the political supporters and the project team as well as representing the investment project internally and externally. Thus, the project management bodies play the role of **process promotors**, who arbitrate between power and technology promotors as depicted in Figure 4-12.

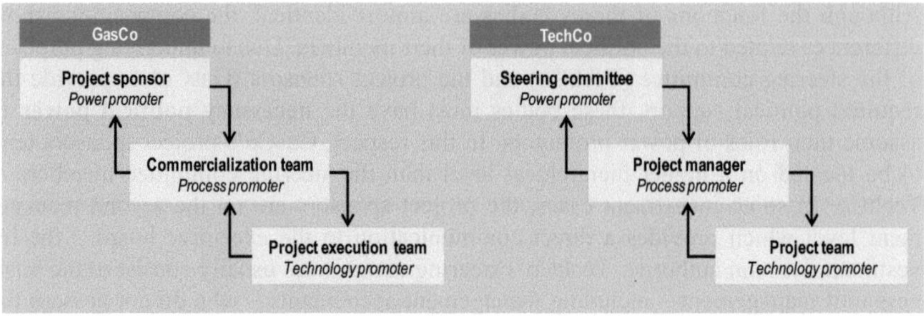

Figure 4-12: Promotor troikas in the implementation phases of GasCo and TechCo

Similar to the initialization phase, GasCo has an institutionalized department – called project execution – which is exclusively focused on the implementation of investment projects. Due to the constant investment flow it is worth to establish a specialist unit to bundle the investment **implementation experience**. Furthermore, the centralization of project implementation capabilities reduces the requirement of interface coordination. At TechCo, the project implementation is typically organized along six different work streams as explained before. The respective project team (TechCo) and the project execution team (GasCo) can be regarded as **technology promotors** who must overcome barriers of capabilities – which means to provide the required project implementation knowledge in terms of technical and local country knowledge.

Due to the **non-recurrent character of investments** at TechCo, it is usual that project team members are involved for the first time in investment projects. This further implies that project team members often work for the first time together due to the one-off characteristic of investment projects, the sheer company size and the variety of different functional backgrounds of the team members.

The different constitutions of project implementation teams may lead to the expectation that TechCo faces higher coordination problems compared to GasCo. Especially, at the early stage of the implementation process, TechCo's project implementation team needs a longer **familiarization phase** due to this one-off character of investments as explained above. The project experience conservation is even more complicated due to frequent job rotations across functions and product divisions, which are a core measure to prepare high potentials for management careers at TechCo. Thus, GasCo's specialized investment implementation units with country-specific investment expertise meet the theoretical prerequisites of technology promotors to overcome barriers of capabilities. In contrast, the non-recurrent character of investments at TechCo implies lower implementation experiences of involved project team members. Therefore, the project team at TechCo may pass a longer development process to assume the role of the technology promotor – which affects the decision process comprehensiveness and decision process speed.

Furthermore, investments of TechCo and GasCo share the common characteristic that a significant part of the investment implementation is realized by an internal supplier. GasCo's investment implementation team appoints the engineering division to set up the core plant technologies and processes, whereas TechCo has a corporate-wide real estate unit which covers the entire construction- and property-related work. Both internal service providers are managed as profit centers. Therefore, both corporations often face painful **transfer pricing** negotiations because. Informants from GasCo and TechCo emphasized that these internal negotiations between corporate divisions cause slower decision processes without creating additional values or increasing the decision quality.

Looking from an agency perspective on these internal supply relationships, the investing unit represents the principal that delegates a part of the implementation work to an internal service provider who acts as the agent. These two cooperating parties have conflicting goals. All things being equal increasing transfer prices lead to higher profits at the service provider, whereas decreasing transfer prices enhance the performance of the investing unit. This is a common mechanism between contractual partners, but in this context the two parties belong to the same organization. Therefore, the two units should act in the interest of the entire corporation and prevent **local profit maximization**, e.g. if accretive investments are neglected due to coordination conflicts between internal corporate units.

Aligning the interests of two internal organizational units can be a measure to solve these agency problems and accelerate decision process. The agency approach delivers basic recommendations by proposing the introduction of governance mechanisms. **Outcome-based contracts** between TechCo's and GasCo's internal service providers and the investing units may reduce the agents' incentives for opportunistic behavior by co-aligning their preferences. For instance, supply contracts and transfer prices between the two internal units can be tied to different investment success indicators, like actual IRR or EVA.

Value chain dispersion

The global value chain dispersion has a significant influence on the **coordination requirements** and interface management during the implementation process of Greenfield investments. A main content-related process difference between GasCo and TechCo is the degree of global value chain dispersion. The value chain dispersion affects the implementation process complexity and the underlying decision process speed. For instance, investment implementation processes of production facilities as parts of a global value chain need to consider interdependencies to other production units in different geographical areas to establish coordinated production processes.

While GasCo's value chain is completely locally concentrated at the new facilities, TechCo's approach is to operate with globally dispersed supply chains to leverage different country-specific advantages, like low cost suppliers for preliminary products. As opposed to TechCo, GasCo's **product portfolio characteristics** do not allow different options than to centralize the complete value chain at one location. GasCo's value chain constitutes integrated physical processes which should not be interrupted for an efficient plant operation. Furthermore, higher product volumes of GasCo cannot be transported at reasonable costs over longer distances. For this reason, GasCo decision alternatives are limited so that decision-makers are confronted with lower decision complexity. Hence, they may feel more confident to decide which accelerates the overall decision-making process.

TechCo's implementation process requires more coordination activities due to a higher number of interfaces within the global supply chain. GasCo's new facilities can be implemented more or less independently because the production units only supply a limited geographical area in the vicinity of the plant. Considering the degree of value chain dispersion indicates that GasCo implementation process faces lower complexity and tends to be faster.

To sum up, both implementation processes indicate **troika constellations** of power, technology and process promotors which imply effective and efficient implementation processes. Marginal differences are observable regarding the importance of the three role typologies within the two implementation processes. GasCo's implementation process tends to be more strongly shaped by process and power promotors, whereas technology promotors play a greater role at TechCo. Similarly, the theoretically assumed requirements of the three role typologies are not satisfied to the same extent. Especially, TechCo's power promotors are relatively weak compared to those of GasCo – which may limit their potential to overcome barriers of will. Therefore, the decision process can be subject to delays due to further approval requirements by higher management levels. Furthermore, TechCo's implementation process is more complex due to the interdependencies to its global supply chain.

4.1.3.1.4 Start-up and control

The start-up and control processes at GasCo and TechCo share some common characteristics related to the transition from the implementation to the start-up and control phase and the adoption of lesson-learned measures to conserve organizational know-how. In contrast, the two localization processes during the start-up and control phase show main differences. Similar to the implementation processes, the product characteristics and the underlying business models exert a significant influence on the decision processes.

Start-up & control	GasCo	TechCo
Transition	Ends after first year of commercial operation	Ideally, project manager = plant manager
Lessons-learned	Not systematically applied	Not systematically applied
Localization	Standardized products	Locally-adapted products ("SMART")

Table 4-4: Start-up and control process influences of GasCo and TechCo

Transition

Both processes have in common that the investments projects are not closed until the commercial operation has been achieved. Thereby, both corporations underline that implemented investment projects are "transitioned" to the operational management and not "handed over". This can be regarded as a measure to prevent an uncoordinated

change of responsibilities. The gradual transition of responsibilities from the project team to the new local management may reduce agency costs. From an agency perspective, the advantage of a transition in comparison to a hand-over is that the agency conflict potential is reduced by aligning the interests of the investment implementation team with the operational management.

The ideal solution for these changing responsibilities is to appoint a project manager who is designated to assume the responsibility for the new plant management. TechCo intends to pursue the approach to appoint the designated new production facility manager for the project management which is – especially in BRIC countries – subject to shortages of qualified employees who are willing to fulfill these responsibilities.

Lessons-learned

A further parallel between GasCo and TechCo during the last stage of the investment decision process is that a systematic lessons-learned approach is not applied. Although GasCo has defined **lessons-learned processes**, the interview evidence shows that these learning processes are more or less neglected at the follow-up of investments. In most cases, the respective team members are already involved in new investment projects which have a higher internal priority than completing the wrap-up of successfully implemented investments. The interview evidence of TechCo also suggests that lessons-learned are not systematically applied. Hence, it is difficult for involved employees to consider the experience of past investments for actual or future projects.

Particularly, TechCo with frequent job rotations can benefit from a consequent organizational learning process. GasCo needs for lesson-learned processes tend to be lower due to the specialized investment departments, like business development or project execution, which are solely involved in investment projects. Both critical success factors – decision process speed and decision process comprehensiveness – are expected to be positively influenced by organizational learning processes. Furthermore, project team members can be prepared faster to assume the role of **technology promotors**. Considering the dynamic Uppsala model, consistently adopted organizational learning processes may increase the decision process comprehensiveness *and* the decision process speed. The perceived uncertainty in future investment decision processes can be reduced by a systematic accumulation of foreign investment knowledge.

Nevertheless, GasCo's central FiCo as the main reviewing body for investment papers has established an investment project archive, where all obligatory investment documents have to be submitted by the investment applicant. Within the context of organizational learning, FiCo uses the project files to develop a **benchmark database** in order to improve the quality of future review processes. But a more systematic learning approach seems to be appropriate for investment case developers in order to prevent planning mistakes already in the early stages. Especially experienced-based capabilities for implementing foreign investments demand to consistently transform tacit know-how of single key persons into organizational knowledge.

Localization

The **localization process complexity** represents a central difference between the two company-specific start-up and control processes which is attributable to the product portfolio characteristics. GasCo produces and sells worldwide standardized products like oxygen, nitrogen or argon. The entire value chain is concentrated at the new production site with identical production processes around the world. Since the physical processes have been initialized and a stable output has been achieved, the plant operations can be managed with a relatively small workforce.

TechCo is obliged to adapt its manufacturing products to the specific market requirements as well as the production processes to the access of qualified employees in emerging countries. Therefore, TechCo has introduced a tailored localization process model for emerging markets to address lower qualification levels, different product requirements and higher price sensitivities. As explained in section 4.1.2.3.4, TechCo's new emerging market localization approach is focused on the **product design**. Local R&D engineers gradually de-feature global high-end products until new products are customized to the local requirements ("SMART products"). Ideally, the entire value chain is localized within emerging countries for these entry-level products. Thereby, it is possible that some parts are produced in India and assembled in China to serve neighboring countries.

GasCo uses a **business transfer approach** which means that the entire value creation is geographically centralized at the new production locations. Independently operating production facilities create lower coordination requirements due to fewer interfaces with other organizational units. TechCo is globally more strongly integrated and connected which may be attributed to product specifics and the underlying production procedures. TechCo's product specifics are appropriate to adopt global value chains to reap local advantages, e.g. components for gas turbines can be produced in different places around the world and assembled at the point of sale. GasCo's industrial gases have to be produced in vicinity of the customers which limits the value chain configuration alternatives.

These configurations of international investments are part of the **allocation decision** which influences the entire investment decision process.[798] GasCo's complete business transfer only requires limited interface management within the organization, the different production locations are managed under the responsibilities of the country management, which report to the regional management. TechCo's globally integrated approach causes more internal complexities due to the required interface management and coordination efforts with different corporate units and functions around the world. These basic localization differences of GasCo and TechCo also influence the recruiting approach.

Due to the standardized products and production processes GasCo can easily hire people from competitors who do not require long orientation and training periods to become contributing members. Therefore, the **recruiting** for the plant operation usually

798 See section 1.3.3.3.

does not represent a critical issue compared to TechCo – which has higher quantity and qualification requirements. At TechCo the start-up phase is characterized by a higher complexity because the new production facilities tend to be more strongly connected to other internal units and functions due to the global value chain dispersion. For this reason, it is necessary to work with experienced people who are internally well-connected and familiar with TechCo's internal requirements. Furthermore, the localization process involves more engineering know-how and experiences with the company's product portfolio. Due to the localization process complexity, the related product know-how and the necessary coordination needs with different internal entities requires TechCo to focus more on **expats** and delegation in the early stage.

Nevertheless, TechCo adopted the strategy to prepare talents or high potentials from BRIC countries for **global management careers.** First these people are developed to understand the organization by sending them around the world. As these people are internalizing the corporate cultures and technologies, they can start to expand the corporate businesses in their home countries because they have the advantage compared to expatriates to be more familiar with the local market conditions. Developed talents from the BRIC countries are trained to manage the localization process which creates also cost reductions because expatriates from Europe are usually associated with significantly higher costs.

4.1.3.2 Discussion

In the following sections, potential measures are discussed which may enhance the decision process speed or/and the decision process comprehensiveness. Although decision process speed and decision process comprehensiveness are discussed in two separate sections, it has to be underlined that the management of these two indicators requires an integrated view due to existing interdependencies. Figure 4-13 illustrates the assumed reciprocal relationship between decision process speed and decision process comprehensiveness.

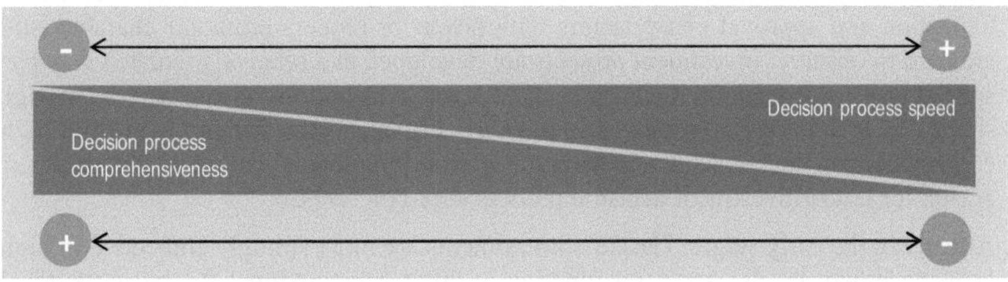

Figure 4-13: Trade-off between decision process speed and decision process comprehensiveness

A main assumption is that increasing the comprehensiveness is associated with lower decision process speed. Extensive analyses require time and may even end in "paralysis".[799] Assuming a static view on capabilities and knowledge of involved decision process actors, the reciprocal relationship between speed and comprehensiveness of

[799] Cf. *Talaulicar et al.* (2005), p. 526.

decision processes appears to be reasonable.[800] In the following these two critical success factors are discussed.

4.1.3.2.1 Decision process speed

Several empirical strategic management studies found that decision process speed affects firm performance.[801] In particular corporations operating in high-velocity environments may enhance the corporate success by speedier decision-making.[802] Considering the actual context of MNCs, where the management faces significant **external pressures** arising from capital markets, shortening product life cycles or growing competition from emerging markets, the decision-making speed and the corporate agility are expected to become even more important in the future.[803] Equally in the context of investment decision processes, efficient time management – in terms of making fast decisions – is expected to be crucial to create competitive advantages as external pressures and environmental dynamics further intensify ("survival of the fastest").

The existence of promotor troikas in each of the four investment phases may support a fast decision-making process and ensure acceptable decision process comprehensiveness. Technology promotors are responsible to develop accretive investment cases whereas the **process and power promotors** are more concerned with the necessary speed and overall efficiency of decision processes.[804] In particular decision processes in complex organizations, like TechCo or GasCo, require a process promotor who disposes over the necessary organizational process know-how and communication skills to overcome administrative barriers of non-responsibility.[805]

Reviewing the two company-specific decision process speeds by taking a promotor perspective, different **promotor constellations** as well as varying balances between the role typologies are identifiable. GasCo shows a relatively balanced mix of technology, process and power promotors along the entire foreign investment decision process. In contrast, TechCo's investigated foreign investment decision process indicates that process and power promotors tend to be underrepresented. Particularly at the initialization and approval phase, actors with power or process promotor characteristics are hard to observe. Investment projects are developed in a relatively isolated way by a special task force team on the business unit level. This bottom-up approach is strongly shaped by technology promotors without early organizational commitment from higher management levels. This constellation of role typologies can be regarded as one reason for lower investment decision process speed of TechCo.

Already in the early stages, GasCo's investments are more strongly embedded in higher management levels. A central function in this respect assumes the business development function which meets the requirements for an effective **process promotor**.

800 Cf. *Fredrickson* (1984), p. 448.
801 Cf. *Baum/Wally* (2003), p. 1124.
802 Cf. *Judge/Miller* (1991), p. 459.
803 Cf. *Hauschildt/Schewe* (2000), p. 101.
804 Cf. *Chakrabarti* (2007), p. 169.
805 Cf. *Hauschildt/Kirchmann* (2002), p. 42.

Business developers are specialized on developing and positioning investment proposals within the investment committee as the main investment decision authority. Thus, business developers dispose over the necessary process and organizational know-how to effectively bridge organizational gaps between power and technology promotors in order to accelerate investment decision processes. Whereas at TechCo the people with process promotor qualifications are difficult to identify due to the one-off character of investment projects and lower process experience of employees.

The requirements of process promotors may be reduced by implementing a **standardized process-orientation** which delivers guidance for employees in order to safeguard coordinated actions and behaviors under complex and uncertain decision process conditions. In stable or predictable decision environments strictly process-oriented behaviors and actions may accelerate investment decision processes. A too narrow process-orientation faces the risk that human potentials cannot be completely exploited. Decreasing employee motivation and proactivity may be induced by prescribed standard procedures.

In particular investments in volatile environments require a certain flexibility of investment decision processes to anticipate external influences on the investment project. Thus, flexible decision processes tend to be faster in volatile environments. Therefore, a reasonable balance between decision process standardization and decision process flexibility has to be found. Investments in BRIC countries are exposed to formal and informal institutional uncertainties which implicate that **investment decision process flexibility** and standardization need to be rebalanced due to the lower predictability of externally-driven influences on the investment project – in particular during the implementation phase.

The degree of **investment decision process centralization** in terms of decision authorities represents a further adjusting screw to accelerate investment decision processes. Al-though the discussed investment projects in both companies required executive board approvals, a main difference on the organizational path to receive the final board approval can be detected. Three approval cycles at TechCo compared to one main approval cycle at GasCo is doubtlessly a main reason for the different pace of decision processes. Distributing higher approval levels that are adequately coordinated with the size of operational units may have the potential to increase the speed of decision-making. Lower internal coordination requirements, fewer involved actors and organizational barriers are associated with more decentralized investment decisions reducing the complexity of decision processes. Decision process comprehensiveness – as the other side of the coin – is discussed in the following section.

4.1.3.2.2 Decision process comprehensiveness

Decision process comprehensiveness is often cited within strategic management literature as *"the extent to which an organization attempts to be exhaustive or inclusive in making strategic decisions."*[806] The prior sections indicate that TechCo's investment

[806] *Fredrickson/Mitchell* (1984), p. 402.

decision process is characterized by a higher decision process comprehensiveness than GasCo's. However, the comprehensiveness of decision processes does not really represent an either/or choice. It is rather a **question of appropriateness** depending on the context of investment decision processes. The different industry characteristics and underlying business models are demanding different levels of comprehensiveness. Whereas the different levels of comprehensiveness between GasCo and TechCo can be explained, it is difficult to assess the appropriate or required level of decision process comprehensiveness within each specific company context and decision setting.

Due to the interplay between the decision context and the appropriate level of decision process comprehensiveness, it may be reasonable to define **decision processes variations**. Both companies have applied a uniform investment decision process without significant gradations. Due to the fact that Greenfield investment projects typically exceed the Capex limit of € 5 million, all investments are finally decided by the executive board and have to fulfill the same formal requirements. Thereby, it is possible that € 5 million projects involve the same depth and breadth of analysis as € 100 million investments.

A possible solution may be to define **gradual decision process comprehensiveness** requirements dependent on the involved investment volume – like small, medium and large investment decision processes in order to anticipate the different decision settings. This seems to be adequate to prevent too detailed analyses ("to crack a nut with a sledge hammer") because these phases also cause significant costs which are usually not included within Capex calculation. To sum up, different investment decision process designs can provide a solution to find a reasonable balance between the extent of search, analysis and evaluation of investment projects and the involved Capex.

Furthermore, the human factor also plays a major role to find an appropriate level of decision process comprehensiveness. The quality of human capital can be decomposed in **employee qualification** and employee motivation to cope with the delegated responsibilities involved within foreign investments. Consistent with internationalization process theories it is assumed that especially experienced-based knowledge determines the quality of actors within foreign investment decision processes. On the one side, experience is important to find an adequate level of decision process comprehensiveness but on the other side broad project experience supports to develop desirable solutions which determine the quality of the decision itself ("making better decisions").

The institutionalization of specialized investment functions promotes the necessary employee qualification by **centralizing investment know-how**. GasCo pursues this approach due to its constant investment project flow. Furthermore, the empirical evidence suggests that both companies possess improvement potentials with respect to lessons-learned processes. Transforming investment experiences into organizational knowledge by implementing organizational learning processes can help to achieve more efficiently a desired level of decision process comprehensiveness for future investments. For example, search costs can be reduced by anticipating prior experiences of past investment projects.

The **motivation of employees** can be enhanced if their interests are tied to the investment project success. Creating aligned incentive structures for involved actors may foster the overall investment decision process success due to co-aligned goals with the investment project owners – who are usually represented by the respective investment decision authorities. In accordance to the applied value based management approach, the employee's compensation may be partially based on the development of value oriented performance measures, like project-specific EVA. An appropriate level of decision process comprehensiveness can be achieved, if search and evaluation costs are integrated within the investment appraisals and performance evaluation reports. From a theoretical point of view, the introduction of an incentive system which is tied to the overall investment project success seems to be able to find adequate levels of decision process comprehensiveness. The ideal case is expected to be that involved employees act as **internal entrepreneurs** with no incentives for opportunistic behavior and strong motivation to achieve the pursued investment goals.

Decisions on **BRIC investments** – taking a German MNC perspective – are expected to require high decision process comprehensiveness due to a variety of unfamiliar external influences on the investment project success. Decision-makers are confronted with higher levels of uncertainty and complexities that may reduce their confidence to act. Therefore, more alternatives and scenarios may be developed and evaluated compared to domestic investments in order to give the decision-makers the required decision confidence.[807]

Besides these behavioral aspects, investments in BRIC countries tend to demand higher decision comprehensiveness due to higher risks of fatal planning mistakes in institutionally distant and strange environments. Recently many prime examples in practice illustrate how insufficient decision process comprehensiveness endangers the existence of entire corporations. This highlights the importance to safeguard a certain level of decision process comprehensiveness – in particular in volatile environments with possibilities of huge losses. Nevertheless, the BRIC countries are growth markets with vibrant competitive environments. Aggressive EMNCs – either state-owned or privately-held national champions – are striving for worldwide leaderships in their industries, which represents a driver for higher investment decision process speed. The detailed country-specific evaluation will be conducted in section 4.3 in order to indicate in which direction the balance between decision process comprehensiveness and decision process speed is tilted.

4.1.3.2.3 Conclusion

The firm-level case analysis comes to the conclusion that decision process comprehensiveness and decision process speed are two main determinants for the efficiency and related success of investment decision processes. Evaluating the two company-specific investment decision processes by applying the above discussed criteria, GasCo has faster investment decision processes than TechCo, while the decision process comprehensiveness is assumed to be higher at TechCo. The cross-company analysis illustrates

807 Cf. *Eisenhardt* (1989c), p. 572.

that the involved decision complexity and uncertainty are main determinants for the design of investment decision processes. But as explained within the prior sections, external context factors, e.g. industry specifics or product characteristics, as well as internal determinants exert a significant influence on the involved complexity and uncertainty. For this reason, MNCs should at least aspire to reduce internally-driven complexity and uncertainty in order to enhance the comprehensiveness and speed of investment decision processes.

Thereby, the main challenge represents to find an **appropriate comprehensiveness-speed-equilibrium** for the design of investment decision processes. The prior firm-level analysis and the subsequent cross-company comparison illustrate that the design of investment decision processes is context-specific. In particular the cross-company comparison between GasCo and TechCo shows how context factors, like industry characteristics and external investment stimuli exert influences on the investment decision process. External environmental conditions determine the involved decision uncertainty and complexity in investment decisions – which indicate the requirement of decision process comprehensiveness and decision process speed, e.g. investment decisions surrounded by unstable institutional environments usually demand higher decision process comprehensiveness in order to give the decision-maker the confidence to finally decide.

Apart from the sheer importance of decision process comprehensiveness and decision process speed, it is of greater relevance from a practical perspective how a **reasonable balance** between these two reciprocal determinants can be achieved to optimize the efficiency of investment decision processes. Analyzing the empirical results from a theoretical perspective implicates that a promotor constellation seems to be able to meet the discussed requirements to ensure overall investment decision process efficiency. It is proposed that a **promotor troika** escorting the entire investment decision process – whereby the role typologies may be assumed by different persons during the different process phases – is expected to be a promising constellation for efficient investment decision process designs in complex MNCs.[808]

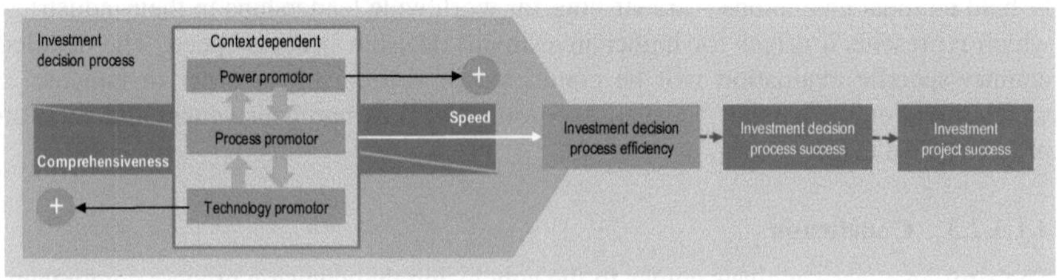

Figure 4-14: Context dependent investment decision process model

It is argued that a promotor troika is germane to find an adequate balance between decision process speed and decision process comprehensiveness which determines the

808 A process promotor is expected to be less important for decision processes within SMEs due to the lower internal complexity and closer organizational connection between technology and power promotors.

overall investment decision process efficiency (see Figure 4-14). Thereby, the adequate balance between decision process speed and decision process comprehensiveness is assumed to be **context dependent** which means that the investment decision processes are influenced by external and internal forces. For instance, foreign investors in BRIC countries are exposed to country-specific challenges which may drive the necessity of decision process speed or decision process comprehensiveness to find an appropriate balance. The cross-level synthesis (section 4.3) will further discuss the identified BRIC country challenges and their influence on the two reciprocal critical success factors of decision process speed and decision process comprehensiveness.

It is argued that **technology promotors** are responsible to guarantee an appropriate comprehensiveness of investment decision processes as depicted in Figure 4-15. Therefore, the technology promotor must possess the required detailed knowledge to overcome barriers of capabilities. He actively promotes the investment decision process by means of specific knowledge, like detailed knowledge about an investment country. Due to these characteristics it can expected that technology promotors actively influence the decision process comprehensiveness. For instance, the role of technology promotors can be assumed by employees with a comprehensive knowledge of a foreign market in this context.

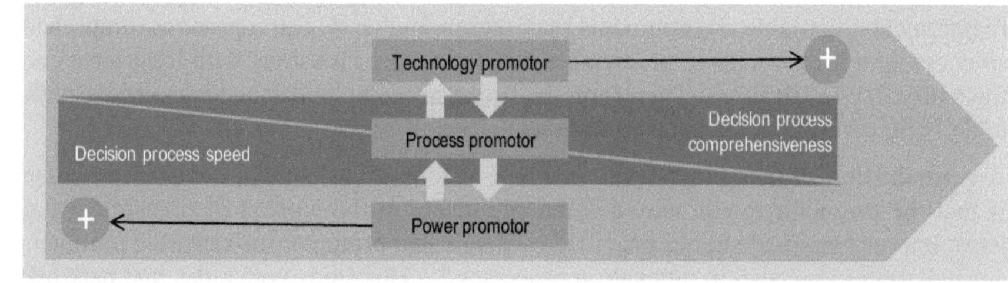

Figure 4-15: Influences of promotors on decision process speed and comprehensiveness

In contrast, the **power promotor** must dispose over the required hierarchical power to make respective decisions by himself in order to accelerate decision-making processes. Otherwise, the promotor by power is not able to influence the decision process speed. For instance, the establishment of a steering committee at TechCo serves to provide the required political support during the investment implementation. Although the provision of political support is a typical responsibility of power promotors, the steering committee does not have the necessary decision authorities (hierarchical power) to accelerate decision processes independently. Thus, the ability to influence the decision process speed depends on the hierarchical power of the power promotor.

Finally, the **process promotor** acts as a mediator between these two role typologies. He coordinates the collaboration between the technology promotor who develops investment decision alternatives and the power promotor who decides about alternatives. Thus, the process promotor requires comprehensive organizational know-how to fulfill his role. In the specific context of investment decision processes, the necessity of a process promotor tends to decrease subsequent to the final investment decision because further decisions during the implementation phase usually do not require the approval of higher management levels.

Only in a few circumstances, like the release of additional investment budgets, significant project scope changes or deviations have to be escalated to the top management. Nevertheless, particular in large MNCs with a huge geographically dispersed workforce – like TechCo and GasCo – the process promotor plays a crucial role to actively mediate between power and technology promotors. The process promotor may only indirectly exert influence on the two critical success factors by a close coordination of the two other role typologies, e.g. the process promotor must be able to "translate" the investment configuration into an understandable "language" to derive fast decisions by the power promotor.

Besides the mere existence of promotor troikas, the investment decision process success depends on the **promotor balance** between the three role typologies. A dominance of process and power promotors tends to favor faster investment decision processes, whereas a preponderance of technology promotors is expected to increase decision process comprehensiveness at the expense of speed. A general recommendation regarding the right balance between the key actors cannot be given due to the assumed context-dependency and the related decision process speed and comprehensiveness requirements. Unstable environments may require higher decision process comprehensiveness than investments in predictable industries, like industries with long-term contractually fixed cash flows. Therefore, the troika needs to be balanced according to the underlying investment decision conditions.

A **contribution** of these firm-level analyses of foreign investment decision processes is that the promotor model may also be applicable to the context of investment projects. Earlier empirical studies provided evidence that promotor troikas are a promising constellation to succeed in innovation processes.[809] This study concludes that networks of technology, process and power promotors within and between process phases provide an adequate constellation to balance investment decision process speed and comprehensiveness as antecedents of investment decision process efficiency and success.

After the foreign investment decision processes were investigated at TechCo and GasCo on the firm-level, the following sections focus on country-specific challenges for MNCs undertaking Greenfield investments in the BRIC economies. For this reason, the interview data was analyzed by taking a **country perspective**. The interview evidence is presented by differentiating between political-economic and socio-cultural country-specific characteristics that are expected to be relevant for foreign investors (section 4.2.1 to 4.2.4). The identified political-economic as well as socio-cultural characteristics are briefly compared between the four countries (section 4.2.5) in order to accomplish the second sub-goal of this study.

---

809 Cf. *Hauschildt/Kirchmann* (2002), p. 48.

4.2 Country-level cases

4.2.1 Brazil case

4.2.1.1 Political-economic characteristics

4.2.1.1.1 Domestic economy

The Federative Republic of Brazil is with over 195 million people the largest country in terms of population and geographical area in South America. The national language is Portuguese due to the Portuguese colonization between 1500 and 1815. Since the mid-1990s, Brazil has achieved to control the problem of **hyperinflation** mainly owing to a strengthening of its macroeconomic framework by several economic reforms which were the basis for the sound development of Brazil during the last decade.[810] An informant from GasCo also argued that the economic stabilization was an important rationale for increasing the local presence:

> *"When Brazil was still very chaotic because of inflation problems, we had placed more attention to the more stable Argentinean market. In the mid 1990s, Brazil got rid of these problems and we shifted our focus to Brazil in South America. But so did our competitors which created a very challenging environment."*[811]

The introduction of a new pegged currency, the Real, in 1994 was crucial to fight hyperinflation. Average inflation rates of 764% a year between 1990 and 1995 came down to single digits within three years.[812] The "*Real plan*"[813] was accompanied by reforms to open the economy to create a more favorable environment for foreign investors. A GasCo manager highlights the importance of the economic stabilization for the local strategy:

> *"The Real Plan with the new currency was crucial for us to intensify our position in Brazil. Macroeconomic volatilities and political uncertainties prevented us to create greater local presences. But I think also, that the invention of the BRIC-concept led to massive surge of capital inflows. The attention is on countries where the growth outlook is. Sometimes – in my opinion – foreign MNCs do not thoroughly reflect their investment deci-*

810 Cf. *Jayme* (2003), p. 65.

811 Interview 43, GasCo, Business Development.

812 Cf. *The Economist* (2009), p. 3.

813 In the 1980s and early 1990s Brazil's economy had to face substantial difficulties due to the world oil crisis resulting in a moratorium for the repayment of external debt and economic stagnation. After several unsuccessful economic stabilization programs, economic stability has been achieved through the introduction of the Real Plan in 1994. The Real Plan was based on the three cornerstones *monetary reform*, *opening of the economy* and *privatization of state-owned companies*, cf. *Chehab* (2010), p. 5.

sions, just because Brazil is a part of the BRIC-story and investing must make sense."[814]

Since the new century, Brazil has experienced strong growth of capital inflows due to foreign direct investments which is widely seen as a source of technology transfer as well as a potential for direct and indirect productivity increases.[815] One major driver of foreign direct investments was the **privatization program** of state-owned enterprises, which allowed foreign investors to participate in former public industry sectors. Brazil was forced to introduce privatization measures in order to reduce foreign debt.[816] A business developer from TechCo emphasizes that the privatization program of state-owned industries provided a variety of opportunities for an industrial conglomerate:

> *"The privatization process offered a lot of chances for us in the 1990s until early 2000s, but recent years indicate a turning point towards foreign capital. The Brazilian public increasingly shows tendencies of nationalization. Brazilians do not want that their traditional corporations, banks or entire industries are dominated by foreigners. Personally, I think the former consolidation pressures created better opportunities for MNCs."*[817]

The share of foreign capital on transferred assets from public to private ownership was up to 60% in some industrial segments like electricity generation or telecommunication, which could be a reason for the nationalization tendencies.[818] In Germany, there was the same debate about restrictions on foreign capital, especially from sovereign wealth funds, in strategic key industries like energy infrastructure or public safety in order to prevent political influences or pressure from other countries.[819] Thus, this public discussion in Brazil does not seem to be exceptional.

In recent years, the expansion of the domestic consumer markets and Brazil's strategic position in Latin America and the vicinity to other fast-growing countries like Argentina or Chile represent additional key drivers for foreign investments.[820] A Brazilian TechCo manager agrees:

> *"Brazil had a long period of sustainable development – I think compared to the majority of EU countries, Brazil would meet the Maastricht criteria [laughter]. But of course, the strategic position within Latin America for exporting to other emerging countries was also an important motive for us."*[821]

---

814 Interview 30, GasCo, Management.

815 Cf. *OECD* (2011a), p. 6.

816 Cf. *Amann/Baer* (2005), p. 423f.

817 Interview 27, TechCo, Business Development.

818 Cf. *Bonelli* (1999), p. 321.

819 Cf. *Müller-Ibold* (2010), p. 103.

820 Cf. *UNCTAD* (2012), p. 53.

821 Interview 4, TechCo, Management.

In 2011, Brazil ranked as the seventh biggest economy in the world with an achieved GDP of USD 2.3 trillion in terms of purchasing power parity[822]. Macroeconomic projections expect annual GDP growth rates around 4% in the medium-term after experienced GDP growth rates of 7.6 % in 2010 and 2.7 % in 2011.[823] Formerly, the resource-rich Brazilian economy benefited from the worldwide resource boom[824] prior to and after the worldwide crisis, particularly due to the surge of oil and iron ore prices. GasCo and TechCo are especially focused on participating in the **flourishing oil and gas sector**:

> *"So we are looking for investments within the oil and gas industry which is booming, especially offshore oil and gas exploration. At the moment, Brazil is still importing gas via pipelines from Bolivia which is expensive due to the infrastructure investments. Brazil wants to reduce its dependence because gas is also crucial for the fertilizer production in order to keep the huge agricultural sector growing."* [825]

> *"Oil and gas is Brazil's core sector. But you now, agricultural products are also a booming segment. The agriculture and agro-industry is growing tremendously. To support this growth they need a lot of fertilizer and processing services. From this point of view, Brazil represents a promising location for us due to our energy-related solutions which are necessary in oil and gas, petrochemical as well as in the agricultural business."*[826]

These statements emphasize that corporations with energy-related products or services may benefit from the high relevance of these industries for the local economy. But the investigation results are biased because both corporations – GasCo and TechCo – are more or less focused on energy-related industries. Therefore, MNCs operating in other industries are expected to face different opportunities and challenges in Brazil.

---

822 Purchasing power parity (PPP) asks how much money would be needed to buy the same basket of goods in two different countries. In the absence of transaction costs the same products must have the identical price in different markets, if the price is expressed in the same currency according to the law of one price. But in reality this law does not hold because prize differences are existent mainly due to different income levels. An intuitive concept to highlight these price differences is the Big Mac Index promoted by *The Economist* which compares Big Mac prizes across the globe denominated in US-Dollar; cf. *Ong* (1997), p. 867. For the purpose of international comparisons across countries, nominal exchange rates need to be adjusted for differences in price levels. These real exchange rates are used to convert different income levels or country GDPs in the same currency. For a detailed discussion of the purchasing power parity concept cf. *Devarajan et al.* (1993); *Rogoff* (1996); or *Taylor* (2002).

823 Cf. *OECD* (2011a), p. 4.

824 The worldwide resource boom was mainly driven by emerging market economies in Asia, especially China, which need to develop their infrastructure to sustain economic growth. This demand for infrastructure development in many emerging markets is associated with high commodity consumption, like iron ore or oil. China had replaced the United States as the country's biggest trading partner due to the high commodity demand in China; cf. *Amann* (2011), p. 34.

825 Interview 43, GasCo, Business Development.

826 Interview 4, TechCo, Management.

Furthermore, the country is the world's largest producer of sugarcane ethanol which is used as a bio-fuel.[827] Rising commodity prices have created significant wealth effects through substantial increases in terms of trade[828] and trade surpluses. Since 1993, Brazil established a **strategic partnership with China**. Brazil is the world's biggest exporter of iron ore and satisfies China's demand as the largest importer of iron ore. Since 2009, China is the biggest export market for Brazilian commodities.[829] A manager from GasCo analyzes:

> *"Brazilian growth in recent years was mainly due to China's appetite for growth and the related rising commodity prices. But now, the domestic economy should focus on creating better domestic economic conditions and reduce the dependence from China. Doing business for foreign companies should be made easier so that the local economy can enhance productivity."*[830]

This statement underlines that the Brazilian economy still heavily **depends on commodity exports** and is prone to worldwide economic downturns. Nonetheless, recent years of stable economic development and continuous advances in microeconomic and institutional reforms led to a growing importance of the domestic market which diversified the economy and made it less vulnerable for global economic shocks.[831] Especially, the rising middle classes started to fuel the domestic economy in recent years – which attracts further market-oriented foreign investments.[832]

4.2.1.1.2 Foreign investment projects

In Brazil, foreign companies face the problem of **increasing costs** – mainly due to significant salary increases. A business developer explains the wage increase by the short supply of qualified people and emphasizes parallels to infrastructure problems:

> *"In Brazil, they have the same problems in education like with the infrastructure. During the last five to ten years Brazil's economy grew quickly, but now we face infrastructure problems and an extreme competition for qualified employees. One consequence is that salaries really exploded and still continue to increase."*[833]

---

827 Cf. *Marr/Reynard* (2010), p. 115.

828 The *terms of trade* are defined as the relation between the price of exportable goods and the prices of importable goods. It is an indicator what quantity of imports can be purchased through the sale of a fixed quantity of exported goods. Terms of trade are used as a rough proxy for the relative social welfare of a country. An increase of the ratio is favorable in the sense that a country can purchase more imports for any given level of exports; for a detailed discussion cf. *Samuelson* (1952); or *Mendoza* (1995).

829 Cf. *Jenkins* (2012), p. 22.

830 Interview 29, GasCo, Management.

831 Cf. *Marr/Reynard* (2010), p. 113.

832 Cf. *Davidson* (1980), p. 13.

833 Interview 41, GasCo, Business Development.

Apart from salary wage increases, rising construction prices are a further driver of the increasing cost pressure on project implementations in Brazil as explained by a GasCo manager:

> *"Construction companies raised their prices because they are just not able to handle the heavy workload due to high demand. The World Cup, Olympic Games etc. demand a lot of construction-related services. Due to local-content regulation we do sometimes have no choice than to accept it to get our facilities constructed."*[834]

A Brazilian-specific problem is that the increasing costs are difficult to avoid, i.e. by engaging foreign companies for implementing investments, due to **local-content requirements**. A TechCo management accountant criticizes:

> *"All foreign companies are obliged to virtuously localize their supply chains in order to produce very expensive products for the Brazilian markets. Sometimes, local supply is disproportionately expensive or inefficient which drives our costs and destroys our global competitiveness. I do not know many firms earning money over there."*[835]

Brazilian corporations can benefit from governmental financing programs if they buy products or invest in assets that have at least 60% of local value creation.[836] Thus, foreign MNCs have an incentive to set up local production facilities in Brazil. Otherwise, Brazilian customers may prefer locally-produced products to get access to better financing conditions by the government. Local-content requirements are of special relevance in industries with high government involvement or regulations, like energy in Brazil. State-owned enterprises (SOE) try to push inward FDIs by dictating local-content requirements for doing business with them. If foreign MNCs want to benefit from the huge budgets and financial strength of these SOEs, there is no other choice than investing in own local production facilities:

> *"Especially, in our oil and gas business we have to deal with state-owned enterprises [...] They want to have at least 40% local value creation – which is not achievable with purchasing volumes. You need to produce locally [in Brazil] – otherwise your competitor gets the deal. And I mean, these corporations have enormous budgets."*[837]

This statement illustrates that foreign investment are often externally driven due to the limited alternatives to supply the Brazilian domestic markets. The former TechCo head of South America underlined that especially Greenfield investments are very welcome in Brazil, compared to the entry mode of cross-border M&A:

> *"Greenfield investments are always very desirable in Brazil. They are really supported by local authorities. As opposed to foreign M&A, Greenfields*

834 Interview 30, GasCo, Management.

835 Interview 14, TechCo, Management Accounting.

836 Cf. *Ivarsson/Alvstam* (2005), p. 1327.

837 Interview 13, TechCo, Management Accounting.

enlarge capacities and bring new state-of-the-art technology to the country. Last but not least – new jobs are created."[838]

But MNCs are exposed to a **high regulatory burden** in Brazil, especially with respect to labor laws and taxes so that Brazil has to struggle with a huge shadow economy.[839] A GasCo business development manager agrees that the tax system is a central obstacle of the Brazilian economy:

> *"As a Brazilian, working my whole professional life executing capital projects, I feel very comfortable to give you a hint: Taxes! Brazil has one of the highest taxes in the world, and unfortunately this high taxation is not returning as reasonable services and infrastructure from the government. This has gradually killed our competitiveness, which impacts the initiatives from MNCs to invest here. In spite of this, we still have a quite high level of investments, but it could be much more. As I see, this is the main challenge we have for the future. The rest, I mean geography, climate, nature, diversity etc, God has given us already!"*[840]

A TechCo management accountant further explains the significant influence of the tax system on the profitability of foreign investment projects in Brazil:

> *"Personally, I do not know many firms earning money in Brazil. Bureaucracy is very high, taxes are a real issue – much more complicated than in China. In Brazil, we must even pay taxes if we ship a compressor from Sao Paulo to Rio."*[841]

Compared to other OECD countries, companies based in Brazil have on average 20% higher tax burden and spend almost tenfold the time to file taxes, which indicates that Brazil is a difficult country for doing business.[842] A TechCo management accountant states about the difficulties in Brazil:

> *"In Brazil we really have to struggle with the tax environment. They have endless different tax regulations – I think plus 50. Additionally, Brazil is extremely expensive in terms of salaries, almost the same level like in the UK. Export and import taxes are further cost drivers of our business and the supplier networks are not better than in India. People often think about low-cost strategies in BRICs, but this is not the reality in Brazil."*[843]

4.2.1.1.3 Infrastructure

The Brazilian government has introduced the Growth Acceleration Program in order to accelerate urban and social development. This program provides subsidies and tax in-

---

838 Interview 4, TechCo, Management.
839 Cf. *Estrin/Prevezer* (2011), p. 59.
840 Interview 44, GasCo, Business Development.
841 Interview 12, TechCo, Management Accounting.
842 Cf. *Cheng et al.* (2007), p. 146.
843 Interview 14, TechCo, Management Accounting.

centives for strategic infrastructure investment projects.[844] Foreign investment decisions, especially the country and location selection, are influenced by the development degree of the infrastructure, e.g. in some regions it is necessary for foreign investors to support the local infrastructure development.

At present, weak physical infrastructure is one of the main obstacles for foreign companies investing in Brazil. MNCs' investment implementations and subsequent day-to-day businesses are negatively affected by the less developed infrastructure. In contrast, German MNCs may benefit from the necessary infrastructure investments by providing the relevant solutions, e.g. TechCo disposes over a separate strategic sector which aspires to collaborate with large cities and public customers in order to develop integrated infrastructure solutions.

In Brazil, **transportation, shipment and seawater** infrastructure is underdeveloped, e.g. during harvest times trucks wait to discharge their loads in queues of 25 miles at congested seawater ports. Years of fiscal consolidation and uncertain regulatory conditions resulted in low investments in infrastructure.[845] The development of the Brazilian infrastructure cannot keep up the pace with the economic growth which created structural bottlenecks, especially related to transportation and electricity generation. *Morgan Stanley* calculated that Brazil's inadequate infrastructure needs approximately annual investments of four percent of GDP over twenty years to catch up with Chile.[846] A GasCo business developer located in Sao Paolo confirms:

> *"Well, they have not invested in the infrastructure of the city [Sao Paolo] as they should have done according to the growth of the city. In Brazilian big cities you have the subway in the center without reaching the outskirts or the airports, so that everybody is going by car which creates massive traffic problems here."*[847]

Further significant infrastructure investments are expected in the near future because Brazil will host the **FIFA World Cup** in 2014 and the Summer **Olympic Games** in 2016, which create investment opportunities for foreign investors.[848] For the first time Olympic Games will be held in South America. Besides the economic benefits for the country due to the indispensible infrastructure investments and money spent by tourists, Brazil gets a huge platform for self-promotion to become more visible in the global arena.

These upcoming major sports events show the increased international importance of Brazil, but on the other side these two international events place extreme pressure on improving the efficiency of its infrastructure.[849] Yet, a business developer from GasCo argues that Brazil has already made planning mistakes within the preparation for these major sports events:

---

844 Cf. *OECD* (2011a), p. 18.
845 Cf. *Amann/Baer* (2012), p. 215.
846 Cf. *OECD* (2011a), p. 17.
847 Interview 43, GasCo, Business Development.
848 Cf. *Amann* (2011), p. 35,
849 Cf. *Amann/Baer* (2012), p. 415.

"Brazil's government started to build the stadiums for the FIFA World Cup, but did not really care about the necessary infrastructure. There are still a lot of upcoming infrastructure challenges. Brazil may have beautiful stadiums but so far no idea how the people should get there in an efficient manner."[850]

As mentioned above, these shortcomings may create business opportunities for foreign MNCs due to the external pressure arising from these two events. Brazil wants to use these chances to gain greater importance in the global arena and cannot afford home-made problems which may endanger the success of these events. It can be assumed that the time pressure enhances the opportunities for foreign firms. The government cannot wait for the development of local corporations which do not yet dispose over the required know-how or technology. A manager of TechCo underlined the upcoming opportunities for his corporation:

"Our strategic sector 'cities' is designated to provide all-embracing infrastructure solutions for mega-cities such as Rio or Sao Paulo – these two main events gave and will give us huge business opportunities. Brazil is under real pressure to provide better infrastructure concepts – otherwise these events are exposed to fail."[851]

After Brazil's political-economic characteristics have been presented, the following sections focus on the socio-cultural specifics which are relevant for foreign investors.

4.2.1.2 Socio-cultural characteristics

4.2.1.2.1 Education

Another important decision criterion for foreign investors is the sophistication of the education system in order to safeguard the **access to qualified employees.** In particular, Greenfield investments require new local workforces. Brazil has made significant progress when it comes to the improvement of educational levels and reduction of poverty by several social programs. The increase of school attendance and educational levels is a positive sign for foreign investors in terms of access to skilled labor. Although Brazil is on the right way to catch up, the country's educational standards still lag behind those in the emerging economies in Asia, like China or India.[852] This is also supported with interview evidence by a TechCo management accountant:

"Although Brazil has made progress to enhance education, the qualifications of employees are not better than in India or China – which would be not problematic, if the cost of labor would be on a similar level."[853]

This statement is consistent with the interview evidence related to regulation and taxes which underlines that the cost levels are relatively high for the development status of

850 Interview 43, GasCo, Business Development.
851 Interview 4, TechCo, Management.
852 Cf. *Amann* (2011), p. 36.
853 Interview 14, TechCo, Management Accounting.

Brazil. For this reason, foreign investors have to thoroughly analyze if **efficiency-seeking** Greenfields are promising in Brazil. Both corporations have explained that qualified engineers are very rare in Brazil, which is a further reason why technical experts are even more expensive than in Germany or the UK:

> *"In Brazil, the supply of engineering employees is very scarce – even more than in Germany. You know, a key success factor is to develop local resources for long-term solutions. Expats are only short-term oriented to get things started and very expensive – but then you have to develop local people to run your business. So we really focus on close collaborations to get qualified people for the future."*[854]

This statement of a TechCo manager underlines that the development of local people is crucial for a sustainable investment because expats usually see their employment as an intermediate station to make an international career. Certainly, the development of local talents is a reasonable approach to create a long-term oriented business, but in Brazil a central challenge for foreign MNCs is to gain and retain local talents:

> *"It's a huge challenge because everybody is competing for the same resources. And I do not mean sugar or oil, but well-trained specialists – who may turn out to be Brazil's most valuable resource."*[855]

Besides the formal qualification of employees, **language and communication skills** of delegated expatriates and the local population are crucial for foreign investment decisions. Portuguese is the official language in Brazil which tends to represent not a critical issue compared to China, India or Russia where language problems are a main source of misunderstandings as described by a TechCo manager:

> *"As opposed to China, India or Russia, we have not such language problems or communication problems in Brazil. It is easier for us to find people fluently in Portuguese and English or even German."*[856]

This statement reflects the overall interview evidence that language and communication barriers are not problematic for a German company investing in Brazil as opposed to the other three countries.

4.2.1.2.2 Society

Similar to the other BRIC countries, especially China, Brazil has experienced a significant increase of its middle class. According to a *KPMG* report between 2008 and 2011 over 45 million people moved into the **emerging middle class**.[857] It can be expected that Brazil will benefit from this development due to the growing consumer base and local purchasing power. Social welfare programs helped to accelerate the

854 Interview 4, TechCo, Management.

855 Interview 28, GasCo, Management.

856 Interview 14, TechCo, Management Accounting.

857 Cf. *KPMG* (2011), p. 12.

emergence of middle classes. A business developer from GasCo highlights that the rising middle classes were an important driver to increase the local market presence:

> *"The increasing demand of the domestic market was decisive to quickly obtain a stronger foothold in the country prior to our competitors. People start consuming everything – cell phones, cars, medical services or global brand products in general, when they achieved to escape from poverty."*[858]

Furthermore, these arguments underline the fact that "first-mover advantages" also played a crucial role for GasCo's investment decisions. Thereby, social welfare programs significantly supported the emergence of these new customers. The "*Bolsa Familia*" cash transfer program introduced in 2003 intends to secure a minimum income of poor families under the condition that their parents enroll their children in school.[859] Also, families receive the necessary medical care and additional social services. This program is one of the world's most effective social welfare programs having helped approximately 20 million people out of poverty between 2003 and 2009.[860] The fight against poverty and income inequality will be increasingly supported by a redistribution of oil revenues. A social fund was set up by government authorities in 2010 to promote a broader range of social and environmental measures including those regions that have no involvement in the oil industry.[861]

4.2.1.2.3 Informal networks

Similar to other emerging countries, cultural aspects play a greater role within the business life – which is often associated with weaker formal institutions. The exchange of favors is known as **Jeito** or **Jeitinho** in Brazil. These informal problem-solving practices are deeply rooted within the Brazilian culture. Thus, the use of favors for business purposes is generally accepted in the local context and viewed as ethically tenable. This typical cultural feature means literally translated "to find a way out" (dar un jeito) and is often transferred to the context of Brazilian management styles and problem-solving characteristics.[862] Particularly, the high regulatory burden of doing business in Brazil as described above, favors to choose Jeito as a mechanism to get around formal rules or institutions.[863]

Jeito is applied by Brazilians to bend or stretch the rules for enhancing flexibility in doing business, e.g. to handle the rigid and excessive bureaucracy.[864] But if Jeito is interpreted too generously or stretched too far, it can quickly receive **corruptive or unethical traits** – which are usually not acceptable to German corporate governance standards of MNCs.[865] As opposed to *Guanxi* in China or *Blat* in Russia, Jeito was not

858 Interview 41, GasCo, Business Development.
859 Cf. *Evans/Kosec* (2012), p. 10.
860 Cf. *Hunter/Power* (2007), p. 18.
861 Cf. *OECD* (2011a), p. 11.
862 Cf. *Amado/Brasil* (1991), p. 54.
863 Cf. *Estrin/Prevezer* (2011), p. 59.
864 Cf. *Puffer et al.* (2012), p. 18.
865 Cf. *Child et al.* (2009), p. 212.

explicitly mentioned by the interviewees. One possible explanation might be that this exchange of favors is not as present as it is in the other three countries. Nonetheless, characteristics or forms of this cultural feature and its importance for doing business can be identified between the lines within the informants' statements:

> *"I mean we must stay politically correct, but we have to admit that business works slightly different from what you have in Europe. In general, personal contacts and relationships are more important in Brazil. Unfortunately, Brazil has to struggle with corruption and not really ethical behaviors in its history. For an MNC it is a really balancing act to be as personal as possible in your relations to the customers without violating our internal compliance standards."*[866]

A GasCo business developer draws attention to the fact that trustful or almost friendly relationship to business partners are very important to get socially integrated as a corporate citizen. He argues that foreign MNCs need to show their willingness to deal with the local culture and everyday-topics:

> *"You need to be very local in Brazil, it is always better to speak Portuguese in customer meetings in order to show your ambition to integrate. It may sound silly, but it is a very deep-rooted tradition to start meetings with a chat about Brazilian football. If you are not into Brazilian football, you are absolutely isolated. It may sound trivial but these are the small things which make the difference."*[867]

This statement indicates that personal relations are very important for being successful in Brazil. As a foreigner personal relations can be more easily established through conversations about local topics, like sports or especially football in Brazil.

4.2.1.3 Summary

Compared to the times of unstable **political-economic** conditions prior to the *Real Plan*, Brazil has experienced a fundamentally positive development since the mid-1990s. Informants from both companies argued that the successful fight against hyper-inflation represents a main reason for their increased investment focus on Brazil. The strong economic growth in recent years is mainly attributable to the export of resources and commodities. Thereby, Brazil's economy is closely connected to China's development as the largest trading partner and consumer of Brazilian natural resources. Brazil benefits from rising commodity prices, but is also strongly exposed to declining prices during global economic downturns. Therefore, one country-specific challenge is to diversify the economy and to strengthen domestic demand.

Informants from both companies emphasized that **growing cost pressures** create obstacles for the profitability of foreign investments in Brazil. Substantially increasing wages and prices of construction-related work are the main cost drivers which are explainable by the limited availability of employees. Currently, Brazil's first priority is to

866 Interview 43, GasCo, Business Development.

867 Interview 43, GasCo, Business Development.

solve infrastructural problems for the FIFA World Cup 2014 and the Summer Olympic Games 2016 – which has different implications for foreign investors. On the one side, the required infrastructure investments create business opportunities for companies like TechCo – also due to shortages within the local infrastructure-related industries. But on the other side, foreign corporations are exposed to infrastructural bottlenecks – in particular during the two last stages of investment decision processes.

Costs are further driven by high **regulatory and tax burdens** imposed by the government, e.g. the effective tax rate is on average 20% higher than in other OECD countries whereas the tax filing process causes additional internal administrative costs. Local content is especially relevant for foreign MNCs that are competing for tenders of SOE like Petrobras or Vale. The central problem is that some intermediate or primary products are loaded with high import-tariffs to push local companies – but in many industries local corporations are not able to provide the required standards

Socio-economic characteristics tend to be less challenging for foreign MNCs investing in Brazil. Interviewees explained that it is not difficult to find people who are fluently in Portuguese, English and German. Therefore, the risks of misunderstanding due to language barriers seem to be limited, which safeguards a certain efficiency of communication. Consistent to studies in other emerging countries, the importance of personal networks for being successful is expected to be higher than in Europe. Corruption may be challenging against the background of German corporate governance standards, but seems to be less relevant and omnipresent for foreign corporations than in other developing countries.

4.2.2 Russia case

4.2.2.1 Political-economic characteristics

4.2.2.1.1 Domestic economy

Since the collapse of the Soviet Union at the end of 1991, the Russian federation is on the difficult way to transition from a communist central-planning system to a market-oriented economy. Although Russia has emerged quickly in the early years of transition, the country experienced only laborious improvements in the institutional and business environment.[868] Despite several attempts to diversify the resource-rich Russian economy, the economic development is still highly correlated with commodity and oil prices resulting in a very **volatile environment**.

At present, Russia faces structural challenges in order to attract more foreign direct investments and to diversify the economy.[869] Corruption, weak rule of law, low competition, oil dependency, state-owned monopolies and administrative burdens require **structural reforms** to improve the investment climate in Russia. These problems are closely connected with each other, e.g. high monopoly rents in the oil industry leave

[868] Cf. *Filatotchev* (2006), p. 111.

[869] Cf. *Klochikhin* (2012), p. 1620f.

enough financial leeway for bribes of government officials. Since the collapse of the Soviet Union, policy-makers are conscious about these deep-set obstacles for foreign investors, but many government actions did not really improve investors' perception of business conditions in Russia until today.[870]

Besides the significant influence of commodity prices on the overall economy potential, foreign investors in Russia must be aware of the important role of politics on business decisions. A challenge for MNCs is that these **political influences** are regionally varying, e.g. regional patriarchs may exert different influences on foreign companies.[871] According to a *KPMG* study, the attractiveness of FDI conditions differs extremely across geographic regions in Russia, which should have an important influence on the location decision of foreign companies.[872] These obstacles in Russia were also mentioned by business development interviewees from GasCo and TechCo:

> *"For us, we often could not choose the specific location within the country because we need to be close to our customers. We are in resource-rich regions as well as in the vicinity to Moscow and St. Petersburg. What you see are totally different attitudes towards foreign capital."*[873]

> *"In Russia it is really difficult to find a promising location due to the strong influence of local authorities and municipalities. This [the influence] is not easy to evaluate prior to the investment implementation. But because we need a lot of engineering employees, we often try to invest close to former armament industries."*[874]

The interview statements suggest that location decisions have to be thoroughly analyzed, but the core problem is that the behavior of local authorities is difficult to assess prior to investment implementation. During the financial crisis between 2008 and 2009 the central government provided huge fiscal support, especially with respect to stabilize the banking system and social protection measures to stimulate the domestic demand.[875] Despite Russia's relatively stable way through the crisis, the decline of oil and commodity prices showed again the **overdependence on natural resource exports**. The dependence on oil and gas has even increased since 2000 from one half of total exports to almost two-thirds in recent years.[876] A manager from TechCo based in Moscow agrees to this overdependence on energy and draws comparisons between Russia and China:

> *"I personally think that China just made some faster progress towards a market-based economy than Russia. They [the Russians] just rely on their*

870 Cf. *OECD* (2011c), p. 83.
871 Cf. *Marr/Reynard* (2010), p. 110.
872 Cf. *KPMG and RSPP* (2010), p. 6.
873 Interview 42, GasCo, Business Development.
874 Interview 23, TechCo, Business Development.
875 Cf. *The World Bank* (2012d).
876 Cf. *OECD* (2011c), p. 91f.

oil and gas. But I think they have seen what happened during the financial crisis, that everything is dependent on oil price and demand."[877]

In particular Russia's natural resource-richness provides huge business opportunities for TechCo with its diversified energy solutions and services portfolio. A regional management accountant of TechCo in Russia highlights the **importance of localization** in order to be able to benefit from these business opportunities:

"TechCo has recognized the importance of the Russian market, but without localization you could not win so many strategic projects, like North Stream or South Stream – projects with political interests. You need to commit to the country to be able to compete. (...) Russia is a huge country, gas is produced in Siberia and must be transported to Germany or the UK – which involves huge investments. We provide the transportation solution."[878]

However, it must be stated that the illustrated business opportunities for TechCo and GasCo are industry-specific. Both companies operate in energy-related industries which occupy special positions in Russia. As explained earlier, a central challenge of Russia is to **diversify the economy** in order to make it less vulnerable to exogenous shocks of declining commodity prices and symptoms of the "*Dutch Disease*"[879], like real exchange rate appreciation and de-industrialization of not resource-related industries. Prior research investigated that abnormal natural resource rents create stagnant attitudes towards reforms, strangle economic progress in other industries and thereby increase the risks of policy corruption.[880]

Modernizing the economy with structural changes is necessary to make Russian products competitive in foreign markets. As long as oil prices linger around USD 75 per barrel, the Russian industry barons earn sufficient oil profits. Thus, investments in new plants, equipment or technologies were postponed.[881] As a consequence, a GasCo manager sees inevitably upcoming business and investment opportunities for his company:

"So, the approach of these companies is very simple, Russia is going to become one of the growth engines for our business. Not as large as China but probably comparable or even bigger than India, at least for the next five years. The oligarchs must start to invest, which will not only secure their

877 Interview 2, TechCo, Management.

878 Interview 11, TechCo, Management Accounting.

879 The expression "Dutch Disease" was first used in an article by *The Economist* in 1977 to explain the economic performance of resource-rich countries and the related consequences of a resource-boom on the local economy. The Netherlands experienced a resource boom in the late 1950s due to natural gas discoveries, which resulted in decreasing competitiveness of the manufacturing sector. The loss of international competitiveness was attributable to a real exchange rate appreciation, increasing wages in resource-oriented industries and the associated relocation of labor forces to the resource sector. For a detailed description and modeling of the "Dutch Disease"; cf. *Corden* (1984).

880 Cf. *Algieri* (2011), p. 266.

881 Cf. *Aslund* (2010), p. 61.

assets for the longer term and their compatibility but will also bring jobs and foreign investments into the country."[882]

Closely connected to the importance of resource-related industries is the **lack of competitive pressures** due to many highly-concentrated markets and low economic activities of small and medium-sized companies. Especially lower entry barriers to start a business in Russia would support the development of small and medium-sized companies, increase economic diversification, competition and overall productivity. Reducing the administrative burden to set up operations is linked to higher allocative efficiency because resources tend to be shifted from low to high productivity firms.[883]

Moreover, higher competition in still regulated industries would increase international competitiveness of Russian corporations in the global marketplace and accelerate economic growth and progress.[884] If Russia increasingly adopts pro-competitive policies, this will have important implications for foreign investors. MNCs could use their greater competitiveness to exploit the opportunities and advantages compared to their Russian competitors. But foreign MNCs may also supplement and support Russia's way through modernization and overall economic development via foreign investments ("spillover-effects").[885]

4.2.2.1.2 Foreign investment projects

Corruption levels are closely connected to the application of the rule of law – which should be based on the principle that governmental authority is legitimately exercised compliant to written and publicly disclosed laws.[886] Comparing survey results related to "telephone justice"[887] between 2007 and 2010 indicates that Russia had made only little progress in strengthening the **rule of law** in recent years.[888] Only 4% of respondents in this nationwide survey believed that the judicial system is not exploited for any unlawful purposes, still unchanged to the results in 2007.[889] A TechCo business developer supports that the weak legal framework is a main reason for the relatively low investment attraction of Russia:

"The Russian legal environment is unpredictable. Judgments are not made independently from political influences – especially in business lawsuits you

---

882 Interview 32, GasCo, Management.

883 Cf. *Conway et al.* (2006), p. 45.

884 Cf. *Djankov et al.* (2006), p. 400.

885 Cf. *Crespo/Fontoura* (2007), p. 410.

886 Cf. *Frye* (2010), p. 80.

887 The Soviet era expression "telephone justice" means that judgments of cases come from instructions issued over phone by holders of political power rather than through the application of law. These procedures in Russia counteract the idealized legal principle that no one is above the law and no one, irrespective of their wealth or political influence, can decide the outcome of cases brought to the courts; *Hendley* (2009), p. 242.

888 Cf. *Ledeneva* (2011), p. 18.

889 Cf. *Ledeneva* (2011), p. 13.

could not expect a fair decision. That is for sure a reason for the investment cautions."[890]

In 2012, the trial of *Pussy Riot* gained great attention and criticism around the world and shows that political interests still determine the results of lawsuits in Russia. The Russian punk group was convicted for two years in jail due to an anti-Putin performance within a church.[891] Weak civil society organizations, the absence of vigorous political opposition and free press are further characteristics of the Russian system, which are not supportive for a strong rule of law which increases the reservation of foreign investors.[892] A TechCo manager highlights that MNCs – operating in industries with high government involvement – are more or less obliged to invest locally:

"TechCo's oil and gas organization has to face industry-specifics in Russia due to the high involvement of the Russian state in energy-related industries. For this reason, it could be more practical in other industries to serve the Russian market from outside, e.g. with exports."[893]

Thereby, an important milestone for foreign investors was Russia's **World Trade Organization (WTO) accession** at the end of 2011. Russia has to fulfill numerous WTO obligations which will require substantial trade and foreign investment liberalization measures.[894] Until 2013, Russia needs to open its economy in all three sectors and ratify the WTO accession protocol in order to comply with WTO standards, which will create new investment opportunities for MNCs.[895] But during the global financial crisis Russia moved in the opposite direction with protectionist measures, e.g. imposed tariffs on imported goods like foods or light manufacturing and export taxes on petrol. Although G20 leaders pledged to abstain from protectionism in times of crisis, Russia introduced more discriminatory trade and investment measures than any other G20 country.[896]

Although Russia has a great endowment of natural resources, relatively well-educated workforce and large potential consumer markets, the country cannot exploit its **FDI potential** due to the risky environment for foreign investors.[897] At present, foreign investors are exposed to institutional instability, especially related to the protection of property rights.[898] A GasCo business developer is convinced that Russia lags behind China due to this very unstable institutional environment:

"A second big card China started to play 20 years ago was to guarantee relatively strong regulations for foreign investors – but even more important – keep it very stable for a long period! In Russia laws are changing

890 Interview 23, TechCo, Business Development.
891 Cf. *Popova* (2012), p. 3.
892 Cf. *OECD* (2011c), p. 78.
893 Interview 5, TechCo, Management.
894 Cf. *UNCTAD* (2012), p. 58.
895 Cf. *Aslund* (2010), p. 50.
896 Cf. *Kee et al.* (2011), p. 15.
897 Cf. *Fabry/Zeghni* (2002), p. 290.
898 Cf. *Fabry/Zeghni* (2006), p. 202.

> *every year. That's what destroyed foreign MNCs' willingness to invest here. Russia has to make it clear to everyone that they will maintain the rules for the next ten years. That will change the behavior of the investors – domestic ones and foreign ones. Now, most of the domestic money is actually exported, it's in banks in Europe or I don't know where."*[899]

Besides these formal deficits, a further obstacle for foreign investors represents the relatively **hostile attitude** of former communist party members towards foreign investor participation, especially related to the exploitation of natural resources.[900] The Russians' suspicion regarding Western capital may be deduced to their problematic former relations to the Western world which seem to be still in the people's minds. A manager with experiences in Russia claims:

> *"During project implementations we have to fight in every project for permissions and schedules with Russian bureaucrats. It's a very exhausting process which could totally blow up your projects. Sometimes, I think government officials are still in the cold war."*[901]

The interview evidence indicates that investments in Russia are exposed to painful approval processes with local authorities to get the necessary permits. A GasCo manager describes this issue as follows:

> *"In terms of permits, my perception is that the process is much more difficult in Russia compared to the other BRICs. Russia is still extremely old-fashioned bureaucratic."*[902]

Due to these complicated permission processes with public institutions strong local organizations and networks are required to handle the administrative burden in Russia. A GasCo manager argues that a weak **local embeddedness** in Russia can be a reason for lower investment performance:

> *"We have so far a less local organization in Russia, which is – in my opinion – the main reason for lower success in developing investments."*[903]

A further GasCo manager argues in the same way that localization is more or less a required fundamental condition to establish operations in Russia:

> *"For me the key success factor is localization of business resources, localization of project execution resources, localization of know-how, operations and particular people. If you are not able to build local organizations, you will never be able to deliver."*[904]

---

899 Interview 51, GasCo, Business Development.
900 Cf. *Luong/Weinthal* (2004), p. 143.
901 Interview 30, GasCo, Management.
902 Interview 32, GasCo, Management.
903 Interview 29, GasCo, Management.
904 Interview 32, GasCo, Management.

This interview statement can be supported by interview evidence from TechCo. A manager argues that MNCs need to create local presences and regional integration to handle arising conflicts locally:

> *"So, you must have a very strong local footprint in Russia itself with Russian managers, otherwise you will fail in implementing investments. Problems must be sorted out locally."*[905]

Furthermore, the localization process is explicitly forced by **local content requirements**. Foreign investors are obliged to localize resources – especially for acquiring long-term supply contracts from large state-owned companies, which represent enormous opportunities for MNCs. Products have to be locally produced to a pre-defined minimum degree of local value creation as emphasized by a management accountant from TechCo:

> *"Especially, in our oil and gas business we have to deal with state-owned enterprises [...] They want to have at least 40% local value creation – which is not achievable with purchasing volumes. You need to produce locally [in Russia] – otherwise your competitor gets the deal."*[906]

A business developer of TechCo underlines that foreign MNCs have to follow the rules dictated by local customers:

> *"Our investment in Russia was necessary to supply a main strategic Russian state-owned company with compressors. They dictate the rules, e.g. if you want to have orders you need to produce in Russia."*[907]

To sum up, doing business for foreign investors seems to be far from easy in Russia. Despite the obstacles of investment implementation, creating regionally integrated or embedded organizations tend to be crucial to succeed in Russia.

4.2.2.1.3 Infrastructure

Russia has a heterogeneous regional infrastructure profile which can partially explain why different regions are not able to attract foreign investment projects, as a less-developed infrastructure induces lower efficiency, e.g. due to higher transportation costs.[908] Russia's great territorial expanses and the heavily Moscow-centered transport system are the main drivers for regionally underdeveloped **transportation infrastructure**. Russia needs to improve the logistic network to bridge the great distances between production and consumption.[909] A GasCo manager explains the regional differences:

905 Interview 2, TechCo, Management.
906 Interview 13, TechCo, Management Accounting.
907 Interview 24, TechCo, Business Development.
908 Cf. *Castiglione et al.* (2012), p. 9.
909 Cf. *Taylor* (1994), p. 19.

> *"In Russia you have both extremes – efficient infrastructure around the big cities like Moscow or St. Petersburg and totally underdeveloped regions."*[910]

Commercial transportation is mainly based on the **railway system**, which is not effectively connected to other means of transportation.[911] Main parts of the railway lines are dedicated to special industries and are not available for common or public use. The railway system is predominantly used by government-related industries, like oil, coal, minerals or timber.[912] Additionally, the railway infrastructure is to a great extent outdated due to decades of insufficient investments.[913] In 2002, Russia introduced a three-stage reform agenda in order to create higher competition via unbundling of ownership and operation of railway infrastructure, but with limited results so far.[914]

Russia faces similar problems related to the **highway system**. The main parts of the road network are not constructed to carry heavy and long-distance truck traffic. Almost 50% of the highway system is dedicated to specific industries or farms, which are not open for public transportation use. [915] Another indicator for the poor quality of the Russian road development and a misallocation of governmental resources is that only one third of the total road system was paved in 2011, which is less than in 1997.[916] The geographic size, the rugged terrain and difficult climate conditions are indeed some major reasons why Russia failed to implement a nation-wide system, but the European parts are much better developed than the area in the Asian part.[917] These characteristics of the Russian road system deliver important implications for the foreign investment decision process, so that transportation considerations within the location selection should play a major role as illustrated by a TechCo manager:

> *"In some areas, you do not even think about to invest. There is everything missing – roads, airports or what else – you will already fail to get there [Laughter]."*[918]

The **waterway system** and the **airport facilities** are better developed than the railway and road network. Especially, the waterway and port system is important to the economy for shipping petroleum products. Furthermore, Russia possesses over 630 airports – thereof 50 facilities are capable to accommodate international flights, but there are still government-imposed entry and exit barriers which reduce competition.[919] Russia's resource-driven economy has an extensive oil and gas pipeline network, e.g. Russia is the major exporter of natural gas to Germany.

---

910 Interview 32, GasCo, Management.

911 Cf. *Pittman* (2007), p. 217.

912 Cf. *Pittman* (2004), p. 186.

913 Cf. *Pittman et al.* (2007), p. 682.

914 Cf. *Pittman et al.* (2007), p. 686.

915 Cf. *The World Bank* (2010), p. 13.

916 Cf. *Blank* (2012), p. 253.

917 Cf. *Pittman* (2004), p. 177.

918 Interview 5, TechCo, Management.

919 Cf. *Andrew* (2012), p. 36.

4.2.2.2 Socio-cultural characteristics

4.2.2.2.1 Education

Despite the relatively low spending of the overall government budget on education, Russia achieved significant improvements in the education system since the Soviet era. In 2000, teacher salaries have increased substantially which helped to create incentives to retain and attract high-quality teachers.[920] In 2005, the continuous development of the education system was placed on the government's priority list as one of four major projects to serve the demands of social changes and economic modernization. Compared to the other BRIC countries, Russia has a relatively well-developed education system, so that the **access to skilled employees** should be not that critical for foreign investors, e.g. Russia produces one of the highest proportions of natural sciences and engineering graduates in world.[921] But opposed to other BRIC countries qualified people do not intend to stay in Russia. A GasCo manager admits:

> *"In Russia, I think, we have a big issue with the brain drain, which means that the best people leave the country. Rich families, who could afford good education, send their children to universities in Munich, London or New York; those guys are not coming back. Same story with Chinese kids, but opposed to the Russians they are coming back – expecting China to become the world's leading nation. Our people base is better in other emerging countries."*[922]

Similarly, the tertiary education system was subject to several reforms. In 2003, Russia joined the Bologna process in order to make academic degree standards and quality assurance standards better comparable throughout Europe, but the implementation progress is still regionally diverse.[923] Despite the rising teacher salaries, teachers earn substantially less than their colleagues in Western countries. Teachers and professors are partially obliged to have second jobs or accept heavy course loads to earn their livelihood which reduces the teaching and research quality.[924] Closely linked to low salaries is the widespread corruption in the education system, which reduces the fairness and quality of the system.[925] Furthermore, the Russian education is not focused on the educational demand of a market-based economy.[926] A TechCo business developer emphasizes that universities must be more strongly oriented on developing problem-solving capabilities:

> *"What we see is that curricula of universities are focused on building encyclopedic knowledge. But we as company need problem solver – I think stu-*

---

920 Cf. *OECD* (2011c), p. 37.
921 Cf. *OECD* (2011c), p. 33.
922 Interview 34, GasCo, Management.
923 Cf. *West/Frumina* (2012), p. 51.
924 Cf. *OECD* (2011c), p. 38.
925 Cf. *Osipian* (2012), p. 82.
926 Cf. *Gerber/Schaefer* (2004), p. 35.

dents need to learn how to use their knowledge to address practical problems. Similar tendencies we see in China."[927]

The improvement of communication has been mentioned as a further educational challenge by the interviewees. In particular, know-how transfers are exposed to **language barriers** as illustrated by two business developers:

> "*Our Russian location is really struggling at the moment. Most of our Russian as well as German technical experts or production professionals like engineers are not native English speakers. But especially for this technical stuff like construction plans, the small things like footnotes make the difference. Language and translation is really an issue in technical areas, especially related to knowledge transfer to ramp-up investments.*"[928]

> "*We have a lot of specialized technical engineers, who first need to translate from German into English. Then you have the problem to get it translated into Russian by people who are perfect in English and Russian, but have no clue about engineering. But we face similar problems in China.*"[929]

A GasCo manager explains the impact of language and communication problems in Russia as well as in China on the design and establishment of production and further operational processes at the new foreign subsidiary:

> "*Language and communication problems are one reason to adapt production processes to the foreign environment. In Germany, everything is documented in handbooks or process descriptions. In Russia, you need to show the people how things are getting done to find a pragmatic solution.*"[930]

As illustrated by the quotes above, language or communication problems have a crucial impact for the start-up and control phase when resources and capabilities are transferred to the new locations. Language differences are also a determinant for adapting production processes to the local requirements because knowledge could not be transferred efficiently due to language differences.[931]

4.2.2.2.2 Society

A special characteristic of Russia's economy is that a small number of industrial tycoons, known as **oligarchs**, dominate the strategic industries of Russia, like steel, coal or the oil and gas business.[932] These businessmen control sufficient resources to influence national politics.[933] Intense corruption, weak rule of law and the Russian oligarchy represent closely connected features of the Russian corporate governance system,

---

927 Interview 15, TechCo, Business Development.
928 Interview 15, TechCo, Business Development.
929 Interview 19, TechCo, Business Development.
930 Interview 29, GasCo, Management.
931 See section 1.3.2.4.
932 Cf. *Guriev/Rachinsky* (2005), p. 131.
933 For an analysis of the relationship between politics and the Oligarchs in Russia, see *Goldman* (2004).

e.g. on the one side, the oligarchs emerged with corruptive measures, on the other side, they further spread corruptive actions through their excessive influences.[934] Most of their conglomerates are horizontally and vertically integrated, which leads to excessive **domestic market power**, often in industries with economies of scale – which even reinforce their market power due to cost advantages. Thus, it is not promising for foreign investors trying to compete within their local markets.

Collaborations or strategic partnerships between oligarchic conglomerates and foreign MNCs are not seldom burdened with unethical, criminal or corruptive practices. MNCs fear to compromise themselves with not compliant business practices or getting expropriated due to the political power of oligarchic conglomerates as expressed by a management accountant of TechCo:

> *"These guys [the oligarchs] set the rules of the game, usually not at their own disadvantage. We try to avoid interdependencies to them on local grounds. We do not want to get involved in questionable practices."*[935]

In 2003, over 60% of Russia's entire stock market capitalization was attributable to the ten richest families, which illustrates the strong ownership concentration.[936]

> *"This means that a few guys, I don't know 20, 30, 40 or 50 people became official private owners of huge assets especially related to steel-making, refineries and petro-chemicals, these three industries. Those people used these assets as cash machines with minimum levels of investments."*[937]

This oligarchy as a special feature of Russia's economy creates uncertainties for foreign MNCs. They are difficult to assess because individuals are able to exert significant influence on the economic reform process and conditions. Similarly, the influence often leads to a lack of support in Russian courts, if foreign MNCs try to legally enforce their claims.[938]

> *"The Oligarchs or we might also call them mafia. These guys use their critical influence to assert their interests. They were basically stealing the rights for the ownership of these former public assets."*[939]

Nonetheless, company representatives also see large opportunities for foreign investors due to the lack of competition within oligarchic industries. GasCo as well as TechCo interviewees highlighted that the oligarchs used their assets and resources as cash cows

---

934 The oligarchs mainly emerged due to the "loans-for-shares" scheme in 1995, when some financially well-positioned individuals gained control over the most important Russian companies. In the mid 1990s, in the course of Russia's privatization, controlled auctions served to allocate controlling stakes of former state-owned companies to private investors in exchange for a loan to the federal government which the latter never intended to redeem. Usually, the nominal loan value was just marginal compared to the value of the company shareholdings; cf. *Estrin/Prevezer* (2011), p. 58.

935 Interview 11, TechCo, Management Accounting.

936 Cf. *Guriev/Rachinsky* (2005), p. 139.

937 Interview 32, GasCo, Management.

938 Cf. *Jones et al.* (2000), p. 194.

939 Interview 42, GasCo, Business Development.

without focusing on investments in future performance potentials. To sustain a minimum level of asset productivity, these industries require investments in new technology, which can often not be provided by local firms.

4.2.2.2.3 Informal networks

Cultural aspects affect the day-to-day operations of MNCs operating in foreign countries. A TechCo management accountant highlights the influence of cultural differences between Germans and Russians in negotiating processes:

> *"Russians and Germans are of different cultures. For us, it is sometimes difficult to see the compelling nature. They often appear opaque to me, possibly they think the same [laughter]. It is usually that agreed topics in prior meetings will be picked up again. Many rounds of negotiations, language problems even with translators and cultural misunderstandings make everything very inefficient. Besides these local specifics, hidden political influences also complicate things."*[940]

The interview evidence from TechCo and GasCo can be further supported by relevant literature showing that negotiations with customers or internal meetings are exposed to communication problems and misunderstandings.[941] A Russian specific is that changing attitudes of negotiation partners are not always purely economically driven but politically. Outsiders are faced with the non transparent formation of opinions due to the mixing of business, political and sometimes private interests.

Corruption or informal exchanges of favors represent a main feature of the Russian culture which influences the local business behaviors. **Intense corruption** – according to the Transparency International Corruption Perception Index Russia is perceived as more corrupt than any other OECD country – discourages foreign investors. Investment decisions and their outcome as well as associated risks are difficult to assess in unstable business climates.[942] Countries with restricted economic freedom and weak rule of law are often subject to corruption due to a misallocation of power, but the corruptive Russian environment is also culturally explained.[943] In Russia, the use of personal relationships to gain advantages, prevent difficulties or to get access to state resources is colloquially known as **Blat** – which is deeply-rooted in the Russian culture.[944] *Fitzpatrick* (2000) understands Blat as an informal exchange mechanism:

> *"Blat is the Russian term for an unofficial system of exchange of goods and services based on principles of reciprocity and sociability."*[945]

These informal networks are established through longstanding relationships, e.g. among families, friends, peers from military or politics.[946] A specific feature of Blat is

---

940 Interview 13, TechCo, Management Accounting.
941 Cf. *Schuster* (2006), p. 420.
942 Cf. *OECD* (2011c), p. 13.
943 Cf. *Ledeneva* (2008), p. 119.
944 Cf. *Ledeneva* (2008), p. 120.
945 *Fitzpatrick* (2000), p. 166.

its reciprocity which means that favor grantors expect an adequate – usually not monetary – consideration in return.[947] A GasCo manager from Russia emphasizes that access to these networks is of special importance in Russia and describes his local company position:

> *"This informal communication with decision-makers is very important in Russia. Our local presence in China seems to me much more developed in these aspects than in Russia today.[...] Networking is probably even more important in Russia to my point of view than it is today in China."*[948]

This entrenched instrumental use of networks in Russia is highly opaque, especially for foreigners, and does not comply with anti-corruption policies and business ethics in developed countries, like Germany.[949] Some empirical studies on foreign companies operating in Russia provide evidence that the capability of joining informal networks with political influence is one of the most important success criteria.[950] Therefore, foreign investor confidence is burdened by the higher tolerance and need for corruption and lower respect for ethical business behavior in Russia.[951] A GasCo manager draws comparisons to China:

> *"If I look at Russia the difference is of course the level of corruption [...] which is today much higher than in China. I mean there is corruption in business in China, but what I have seen in five years is that corruption is not decisive [in China]."*[952]

A central problem related to high corruption is the **unpredictability of business activities** and decisions of local actors which may have an important influence on the success of foreign investments. TechCo and GasCo informants complained that foreign corporations can never be sure to win a deal even when they are offering a predominant solution:

> *"I have never seen someone coming with such an advantage – approximately € 120 million compared to the local solution and the potential beneficiary party says 'I am not going to do that'. In Russia, I do not really understand so many decisions of customers. I think, in this case [...] individual motives outweighed the advantages for the company."*[953]

The exploitation of Blat has been developed in Russia through defects in the political and economic system. For this reason, MNCs are exposed to significant institutional uncertainties which can explain the unexploited FDI potential of Russia. MNCs do not want to be associated with unethical business behavior which is not compliant to international corporate governance standards.

946 Cf. *McCarthy et al.* (2012), p. 31.
947 Cf. *Ledeneva* (1998), p. 37.
948 Interview 32, GasCo, Management.
949 Cf. *Ardichvili et al.* (2012), p. 418.
950 Cf. *Arino/Abramov* (1997); *Fey/Denison* (2003).
951 Cf. *McCarthy/Puffer* (2008), p. 28.
952 Interview 32, GasCo, Management,
953 Interview 2, TechCo, Management,

4.2.2.3 Summary

The country analysis shows that foreign investors are faced with a very challenging environment in Russia. If Russia seeks to be less exposed to the global economic downturns and the development of commodity prices, the country needs to diversify its economy in order to strengthen the domestic markets. Foreign investors can benefit from massive investment requirements to modernize the overall economy and infrastructure – but the interview data indicates that foreign investors have to accept the dictated rules by local stakeholders. **Weak rule of law** and **intense corruption** are responsible for the reservation of foreign MNCs, so that Russia cannot fully exploit its inward FDI potential. The Russian Oligarchy and its huge market power limits local competition and the emergence of small and medium-sized companies which are usually driving innovation and modernization.

In Russia, the **educational level** is relatively high, but the interview data indicated that universities require to be refocused on the development of qualified employees for a market-oriented economy. Language problems are also a socio-cultural barrier. In particular communications regarding technical aspects or engineering-related topics disturb the know-how and resource transfer through misunderstandings. As mentioned above, corruption is to a great extent socially established or almost a feature of the Russian culture. These conflicts to German corporate governance standards have been broadly reflected within the interviews. To sum up, Russia's problems are closely interdependent to each other: huge oil and gas rents, oligarchy, high corruption and weak rule of law.

4.2.3 India case

4.2.3.1 Political-economic characteristics

4.2.3.1.1 Domestic economy

With a population of approximately 1.2 billion people, India is after China the second most populous country in the world and the world's largest democracy. According to the *World Bank*, India has emerged as a major economic player in the global arena with the fourth-largest economy in terms of purchasing power parity GDP.[954] But until the early 1990s India was almost not competitive due to a highly protected and isolated economy with ineffective incentive structures. After India achieved independence from British colonial rule in 1947, the national government followed the Soviet model that gave the state an active role to develop the domestic economy and accelerate growth. In the first years between 1951 and 1965 India's strategy was successful in terms of GDP growth rates at an annual average rate of 4%.[955] But by the mid-1960s India's policymakers increasingly tried to emphasize **self-sufficiency** to avoid external

954 Cf. *The World Bank* (2012c).
955 Cf. *Panagariya* (2007), p. 229.

influences on the domestic economy.[956] Until the early 1990s the Indian economy had to overcome several obstacles related to inefficiencies, high costs, poor management, non-competiveness, excessive reservation, bureaucratization, import controls, lack of export orientation and constrained foreign direct investment policies.[957]

High **public sector involvement** and regulation promoted inefficiency due to the absence of competitive and international pressures. Government permissions were required for producing a special product, setting up a new production unit, extending a production line or even closing a business. Small-scale industries were protected from international as well as from domestic competition.[958] The protective measures included product reservations, preferred access to finance, interest rate subsidy, business and technical services by the government and preferential input supply by the government.[959] These governmental support measures resulted in highly inefficient industries which cannot produce at competitive cost and quality levels.[960]

Although a lot of empirical investigations provide evidence that foreign direct investments are essential for the development of emerging economies, India adopted prohibitive foreign investment policies. [961] In the early 1990s serious changes in the economic environment accelerated.[962] A more **market-oriented framework** was established. In 2006, GasCo took the chance to acquire a major competitor with a leading market position in India. A GasCo manager explains:

> *"We are the leading player in India. There is only one other big competitor in India. In 2006, we created with our acquisition the basis for a leading position in Southeast Asia. Thereupon, we systematically enlarged our footprint in India with Greenfield projects. As opposed to China, we do not have local competitors, which could be a result of the relatively late economic liberalization. In China everyone faces much more competition from locals."*[963]

Although the Indian economy had to struggle with dysfunctional structures and an unfriendly business environment in the past, the country performed very well in terms of annual average **GDP growth** rates of approximately 9% between 2005 and 2010.[964] India's economy was only slightly affected by the global financial crisis due to the strong domestic demand and low integration in the worldwide financial markets. This stable growth during times of worldwide crisis is a rationale for Western MNCs to in-

956 Cf. *Kochhar et al.* (2006), p. 983.
957 Cf. *Beena et al.* (2004), p. 129.
958 Cf. *Panagariya* (2007), p. 230.
959 Cf. *Beena et al.* (2004), p. 128f.
960 For a detailed analysis of the effects associated with protective measures for small-scale industries on the economy in India; cf. *Mohan* (2002).
961 Several empirical investigations detected positive spillover effects of FDI on the host economy in developing markets, for example cf. *Caves* (1974); *Haddad/Harrison* (1993); *Kokko* (1994); *Buckley et al.* (2002b) or *Alfaro et al.* (2004).
962 Cf. *Kochhar et al.* (2006), p. 995.
963 Interview 36, GasCo, Management.
964 Cf. *OECD* (2011b), p. 22.

vest in emerging markets. Informants from GasCo as well as from TechCo emphasized the strategic importance of India as a future market:

> *"In 2006, the executive board took a conscious decision that India represents a main global growth area for the group. The acquisition of one of our competitors helped to gain a strong presence. Since then, every strategic investment was actively supported by the board."*[965]

> *"For us as a company with infrastructure solutions we cannot ignore a market like India. Okay, it is still very chaotic – but India is a clear future market with a lot of potential. The Indian population will overtake the Chinese in the medium-term."*[966]

These statements reflect the overall interview evidence that the Indian market plays a central role for the corporate strategies of TechCo and GasCo in order to establish a strong position in high growth markets. A main motivation of TechCo and GasCo executives was to absorb weakening demand in matured markets like Europe.

4.2.3.1.2 Foreign investment projects

Earlier Indian trade policies intended to substitute imports by local production to attain a greater degree of self-reliance. Import controls were executed by public sector companies which had the exclusive right to import a certain commodity.[967] These import controls combined with import tariffs led to high costs of primary products which made Indian products not competitive on the global market.[968] The **Indian protectionism** on imports was accompanied by severe restrictions on inward foreign investments. Most foreign investors were not allowed to hold an equity share exceeding 40%.[969] A TechCo business developer argues:

> *"Since, the early 1990s we started to develop locations with higher value creations. It did not make sense at all to bring the technology to a country, but without having the property rights to control it. Why should we do that – the local market was also weak."*[970]

Thereupon, foreign investors hesitated to operate with their state-of-the-art technologies in order to protect their intellectual property. The restrictions on foreign capital and investments had the effect that MNCs avoided to invest in India because internationally efficient product volumes and qualities could hardly be achieved. Market-oriented economic reforms led to significant increases in inward foreign investment flows because companies received the authority to decide on investments, expansions, plant locations and product portfolios.[971] The interview evidence suggests that nowa-

965 Interview 49, GasCo, Business Development.
966 Interview 23, TechCo, Business Development.
967 Cf. *Mohammad/Whalley* (1984), p. 392.
968 Cf. *Deshpandé/Farley* (1999), p. 114.
969 Cf. *Aggarwal* (2002), p. 124.
970 Interview 22, TechCo, Business Development.
971 Cf. *Beena et al.* (2004), p. 129.

days MNCs are strongly focused on the Indian economy – especially energy- and infrastructure-related industries. Time delays and price sensitivities of local customers are two main problems which put pressures on the overall project performance.

A challenge for foreign investors is the burgeoning bureaucracy. This legacy of the British colonial rule intended to gain control over the country rather than providing efficient business conditions.[972] In particular Greenfield investments are exposed to tedious decision processes of political institutions. **Time delays** are often due to the problem to get permits of local authorities to start investment implementations. A business developer of GasCo based in India explains:

> *"I mean in this particular investment we did not have these problems with local authorities, because a lot of these issues were taken care of by our local customer. But speaking more generally, there are two big elements where you might often end up in delays in India. One is, when you are acquiring the land for the Greenfield, so the land acquisition very often takes more time than what you budgeted for; the second issue is getting your energy supply."*[973]

As opposed to other corporations, GasCo may leverage its advantage that the company develops investment projects in close cooperation with local customers. Therefore, dealing with local authorities can be delegated to the locally better connected customer who could solve these problems of permissions. Nonetheless, finishing investments on time is one of the critical challenges in India as explained by a GasCo and TechCo informant:

> *"India is a very chaotic country and we Indians are the most optimistic in the whole world. We can do everything which may not be totally wrong, but we do rarely things on time. Productivity is a real problem, almost none of our investments did happen on time – it is more a question of minimizing delays."*[974]

> *"So again we did a lot of work over the two year period going back and forth with them on structuring the investment. That's probably quite long but it does show, I mean, in India things generally take a long time but this is a bit longer than normal."*[975]

As introduced in section 1.3.3.2, timing decisions can also be crucial for the overall investment performance due to scarce resources. In India, GasCo faces the challenge to handle many projects simultaneously because India was and is a key market destination for foreign investments:

> *"One issue we have in India is that we realized so many projects and invested very quickly during the last years, that the local organization and the workforce cannot always keep the pace. But I think many corporations have*

972 Cf. *Holtbrügge/Friedmann* (2011), p. 18.
973 Interview 45, GasCo, Business Development.
974 Interview 49, GasCo, Business Development.
975 Interview 3, TechCo, Management.

this problem when they experienced high growth rates. If you do not have the local resources to implement investments, it takes some time to develop them."[976]

But the overall impression gained from the interviews is that investment projects are virtually never completed on time. Compared to other emerging economies India has still a lot of potential to increase its overall productivity. A lot of activities are not automated and manually handled. A manager compares investment implementations in India with Western countries and China:

"You know if you look at the way projects are implemented in the West or also in China – India lags behind. You have lots of cranes and automated machinery in China. Whereas in India everything is largely done by manual labor, it's not uncommon to see 50 people pulling on a rope to lift something in the air as opposed to having a crane. So you need to understand how to execute projects in India, so I would say that's one of the main success factors."[977]

Foreign MNCs must be aware that Indian customers are very **price sensitive**. Thus, cost of products but as well as the initial Capex must be tightly controlled. Therefore, it is necessary to work with local companies in order to manage the cost levels. Imports – like components for new facilities – from Germany or other regions are too expensive to serve the local market at feasible costs as explained by GasCo business developer:

"Our engineering division faces the challenge to find local suppliers to built plants at satisfying costs. Usually, a substantial chunk of the entire Capex is sourced in India from Indian local companies to bring down the costs. Otherwise we would burn the money in India!"[978]

Another GasCo manager describes that negotiations with Indian customers are also very price-oriented. It is common practice that several biddings with price reductions are necessary to achieve an agreement:

"Again probably one of the obvious things would be the style of negotiation. It seems very price-focused, so it is that you get in and they want one bid and another bid and another bid to try to get the price down. I think in this case we put in six different bids. So I guess this is one point in India – they want to pay Indian prices for European quality."[979]

The same evidence has been highlighted by a TechCo manager:

"In India, we face the challenge to produce at reasonable costs. Therefore, you need to rethink your processes, reengineer and redesign your products

976 Interview 45, GasCo, Business Development.
977 Interview 36, GasCo, Management.
978 Interview 42, GasCo, Business Development.
979 Interview 36, GasCo, Management.

to bring down the costs, if you want to serve the local market with your investment."[980]

Due to the high cost pressure in India, foreign MNCs are obliged to cooperate with local suppliers to implement new investments. Collaborations with Indian suppliers often create productivity and schedule problems as explained by a business developer of TechCo:

"I think productivity is obviously an issue which is related to the quality of work as well as to the schedule, you never get the productivity out of the workers that you want. It is common that schedule commitments are given and then missed or ignored."[981]

As explained in section 4.1.2.3.4, TechCo has introduced its SMART approach to explicitly address these issues of high price sensitivities and different product requirements. TechCo applies a systematic **cost engineering** approach to develop tailored products for emerging markets, like India.

4.2.3.1.3 Infrastructure

India still faces significant infrastructure problems, especially in the area of energy supply and transportation which represents major impediments to sustained growth.[982] Infrastructure development cannot keep the pace with the growing economy. A business developer from TechCo describes the condition of the Indian infrastructure as follows:

"Their [the Indian] infrastructure is appalling – India has such a huge development need in almost every infrastructural area. This makes a lot of our business inefficient just because it took so much time to get something or someone from A to B. Nevertheless, these issues should create opportunities for us, but these problems have to be addressed by the government."[983]

The *World Bank* estimated an investment gap in infrastructure of approximately one trillion US-Dollars for the next five years.[984] Domestic investors as well as foreign MNCs hesitate to set-up large scale-productions due to the **unreliable energy supply**. Besides the problem of regular power cuts and low electricity availability, the Indian industry has to struggle with relatively **high energy costs** because of theft and non-payment behavior of customers.[985] Electricity distributors tend to raise tariffs on the paying consumer base in order to compensate the losses arising from the declining

980 Interview 2, TechCo, Management.
981 Interview 27, TechCo, Business Development.
982 Cf. *Huang/Tang* (2012), p. 93f.
983 Interview 15, TechCo, Business Development.
984 Cf. *The World Bank* (2012c).
985 Cf. *Kochhar et al.* (2006), p. 1013.

willingness to pay.[986] The government is aware of these problems and is committed to invest USD 250 billion in energy infrastructure between 2008 and 2012.[987]

Further measures are to completely deregulate the industry along the supply chain from power generation to power distribution to create greater competition and better availabilities. Energy investments are stimulated by liberalization measures, e.g. private sector companies are allowed to use transmission lines in order to put greater pressure on state-owned companies.[988] Due to the energy background of TechCo and GasCo, India represents a huge market for the two companies, but especially TechCo had to struggle with its time-to-market as explained by a business developer:

> *"For us as company with infrastructure and energy services we cannot say to stay away from the Indian market. But the factory came on board five years ago [...] before everybody in energy saw that India has great potential and built new transformer plants. Now we have to struggle with overcapacities and our competitors were faster than us. Updating the business case in 2011, you could never justify spending the Capex!"*[989]

Transportation is the second serious infrastructural issue in India. To keep the pace of economic development, India needs to expand its network of airports, seaports, roads and railroads. The few airports are chronically congested which makes travelling for foreign investors very inefficient, especially compared to the well-developed airport network in China. The capacity of seawater ports is also relatively low compared to the size of the country, e.g. the largest container terminal in Mumbai accounted for 2.5 million twenty foot equivalent units in 2008, whereas Singapore handled 30 million.[990]

The main parts of the Indian **highway system** can be characterized as being far from well-developed, so that the distribution of cargos between ports and regions within the country takes much more time compared to international standards.[991] A GasCo business developer explains that sometimes components need to be produced at customer sites because it would be too risky to ship them because of the bad condition of roads:

> *"Sometimes, we need to produce our components at the costumer units. If you need to transport very heavy loads, you face huge risks because of the chaotic traffic and road system."*[992]

But since 2007, a private partnership model was introduced in the course of the National Highway Development Program, which boosted the private sector involvement in road projects from 10% in 2007 to nearly 100% in 2012.[993] According to a GasCo

986 Cf. *Panagariya* (2007), p. 241.
987 Cf. *Singhal* (2011), p. 23.
988 Cf. *Panagariya* (2007), p. 242.
989 Interview 15, TechCo, Business Development.
990 Cf. *Singhal* (2011), p. 23.
991 Cf. *Panagariya* (2007), p. 239.
992 Interview 49, GasCo, Business Development.
993 Cf. *OECD* (2011b), p. 43.

business developer, nowadays the main reason for delayed investment projects is still the poor infrastructure:

> *"One of the challenges we always face in India is that projects are not completed on time. We have to struggle with poor infrastructure in a lot of our regions. It starts with problems to get components for your new facilities. But we are quite experienced in India, so as a manager you have to expect these things."*[994]

Apart from the overall poor condition of the infrastructure, **regional differences** related to the development of infrastructure further complicate the investment decision process. A TechCo manager summarizes that India's infrastructure even aggravates the regional problems:

> *"Besides the question of talents and markets, we also have a problem with logistics in some areas. If roads are not paved, airports far away and no connection to the sea you face strategic disadvantages because it brings down your productivity."*[995]

But another statement of a TechCo business developer clarifies that a lot of location decisions in the past were more driven by **government incentives** to invest in certain regional areas than by pure economic evaluations of the current situations:

> *"Often our decisions were made on incentives we received by the government to invest, like tax incentives or subsidies. The government tries to push certain areas, but we as a corporation must also act as a kind of development supporter. For us from European countries, it is sometimes difficult to understand but the right region is much more important also because of the poor infrastructure in India."*[996]

Furthermore, it is very difficult to convince expatriates to work in these less-developed areas due to the relatively low life quality compared to metropolis like Mumbai or Delhi. A TechCo business developer evaluates the access to skilled local employees in some regions as problematic:

> *"Young good qualified Indians want to live in the big cities. But we really struggle to find employees to live in the middle of nowhere where they have to take three planes to get home once a month – otherwise they spend the entire weekend for travelling. In India, you really have to think about the location."*[997]

The analysis of India's political-economic characteristics shows a great upcoming market potential just due to the sheer population size, but the country is far from providing efficient business conditions. The interviews indicated that "earning money" in India is very difficult due to poor infrastructure, unreliable commitments of suppli-

---

994 Interview 45, GasCo, Business Development.
995 Interview 3, TechCo, Management.
996 Interview 15, TechCo, Business Development.
997 Interview 15, TechCo, Business Development.

ers and customers and excessive price sensitivity. India represents a challenging environment for MNCs which requires a strict cost management and tight controls to efficiently implement investments.

4.2.3.2 Socio-cultural characteristics

4.2.3.2.1 Education

The country's educational level has a significant influence on the availability of qualified employees and the performance of the economy.[998] It determines which operational activities can be performed in the foreign country. India experienced considerable improvements related to school attendance. In 2010, the **Free and Compulsory Education Act (RTE)** came into force. Since then, primary education is compulsory and free for Indian children aged between six and fourteen years.[999] Steadily increased government spending and better access to funding for private organizations led to a substantial growth in the supply of education services, e.g. India met its target to establish sixteen new central universities and thirteen new elite institutes of technology and management by 2012.[1000] But India still has the problem that **higher education** is dominated by private commercial providers so that it is only affordable to the upper class of the society.[1001] Furthermore, India produces a flood of degree-holders, but most recent graduates are not adequately trained to meet the requirements of MNCs.[1002] A TechCo manager explains that people with fundamental knowledge are quite easy to find, but it is more critical to find talents which are used to the working conditions in international MNCs:

> *"Let me take India: you get well-educated talents with great degrees in engineering or IT and high quality in terms of technical understanding. But we struggle to find people who understand how to work in a big conglomerate like TechCo."*[1003]

A business developer from GasCo explains that his company intends to localize talents and familiarize them with the global corporate culture by on-the-job-training:

> *"What we have done is to hire very fresh guys from universities with quick perceptions and we tried to educate them on-the-job. Furthermore, we send them around the world to understand the corporation and our culture. But for sure, you need to invest in people – it takes some time until they add value."*[1004]

---

998 Cf. *Hanushek/Woessmann* (2008), p. 657.
999 Cf. *OECD* (2011b), p. 155.
1000 Cf. *OECD* (2011b), p. 159.
1001 Cf. *Wood/Gopalakrishna* (2012), p. 147.
1002 Cf. *Kochhar et al.* (2006), p. 1017.
1003 Interview 5, TechCo, Management.
1004 Interview 28, GasCo, Management.

After India has established the necessary quantity of educational institutions and services, the country needs to focus on improving the **educational quality** now. This is important for the individual contribution to economic growth at the macro-level and the attraction of foreign investments.[1005] Skilled employees for value-adding activities are still the most important bottleneck besides the poor infrastructure, which must be considered within foreign investment decisions.[1006] A GasCo business developer argues that recruiting is quite challenging due to the fast growing economy:

> *"There is a lot of tension in the Indian job market. That is a typical problem if you have a strongly growing economy. So many companies are expanding in India. Everyone working in an MNC gets a lot of job offers – so retention is a big challenge for companies."*[1007]

India has a huge low-cost labor force which attracts foreign investors with efficiency-seeking motives for mass productions. An exception represents the **IT-related industries** in India. A special characteristic of FDI pattern in India is that foreign investors use the country increasingly as a business-processing and IT-services hub. Also TechCo has centralized its internal IT services and software development in India. A manager of TechCo explains the cornerstones of this off-shoring project:

> *"In 1992, we hired round about one hundred Indians for our software engineering. They were trained-on-the-job for two years in Munich or other German locations. After two years they went back to India and we bundled our company-wide IT services in India, mainly for in-house services but partially we also exported external IT-related services, like SAP implementations, from India to Europe."*[1008]

He further emphasizes that the access to skilled employees in the IT sector continuously gained relevance for TechCo:

> *"Besides efficiency-seeking motives, the access to strategic resources – I mean the access to talented people – is increasingly relevant for our organization. Trying to set up a new software engineering team from the ground up with 20 or 30 people is not possible in Germany. In India the availability of skilled personnel, especially in IT-related industries, is significantly better than in Germany."*[1009]

Strategic-resource or market-seeking investment motives – as illustrated by the interview statement – are expected to become also increasingly important for other industries than the Indian IT sector.[1010]

Language and communication problems tend to be lower in India. The huge linguistic heterogeneity with 21 different languages requires communicating in English.[1011] Be-

---

1005 Cf. *Hanushek/Woessmann* (2007), p. 46.
1006 Cf. *Panagariya* (2007), p. 247.
1007 Interview 45, GasCo, Business Development.
1008 Interview 5, TechCo, Management.
1009 Interview 6, TechCo, Management.
1010 Cf. *Zheng* (2009), p. 275.

cause of the long-term British colonization a relatively large part of the population is fluent in English. A business developer from TechCo compares India and China with respect to communication problems:

> *"A real advantage of India compared to China is that communication is much ea-sier due to good English skills."*[1012]

These strong English-language skills in India are an important determinant for attracting foreign capital.[1013] For both German MNCs, these capabilities represent an important argument to invest in India. In particular engineering-related and technologically sophisticated industries are exposed to language barriers which can interfere with the implementation and resource transfer process.

4.2.3.2.2 Society

A country-specific challenge is the extreme **cultural diversity** in India which has also implications for foreign market entries. It is not trivial to adapt the operations, processes, products and marketing campaigns to the local conditions. As mentioned earlier, the huge diversity of the country is also illustrated by a variety of different languages and accents. An Indian business developer from GasCo states:

> *"I have to admit that I have to communicate with most of my Indian colleagues in English because I just do not understand their dialect. For an MNC like GasCo this is not bad because most Indians have good English-speaking skills."*[1014]

Although English skills may be an important bridge within the adaption process, India is very special and diverse in cultural terms which represents a challenge for MNCs in Greenfield projects in India. A GasCo manager explains the relevance of culture for **HR management**:

> *"In India you need the so-called management-by-differentiation to establish your company. Culture has a higher influence on working habits than in Germany or the UK. As an expatriate you need to balance the conflict between imposing your work culture and tolerating the characteristics of the local people, but an Indian-specific is that there are so many facets."*[1015]

Cross-cultural literacy is required to understand the complex socio-cultural characteristics of the Indian work culture, consumption preferences and management practices. These aspects are of special relevance during the implementation and start-up & control stages, when local employees are hired and products must be sold to the domestic market, e.g. marketing programs must understand the Indian cultural diversity in order to introduce culturally sensitive campaigns. A business developer from GasCo underlines the extraordinary importance of local adaption:

1011 Cf. *Holtbrügge/Friedmann* (2011), p. 31f.
1012 Interview 27, TechCo, Business Development.
1013 Cf. *Zheng* (2009), p. 276.
1014 Interview 41, GasCo, Business Development.
1015 Interview 36, GasCo, Management.

> *"Foreign companies need to acquire local market knowledge and localize the operations. Understanding the local market situations, learning how to operate in India – I think this is the biggest challenge and needs time. Many foreign MNCs assess the market conditions as difficult and very special in India."*[1016]

But a manager from GasCo argues that the use of expatriates in India is problematic compared to other regions like Singapore:

> *"You know if you look at our business in Singapore or in Malaysia. Business is a more straightforward. You could put pretty easily expats in charge of these businesses. But in India because things are not always straightforward, it's better to have someone with local experience. [...] India has its own very diverse culture. If you look in the West, things are black or white. You know, it's very clear what the rules are. In India, you know, the rules can be bent or stretched, things are not always clear, things are not always what they seem to be."*[1017]

A business developer at TechCo highlights the importance of **intercultural competence** for expatriates within new investment projects:

> *"Luckily, the two expats I worked with were very quick in understanding the Indian culture. They could really use their technical knowledge locally because they understood what is feasible and what is just impossible. Making the technical knowledge work in a strange environment is also a matter of cultural awareness."*[1018]

The transfer of resources is an important challenge for expatriates, when new investment projects are implemented and ramped up. Expatriates in India must understand that resources – as illustrated by technical knowledge above – may require adaptations to the local conditions. Furthermore, lower employee qualification levels as well as cultural specifics have important implications for **leadership styles** in India. Despite the tendency that the importance of the caste-based thinking is declining in India, it still influences leadership styles. The caste system can be regarded as a reason for the strong hierarchy orientation. A manager from TechCo explains:

> *"One extreme of Indians is that they think in strict hierarchies [...] For me as a manager, this means, that you have to speak a lot with your employees in order to gain an idea about what is really going on in your company. In Germany, the communication between different hierarchical levels is more direct. This yes-man mentality requires more control activities."*[1019]

This statement suggests that foreign managers in India undertake more control activities due to culturally-based power distance to superiors. Similarly, a GasCo manager

1016 Interview 45, GasCo, Business Development.
1017 Interview 36, GasCo, Management.
1018 Interview 23, TechCo, Business Development.
1019 Interview 6, TechCo, Management.

describes the relatively low individual initiatives of young employees, thus requiring clear instructions and measures to foster a more independent working style:

> *"Especially the more junior employees in India show almost no proactive initiatives, reflection or own ideas and concepts compared to young professionals in Europe. Young Indians understand themselves as recipients of orders or commands."*[1020]

Since Indians also tend to prevent open criticism in larger groups and in the presence of fellow employees. This cultural specific is of special relevance for the **conflict management** to solve arising problems as explained by a manager from TechCo:

> *"Similar to the Chinese, Indians attach great value that nobody 'loses his face' which has important implications for our business. For example, a project faces some problems or delays, Indians only communicate the bad news, if it is unavoidable. This can cause serious, but preventable problems. Therefore, I have to exercise much tighter control than in Germany."*[1021]

A TechCo business developer supplements the prior statements by highlighting the tighter control mechanisms and well-specified instructions:

> *"Our processes that worked amazingly in Austria could not be just copied to the Indian setting. Actually this is not the best solution to do it. You can't have the Indian work in the same way as the Austrian work, because then you have chaos, absolute chaos. I mean we tried [laughter]."*[1022]

Foreign MNCs need to adapt Western management and leadership styles to the cultural specifics in India. The interview evidence shows that leadership in India is characterized by **top-down** rather than bottom-up **communication**. Employees tend to expect clearly-defined tasks and targets from superiors. As highlighted by some interviewees business processes need to be tailored to these Indian working habits in order to safeguard efficient operations. Understanding the "Indian mindset" is a challenging task for expatriates during the implementation and start-up of Greenfield investments when local resources are developed.

4.2.3.2.3 Informal networks

The ability of Indians to adapt to different cultures is often explained by the historic experience of British colonization for approximately two centuries. These specific capabilities are described by *Schuster* (2006) as:

> *"The native Indians have a bicultural business system in that many people can and do proceed with business in the Western tradition when the need*

[1020] Interview 30, GasCo, Management.
[1021] Interview 6, TechCo, Management.
[1022] Interview 15, TechCo, Business Development.

arises; however, they do not necessarily value this process or use it when doing business among themselves."[1023]

A traditional feature of the country's complex multi-facetted culture is the practice of **Jaan-pehchaan** which literally means "you get someone done by somebody you know".[1024] The former caste system in India served as a foundation of the development of different informal networks within these society groups. Relationship-building to the right people is crucial for Indian-based managers. Foreign investment performance can be positively as well as negatively impacted by these Jaan-pehchaan networks depending on the respective local connections. This is supported by an interviewee from GasCo:

> *"I expect that our good personal relationships to the Indian steel industry, especially those of our Indian board member, were crucial for winning the tender for that investment. These relationships often make the difference."*[1025]

A GasCo manager explains that customer negotiations and decisions are sometimes not purely driven by objective transaction criteria:

> *"So, it is not driven as much on a pure transactional approach, sometimes it's relationship-based. I would say that's true in China even more."*[1026]

Furthermore, a GasCo business developer draws the attention to the important role of local networks and investing in relationship-building:

> *"So again, our network at the ground level were extremely strong. I think for myself, I have been in India about 50 times in between 2008 and 2009, so it's quite a lot of engagement to build trustful relationships. Networks play significant roles – we have the advantages to have a very local organization with a lot of highly-skilled Indians."*[1027]

GasCo intends to overcome the specific challenges of foreign investments by localizing its organization in India, e.g. by hiring Indians for key positions with customer contact. A business developer from GasCo with former positions in India explains that local knowledge and experience are one of the success factors for foreign companies in India:

> *"Employing people who are experienced with the Indian conditions is decisive. India is a very diverse market that requires local business know-how. If you look in our region that we have here in Southeast Asia, I would say India is one of the countries where you definitely would want to have a local person in charge."*[1028]

1023 *Schuster* (2006), p. 422.
1024 Cf. *McCarthy et al.* (2012), p. 32.
1025 Interview 49, GasCo, Business Development.
1026 Interview 3, TechCo, Management.
1027 Interview 36, GasCo, Management.
1028 Interview 36, GasCo, Management.

To sum up, the descriptions of the socio-cultural specifics highlighted the cultural diversity in India which tends to have a significant influence on the applied business practices. The interview evidence suggests that expatriates require adapting their leadership styles and conflicting management to the Indian cultural specifics by proactively approaching Indian employees.

4.2.3.3 Summary

The country-level interview analysis indicates that India has an enormous market potential and growth prospects due to its sheer demographic size. The country still requires massive investments and structural reforms to resolve the **chaotic infrastructural conditions**. Although India lags behind China in terms of industrial development or income, interviewees expect that India will catch up and compete with China in the near future. One reason mentioned by the informants is the strong Indian entrepreneurial culture that is regarded as decisive to emerge from a low-cost mass producer to an innovative knowledge-based economy.

MNCs face serious challenges to achieve the planned investment profitability. **Time delays** and high price sensitivities put pressure on investment cases. The interview data shows that almost no investment project was completed within the previously assumed time schedule because prior agreements with local suppliers or authorities are often not met. High price sensitivities of local customers create intense **cost pressures** for MNCs. In particular interview data from TechCo indicates that value can only be created by strictly applied cost engineering in India. Nevertheless, GasCo and TechCo placed India at the top positions on their priority lists of target markets because the sheer demographic size creates significant business opportunities.[1029]

The analysis of socio-cultural aspects shows that culture plays an important role within the business life in India. Besides the importance of culture, the complexity of the Indian culture represents a country-specific challenge for Western MNCs. In particular the former caste system led to hierarchy-oriented working habits. Expatriates from Europe cannot expect that employees proactively approach their superiors to address issues or to encourage new ideas. Therefore, expat's **leadership styles** are more strongly focused on controls because arising problems are first escalated when it is already too late to take countermeasures. Conflict management requires intercultural competence in India.

1029 In particular TechCo provides infrastructural solutions for public clients.

4.2.4 China case

4.2.4.1 Political-economic characteristics

4.2.4.1.1 Domestic economy

The People's Republic of China was founded in 1949. Since then, the most populous economy in the world (1.35 billion inhabitants[1030]) has been ruled by the Chinese Communist Party. In 1978, the one-party state started to introduce free market-oriented reforms which initiated the transformation process from a rigid centrally-planned economy to an open market-based one.[1031] The reforms were gradually introduced, but they have been remarkably successful – as opposed to the dominant school of economics which favors the "big-bang" policy accompanied by a grand master plan like the former Soviet Union.[1032]

After experiencing a dynamic economic development, China surpassed Germany as well as Japan and became the world's second largest economy in terms of purchasing power parity in 2010.[1033] Due to the growing economic power in recent years and the high expectations of future development, China's political and economic influence in the global arena is increasing rapidly.[1034] But China is still a **centrally-planned economy** which has implications for foreign investors as explained by an informant from GasCo:

> *"Okay – probably in China investment decisions are quicker to be made because the politics heavily incentivize foreign investments. China I think is a specific case, because China is always quicker than other places. The government heavily sponsors investments in industrial areas, because they desperately need growth in China."*[1035]

Due to the centralized political power decisions processes tend to be quicker than in democratic political systems. The Chinese focus on economic growth creates huge investment opportunities for foreign MNCs, but corporations also need to accelerate decision-making processes in order to keep up the pace with the **dynamic Chinese environment**. In particular interviewees from TechCo stated that investment approvals take too much time which may negatively influence the acquisition of new projects, e.g. a business developer stated:

> *"China is a very specific environment – you need to make fast decisions because everybody – from local companies to worldwide MNCs – wants to do business there. You need fast decision-making processes to be not too late in the market. We have the internal problem that many large MNCs face –*

1030 Cf. *The World Bank* (2012a).
1031 Cf. *Borensztein/Ostry* (1996), p. 224.
1032 Cf. *McMillan/Naughton* (1992), p. 131.
1033 Cf. *Fukumoto/Muto* (2012), p. 63.
1034 Cf. *OECD* (2010a), p. 23.
1035 Interview 43, GasCo, Business Development.

indeed we have the technology and everything but sometimes we are just too slow!"[1036]

A business developer from GasCo explains that the strong domestic growth created **strong local companies** that are expected to be serious competitors in the developed markets in the future:

"Today Chinese companies go into markets like Africa, Middle East, CIS but the more you will see them in Europe and America – I am absolutely convinced. They are the most advanced in terms of management, in terms of skills, organization and globalization. If you take some time, I don't think we will see that in two or three years but give another 15 years to China and you will see that their big names have a significant market share in the overall world. The Chinese will do it by acquisitions due to their very practical way of thinking."[1037]

This statement underlines that currently Chinese corporations mainly expand into other emerging markets. Investment projects are strongly resource-driven in order to fuel the domestic growth of the economy, especially in Africa.[1038] But increasing foreign investments in mature markets like Germany create new competitors for established MNCs, like TechCo or GasCo. Nonetheless, a TechCo manager states that MNCs also try to absorb the growth in the emerging markets to be prepared for stronger competition in the domestic market:

"If we are not doing the business, local corporations or other MNCs will get it. You need to participate in these growth markets – otherwise you will be overtaken by your competitors and local Chinese companies or so called emerging MNCs. This is because the future growth will take place in these BRICs or other emerging economies and you need to get a piece of the cake, if you want to stay ahead on a global scale."[1039]

A current investigation of the Boston Consulting Group (BCG) comes to the same conclusion that MNCs increasingly face "new challengers" from rapidly growing economies – especially from China – on the world and home market. Corporations start to expand abroad to become global leaders within their industries.[1040]

As opposed to the ongoing economic liberalization in China, a diversification and democratization of the political landscape has not yet taken place. Although recent trends show a significant increase of protests, mistrust and democratic tendencies of the emerging middle classes and especially younger Chinese, the People's Republic is still one of the few countries in the world with an **authoritarian one-party system**.[1041] A TechCo business developer explains the consequences for foreign investments:

1036 Interview 22, TechCo, Business Development.
1037 Interview 32, GasCo, Management.
1038 Cf. *Broadman* (2008), p. 96.
1039 Interview 3, TechCo, Management.
1040 Cf. *The Boston Consulting Group* (2013), p. 5.
1041 Cf. *Liu/Chen* (2012), p. 48.

"As a foreign company in China you must be aware that the power is centralized in China. The party is the key decision-maker with respect to the development of economic conditions. If you try to do business in industries which are actively promoted by the government, you may have a lot of benefits. All dealings with local authorities like land acquisitions or other permission processes are more smoothly and faster – this is crucial for your project schedule. But government's interests could also quickly change."[1042]

These statements underline that foreign investment implementations are exposed to external influences due to **political interests** of the Chinese government. Although investment schedules may benefit from actively supported industries or regions, corporations must be aware to take this additional influencing factor into account in a centrally-planned economy. A business developer illustrates the impact of a high-speed train crash on a TechCo investment in China:

"So we somehow agreed with the government, we will deliver these first trains from Germany and then we build the factory in China. But just about one and a half years ago, a high-speed train crashed in China and of course then all of their investments in high-speed rails were put on hold until they find out why the train crashed. So, you got no business all of a sudden. Right now, I have a lovely, beautiful – empty – factory."[1043]

The high-speed train example shows that foreign companies especially in infrastructure-related industries are exposed to changes within the government's economic strategy. Corporations in consumer industries are expected to be less exposed to changing government interests. In this specific case, it did not make sense for TechCo to finish the new investment due to the reservation of the government as the single potential customer.

MNCs must be aware that policy-makers of the Chinese Communist Party are able to exert significant influence on foreign investment projects with burdensome regulations and weak property rights.[1044] Similarly, the Chinese policy is marked by **informal exercise of power** with not transparent hierarchies and decision processes.[1045] These political risks represent an issue for the evaluation of investment projects as described by a management accountant from GasCo:

"These political influences in economies like China also represent a problem for me as management accountant. I need to do the project evaluation and it is not easy to consider these kinds of risks in your business plan. Shifting government focuses may have significant influences on your top line [revenues]."[1046]

1042 Interview 23, TechCo, Business Development.
1043 Interview 15, TechCo, Business Development.
1044 Cf. *Fan/Chan-Kang* (2008), p. 855.
1045 Cf. *Holtbrügge/Puck* (2008), p. 14.
1046 Interview 37, GasCo, Management Accounting.

Generally, GasCo as well as TechCo anticipate these risks by integrating contingencies of a certain percentage of total Capex. The interview evidence underlines that investment and business planning processes are more demanding than in the home country because more external influences may have an impact on the investment development.

4.2.4.1.2 Foreign investment projects

In China, the government and the party may are important external determinants of uncertainty. Nevertheless, a central government concern was to create an investor-friendly environment to foster competition and attract oversea investments, e.g. "**special economic zones**"[1047] were introduced where MNCs can set up their operations to take full advantage of lower labor and production costs.[1048] Thereupon, the Chinese economy grew at an average rate of almost 10% per year with extraordinary annual growth rates between 2003 and 2012 of almost 11%.[1049] These special economic zones play indeed an important role for the location decisions within the two investigated companies. A GasCo manager highlights the influence of the customer locations:

> *"Absolutely, we try to do business in special economic zones. But the problem is that most of China, most of our local customers and businesses are not in these zones. We need to invest close to our customers. Therefore, this decision is not totally in our hands."*[1050]

GasCo's business model calls for the necessity to produce close to the customers or even on their production sites. For this reason, these industry sector-specifics may reduce the importance of special economic zones within the foreign investment decision process. But if location decisions can be made more independently, choosing special economic zones can enhance the overall project performance[1051] for foreign investors in China. According to a business developer from TechCo these special foreign investor regulations are crucial for the specific location decision:

> *"Of course, we want to benefit from special local regulations in China. If the government wants to push a certain industry segment or regional clusters, they grant subsidies to accelerate the developments in the favored directions. As a foreign company, you need to stay receptive for these topics in order to anticipate and benefit from this support."*[1052]

1047 Before China started to open its economy it tested an "open door policy" in its two coastal areas Guangdong and Fujian. The introduction of "special economic zones" within these areas guaranteed foreign investors preferred rights, such as tax incentives. Subsequently, China's government adopted this model in 14 other coastal regions because positive spillover effects to the inland areas had been expected; cf. *Brun et al.* (2002), p. 162.

1048 Cf. *Marr/Reynard* (2010), p. 85.

1049 Cf. *The World Bank* (2012a).

1050 Interview 28, GasCo, Management.

1051 In this context *performance* means that the project creates more shareholder value due to lower transaction costs compared to investments in other Chinese regions without special foreign investor-friendly regulations.

1052 Interview 23, TechCo, Business Development.

A manager from GasCo highlights that the establishment of special economic zones is a core measure of the government to provide stable as well as **compliant business conditions** for foreign companies:

> *"Special economic zones are powerfully developed. They [the government] stopped the big corruption in there or at least to hide it from foreign investors to enhance their confidence. But unfortunately most of China is not in a special economic zone."*[1053]

Outside from special economic zones, China's legal system primarily serves to enforce political interests. For this reason, China does not have the conception of the separation of power and is characterized by a historically **weak judicial culture**.[1054] A business developer from GasCo explains:

> *"You have to be prepared that a signed contract is no guarantee for cash inflows in China. Signed contracts are the beginning of a negotiation – not the result. Fixed topics are often subject to discussion in the next meeting. Contract management involves high maintenance in China – especially when you have contracts with unbalanced benefits or one-sided win-positions, you are exposed to huge contractual risks."*[1055]

This statement underlines that signed contracts do not have the final character like in Germany. Furthermore, the interviewee highlights that this Chinese mentality could create payment risks when contracts do not create win-win-situations. Moreover, the interviews provided evidence that the Chinese mentality tends to view laws more as guidance than as binding rules. Therefore, laws and contracts are often ambiguously formulated to leave scope for interpretations:

> *"Chinese contracts are not really specified, e.g. what are the penalties if contractual agreements are not fulfilled. A contract is more or less regarded as a general agreement to do business with each other – without specifying the details. It is difficult to enforce these types of contracts due to the variety of different interpretation lines."*[1056]

Filing a suit against Chinese stakeholders, e.g. local authorities or Chinese suppliers with relation to the communist party, is not promising due to the political influence on the legal system. Additionally, contractual violations are rather settled out of court which is induced by the weak judicial culture but also by the deeply-rooted fear of losing "face".[1057] A manager from GasCo explains the approach of his corporation to handle contractual violations:

> *"Our approach is to avoid litigations in China because legal disputes could seriously affect your corporate networks and personal business relations due to this face concept etc. You never really know whose toes you tread on.*

1053 Interview 32, GasCo, Management.

1054 Cf. *Holtbrügge/Puck* (2008), p. 16.

1055 Interview 47, GasCo, Business Development.

1056 Interview 5, TechCo, Management.

1057 For the Chinese concept of "face" see section 4.2.4.2.

We are always eager to find an amicable solution. But in some cases you have no choice."[1058]

Foreign MNCs need to pursue a cautious **conflict management** due to the not transparent relationship between political and corporate decision-making. Trustful relations to political authorities and their decision-makers seem to be a success factor for Greenfield investors. This could sometimes be problematic for German corporations due to the thin line between compliant business behaviors, lobbying and corruption or bribery. Therefore, TechCo and GasCo have developed an unambiguous code of conduct for dealing with government agencies and other local stakeholders in order to prevent corporate governance violations.

Closely related to the relatively weak rule of law is the protection of **intellectual property rights**. According to studies of American Anti-Counterfeiting organizations, the worldwide losses of copyright violations from China are estimated to be up to USD 50 billion annually.[1059] Almost 20% of consumer goods manufacturing operations are based on counterfeiting in China.[1060] A business developer elaborates that the technology of the largest local competitor within the construction of mechanical engineering facilities was originally copied from GasCo:

"The largest local mechanical engineering company – by far our strongest competitor in China – has copied the core technology from GasCo in 1980. The technology was further standardized to provide it on a broader scale. So we created with our investments our strongest local competitor."[1061]

A GasCo manager explains that the market entry mode is one instrument to absorb these risks:

"We always try to operate with wholly-owned subsidiaries in China, if we are really exposed to IPR violations. In joint ventures we already faced problems with IPR violations."[1062]

Almost every industry from simple to complex products has to handle the risk of piracy and counterfeiting in China. The widespread problem to protect IPRs is often culturally explained. Imitations are not negatively perceived – moreover it expresses the respect for the originating company. Therefore, the Chinese public does only have little awareness of wrongdoing.[1063] Although China has passed some laws pertaining to the protection of intellectual property rights, the enforcement of copyright laws is weak and penalties for copyright violation are relatively low. Despite these legal problems foreign investors made significant contributions to the strong economic development. Due to the WTO accession in 2001 and generous incentives offered to foreign investors, China's export growth virtually exploded with extraordinary growth rates of

1058 Interview 29, GasCo, Management.

1059 Cf. *Handelsblatt* (2007).

1060 Cf. *Hung* (2003), p. 59.

1061 Interview 47, GasCo, Business Development.

1062 Interview 23, TechCo, Business Development.

1063 Cf. *Murphy* (1995), p. 30.

almost 30% between 2002 and 2007.[1064] Foreign investors entered China to establish **low-cost manufacturing platforms** in order to export the products.[1065] A GasCo manager emphasizes:

> *"China has really done its homework, 20 or 25 years ago and implemented a relatively stable institutional environment in a very strong and visible manner. Furthermore, China got rid of its corrupt methods in the big economic centers, like Shanghai or Beijing. Foreign investors feel quite secure compared to countries like Russia."*[1066]

In 2007, foreign companies produced 57% of China's merchandise exports compared to 20% in 1992. The export value increased from USD 17 billion in 1992 to approximately USD 700 billion in 2007.[1067] But recent trends indicate that foreign investments increasingly driven by market-seeking considerations as local purchasing power increases.[1068] In earlier days, the access to cheap labor was used by foreign corporations for the production of labor-intensive mass products in order to export them to the rest of the world.[1069]

A positive side-effect of the openness to foreign firms for China is that local companies have experienced productive **spillover-effects** from the sheer presence of foreign investments, strengthening competition between foreign and local firms and the exchange of employees between foreign subsidiaries and domestic companies.[1070] On the one side, these spillover-effects are positive for the Chinese corporations but on the other side, foreign corporations face immense **price decreases** in some industries as described by a TechCo business developer:

> *"We lost a lot of people to local competitors which make our business much more complicated. Due to the strong local competition, prices are 40% lower than three years ago, I repeat 40%! We brought the know-how to the country and now we almost have to do twice the volume in order to be able to meet the business case."*[1071]

The significant role of foreign MNCs in China's economy implicates positive consequences for future foreign investment decision processes. Due to the fact that China attracts the second largest amount of foreign investments after the USA, investment knowledge must have been accumulated which reduces the uncertainty for potential investors. Similarly, successful pioneer MNCs operating in China for several years also shaped the local economy and helped to develop the hard and soft infrastructure

---

1064 Cf. *The Economist Intelligence Unit* (2009), p. 30.
1065 Cf. *Zhang/Song* (2001), p. 386.
1066 Interview 32, GasCo, Management.
1067 Cf. *The Economist Intelligence Unit* (2009), p. 30.
1068 Cf. *Liu et al.* (2005), p. 99.
1069 Cf. *Rodrik* (2006), p. 17.
1070 Cf. *Li et al.* (2001), p. 318. For additional empirical investigations related to spillover effects in China due to foreign investments; cf. *Li et al.* (2001); *Buckley et al.* (2002a); *Liu* (2002); *Hu/Jefferson* (2002) or *Buckley* (2007).
1071 Interview 15, TechCo, Business Development.

that led to a stabilization of the local business environment.[1072] The strong footprint of foreign companies in China since the late 1970s also created a better acceptance of local stakeholders for oversea investments and international corporations.[1073]

But **investment implementations** also require local commitments and sufficient project management capabilities in the host country. Managing from a distance is not regarded as a promising option. A GasCo manager expresses that investment implementations in China and Russia are exposed to different work attitudes and quality standards compared to Europe:

> *"In both regions – China and Russia – it has nothing to do with European mentality in terms of implementing projects, in terms of contractors, in terms of standards, etc. And I believe no company today can be successful in China if you want to manage a project from Europe. These are completely different worlds: the culture, the typical standards and the cost levels are different compared to Germany and if you are not able to meet them and locate resources in China and Russia – you are going to fail."*[1074]

A GasCo business developer explains that usually project implementations in China are still exposed to delays but less than investments in India or Russia:

> *"Today, Chinese project executions are not that complicated to finish on time and budget like in India or Russia. In China, the infrastructure is much more developed. You have really huge ports with a good availability from industrial areas – which is necessary for China's export economy."*[1075]

As opposed to India, project implementations in China seem to be more straightforward due to a more sophisticated infrastructure especially in terms of power supply. Huge seaport capacities with good road connections to industrial clusters provide the necessary framework for a swift movement of goods, e.g. when components for investment implementations are imported.

4.2.4.1.3 Infrastructure

China has undertaken massive government investments and spending in infrastructure projects to sustain a framework for fast economic growth. Nowadays, China disposes over an impressive national road network, but nevertheless the government has adopted additional development programs in order to serve China's high transport requirements and absorb the explosive growth of car ownerships.[1076] A manager from TechCo describes the development of the infrastructure in China as follows:

> *"China has made its homework compared to the other BRIC countries – but infrastructure is still an issue because car ownerships and passengers in-*

1072 Cf. *Dunfee/Warren* (2001), p. 195.

1073 Cf. *Luo/Park* (2001), p. 142.

1074 Interview 32, GasCo, Management.

1075 Interview 42, GasCo, Business Development.

1076 For a panel study related to the growth of car ownership in emerging markets, especially in China and India; cf. *Chamon et al.* (2008).

crease so fast that this is almost an impossible mission to keep the pace. If you experience growth rates of more than 10% for many years – I think that this is not unusual. You cannot set up the infrastructure prior to economic booms – it is an evolutionary process."[1077]

The statement underlines that infrastructural bottlenecks are not surprising in high growth regions. Although China implemented huge infrastructure projects, the country is now still facing **traffic problems** in the big megacities like Shanghai or Beijing. Closely related to the strong traffic growth and energy demand is the **increasing air pollution**, like the smog problem in Beijing in January 2013.[1078] Furthermore, 900,000 kilometers of rural roads are currently under construction due to its importance for poverty reduction.[1079] China's sea port facilities have also improved rapidly with just 483 million tons of handled goods in 1990 compared to 3.9 billion tons in 2007. In 2012, already six of the ten largest seaports were located in China.[1080]

However, the government has introduced further flagship projects, e.g. a USD 16 billion offshore deepwater seaport in the vicinity of Shanghai in Yangshan.[1081] The **seaport infrastructure** and capacity in China is of great importance to keep up the export-driven GDP growth.[1082] The aviation infrastructure has also experienced a fast development during the last decades with explosive growth rates with respect to civil aviation. In 2010, China's civil airports handled approximately 200 million passengers compared to 67 million in 2000.[1083] Similarly to the transport network, main parts of the country are already covered with electricity and telecommunication connections.

4.2.4.2 Socio-cultural characteristics

4.2.4.2.1 Education

China's dynamic economic growth has been marked by **disparate regional developments** which are attributable to the establishment of special economic zones and selective introduction of industrial reforms.[1084] While coastal and urban regions in east China flourish, the western more rural regions lag behind.[1085] The heterogeneous regional development also influences the education quality and the access to employees as emphasized by a TechCo management accountant:

"In Huludao, we have underestimated that people prefer larger cities compared to smaller villages [...] It was an unsolvable problem to find quali-

1077 Interview 2, TechCo, Management.

1078 Cf. *Reuters* (2013).

1079 Cf. *Fan/Chan-Kang* (2008), p. 313.

1080 Cf. *Chiu* (2013).

1081 Cf. *The Economist Intelligence Unit* (2009), p. 19.

1082 Cf. *Albarran et al.* (2011), p. 5.

1083 Cf. *Xiao et al.* (2012), p. 267.

1084 Cf. *Brun et al.* (2002), p. 163.

1085 Cf. *Cheung* (2012), p. 1.

> *fied engineers who would stay for longer periods. Therefore, we employed engineers close to Beijing. Corporations need to evaluate location decisions very thoroughly because China is a big country with immense regional differences – especially with respect to employee access."*[1086]

In contrast, the access to skilled employees is not critical in urban regions like Shanghai or Beijing with millions of skilled college graduates.[1087] A GasCo manager supplements that rural areas are facing a lack of skilled employees:

> *"According to my experiences, in China it is not difficult to acquire world-class skilled employees with MNCS experience in cities like Shanghai, Beijing or Hong Kong – they have millions of top-educated people."*[1088]

The education quality is closely related to the future income generating potential – which can even aggravate the regional heterogeneity when rural areas cannot improve their education quality.[1089] An indicator for lower education standards in the Western area can be derived from the qualifications of teachers, e.g. only 20% of high school teachers have attended university in rural regions compared to three-quarters in Beijing.[1090] Furthermore, it is quite difficult for MNCs to find qualified engineers in rural areas, but recruiting technically-skilled people who are also able to speak English is a real challenge as expressed by a TechCo business developer:

> *"In China the regional differences are very extreme. You can barely find qualified people – Chinese, German or whatever – who are willing to go to the midlands. One side is the technical part, but English or German {laughter] skills are of the same importance – otherwise you just cannot communicate. Finding these people is really challenging."*[1091]

One important aspect to consider is that the government actively promotes foreign investments in some rural areas in order to create positive spillover-effects for the regional or environmental development. This is often an incentive for foreign MNCs to invest in regions without a secured access to a pool of qualified employees. Especially MNCs with sophisticated products and production techniques like TechCo or GasCo, China's cheap labor markets of migrant workers were never a real option. Nowadays, TechCo faces retention problems and fast-growing labor costs as explained by a business developer:

> *"Unqualified migrant workers for repetitive tasks you can find everywhere in China – also in the rural areas. But for us as an international company with high-end products and state-of-the-art productions we need a solid base of skilled workforces. In the big cities we have to face fast-growing*

1086 Interview 12, TechCo, Management Accounting.
1087 Cf. *Marr/Reynard* (2010), p. 88.
1088 Interview 33, GasCo, Management.
1089 Cf. *Tolley/Olson* (1971), p. 461f.
1090 Cf. *OECD* (2010a), p. 133.
1091 Interview 24, TechCo, Business Development.

salaries and fluctuation problems. People with TechCo on the CV are very welcome in local firms."[1092]

The retention problems also cause higher risks of counterfeit and piracy, if former employees take the acquired knowledge to their new – often Chinese – employers. Another reason for the retention problems in China is the strong growth of the economy and its corporations during the last decades which causes a huge demand of skilled-employees. Furthermore, a TechCo manager elaborates that corporations need to find management talents who are able to develop quickly enough to keep the pace with the corporate development:

"Now this is completely different to having someone who is just managing a thirty million business ongoing. So you need somebody who is willing to take a job managing a thirty million business today, but who is going to be able to grow fast enough to be able to manage an eighty million location in three years time. That's really a gamble, really a gamble. The other problem we have in China, I mean the economy has grown so much in the last few years, that there is a real sucking of the talent from out of the thirty to forty-five bracket."[1093]

As opposed to the early days of internationalization, the interview data show that MNCs have modified their **international management philosophies**[1094] as explained by a manager from TechCo:

"In earlier days, we positioned German managers in Chinese subsidiaries more or less as watchdogs. But now we focus on developing local people for global management challenges by sending them around the world. After some stations they should lead the local management teams in their countries. We try to give them clear career paths – also as a measure for retention."[1095]

These statements highlight that TechCo management philosophies shifted from an ethnocentric to a regiocentric perspective. TechCo intends to **localize management capabilities** to reduce costs and achieve a higher productivity due to locally better connected people. A TechCo management accountant evaluates that the localization requirements are driven by cost pressures in order to be able to compete in these markets. He highlights that it is extremely important to develop local people and to pursue local sourcing strategies in order to offer products at reasonable prices:

"Localization is the key to be successful in China in terms of profitability. You need to reduce your costs because the price for your products can be assumed as given. Chinese customers want to have the same quality but at significant lower price levels. Price and quality expectations are often not aligned. If you try to make your products like in Germany, you are desig-

1092 Interview 24, TechCo, Business Development.
1093 Interview 3, TechCo, Management.
1094 See section 1.3.1.3.
1095 Interview 3, TechCo, Management.

nated to fail. You cannot afford the same processes. Localization of material and localization of people are the two central drivers to reduce the costs."[1096]

A further management accountant of TechCo also emphasizes the importance of local productions to reduce costs, but he also underlines that localization is required to participate in the huge market potential:

"If you want to serve the Chinese and surrounding markets, then you have the questions of costs. You cannot produce for these markets from Germany or the old Europe to be competitive – you need local production and local supply chains, no matter if you produce pencils or gas turbines."[1097]

Besides the localization of supply chains, the interviews showed that MNCs increasingly try to **develop local talents** for global management careers. These tendencies in China are also driven by language barriers. For foreigners from European countries, the Chinese language is difficult to learn and understand. It is very rare that Western managers are able to speak Chinese.[1098] In the context of foreign investments, language and communication skills are essential for a mutual understanding, e.g. regarding knowledge transfer or sharing.[1099] A TechCo business developer expresses the importance of language skills:

"No, it is really difficult. We have got really all of the processes in German and English. You might think it's easy to translate it. But actually somebody with technical knowledge, who can translate it into Chinese without losing anything in translation, is very rare."[1100]

A further TechCo business developer highlights that Chinese should occupy key positions in China because expatriates or other outsiders are not used to the local conditions and informal communications:

"Our Greenfield in China is managed by a Chinese CEO. I think you need Chinese people in key positions to improve the local awareness. For example, sometimes in customer meetings we speak English, but you have so many surrounding situations in which they switch to Chinese. A foreigner is not able to get all these informal things."[1101]

4.2.4.2.2 Society

China's economic growth was mainly based on high levels of investment and soaring exports rather than on private consumption.[1102] High saving rates of the Chinese are influenced by the relatively weak social security system, so that people are concerned

1096 Interview 12, TechCo, Management Accounting.
1097 Interview 13, TechCo, Management Accounting.
1098 Cf. *Gamble* (2000), p. 899.
1099 Cf. *Buckley et al.* (2004), p. 47.
1100 Interview 15, TechCo, Business Development.
1101 Interview 24, TechCo. Business Development.
1102 Cf. *Wei* (2005), p. 720.

with health, education and retirement issues.[1103] Recent socio-economic reforms intend to create a broader base for a domestic demand-driven economy on the other hand. Nowadays, the absolute size of the middle class is already larger than the entire population of the USA with approximately 400 million people in 2010.[1104] But in recent years, the Chinese **emerging middle classes** start to consume. Young people work very hard to be able to afford status symbols like cars or international designer brands.[1105] A GasCo business developer living since many years in China appreciates the drive of the local people:

> *"The people are very hungry – hungry for success. They work very hard for their careers. They are keen to afford a better life. Now, the hard work of the last decades bears fruits [...] The population starts to buy European cars, shopping malls spring up like mushrooms – all is getting more consumption-oriented."*[1106]

The rapid development of China and its attributed importance for the world economy affect foreign investment decisions of MNCs as this growth market cannot be ignored within the strategic planning process.[1107] The domestic market potential determines the investment needs to serve the local demand.[1108] A GasCo manager explains the strategic importance of the Chinese market:

> *"Ten years ago, our executive board made the landmark decision to place special attention on China. Domestic demand is increasing and people start to spend money which should have positive effects for the entire Chinese economy. In the past, China mainly produced for its massive exports and now the economy also increasingly needs to serve the local demand. The emerging consumer markets require further investments, if the demand should not be satisfied with imports."*[1109]

The ongoing strong momentum has transitioned China from a low-income to a middle-income country. But due to the rapid economic rise, China faces complex development needs related to poverty reduction, an ageing population, internal migration of labor, rapid urbanization and environmental sustainability.[1110] The history shows that the transition from a middle-income to a high-income country is more challenging than stepping up from low- to middle-income levels.[1111] Policymakers are increasingly aware that more **people-oriented programs** are necessary to balance economic

---

1103 Cf. *He/Cao* (2007), p. 12.
1104 Cf. *Marr/Reynard* (2010), p. 87.
1105 Cf. *Ngai* (2003), p. 476.
1106 Interview 41, GasCo, Business Development.
1107 Cf. *Luo/Park* (2001), p. 153.
1108 Cf. *Agarwal/Ramaswami* (1992), p. 5.
1109 Interview 29, GasCo, Management.
1110 Cf. *Yan/Yi Qian* (2004), p. 615.
1111 This phenomenon is known as "the middle income trap". Many countries are not able to move up to a high-income country because of insufficient capabilities to create new products and a lack of sophisticated labor forces; cf. *Ohno* (2009), p. 28.

growth with distributional and ecological sustainability.[1112] The 11th (2006-2010) and 12th (2011-2015) five year plans are focused on creating a harmonious society by improving public services in social protection, education and health as well as by increasing income and improving living standards.[1113]

Social discrepancies also affect the delegation of expatriates. In some areas of China, it is almost impossible to find people who agree to support the implementation process locally. Thus, the location selection[1114] is a main decision for foreign investments in China because the involvement of expatriates is still required for the transfer of resources as explained by a TechCo business developer:

> *"It is a real challenge to convince expats to go to the rural parts of China. It is still not simple to find Chinese people. But for our Greenfield projects we need expats to transfer the required know-how to the new locations to get our business started."*[1115]

When expatriates are willing to supplement implementation processes they are confronted with strong cultural influences on the working habits. A major feature of the Chinese Confucianism shaped culture is the respect for a **precisely ordered hierarchy**. Authoritarian and strict education styles influence the leadership culture and decision behavior in Chinese organizations.[1116] Problems are not openly discussed due to the strict integrity towards superiors which makes it difficult for German MNCs to manage their Chinese subsidiaries from a distance.[1117] A GasCo management accountant describes his experience:

> *"Our Chinese employees do not proactively address issues or problems. Therefore, we had to enhance and intensify our project monitoring. But you see the differences when people studied in America or Europe and lived there for many years. These people articulate problems more confidently."*[1118]

A TechCo business developer underlines that particularly the training of people without English-speaking capabilities requires a lot of patience because basic principles and tasks have to be repeated regularly:

> *"It is like a morning roll call – people are assembling and you have to show them examples again and again. These things belong to this container and so on. You really need supervisors to closely monitor the work. I mean this for simple tasks – for qualified people like engineers it is different."*[1119]

1112 Cf. *Kuijs/Wang* (2006), p. 14.
1113 Cf. *OECD* (2010a), p. 130.
1114 For an empirical investigation with respect to the determinants of location decision within foreign investment processes in China; cf. *Cheng/Kwan* (2000).
1115 Interview 17, TechCo, Business Development.
1116 Cf. *Rothlauf* (2012), p. 494.
1117 Cf. *Cheng et al.* (2004), p. 96.
1118 Interview 37, GasCo, Management Accounting.
1119 Interview 24, TechCo, Business Development.

A Chinese cultural specific is **Mianzi** (face). The concept of Mianzi is closely connected to Guanxi because it is defined as the recognition by others of an individual's social standing and position. Therefore, saving Mianzi determines the individual Guanxi potential on the one hand, whereas the status of the individual Guanxi network influences the social position.[1120] The loss of face (Mianzi) means that individuals are no longer able to use their personal networks for the exchange of favors.[1121] Foreign MNCs must be aware of this cultural specific – especially within meetings, groups or other plenary situations – to prevent people from being exposed. Supporting evidence could be derived from an interview with a GasCo manager who explains the influence of local culture on personnel management:

> *"Leadership styles must be adapted to the Chinese culture – open criticism of individuals especially in groups is not usual for Chinese people. If we try to setup a new business with expats, they receive intercultural trainings to get a very rough understanding – but it is not possible to learn these intercultural competences in classroom trainings."*[1122]

This statement illustrates the impact of the Mianzi concept for HR management and **leadership styles**. Within the foreign investment decision process, these implications are expected to be more important for the start-up and control stages when the production starts and local people are employed to run the new facilities. A GasCo manager stated that Mianzi has also consequences for the company's recruiting strategy in China:

> *"The face issue means for our recruiting in China, that Chinese people always want to work for the 'winner'. These people want to be recognized as successful managers working for the most visible or successful company in the market. So, if we want to hire the best people in the market, we need to develop this winning culture. No Chinese wants to work for the loser."*[1123]

This statement underlines that the Chinese concept of face has important implications for managers of MNC with respect to leadership and communication styles, e.g. because "losing face" is synonymous with social isolation, it is unusual to criticize others in public.[1124] MNCs need to be aware and prepared that the Chinese cultural habits have a significant influence on the way of doing business and therefore on the performance of investment projects in China. Due to the strong cultural influence on the Chinese working behaviors and leadership styles in organizations, expatriates of TechCo receive an **intercultural training** as described by an informant:

> *"Prior to our expatriation, we had a four-day intercultural training called 'international cooperation in China'. This workshop is focused on the Chi-*

1120 Cf. *Buckley et al.* (2006), p. 276.
1121 Cf. *Luk et al.* (1999), p. 260.
1122 Interview 33, GasCo, Management.
1123 Interview 32, GasCo, Management.
1124 Cf. *Depner/Bathelt* (2005), p. 73.

nese culture, economy and politics as well as on more specific topics like personnel management or negotiating in China."[1125]

But all interviewed employees are not convinced that these course-teaching methods are useful preparation methods for expatriates. Moreover, they have serious doubts that a preparation is possible at all. It is crucial to gain experience within the country in everyday life to develop an understanding of its culture. The GasCo head of business development for China expressed:

> *"I had an intercultural training in Germany, which was completely useless. We had a two-day workshop for 6.000 Euros. Every day in China I learned more about the Chinese characteristics than during these two days."*[1126]

Similar statements have been made by a TechCo manager in China:

> *"Personally, I think these trainings are not worth the time and money. You cannot fill the gap of intercultural competence with textbook lessons. Learning by doing and collecting local experiences is the single way to get into it."*[1127]

These statements are consistent to the Uppsala internationalization process model which assumes that local knowledge needs to be acquired by personal experiences ("experiential knowledge") in foreign markets.[1128] The well-established **regional organization** of GasCo and TechCo within their matrix organizations bundle the local market knowledge. A TechCo management accountant illustrates the crucial relationships between the local market and the global product lines through the regional organization:

> *"Our regional organization – TechCo China – is the central link between the local market, local stakeholders and the global product or industry business units, e.g. for finding joint venture partners or targets. They are really close to the market which could not be achieved from a distance in Germany."*[1129]

Consistent with this statement a TechCo business developer emphasizes the importance of a regional organization due to the high communication efforts and the necessity to show a greater local presence:

> *"A core challenge is the question of 'how' to do business due to the cultural specifics. Chinese business partners require a lot of communication – you need to permanently explain why things are handled this way and not that way. This is a very time-consuming process – but for this relationship management we use the local organization, which is also by far much more qualified. I think that is a core advantage compared to smaller competitors*

1125 Interview 22, TechCo, Business Development.
1126 Interview 47, GasCo, Business Development.
1127 Interview 2, TechCo, Management.
1128 See section 2.2.1.
1129 Interview 13, TechCo, Management Accounting.

which cannot delegate these issues to a local team. We just have the necessary resources."[1130]

The interviewees highlight that the strong local organizations constitute a core advantage compared to SMEs. These corporations do not have the required personal as well as material resources to implement investments efficiently without constraining the day-to-day operations.

4.2.4.2.3 Informal networks

As opposed to Western management standards with formal rules and discrete transactions, the Chinese way of doing business is based on informal rules, interpersonal relationships and trust.[1131] **Guanxi** (personal networks) is a central cultural characteristic that represents an integrative part of the Chinese business environment.[1132] Guanxi is an elusive cultural concept which has also been investigated by a large body of literature from different research fields in recent years.[1133] The head of GasCo's business development in China underlines:

> *"China is completely different compared to Germany, especially the way of doing business here. It starts in the early beginning of the childhood. In China, it is not unusual that parents give cash envelopes or other gifts to teachers – that is totally accepted in the society. Therefore, China represents a difficult market for international corporations like us. But I want to clarify our position: Corruption, like briberies, is absolutely not acceptable for us, although it would make many things easier and quicker. We try to succeed with superior and sustainable technologies. But for sure, compared to Germany we are more strongly oriented to develop strong personal and trustful relations to the customers – the basis for doing business!"*[1134]

This quotation illustrates that investments in China may lead to **conflicts of interests**. On the one side, international corporations like TechCo and GasCo are obliged to comply with corporate governance standards from the home country. But on the other side, it can be very challenging to be successful with the domestic, compliant business models in markets like China. Foreign MNCs must be aware and consequently communicate how these conflicting forces are handled within the organization, e.g. by the development of a global code of conduct. This trade-off is further complicated by increased competition from local or foreign EMNCs. These corporations tend to have lower corporate governance standards or different business ethics, which can be a major source of advantages in emerging markets with weaker institutional environments as stated by a TechCo manager:

1130 Interview 17, TechCo, Business Development.

1131 Cf. *Lovett et al.* (1999), p. 232.

1132 Cf. *Buckley et al.* (2006), p. 276.

1133 For different attempts to define *Guanxi*; cf.*Lovett et al.* (1999), p. 233; or *Dunfee/Warren* (2001), p. 192f.

1134 Interview 50, GasCo, Business Development.

> *"Very large international corporations from other emerging markets play with different rules of the game which are not tolerated in our society. This makes it sometimes hard for us to compete in certain areas. It will be even harder in the future because these firms are developing fast. Nowadays, in many industrial areas only established MNCs could provide reliable solutions, which leave the customers no choice. But emerging market firms are catching up quickly."*[1135]

In the context of business decisions Guanxi means that individuals within networks created reciprocal obligations for the continued **exchange of favors**, e.g. providing access to customers or offering job opportunities. Guanxi networks are based on friendship and affection which commit its network members by unwritten codes and informal rules. In China, economic or personal success is closely related to the strength of Guanxi networks which is determined by the social status and the decision authorities of the network members.[1136] A representative of GasCo attaches high importance to Guanxi:

> *"My opinion is that Guanxi can open doors for you, but then you have to create value for someone. If you destroy value or offer a bad deal, Guanxi will not help you anymore."*[1137]

As described in the first part of the study, GasCo's investments are mainly driven by single strategic customers, e.g. a Chinese steel corporation intends to build a new steel mill, GasCo participates in tenders to provide the long-term gas supply via opening new production facilities nearby. Due to this specific business model of GasCo, Guanxi is extremely important during the initialization of investment processes. Winning the tender is the starting point or trigger for new investments. Therefore, compliance is a central subject for GasCo's investment processes in China. A GasCo business developer explains how new investments can be acquired and managed in a compliant way:

> *"What we have learned here in China is that you need to establish the contact to the company owners – when you are doing business with private companies. [...] He wants the best for his company. But it is also very helpful during the implementation because you can very quickly address and solve issues."*[1138]

GasCo's approach to **focus communication on the owners** in private companies is effective to avoid corruptive measures. A main reason is that the owner usually intends to optimize the value for his company by leaving no money on the table. Therefore, owners do not have incentives to choose suboptimal solutions because it would affect their personal wealth. This procedure of GasCo can be understood as a means to reduce agency-relations as the business is directly negotiated between the owner and the

1135 Interview 3, TechCo, Management.
1136 Cf. *Pearce II* (2000), p. 32.
1137 Interview 46, GasCo, Business Development.
1138 Interview 47, GasCo, Business Development.

potential supplier (GasCo). But a required precondition for foreign investors is to dispose over intercultural competences in order to initiate and maintain social contacts, e.g. managers of MNCs must adapt their communication styles to the Chinese culture.[1139] A business developer from TechCo describes:

> *"Cultural awareness is a necessary capability of expats in China. Sometimes, we need to replace people due to complaints of Chinese customers. Our communication in Europe can be characterized as very direct which can deter Chinese stakeholders. [...] You need to know about what to say to whom in which situation."*[1140]

But if foreign investors skillfully cultivate the Guanxi system, it can be used as a strategic capability in China, e.g. as a substitute for formal institutions to get market access or to accelerate dealings with government agencies.[1141] A very practical way to use Guanxi as a strategic resource is to appoint Chinese people for representative positions in order to be more strongly perceived as a Chinese company and localize know-how.[1142] Interview statements from GasCo and TechCo confirm that strong relations to customers and suppliers can fill institutional voids[1143]:

> *"A network-based approach is important in China. Long-term relationships create trust for each other. So, we can live with lower legal enforceability. It is more about trusting each other."*[1144]

> *"Our regional organization TechCo China serves to provide the necessary network in the country for our global product business. Managing business from a distance is not very promising in China. You need to show local presence at the right places with the right people and networks to manage the uncertain legal conditions."*[1145]

The interview statements above are two concise examples that illustrate the importance of strong networks in less-developed institutional environments. Trustworthiness and long-term reliable relationships with Chinese partners are assumed to be an effective instrument to manage institutional risks. As stated earlier, the regional organizations of TechCo and GasCo in China undertake these responsibilities to create a strong local visibility and network.

1139 Cf. *Hwang* (1998), p. 29.

1140 Interview 17, TechCo, Business Development.

1141 Cf. *Pearce II* (2000), p. 36.

1142 Cf. *Tsang* (1998), p. 71.

1143 In this context institutional voids mean the absence of formal institutions such as regulatory frameworks; cf. *Peng/Zhou* (2005), p. 328. Especially in China, informal rules, relationships and institutions may provide effective means of adapting the business models to the host country; cf. *Puffer et al.* (2010), p. 460.

1144 Interview 35, GasCo, Management.

1145 Interview 25, TechCo, Business Development.

4.2.4.3 Summary

China received doubtlessly the greatest public attention among the BRICs due to its enormous development in recent years. Double digit GDP growth rates were rather the rule than the exception. China's success story was mainly based on high **public sector investments and export-driven growth**. Therefore, foreign MNCs were consequently attracted to support the development of the local economy. Special economic zones with favorable FDI policies for MNCs intensified regionally disparate developments between rural and urban or inland and coastal areas. The communist party was dedicated to accelerate growth, but now China as the second largest economy needs to support innovations to achieve the next level of economic development even though strict rules and obedience may have a restraining effect on creativity and innovations.

Although foreign investors may benefit from favorable FDI regulations and relatively well-developed infrastructure, **violations of intellectual property rights** still create significant risks for MNCs. The interviews confirm the impression that China tries to systematically attract foreign companies to develop local corporations by copying foreign products and production procedures. In particular retention problems of MNCs increase the risk of intellectual property violations – if acquired knowledge is applied within local Chinese competitors. Weak Chinese law enforcement makes an effective legal prosecution more complicated.

Looking from a socio-cultural perspective, China can be regarded as a very complex country for MNCs. The strictly hierarchy-oriented Chinese culture has a significant influence on business practices, negotiation processes or leadership styles. **Guanxi** and **Mianzi** are the two core cultural concepts that set the framework for the Chinese business life. The importance of personal relationships and networks for business success in China is attributable to Guanxi, while a cautious conflict management and leadership style is deducible to the concept of Mianzi.

4.2.5 Cross-country discussion

4.2.5.1 Political-economic characteristics

The country-specific political-economic characteristics are summarized in Table 4-5. The different signs indicate country-specific advantages/ strengths (+) or disadvantages/ weaknesses (-), whereas the former (latter) are expected to reduce (intensify) country-specific challenges for MNCs. A "0" means that the influence cannot be determined clearly.

Comparing the **domestic economies**, the four countries have experienced high GDP growth during the last decade and received great attention by German MNCs. The economic growth in Brazil and Russia is mainly attributable to the export of natural resources and rising commodity prices, whereas China and India increasingly benefit from domestic market growth and manufacturing exports.

Political-economic	Brazil	Russia	India	China
Domestic Economy	+ Natural resources + Growing domestic market - Diversification needs	+ Natural resources - Diversification needs - Concentrated markets - Regulation	+ Domestic market + IT-related industries - Bureaucratization	+ Domestic market + Export - Centrally-planned - High local competition
Foreign Investments	- High regulation/taxes - Local content - Cost pressures	- Political influence - Local content - Rule of law	- Cost pressures - Schedule problems	+ FDI policies + SEZ - IPR - Rule of law
Infrastructure	- Weak + World Cup/ Olympic Games	o Moscow-centered - Modernization needs	- Unstable energy supply - Chaotic transportation	+ Coastal/urban - Inland/rural

Table 4-5: Political-economic characteristics of BRIC countries

Former efficiency-seeking motives in China ("workbench of the world") and India ("office of the world") are gradually replaced by market-seeking foreign investments due to the emerging middle classes. The domestic economies in Brazil and Russia are exposed to commodity price developments which result in volatile environments. Until today, both countries failed to diversify their economies to reduce the dependence on global economic activity. In Russia, concentrated markets induced by the oligarchy limit positive competitive forces. Political influences arising from the centrally-planned economy enhance the uncertainty for foreign MNCs in China. Furthermore, the interviews indicate that local Chinese corporations create stronger pressures on foreign MNCs compared to their counterparts within the other three countries.

The strong local competition in China can aggravate the impact of the **liability of foreignness** on the investment performance of MNCs. It is not surprising that MNCs in China are subject to unfamiliarity, discrimination or relational hazards, but more intense competition from local companies creates a higher pressure to overcome these obstacles quickly, e.g. MNCs in China are exposed to high time pressure to develop local market knowledge in order to accelerate the socio-economic process of trust-building with local stakeholders. Nevertheless, MNCs also face the liability of foreignness in the other three countries, but lower local competition reduces the external pressure to cope with it.

In particular, the political risks in China and Russia can be characterized as more influential compared to Brazil and India. As opposed to Russia and China, Brazil and India are democracies which reduce the probability of arbitrarily discriminatory behavior of host governments. As a consequence, MNCs investing in Russia and China are more likely exposed to the **disadvantage of foreignness**. Furthermore, the interviews focusing Russia leave the impression that many Russians are backward-oriented and have significant doubts related to Western MNCs. Therefore, especially consumer-oriented MNCs may face a disadvantage of foreignness due to a discriminatory treatment by customers.

The environments for **foreign investments** show a heterogeneous picture among the four countries. Interviews related to Brazil and India implicate that foreign investment projects face strong cost pressures which affect the overall performance of investments. In Brazil, cost pressures are driven by huge salary increases – especially for technical jobs – and growing prices of construction-related services. High regulation, taxes and local content requirements are further cost drivers. In India, cost pressures mainly arise due to the high price sensitivity of customers, relatively high energy costs and infrastructural inefficiency.

Foreign investors in Russia and China are confronted with a weak rule of law. Intellectual property violations are closely connected to low legal standards in China. Interviewees highlighted the Chinese-specific advantage of special economic zones that provide very stable FDI environments comparable to mature markets. On the other side especially China's country case illustrated the importance of institutional distance for foreign investments in China. In particular, the **normative and cognitive pillars** – as the two main determinants of the liability of foreignness – show significant Chinese specifics. For instance, intellectual property violations are perceived as completely different by Chinese – they evaluate product or technology imitation as an expression of respect for the initial inventor not as a criminal act. For instance, the emergence of GasCo's strongest local competitor in China was based on intellectual property right violations. Due to the imitation of the technology, GasCo experienced a noticeable decrease of new business by local Chinese customers.

Foreign MNCs are exposed to diverse **infrastructures** within the BRIC countries that require adapting value chains to the country- or region-specific conditions. The interview reflects that China – in particular the coastal areas – provides a more efficient physical infrastructure than the other countries. Informants often argued that China was preferred to India due to the better infrastructure. Nevertheless, all countries share the common feature of large geographic areas and population sizes that create difficult infrastructure-related challenges and regional heterogeneity, e.g. a county-wide homogenous provision of efficient infrastructure is almost unsolvable due to the countries' enormous geographical dimensions.

The extremely different infrastructure conditions may create specific challenges for foreign firms according to the **cost of doing business abroad** approach. Thereby, MNCs can face disadvantages compared to local competitors due to the lower experience to cope with these challenges. In some geographic areas with poor infrastructure, local firms are adapted to these external conditions and their obstacles. Thus, MNCs must undergo a learning process to make their resources and capabilities work in inefficient infrastructural conditions. The huge geographic diversity of these four countries even aggravates the challenges related to poor infrastructure conditions. In particular, the design of corporate supply chains must consider infrastructural bottlenecks – which are more difficult to assess for MNCs than for local companies which are used to these environments.

A statement given by a TechCo management accountant summarizes the cross-country comparison of political-economic characteristics:

> *"Among the BRIC countries, I would say China and India are different to Russia and Brazil in the way they are thinking. Chinese and Indians are really business-driven, they want to grow and make profits. You feel the dynamics in these countries, they really want to push the business and make progresses."*[1146]

4.2.5.2 Socio-cultural characteristics

The socio-cultural characteristics investigated within the four single countries are presented in Table 4-6. The signs in front of the illustrated aspects have the same meaning as in the prior section. In accordance to the political-economic characteristics, the country-specific socio-cultural aspects indicate heterogeneous conditions for MNCs investing in BRIC countries. The interview data suggests similarities between the country-specific **education** level and physical infrastructure conditions.

Socio-cultural	Brazil	Russia	India	China
Education	+ Low language barriers - Lack of engineers o Access to employees differs geographically	- High language barriers + Relatively high education level o Access to employees differs geographically	+ English-speaking skills + IT specialists o Access to employees differs regionally	- High language barriers o Access to employees differs regionally
Society	+ Emerging middle class + Social welfare programs - Regional inequalities	- Oligarchy - Regional inequalities	- Cultural diversity + Entrepreneurial culture - Regional inequalities o Caste-based thinking	+ Emerging middle class o Hierarchy-oriented - Regional inequalities
Informal networks	o Importance of personal networks	- High corruption (Blat) - Importance of political lobbying	o Importance of personal networks	- High corruption in inland/rural areas - Importance of political lobbying

Table 4-6: Socio-cultural characteristics of BRIC countries

Each country is characterized by regional differences regarding education quality and the related access to employees. Regions with high educational standards and good availability usually dispose over efficient infrastructural conditions. A clear tendency is that investments in rural areas – which are often actively supported by governmental

1146 Interview 12, TechCo, Management Accounting.

measures to attract foreign investments – are exposed to weak education conditions as well as to inefficient physical infrastructure. In particular interviewees from TechCo explained that foreign corporations are attracted to foster the regional development by investing in soft and hard infrastructure that may reduce the overall investment project success in the short term. In the long term, it can beneficial for MNCs in the BRIC countries to support the regional development in order to improve the local appearance and image of the company. Moreover, educational projects, like supporting the building of schools, provide the opportunity to enhance the **local embeddedness** of MNCs in these countries which reduces the liability of foreignness. Besides these general educational characteristics, country-specifics were also identified.

The availability of highly skilled IT experts in India and engineers in Russia has been highlighted as country-specific advantages with respect to education, while the interviews did not indicate any educational specifics in China. As opposed to the positive education-related specifics in India and Russia, a negative Brazilian specific is that engineering employees are extremely scarce. Thus, the cost of engineering-related labor experienced significant increases in recent years. Cost-driven foreign investments in Brazil are exposed to significant price increase which may question the entire investment rationale at all. In general, MNCs in BRIC countries face the liability of foreignness with respect to recruiting processes in the early stages of implemented investments. Due to **relational hazards** – as a key component of the liability of foreignness – MNCs have to handle higher external uncertainties in recruiting processes. Cultural distance causes internal governance costs because job candidates are more difficult to evaluate due to culturally-driven barriers.

Language and the associated communication efficiency were often mentioned as problematic in Russia and China. In contrast, language barriers within investment projects in Brazil and India are not considered as a significant obstacle by the interviewees. Language problems in Russia were not explicitly expected for German MNCs because many bilingual Russians live in Germany since many years. Due to high lingual diversity in India, local people are used to speak English with each other which facilitate the overall communication within investment projects in India.

Nevertheless, language barriers or problems aggravate the liability of foreignness as well the **liability of outsidership** in the BRIC countries. For instance, the interview evidence from China and Russia suggests that meetings are often held in English but local customers or other stakeholders permanently switch to Chinese respectively Russian to discuss topics among themselves. This behavior may hinder the **trust-building process** on both sides. When expatriates of MNCs are not able to speak the local language in the BRIC countries, they are exposed to the liability of outsidership. Therefore, MNCs have a central advantage when their managers are able to speak the local language in the respective countries, especially due to the importance of informal relationships to local stakeholders. In particular TechCo informants underlined its new approach to develop local talents for global management careers. TechCo prepares local employees who are used to the environments in these emerging countries due to the strategic importance and future relevance of the BRIC countries.

Language barriers are of special relevance for technology corporations, like TechCo and GasCo. Technical know-how and detailed engineering capabilities are more complicated to convey in a foreign language. TechCo interviewees emphasized language problems in Russia and China with respect to the transfer of technical resources and capabilities. These communication barriers are theoretically rooted in the concept of **psychic distance** which creates additional costs of learning for foreign investors.

The most far-reaching **society** developments are doubtlessly the emerging middle classes, especially within China and Brazil. These new consumer bases create significant market potentials for MNCs – just due to the sheer population size. Interviewees emphasized similar tendencies in India's urban regions, but poverty levels are still very high in the rural areas. The oligarchy in Russia represents a country-specific stemming from corruptive privatization programs in the post-soviet era which created an extremely wealthy and influential upper class. Due to the new purchasing power from emerging markets, foreign investments are increasingly driven by market-seeking motives. For this reason, the disadvantage of foreignness is expected to become more apparent for foreign investors. As opposed to purely cost-driven investments, market-seeking investments require that products are accepted and appreciated by local customers. Hence, MNCs need to establish a good reputation in the local markets to prevent discriminatory treatments of customers.

Similar to the other discussed country-specific characteristics, each country shows significant regional diversity related to social aspects. Culture plays an extraordinary role within the business life in China and India. **Chinese as well as Indian working habits** – in particular the relations to superiors and conflict management – reflect the fundamental Indian and Chinese cultural values. Strict hierarchy-orientations, absolute obedience and indirect communications shape the working styles of local hires. For Russia and Brazil the interviews did not indicate any crucial culturally-driven implications for working habits.

Due to the strict-hierarchy orientation and the concept of "losing face" investments in China and India are associated with **intra-organizational relational hazards**. In particular, expatriates of GasCo and TechCo highlighted the different work habits of Chinese and Indian employees. Delegated expatriates – who are usually in managerial positions – need to adapt their leadership styles to the foreign specifics in order to prevent retention problems or cultural conflicts to avoid internal governance costs.

The interview data reflects that **informal networks** and personal relationships are of higher relevance in BRIC countries compared to Europe where business relations are more strongly focused on transactional approaches by applying more objective and rational decision criteria. Besides the sheer importance of these informal relationships and "use of favors" to do business, the four country-specific informal mechanisms are applied in different contexts. In China and Russia the use of informal networks is often required to deal with government agencies and (former) state-owned entities. Thereby, GasCo as well as TechCo interviewees accentuate that personal involvements are strictly avoided that are not compliant with global corporate governance standards. For India and Brazil the interviews indicate that business relationships with private as well as public stakeholders are not to the same extent burdened with corruptive and unethical features.

Although the business environment in China may create conflicts with German corporate governance standards, the interview data indicates that these ethical conflicts are even more omnipresent in Russia. Furthermore, the interviewees emphasized that Chinese corruption differs regionally – particularly in special economic zones corruptive features are almost not observable for foreign investors. Nevertheless, the four presented informal networks of the BRIC countries imply that MNCs are fundamentally confronted with the **liability of outsidership**.

All of the four BRIC countries can be regarded as complex networks of opaque relationships of local stakeholders. In particular, Blat in Russia and Guanxi in Russia are culturally-rooted, complex informal networks which evolved over decades. Due to the importance of informal networks for business success, MNCs need to develop a visible position in these informal networks. Thereby, the required trust-building process to become a part of this network is also influenced by institutional distances, like culturally-driven cognitive distances. Different comprehensions of ethical and unethical business behavior between MNCs and local network members even aggravate the process to cope with the liability of outsidership. Costs of trust-building or to familiarize with the foreign markets are also regarded as determinants for the liability of foreignness of MNCs in foreign countries.

Overall, the extent to which informal networks and favors are used differs across the BRIC countries. A central challenge in BRIC countries is to deal with these culturally-based informal mechanisms in a compliant manner with German business ethics. Nevertheless, it should be mentioned that the presentation of these informal networks can only be interpreted as a **limited snapshot**. Each multi-facetted country culture and the associated use of informal networks require a deeper analysis to derive more differentiated propositions which would go beyond the scope of this work.

To sum up, each of the illustrated political-economic as well as socio-cultural criteria is subject to regional heterogeneities within the single four countries. Therefore, these criteria have to be assessed on a case by case basis for every new arising investment project. The **political-economic** as well as the **socio-cultural diversities** in combination with **huge geographies** in the single BRIC countries do not allow deducing general propositions or evaluations concerning the above discussed criteria. Nonetheless, the country-level cases provide a first impression of potential country-specific challenges for MNCs or corporation with low international experience which want to invest within these countries. Due to the underlying holistic approach of this study to gain broad explorative results, further research projects may focus only one of the countries or single country-specific characteristics, e.g. like the role of informal networks and their relationship with foreign investment performance.[1147]

The following section intends to merge the firm-level results (section 4.1) with the findings of the country-level cases (section 4.2).

1147 See section 5.3.

4.3 Cross-level synthesis

4.3.1 Overview

In this section the identified country-specific characteristics and challenges are evaluated from an investment decision process perspective. The firm-level discussion proposed that the investment decision process success is determined by its efficiency. **Decision process speed** and **decision process comprehensiveness** have been proposed as the two main drivers of investment decision process efficiency.

Prior empirical studies provided evidence that strategic decision processes must be adapted to the respective environmental conditions in order to achieve superior performance.[1148] Finding an appropriate balance between these negatively correlated drivers depends on the specific investment context, like the foreign country characteristics at this point. For this reason, this section discusses how the environmental conditions of the BRIC countries exert influence on the balance or the **trade-off** between decision process speed and decision process comprehensiveness (see Figure 4-16).

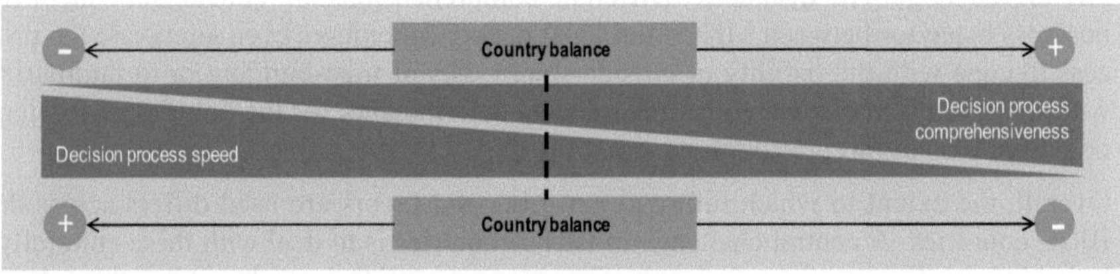

Figure 4-16: Country balance of speed and comprehensiveness

Thereby, it must be emphasized that phases which are assumed to require higher speed (comprehensiveness) shall not imply that comprehensiveness (speed) can be neglected – it just indicates a rough direction to find an efficient balance of investment decision processes in a specific country context. The **reference point** for the following discussion is the established balance between comprehensiveness and speed in the familiar home country environment, like Germany in this case.[1149]

This means when country-specific challenges indicate "higher" decision process speed, "higher" suggests that the country balance is tilted to decision process speed at the expense of decision process comprehensiveness compared to familiar home country environment in Germany. According to Figure 4-16 "higher" decision process speed implies that the country balance shifts to the left side which is associated with lower decision process comprehension compared to the initial balance. Subsequently, each of the four investment phases is discussed along the four BRIC countries and their drivers for investment decision process speed or comprehensiveness.

1148 For empirical studies which investigate the relationship between the design of strategic decision processes and environmental conditions; cf. *Eisenhardt/Bourgeois III* (1988); *Eisenhardt* (1989c); *Fredrickson* (1984); or *Fredrickson/Mitchell* (1984).

1149 GasCo and TechCo are German MNCs. For this reason, the empirical study implicitly investigates country-specific challenges from a German perspective.

4.3.2 Phase-specific comparison

Firm- and country-level results are consolidated by analytical considerations – not by means of statistical inferences as explained in section 3.1.2. The main idea is to discuss the impact of explored country-specific challenges in the context of foreign investment decision processes. Propositions concerning phase-specific prevailing investment decision process success drivers for each country are presented hereinafter. The term "proposition" is used deliberately to highlight the **interpretative character** of the following elaborations.

The following country-specific process illustrations have to be interpreted in the following way. Countries on the left side of the initial balance – as presented with the dotted line – tend to require a stronger focus on decision process comprehensiveness at the expense of decision process speed. As opposed to the left side of the initial balance, the right side indicates that country-specific challenges drive decision process speed. The underlying rationales for these indications are explained by the country case results in the following four sections. Furthermore, **country-specific suggestions** are briefly discussed that may have the potential to enhance the decision process speed or comprehensiveness within the single country contexts.

4.3.2.1 Initialization

Not surprisingly, all of the four countries tend to require higher decision process comprehensiveness in the initialization phase at the expense of decision process speed (see Figure 4-17). Investments in BRIC countries involve careful planning processes due to the weaker institutional environments and higher unfamiliarity in culturally-distant countries as opposed to well-known home country environments.

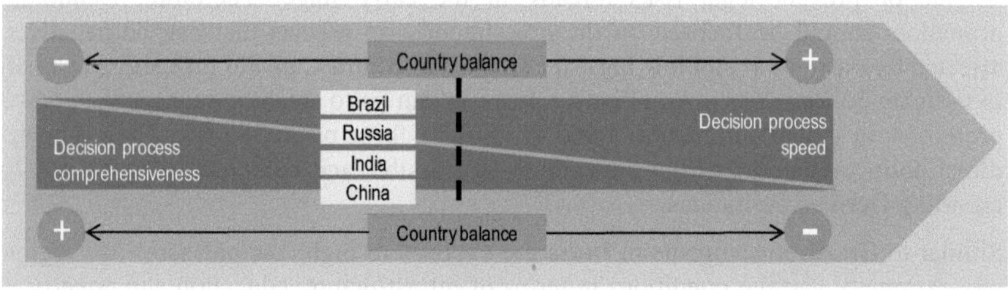

Figure 4-17: Country-specific initialization process speed and comprehensiveness

Associated higher liabilities of foreignness and outsidership require more detailed up-front analyses and information search with respect to local market conditions. In particular the location decisions should be discussed in detail due to extremely varying external conditions within the single BRIC countries. Foreign investors are exposed to **considerable regional differences**, e.g. the investment performance in China can be significantly influenced by investing in special economic zones. The huge geographic country dimensions lead to heterogeneous foreign investment conditions which should be anticipated in the very early stage within foreign investment decision processes. A carefully developed, planned and evaluated investment case clearly represents a critical success factor within every investment process regardless of the target country. Insufficient investment evaluations and planning mistakes can quickly cause significant losses due to the irreversible character of investment projects.

Investment projects in **Brazil** are expected to call for higher decision process comprehensiveness due to several identified country-specifics. In recent years, many MNCs cannot exploit the assumed investment potentials and lost money in Brazil. A potential reason is that investment decisions were not sufficiently planned and evaluated. Huge regional differences in terms of hard and soft infrastructure, increasing cost pressure due to high salaries and regulative burden require careful investment planning. Interviewees indicated that influences of local content regulations on cost levels are difficult to evaluate which drives the perceived uncertainty and asks for higher decision process comprehensiveness.

The interviews clearly indicated that a weak rule of law and intense corruption are omnipresent in **Russia**. Due to the fact that Russia is one of the largest oil and gas producing countries[1150], potential foreign investors may intend to undertake resource-driven investments which implicate a high involvement of public sectors and the importance of political lobbying. For this reason, investment decisions must be thoroughly analyzed prior to the approval phase to anticipate country-specifics that may contradict global corporate governance standards. In energy-related industries, MNCs are exposed to disadvantages of foreignness due the dependent relationships to industries dominated by Oligarchs or the public sector. Both local stakeholders can exert significant influence on the investment projects – which requires a more comprehensive investment decision process to expect potential adverse influences.

A weak rule of law requires high decision process comprehensiveness in order to anticipate or prevent legal risks already in the early stage. Therefore, technology promotors should be focused on the investment case aspects that can be negatively affected by corruption and low legal protection. In contrast, power promotors can help to mitigate political risks. An effective measure can be to send top managers as power promotors to global summits to avoid or mitigate these political risks. They can seek direct political support within the country in a visible and compliant manner, e.g. by escorting German politicians.

Similar to Brazil, investments in **India** are exposed to high cost pressures and regionally extremely varying conditions in terms of infrastructure, education and poverty. A main difference is that these pressures are induced by highly price sensitive local customers – which require detailed calculations whether the corporate products and services can be offered at these competitive price levels. Partially chaotic infrastructural conditions drive costs due to arising inefficiencies. The emerging middle classes in India gain increasingly attention of foreign investors – but still low purchasing power requires locally-adapted product designs in order meet the required price levels. These challenging foreign investment conditions entail a more comprehensive initialization process as opposed to familiar home country environments.

1150 Based on 2009 statistics; cf. *Locatelli/Rossiaud* (2011), p. 5590.

The interview data indicates similarities between **China** and Russia within the early stages of investment decision processes. Weak rule of law, high importance of political lobbying and problems with corruption in rural or inland areas ask for more comprehensive investment decision processes. A Chinese specific problem represents the protection of intellectual property – which is a main driver for Greenfield investments. The risks of intellectual property violations have to be thoroughly evaluated and anticipated during the investment configuration, in particular within the resources and technologies transfer planning. As explained for Russia, CEOs may act as power promotors by visiting the country's policy makers to absorb the risks arising from corruption and a weak legal framework on the top decision level.

4.3.2.2 Approval

The country- specific speed and comprehensiveness propositions in the approval phase are almost identical to the initialization processes. The investigated country-specifics call for higher decision process comprehensiveness within the approval phases – except **China**. Investment decision process speed is expected to outweigh comprehensiveness in the approval phase due to the very dynamic business environment in China (see Figure 4-18).

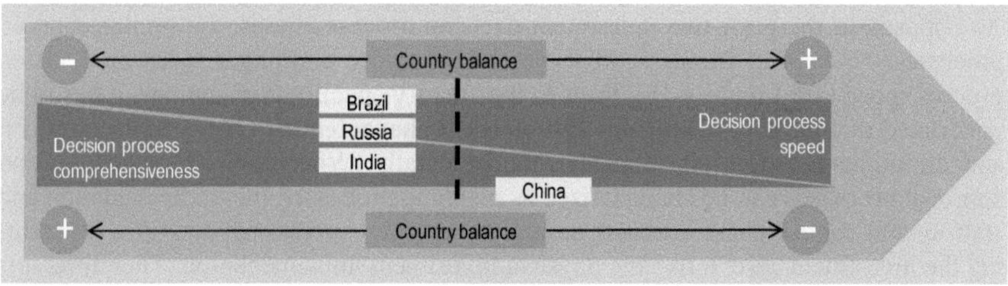

Figure 4-18: Country-specific approval process speed and comprehensiveness

A Chinese specific among the BRIC countries is the centrally-planned economy. The related political influence on the local industry and the entire economy creates higher volatility for foreign MNCs. In particular the approval phase may be subject to enormous time pressures, if some industries, regions or products are placed on the government's priority list. Governmental invitations of tenders are often subject to local investment commitments. For this reason, investment decisions have to be made fast. Moreover, foreign investments in China are also subject to changing priorities of the governments in the other way round. Performance potentials of investment projects can be adversely affected which also requires fast change management actions.

Furthermore, strong competition from Chinese corporations requires fast investment decision processes. Changes within the competitive environments arise quickly, so that developed investment proposals and underlying assumptions may require updates, if final approvals take too much time. As concluded in section 4.1.3, a higher involvement of power promotors may accelerate the decision processes at this point. MNCs already send their CEOs to the political leaders in emerging countries like China or

Russia – in which political lobbying is important – to demonstrate serious interest in the development of the country and to fix investment agreements with local stakeholders. Thereby, these power promotors can help to overcome the liability of foreignness or even prevent the disadvantage of foreignness, e.g. trustful collaboration between a host country's government and the top management of a MNCs can reduce the probability of discriminatory treatments by the government.

In contrast to developed countries, MNCs also face dynamic environments in **Russia**, **India** and **Brazil**, but not to an extent that would justify a stronger focus on enhancing the investment decision process speed at the expense of comprehensiveness. Although China is also a challenging environment for foreign MNCs, the interviews clearly indicated that FDI policies can be regarded as more stable and predictable compared to the other three countries. Furthermore, the Chinese growth story in recent decades was to a great extent attributable to the commitment of foreign investors which used the country as a mass production platform to export the locally produced output to the entire world. This contribution of foreign MNCs to the Chinese development establishes relatively stable investment conditions.

4.3.2.3 Implementation

As opposed to the prior two investment decision process phases, the implementation processes – except in Russia – are expected to require a stronger focus on decision process speed (see Figure 4-18). Prior to the country-specific explanations, it has to be underlined that the **investment decision process characteristics** between the approval and the implementation phase change fundamentally. Whereas the initialization and approval processes can be characterized as planning processes, the implementation and start-up and control phase are more strongly shaped by operational activities ("executing the investment case"), like the physical investment implementation. Therefore, it is argued that implementation processes can be focused on decision process speed as long as investment cases are comprehensively analyzed and planned in the two preceding phases.

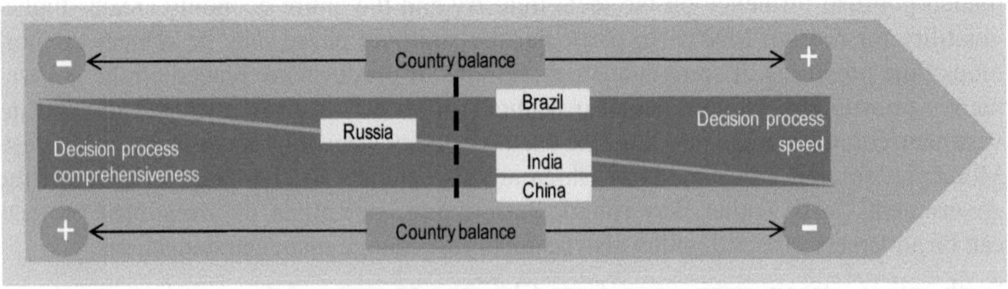

Figure 4-19: Country-specific implementation process speed and comprehensiveness

Localization and local adaptation pressures represent important determinants for the implementation process within **BRIC** countries. The interviews clearly show that the development of local resources and locally adapted products are not solely a clear success factor for foreign investments, but obligatory in many industries due to local content regulations. For this reason, the entire implementation process has to consider these external influences to meet the regulatory requirements. As a consequence, the implementation has to be designed in the way to achieve a certain degree of local value creation in order to produce locally responsive products.

Thereby, MNCs are often bounded to develop local suppliers, just because the local corporations are not able to deliver the required supply in adequate qualities. This development of local resources has to undergo complicated processes – due to unfamiliarity with local suppliers, cultural differences and communication barriers. Whether these requirements cause a stronger tilted balance towards decision process speed or decision process comprehensiveness is difficult to indicate, but the necessity for localization clearly intensifies the time pressure of the investment implementations.

Based on a carefully planned and evaluated investment decision, the implementation phases can be characterized as more strongly driven by investment decision process speed in Brazil, China and India. In contrast, Russia takes a unique position. Interviews indicated that investment decision processes in **Russia** still demand higher comprehensiveness to anticipate problems with oligarchy and corruption. Relations to external stakeholders, like SOE customers, local authorities, policymakers or suppliers, need a well-considered and cautious management. Opaque, not transparent and deeply-rooted informal networks between these external stakeholders may create unsolvable obstacles, e.g. when the "wrong people" are annoyed by foreign MNCs. This **liability of outsidership**[1151] that foreign MNCs have to face in Russia exposes expatriates to a dilemma. Corporations which understand to cope with these disadvantages have to fear legal consequences in their home countries due to the very thin line between loyalties to certain stakeholders and corruption.

Additionally, the Russian oligarchy created highly concentrated industries which amplify the risks that national champions use their power at the expense of foreign MNCs. Therefore, every step during the implementation phase has to be thoroughly evaluated by comprehensive decision processes. A general problem related to Russia is that faster decision processes can require specific business practices, like bribes, that are not acceptable for MNCs. In particular, these **institutional voids** in Russia require comprehensive implementation processes. On the one hand, comprehensiveness is important to avoid discriminatory treatments by local authorities and on the other hand to act consistently with international corporate governance standards. Regional country organizations in Russia may act as a kind of technology promotor by providing the required local market knowledge to make informal networks more transparent. Expatriates can play the roles of process promotors to arbitrate between the headquarter and regional organizations in order to safeguard that business practices are applied in a compliant way.

Investment decision process speed tends to prevail in **India** due the country's reputation for schedule problems within investment implementations. The interviews indicated that almost no investment has been completed on time although the project im-

1151 See section 2.2.2.

plementations have been tightly controlled. As explained above, the chaotic infrastructure, inefficient supply chains, excessive bureaucracy and cultural specifics are drivers for these problems. In particular the cultural context has a significant influence on the Indian working habits. Strictly hierarchy-oriented working practices limit the individual initiatives of local employees. But investment implementations are often associated with unexpected issues which require direct communication to introduce fast change management measures to keep the pace within the implementation process. Project managers – who have been identified as process promotors – need to exercise very close controls and actively approach local hires to be able to anticipate upcoming project issues.

The importance of decision process speed during investment implementations in **China** is mainly driven by the same country-specific characteristics as in the approval phase. The hierarchy-oriented working habits which are attributable to the Chinese culture and the precisely ordered society represent an analogy to India. Chinese employees on the lower hierarchical levels or at the beginning of their careers tend to expect clear instructions of superiors. These working characteristics may cause delays when tasks are not clearly defined. Certain project aspects that require individual initiatives, like unexpected implementation changes may also lead to schedule problems. Therefore, it is crucial to appoint qualified (local) people who are confident enough to make own decisions. The interviews indicate that these positions can be effectively and efficiently assumed by Chinese talents who accumulated international experiences and developed a global mindset.

Decision process speed seems to outweigh comprehensiveness within the investment implementation phases in **Brazil**. Interviewees emphasized that investment implementations by foreign MNCs are confronted with costly and time-consuming regulatory burdens, e.g. like dealings with labor regulations or tax administrations. A further important country-specific for investment implementations in Brazil is the limited availability of engineers and technical experts – which created excessive salary increases. Therefore, MNCs are obliged to implement investments with a relatively high involvement of expatriates. But as mentioned above, strict labor regulations complicate the work permission processes which intensify the schedule pressure on implementation processes. In this respect, legal specialists, who are familiar with local working regulations and administration, may act as process promotors to accelerate these complicated permission processes.

4.3.2.4 Start-up and control

The country-specific balances between speed and comprehensiveness in the start-up and control phase are assumed to be identical to the implementation process (see Figure 4-20).

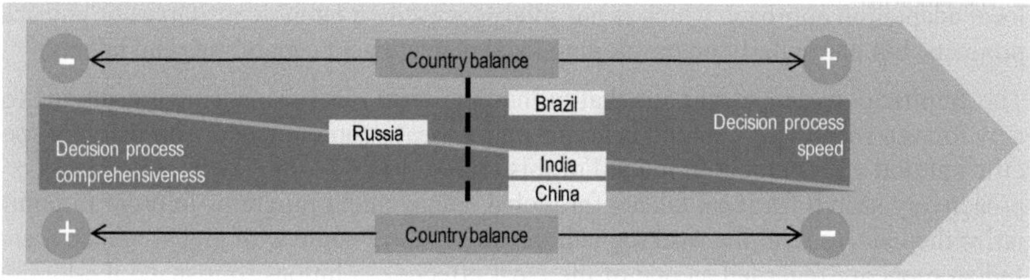

Figure 4-20: Country-specific start-up and control process speed and comprehensiveness

Brazil, India and China share the common characteristic of **emerging middle classes** that create new mass markets due to the sheer population sizes, e.g. already in 2010 Chinas middle class accounted for 400 million people – larger than the entire USA.[1152] MNCs and EMNCs concentrate on these new consumers which causes high competition. Fast MNCs with a strong local country commitment as a corporate citizen may benefit **from first-mover advantages**.

Interviewees emphasized that MNCs increasingly cooperate with universities in India and China not solely to safeguard the access to qualified employees but also establish the company as a brand within the universities. People start to consume certain products, like cars or cell phones, for the first time in their life which underlines the necessity of **fast time-to-market** processes. An emerging market-specific is that the fastest corporations may benefit due to the lack of rival products in the early stages of industrial development and increasing private wealth. These country-specifics require higher decision process speed within the start-up and control phase to realize first-mover advantages.

The start-up and control phase in **Brazil** is expected to call for higher decision process speed – again due to the relatively burdensome regulatory environment. Interviewees emphasized that Brazil cannot fully exploit its potential due to inefficient and highly regulated business environments. The demand for decision process comprehensiveness tends to be lower due the established democratic values and the relatively stable legal framework. As mentioned above, the country faces bottlenecks with respect to the availability of engineers which may lead to delayed recruiting processes during the start-up phases. Excessive labor regulations further aggravate these problems because it is complicated to receive working permits for expatriates. For this reason, HR-related subjects like hiring local employees or delegating expatriates for investment projects in Brazil have to be addressed early to prevent delays in the final stages.

Foreign investments implemented in **India** are forced to localize resources quickly in order to cope with the cost pressures arising from price sensitive customers. As long as too much value creation is attributable to imported goods from outside countries or even from Germany, foreign MNCs have to fear unprofitable operations in India. For this reason, investment decision process speed tends to outweigh comprehensiveness within the start-up and control phase. The Indian country-specific challenges require a

1152 See section 4.2.4.2.2.

local adaptation approach which is not solely focused on tangible resources or physical products, but particularly on developing local management capabilities and talents.

The empirical evidence suggests that in the long term local management positions for new foreign subsidiaries should be assumed by local people to cope with the very specific cultural environment in India. For this reason, MNCs – like TechCo and GasCo – proactively search for local talents for global management programs in order to familiarize themselves with the working cultures in MNCs. People with global mindsets and Indian roots are regarded as one of the most effective solutions to manage the foreign operations by the interviewees. These local talents may act as process promotors to implement the working culture and management styles of MNCs adapted to the local conditions in India. They can combine the necessary local market know-how with the organizational knowledge in order to accelerate decision processes and enhance their efficiency. Expatriates face the challenges to adapt their leadership styles to the cultural-specifics in India. More control-oriented leadership is required in order to anticipate arising problems or issues early.

The country-specifics in **China** also require higher decision process speed for the start-up and control process. Strong local competition in many industries in China tends to call for higher investment decision speed. Besides powerful state-owned entities, local SMEs increasingly intensify the competitive pressures. Interviewees indicated that this fast developing local competition is mainly attributed to retention problems and intellectual property violations. Chinese employees working for MNCs use their accumulated insider knowledge to establish new corporations.

Cultural considerations tend to have the same effect on the investment decision process speed like in India. Cultural barriers or misunderstandings between expatriates and Chinese may cause inefficient or more time consuming coordination activities. For this reason, MNCs are more concerned with faster investment decision processes. Similar to India, MNCs start to systemically develop Chinese high potentials for global management careers. In the long run, these internationally experienced people combine company-specific organizational knowledge with local cultural competence in order to replace less effective expatriates.

Similar to the other investment phases in **Russia,** the high-risk environment of oligarchy, corruption and weak legal protection requires highly comprehensive decision processes to anticipate upcoming external threats. Managing foreign subsidiaries from a distance is designated to fail because these unstable business conditions have to be closely controlled by regional presence. Strong regional country organizations – as represented by horizontal dimensions within the matrix organizations of TechCo and GasCo – are indispensable in Russia to mitigate these political, legal and cultural risks, but also for political lobbying purposes by signaling serious commitment to the country. Due to these required networking activities to overcome the liability of foreignness in Russia, it has to be carefully considered whether the applied business practices meet global compliance standards.

To sum up, the final cross-level synthesis served to discuss the identified BRIC country challenges at the background of the firm-level results. Thereby, it has to be underlined again that the propositions in this cross-level section are of interpretative character. They only provide an indication for prevailing investment decision process success drivers in the specific country context. Each of the four countries is very diverse and characterized by extremely varying regional foreign investment conditions, which requires investigating foreign investments on a **case-by-case basis** to derive more differentiated propositions. Although the BRIC countries emerged as a group of nations, the country cases illustrated significant economic, social and cultural differences among the four countries.

5 Conclusions

5.1 Main results

The **overall research objective** of the present study was to empirically investigate foreign investment decision processes within MNCs by applying a case study approach. Due to the strategic relevance of emerging markets for MNCs, the regional focus was on investments in the BRIC countries. Three sub-goals have been defined to specify the overall research objective. The first sub-goal was to describe the company-specific foreign investment decision processes and discuss the underlying success factors **(firm-level)**. The second sub-goal was to explore country-specific challenges for foreign investors in the BRIC countries **(country-level)**. Finally, the third sub-goal aimed to merge the main findings by evaluating the country-specific challenges within the context of foreign investment decision processes and associated critical success factors **(cross-level)**.

A qualitative **case study design** was adopted to achieve the three main research objectives. Thereby, a research partnership with two very internationally experienced German MNCs was established to guarantee the practical feasibility of this study. GasCo and TechCo granted the exclusive opportunity to investigate their foreign investment decision pro-cesses. Moreover, GasCo and TechCo are strategically focused on achieving emerging market revenue growth – which further underlines their suitability for research purpose of this study. The empirical results are based on 52 interviews with managers, management accountants and business developers who have practical experience related to investment projects in BRIC countries. A main strength of this study is attributable to this multi-perspective view on investment decision processes which provided a comprehensive description of the research object. Subsequently, the main findings are presented according to the three sub-goals of this study.

Firm-level cases

The firm-level cases were focused on providing a detailed description of the two company-specific foreign investment decision processes. GasCo is a specialized gases and engineering MNC, whereas TechCo can be characterized as a diversified conglomerate operating in a variety of industries. The empirical results indicate that the different **industry characteristics** influence the investment decision processes. The most striking difference between the underlying business models is that GasCo invests in a certain "customer or cluster of customers" (pull investments), whereas TechCo invests in a "market" (push investment). GasCo's investments are triggered by specific customer requirements which reduce the involved decision uncertainty and complexity due to the limited alternatives of reasonable investment configurations. Key assumptions of investment evaluations, like the revenue estimation, are almost predetermined by the long term supply contract with the respective customer.

Moreover, **GasCo's** specific business model causes a frequent flow of foreign investment projects because new business opportunities arising from single customers usually require the establishment of investments to serve the new demand. As a consequence investments are treated as parts of the company's core activities. For this reason, the underlying foreign investment decision process follows standardized procedures and is managed by specialized corporate departments that are exclusively focused on initializing and implementing investment projects abroad. Furthermore, the accumulation of foreign investment experience in specialized corporate units implies that foreign investment decision processes are driven by investment specialists with detailed foreign market experience.

At **TechCo**, foreign investments tend to possess a one-off character. Therefore, the involved actors are confronted with **higher perceived uncertainties** which reduce the confidence in the decision-making process. Apart from the deviating investment project frequency between the two companies, the external industry-specific uncertainties create higher control-oriented investment decision processes at TechCo. Furthermore, TechCo is significantly larger in terms of revenues and employees than GasCo. TechCo has a steeper hierarchy than GasCo with more approval cycles which reduce the speed of investment decision processes. Additionally, the TechCo interviewees underlined company-specific improvement potentials, in particular with respect to shorten and reduce approval cycles.

Similarly, TechCo's globally-dispersed value chains entail additional interfaces with other operating units around the world. Thus, the **involved complexity** in the foreign investment decision process increases due to the interdependencies to other (geographically-distant) production facilities. GasCo operates with completely independent value chains at the new investment locations which reduce the complexity of investment decision processes due to the absence of interdependencies to other corporate units.

Based on prior strategy process research and the empirically investigated real-typical investment decision processes, two critical success factors of investment decision processes have been proposed. It has been argued that investment project success is driven by its underlying investment decision process success which is determined by the respective investment decision process efficiency as depicted in Figure 5-1.

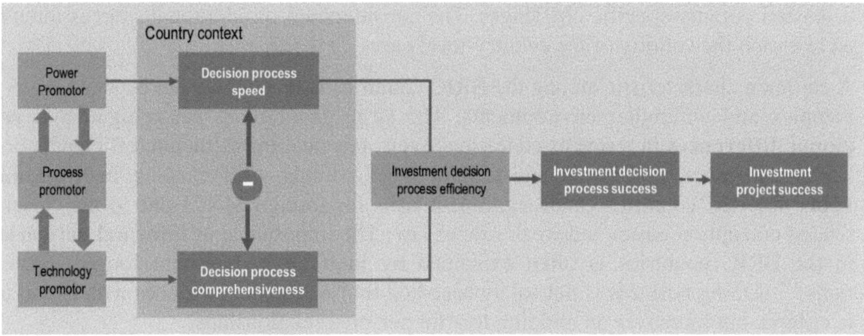

Figure 5-1: Firm-level results

Thereby, **decision process speed** and **decision process comprehensiveness** have been analytically suggested as the main determinants of the investment decision process efficiency. Due to the assumed negative interrelation between speed and comprehensiveness, a context-specific trade-off has to be balanced. Country-specific challenges related to foreign investments may require more comprehensive or faster investment decision processes.

Furthermore, the establishment of a **promotor troika** has been suggested as a possible solution to safeguard an adequate balance between decision process speed and decision process comprehensiveness. Power promotors (e.g. the executive board) tend to accelerate decision processes whereas technology promotors (e.g. management accountants, engineers etc.) drive the underlying decision process comprehensiveness. In large and complex MNCs, process promotors need to mediate between these two parties to overcome organizational barriers and achieve an efficient collaboration between power and technology promotor. Ideally, the power promotor can make fast investment decisions based on comprehensively developed investment cases by technology promotors.

The firm-level cases concluded that a troika constellation of technology, process and po-wer promotors within the foreign investment decision process can serve to find an adequate trade-off between investment decision process speed and investment decision process comprehensiveness as antecedents for the investment decision process efficiency and success.

Country-level cases

Subsequent to the firm-level analysis, the interview data was analyzed from a country perspective to achieve the second sub-goal of this study. Country-specific challenges have been identified based on three implemented investments in each of the BRIC countries. Political-economic as well as socio-cultural characteristics that have been emphasized during the interviews were elaborated in the country-level cases. Thereby, the interview data was complemented with published country studies of international organizations, like the *UN* or *OECD*, in order to gain a deeper understanding for the discussed country-specific challenges. The consideration of additional sources intended to enrich the validity of the country-level cases.

A common characteristic among the BRIC countries is that MNCs are exposed to very complex and unfamiliar environments. The large geographies cause significant **regional differences** in terms of education levels, physical infrastructure efficiency, political influences, corruption and cultural backgrounds. Still existing **institutional voids** in BRIC countries entail significant risks for foreign MNCs due to the closely related corruption issues and weak rule of law. The importance of **informal networks** in the BRIC countries is often explained by ineffective or absent formal institutions.[1153] Doing business is not solely based on transactional approaches with economic criteria, but moreover on building trustful personal relationships.

Furthermore, foreign MNCs face the challenge to compete with **EMNCs** in their host markets. Competitive disadvantages for MNCs may arise due to the different percep-

1153 Cf. *Estrin/Prevezer* (2011), p. 42.

tions of ethical and unethical business behaviors – higher global corporate governance standards require MNCs to find compliant ways to compete. Strong regional headquarters – as the second dimension within the matrix organizations – and localization of resources are necessary to show the commitment to the country in order to create local responsiveness. Moreover, regional headquarters serve to manage arising country-specific challenges locally.

Investors in **Brazil** are exposed to excessive bureaucracy, relatively high salaries and burdensome tax regulations. **Russia** represents by far the most challenging environment due to high corruption (Blat), low legal enforceability and oligarchy. **India** is perceived as the country with the highest economic potential due to the entrepreneurial culture, emerging domestic market and high demographic growth. But currently MNCs struggle with chaotic infrastructural conditions, ineffective foreign investment regulations and high price sensitivities of local customers in India.

China is certainly the most striking example in terms of economic growth within the BRIC countries.[1154] In particular in special economic zones foreign investors can combine stable FDI policies comparable to developed countries with the advantages of an emerging economy, like relatively cheap labor or high growth. A negative China-specific is the high risk of intellectual property right violations that are creating new local competitors. Furthermore, China and India are perceived as the two countries with the strongest influence of cultural backgrounds on working habits which complicates the day-to-day operations and therefore requires culturally responsive leadership styles of expatriates.

To sum up, the illustrated country-specific challenges indicate that foreign investors are exposed to regional heterogeneities within the single countries. Therefore, these country characteristics have to be assessed on a **case-by-case basis** for every new arising investment project. Nonetheless, the country-level cases provide an impression of potential arising country-specific challenges for internationally oriented companies which want to invest in these countries.

Cross-level synthesis

Finally, a cross-level synthesis served to consolidate the firm-level and country-level results. Therefore, the country-specific challenges were evaluated within the context of foreign investment decision processes. The basic principle was to discuss whether the identified country-specifics demand higher decision process speed or decision process comprehensiveness to find an efficient country balance between these conflicting forces. The evaluation of prevailing critical success factors is summarized in Figure 5-2. Prior to the presentation of the results it has to be reflected that these indications are based on analytical-interpretative consideration and not by means of statistical inferences or significances, which will be discussed in more detail in section 5.3.

1154 Cf. *Subacchi* (2008), p. 485.

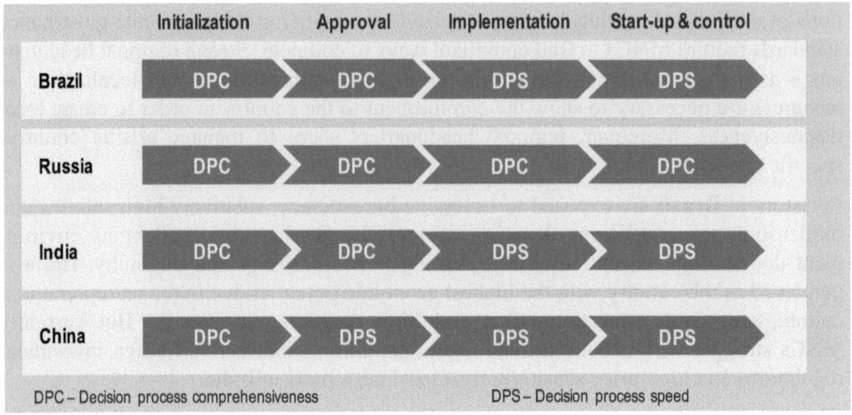

Figure 5-2: Cross-level results

Not surprisingly, all country-specific **initialization** stages tend to require higher decision process comprehensiveness which can be assumed for every investment project no matter which country is targeted. But thoroughly developed and evaluated investment cases are of special relevance in target countries with weaker institutional environments, regional differences and distant cultures, like the BRICs. During the **approval** phases the balances are also tilted towards decision process comprehensiveness – except for decision processes related to investments in China. Due to the combination of the centrally-planned economy and the dynamic competitive environment, investment decisions have to be made fast. Foreign investors can enjoy stable FDI policies based on long-term development plans – thus reducing the need for comprehensiveness – but have to handle highly competitive markets – that reinforces the requirements for the decision process speed.

For the **implementation** as well as for **start-up and control** stages country-specific challenges in Brazil, India and China indicate a stronger tilted balance towards investment decision process speed. Assuming that investment projects were carefully planned and thoroughly evaluated prior to the final investment decisions by the executive boards, the last two – more operational – phases tend to require a stronger focus on decision process speed to achieve short times-to-market. In particular in emerging markets first mover advantages may be significant, when people start to consume some products for the first time in their life.[1155] Russia's identified country-characteristics demand for a high level of decision process comprehensiveness during the entire process. As mentioned earlier, omnipresent corruption, oligarchy, weak rule of law and deeply-rooted informal networks constitute a challenging environment for foreign MNCs. For this reason, it is assumed that comprehensiveness tends to overcompensate the requirements for decision process speed.

1155 Cf. *Rahman/Bhattacharyya* (2003), p. 146.

All in all, this is one the first studies that empirically investigates the foreign investment decision process in German MNCs. The review of prior literature illustrated that empirical studies explicitly focusing on foreign investment decision processes are either conceptual-based or outdated. This study addressed this research gap by developing two **real-typical foreign investment decision process models** based on in-depth interviews with managers, business developers and management accountants. Therefore, this explorative study contributes to gain a more comprehensive and contemporary understanding how foreign investment decision processes unfold in MNCs. Furthermore, this work contributes to the interdisciplinary research field of foreign investment decision processes by proposing a modified promotor model to improve the efficiency of decision processes. Therefore, this work contributes by extending existing decision process theory and provides starting points for further discussions and refinements.

5.2 Managerial implications

Business administration aspires to be an applied science.[1156] Thus, a major concern of this study was to achieve practical relevance. GasCo and TechCo are two of the most internationally experienced MNCs in Germany. They provided the exclusive opportunity to investigate foreign investment decision processes in their real-life contexts. In particular the firm-level cases in section 4.1 demonstrated how experienced MNCs cope with the associated challenges of foreign investment decision processes. Due to the assumed high strategic relevance for the majority of corporations, the regional focus was on investment projects in BRIC countries to enhance the practical value of this study. Possibly, export-oriented **German SMEs**, which are already world leaders in their niche markets, may take the next step to establish own foreign subsidiaries in these countries. This study is able to provide a broad overview of possible upcoming challenges with respect to investments in the BRIC countries.

The application of the promotor model in the present context of investments represents a managerial implication of this study. Prior research proposed that a troika of power, process and technology promotors is the most effective and efficient constellation to implement innovations in large corporations.[1157] This work transferred the promotor concept to the context of foreign investment projects. The firm-level analysis concluded that a promotor troika seems to be a reasonable constellation to manage the conflicting investment decision process success drivers of speed and comprehensiveness. Thereby, the promotor balance between these three role typologies is context-dependent. The application of the promotor model provides managerial implications for **designing foreign investment decision processes**. Top managers who have the power to shape the corporate investment decision processes and appoint responsible people should be aware of creating context-specific balanced constellations of power, process and technology promotors. For instance, if a project steering committee shall provide the political support of investment projects, the respective committee members

1156 Cf. *Kornmeier* (2007), p. 22.
1157 Cf. *Hauschildt* (2001), p. 337.

(power promotors) must possess the required hierarchical power to accelerate decision processes.

Furthermore, the broad descriptions of the two company-specific investment decision processes represent potential solutions or alternatives to cope with these arising emerging market challenges. For instance, TechCo's "SMART"[1158] product concept has been specifically developed to address emerging market needs by applying consistent localization processes and cost engineering.[1159] Similarly, this work explored that the development of local, talented people represents an effective way to implement foreign investments and establish the new businesses in the host countries.[1160] In particular in China and India, GasCo and TechCo actively search for **local high potentials** to prepare them for global management careers. This approach combines several advantages. Local people do not have to overcome communication barriers due to cultural misunderstandings or language problems. The necessary organizational knowledge and underlying management approaches are imparted to these local talents by global management trainee programs. Especially, the emerging middle classes in China and India imply growing market-seeking foreign investment projects which require a sophisticated understanding of local market preferences. It is beneficial for foreign MNCs to make use of local human resources to cope with the disadvantages of foreign corporations in psychically-distant countries. Thereby, local management talents have to be sensitized for global corporate governance standards due to the different comprehensions of business ethics.

The last main managerial implication is attributable to the important role of culture within the business world. The country-level cases illustrated that cultural considerations are of special importance with respect to HR management in China and India as opposed to Russia and India. A strictly hierarchy-orientated society and the concept of losing "face" seem to represent the two most significant cultural influences on the working habits in these countries. Due to indirect communication and reactive working styles, expatriates must be aware of adapting their **leadership styles** to the foreign habits. Managers of foreign MNCs need to be more control-focused to be able to anticipate arising problems. Open criticisms within the presence of other people are unusual due to the fear of losing "face" which is synonymous with social isolation. Therefore, expatriates must adopt culturally adapted leadership styles by pursuing a cautious conflict management. Due to these cultural barriers, highly qualified local people are usually more effective in their host environments. For this reason, MNCs shift their attitudes to develop local management talents with global mindsets.

5.3 Limitations and perspectives

Like all empirical investigations, this study is subject to certain conceptual and methodological **limitations**. These limitations have to be considered in order to reflect and

1158 SMART means simple, maintenance-friendly, affordable, reliable and timely-to-market.

1159 See section 4.1.2.3.4.

1160 In earlier days, foreign investments in developing countries were primarily interested in gaining natural resources or cheap labor for simple activities.

evaluate the discussed empirical results and managerial implications above. Although the current research approach has been selected as the most adequate design for the pursued objectives, every empirical study is exposed to limitations. The most significant limitations are attributable to the restricted generalization opportunities, possible interview and interpretation biases as well as to the complex nature of the research objectives.

The most prevailing limitation is that the investigated decision process success drivers as well as the country-specific characteristics are based on two corporations within specific contexts. Although qualitative research does not intend to anchor empirical results within statistically representative samples, the focus on two specific corporations is associated with several limitations, especially with **limited generalization** opportunities. In particular the explored company-specific foreign investment decision processes are only partially transferrable to other corporations. For instance, it can be expected that investment decision processes of MNCs operating in other industries may exhibit different characteristics. The cross-company analysis between GasCo and TechCo already indicates that industry characteristics and underlying business models shape foreign investment decision pro-cesses. Closely-related to industry influence on decision processes is the individual perception of country-specific challenges. MNCs based in different business segments may face different challenges in these countries due to industry-specific foreign investment policies in particular. For instance, China tends to actively attract foreign corporations by initially granting preferred treatments for single industries that are locally less developed.

The second main limitation is attributable to possible **interview data** and **interpretation biases**. For the firm-level cases, the interview data may be biased due to the overrepresentation of business development interviews. This may have the consequences that the role of business development is overestimated within the foreign investment decision process. But due to the "snowballing" interview sampling approach[1161], which followed random patterns, it can be assumed that the business development teams are the driving forces within investment decision processes on the operational levels.

Moreover, the majority of interviews were held by **telephone.** Therefore, visual cues of the interviewees cannot be captured. Information conveyed in gestures is lost in telephone interviews which may influence the interpretation of the interview data. Due to the international focus of this study it was not possible to conduct the entire interviews personally in the respective countries which is a shortcoming related to the data collection process. Furthermore, single interviews are exposed to subjective opinions and statements given by the interviewee. Although the researcher intends to stay objective, the high personal involvement and intensive cooperation with the research partners may have created interpretation biases.

The final cross-level synthesis in section 4.3 is also associated with different **interpretation alternatives**. Possibly, other researchers would evaluate the country-specific

1161 See section 3.3.1.

forces that drive decision process speed or comprehensiveness in a different way. But this study provided a detailed description of country-specific challenges, firm-level investment decision processes as well as the line of argumentation and interpretation in order to create a better traceability for third parties and interested readers. Furthermore, a detailed documentation of the research process has been elaborated in section 3.3.

A last central limitation of this study is attributable to the **complex nature of the research topic**. The overall objective was to provide realistic and comprehensive insights into investment decision processes within MNCs and related country-specific challenges in BRIC countries. First, foreign investment decision processes affect a variety of corporate functions, hierarchy levels and regional units. These multi-personal processes in large MNCs cause multitudes of interfaces, interdependencies and underlying process contents, e.g. to develop the technical, financial, strategic or legal concept of investment cases. The second main driver of complexity is the consideration of four heterogeneous countries of Brazil, Russia, India and China. Due to this holistic research approach and complex research object not every aspect – whether on the firm- or country-level – can be investigated in detail in this study. Thus, this work provides interesting starting points for further research projects. The most prevailing further research opportunities are presented below to finalize this work.

Further qualitative case studies targeting MNCs corporations operating in other industries would be interesting to investigate whether the empirical results of this work are transferrable to other industry segments. In particular it would be worth investigating investments of **business-to-consumer MNCs** in BRIC countries in order to explore how these companies address local end customer preferences. It can be expected that cultural aspects are even more prevailing due to the importance of individual preferences in these business segments.

As described above, **German SMEs** have emerged as world leaders within their niche markets. These dynamic corporations continue to further enhance their global outlooks. Greenfield investments in BRIC countries may serve as an effective means of expanding their global leadership. For the reasons given above, it is worth investigating how these significantly smaller corporations manage these complex internationalization processes with lower organizational capabilities, like management resources. An in-depth case study may provide valuable insights into these questions.

Quantitative investigations may incorporate the results of this study within a survey-based design to test them on a broader empirical basis. For example, the identified **country-specific challenges** provide valuable starting points to design a quantitative study. Larger samples of MNCs with Greenfield investment experiences in BRIC countries can be approached to test the validity of the present research results. Thereby, this study can provide a basis to derive hypotheses. Besides the sheer identification or evaluation of country-specific challenges it would be of even greater practical relevance to explore how other experienced MNCs overcome these obstacles.

Equally, the importance or general relevance of the analytically deducted critical success factors for investment decision processes could be addressed within survey-based investigations. Decision process speed and decision process comprehensiveness have been suggested as the main drivers of successful investment decision processes. This work transferred the promotor model to the context of investment decision processes in order to propose an analytical solution to balance the conflicting forces of speed and comprehensiveness.

Furthermore, it is interesting to empirically explore the influence of **promotor troika** constellations within decision processes on the overall investment performance. A broader empirical basis in quantitative designs can focus on the identification of the role typologies in investment decision processes. Thereby, the influence of the power, technology or process promotors on the decision process speed and the decision process comprehensiveness can be tested in order to validate the results of this study.

Unambiguously, the BRIC countries possess excellent economic perspectives. Their emerging middle classes will change the global patterns of consumption and economic power. These countries accounting for more than 40% of the world population – will be even more focused by MNCs in order to stay ahead of their emerging market competitors. These expected tendencies will inevitably lead to massive **increases of investment flows to the BRICs**. For the reason given above, the research field of Greenfield investments in BRIC countries will certainly provide further exciting research opportunities.

Appendix A: Prior Research

Empirical research related to foreign investment evaluations

Author(s)	**Sample/Response rate**	**Aim of the research / research question**	**Main results**
Oblak/Helm (1980)	226 U.S. corporations of the Fortune 500 Index 58 (26%)	This paper investigates the capital budgeting methods that large U.S. MNCs use, as well as their procedures to estimate project returns, risk, and the required rate of return for foreign investment projects.	The results of the survey indicate that MNC are conducting more detailed analysis of their foreign projects. Compared to earlier results in 1966, they found that higher percentage of MNC use DCF methods and adjust for risk in foreign direct investments.
Kelly/ Philippatos (1982)	255 U.S. manufacturing MNC of the Fortune 500 Index 136 (54%)	The paper investigates the foreign investment valuations practices employed by large U.S. based multinational manufacturing companies.	IRR is the most common method. The authors come to the result that firms experiencing losses related to foreign risk would have developed more sophisticated risk evaluation methods. Many companies use a parent and subsidiary viewpoint. Furthermore the concrete implementation of capital budgeting methods depends on the target region.
Wilson (1993)	729 UK MNC of the Times 1000 Index 59 (8%) 20 interviews for further investigation	The study intends to examine the capital budgeting methods used by UK based MNC. A special focus is on the integration of risk in the financial evaluation techniques.	UK MNCs are not familiar with the incorporation of risk in the financial evaluation. UK MNCs are less sophisticated than Americans. A possible reason for not employing the theoretical concepts is that the organizational context of the decision process is not considered by theory.
Scholz (1996)	100 largest German companies with substantial foreign assets 61 (61%)	The study investigates the questions how risk is assessed by German companies for evaluating foreign projects.	The study provides evidence that a special risk assessment for evaluating foreign projects is not common in practice. Nevertheless, practitioners appreciate that more sophisticated techniques are needed.

To be continued

Fox (1999)	367 German-based companies of the "Germany's Top 500 Index" which have substantial foreign assets 231 (63%)	The author investigates the whole foreign direct investment process, especially how foreign direct investments are evaluated.	The results of the survey indicate that capital budgeting methods are modified subjectively to assess the special risks involved in foreign projects.
Block (2000)	483 MNC of the U.S. Fortune 1000 Index 146 (30%)	The study observes the latest capital budgeting methods used by U.S. MNC for international decisions.	In contrast to financial theory companies overstate the risk of FDI. They rather take the project perspective than the portfolio view. The study observes a mismatch between the cash flows and the discount rate. Project cash flows are inconsistently discounted with the corporate wide WACC.

Empirical research related to domestic investment evaluations – descriptive studies

Author(s)	**Sample/Response rate**	**Aim of the research / research question**	**Main results**
Mao (1970)	8 U.S. corporations Case study	The purpose of the study is to compare the current capital budgeting theory with the concepts adopted in practice.	The investigation provides evidence that there is a gap between the preferred capital budgeting methods by theory and practice. The paper offers six proposals with which current theory can be modified to make it better implementable and acceptable by practitioners.
Klammer (1972)	369 large U.S. manufacturing companies 184 (50%)	The author investigates the question if the evolution of more sophisticated capital budgeting methods during the last decades has changed the adopted concepts of practitioners.	The sophisticated capital budgeting methods of the 1950s obtained acceptance in the early 1970s. Nevertheless the theoretically inferior investment appraisal techniques like payback are still common practice.
Brigham (1975)	33 large U.S. corporation with representatives participating in MBA classes in five different universities 33 (100%)	The purpose of the paper is to explore to what extent the capital budgeting practices of practitioners are congruent with the financial literature.	The main conclusion is that the corporations are open-minded for the relatively new DCF methodology but the implementation is not consistent with the academic literature. Many firms use historical returns for hurdle rates instead of the weighted average cost of capital.
Schall et al. (1978)	424 U.S. corporation 189 (46%)	The authors inquire the capital budgeting techniques employed, the calculation of the discount rate and cash flows, and the method of estimating and adjusting for project risk.	The paper provides evidence that the trend toward use of sophisticated capital budgeting techniques continues. Most of the firms are combining DCF models with payback or accounting rate of return. After-tax weighted average cost of capital is the common method of determining the required rate of return. Project risk is usually assessed subjectively.

To be continued

Rosenblatt/ Jucker (1979)	Summary of empirical research concerning the capital budgeting process and techniques n/a	The aim of the research is to outline the different surveys concerning capital budgeting techniques and to identify trends through time.	The different surveys indicate that the practice is getting more familiar with time-value-of-money concepts like NPV or IRR through time. Nevertheless static measures like the payback period are still the most frequently used.
Gitman/ Mercurio (1982)	1000 U.S. corporations of the Fortune 1000 - Index (the 1000 largest US companies) 177 (18%)	The study intends to discover the cost of capital concepts employed by major U.S. corporations. The findings provide indications for further targeted management education to close the gap between theory and practice.	The paper displays a significant gap between financial theory and practice. A minority of firms understand to implement the cost of capital techniques presented in recent financial research. The authors propose that the exchange between theory and practice must be more effectively organized.
Moore/ Reichert (1983)	500 U.S. corporations of the Fortune 500 Index 298 (60%)	The aim of the study is to examine the extent and manner in which sophisticated financial management methods are implemented by large corporations.	Sophisticated capital budgeting techniques are used by the main part of major U.S. corporations. Equally firm size and the utilization rates of sophisticated capital budgeting methods are directly related. Differences between industries concerning the implementation of modern capital budgeting tools are explained by firm size. Some industries have significantly smaller corporations which is an indicator for lower utilization rates.
Ross (1986)	15 large manufacturing companies 15 (Interviews)	The study intends to examine capital allocation practices by in-depth analysis of 15 large manufacturing companies.	Most companies of the sample use DCF methods. For smaller projects most firms simplify their DCF practices or just focus on payback. The results indicate that different practices are in use depending on the project size and the decision responsibility.

To be continued

Barton et al. (1992)	500 UK corporations of the Times 1000 Index 100 (20%)	The paper analyses the view of CEOs and COOs of the respective subsidiaries on the investment decision making process.	Many decentral divisions see the parent as a constraining factor to create competitive advantages through rationing capital or rapid payback. The parent companies understand their roles in preventing ill-judged investments by imposed capital budgets and strict financial criteria. There are essential differences of opinion between divisions and their parents about the roles they play in the strategic investment decision process.
Sangster (1993)	491 Scottish companies of Jordan's Scotland's Top 500 Companies 94 (22%)	The paper investigates the current investment appraisal techniques employed by the largest Scottish companies. Furthermore the results are compared to earlier studies concerning capital budgeting methods of UK companies to identify trends through time.	The results are that payback is the most popular model followed by IRR. Consistent to earlier findings IRR is preferred to NPV despite the theoretical superiority of the latter. In general the adoption of time-value-of-money increased during the last decade. The author explains this trend towards more sophisticated methods by the fast development of information technology and the growth of management education.
Pike (1996)	129 largest UK listed companies 99 (78%)	The paper intends to present the findings from a longitudinal study based on surveys conducted at five-year intervals between 1975 and 1992. The author tries to investigate trends through time in capital budgeting methods implementation.	The authors explored the greatest changes in the area of risk analysis, net present value analysis and post-completion audits. Furthermore the adoption of so-called sophisticated capital budgeting methods is increased so that the observed gap between theory and practice is insignificant. He explains this development by the evolution of information technology and management education.

To be continued

Farragher/ Kleiman (1999)	379 U.S. corporations of the Standard & Poor's Industrial Index 128 (34%)	The paper considers the entire investment decision process. Capital investment practices of U.S.-based companies are analyzed and compared to the results of former studies.	The companies under investigation use fairly sophisticated capital investment processes. Most responding companies connect corporate strategy and capital investment analysis. Almost all companies forecast their project returns on a cash, rather than income, basis. The main method is the DCF evaluation, but post-audit are not often operated on this basis.
Arnold/ Hatzopoulos (2000)	300 UK corporations of the Times 1000 Index 96 (32%)	The study investigates the extent to which sophisticated investment appraisal techniques are employed by UK based corporations.	The results indicate that UK corporations have increasingly adopted investment appraisal techniques preferred by theory, especially DCF methods. Just a small minority does not use sophisticated methods like formal risk analysis or dynamic capital budgeting methods.
Filbeck (2000)	130 U.S. family businesses 61 (47%)	The aim of the research is to explore which capital budgeting, working capital management and risk adjustment techniques are established.	Larger family businesses or corporations with outside influence tend to use more sophisticated and modern capital budgeting techniques than smaller firms with no outside influence.

To be continued

Gitman/ Vandenberg (2000)	1000 U.S. corporations of the U.S. Fortune 1000 Index 111 (11%)	The paper surveys the cost of capital practices of major U.S. companies and compares the results with an earlier study of the author. The findings are integrated in the investigations of earlier studies during the last 17 years.	The study provides a longitudinal comparison by using a similar sample and questionnaire. The key results are that practitioners are getting more familiar with sophisticated cost of capital concepts like the CAPM. Many firms changed their methodology during the last 17 years and move towards the proposed concepts by theory.
Manigart (2000)	USA: 73 (24%) UK: 66 (58%) France: 32 (24%) Holland:24 (41%) Belgium:14 (50%)	The paper examines the differences of investment appraisal techniques used by venture capitalists based in the USA, UK, France, Belgium and Holland.	Between-country differences concerning the due diligence and valuation stages and the importance of accounting and financial information are discovered. The paper provides further evidence of the fragmented nature of the venture capital industry.
Ryan/Ryan (2002)	all U.S. corporations of the Fortune 1000 Index 205 (21%)	This study examines the capital budgeting decision methods used by the U.S. Fortune 1000 companies.	Discounted capital budgeting methods are generally preferred over non-discounted techniques. NPV is the most popular method followed by IRR. The vast majority of respondents agree that WACC is the best starting point to determine the appropriate discount rate.
Block (2005)	1000 U.S. corporations of the U.S. Fortune 1000 Index 302 (30%)	The paper analyzes if the increased sophistication of capital budgeting methods used in practice take place across all industries.	Dependencies between industries for goal setting, determining the required rate of return and utilizing portfolio effect considerations are detected. The results could partially be explained by different finance patterns across industries that affect the hurdle rate.

Empirical research related to domestic investment evaluations – explanatory studies

Author(s)	**Sample/Response rate**	**Aim of the research / research question**	**Main results**
Haka et al. (1985)	50 Pairs of U.S.-listed companies (Interviews) 30 (60%)	The study investigates the effect on a corporation's market performance of switching from naive to sophisticated capital budgeting techniques.	The results of the study provide no significant relationship between the adoption of sophisticated capital budgeting methods and superior market performance. One possible explanation is that companies implement new capital budgeting techniques during times of economic stress.
Moore/ Reichert (1989)	500 U.S. corporations of the Fortune 500 Index 313 (63%)	The study investigates the relationship of firm performance and the adoption of modern analytical tools and financial techniques.	Superior firm performance is correlated with managerial sophistication. Better than average firm performance is measured as ROI compared to the industry sector. Modern capital budgeting techniques are indicators for managerial sophistication.
Farragher et al. (2001)	379 U.S. corporations of the Standard & Poor's Industrial Index 128 (34%)	The study tries to measure the relationship between capital budgeting sophistication and corporate performance. The difference to previous investigations is that the authors use a more comprehensive measure of capital budgeting sophistication.	There is no significant relationship between degree of capital budgeting sophistication and corporate performance discovered. Corporate performance is measured as operating rate of return. Further analysis should be focused on the relationship between business performance and newer capital budgeting methods like economic value added or real options.

Appendix B: Kick-off interview questions

1. Entire process

No.	Questions	Key area
1	a. Could you please explain your investment strategy? b. What were the main investment regions during the last five years? What are the most important investment regions in the medium and long term for your company? c. Does your company have an investment strategy for BRIC countries? If yes, could you please explain the main features of this strategy? d. Could you please provide a list of implemented and completed investments of the last three to five years?	Investment strategy
2	a. Could you describe how investment decision processes are organized within your company? b. Does your company differentiate between foreign and domestic investments? If yes, what are the major process-related differences? c. How would you evaluate the degree of standardization? d. Does your company have formalized investment handbooks? If yes, who has developed them and what are the main contents?	Investment decision process
3	a. How does your company coordinate investment opportunities? b. Which corporate units are usually involved in investment processes?	Investment coordination
4	a. How are investments linked to the strategic planning process? b. How is the interface between investments and capital allocation designed?	Strategy – capital allocation – investments
5	a. What kind of role does management accounting play in foreign investment decision processes? b. Which tasks are performed by management accountants and what are their responsibilities?	Management accounting

2. Initialization phase

No.	Questions	Key area
1	a. How do investment ideas or opportunities arise within your organization? b. Where do investment stimuli come from (hierarchy level, business function, operating unit etc.)? c. What are the differences between foreign and domestic investments in this early stage? d. Has your company implemented an institutionalized screening process for investments? If yes, how is this process designed and who is involved?	Investment stimuli
2	a. What kind of parties are usually involved within the investment decision process in the early stage? b. Has your company institutionalized investment committees? If yes, could you please describe the different committees' compositions, their purposes and decision authorities?	Related parties
3	a. How does your company summarize investment ideas to business cases or investment proposals? b. What are the major content-related differences between domestic and foreign investment proposals? c. What kind of forecast related to investments does your company conduct? Could you please describe differences between foreign and domestic investments? d. What are the most important milestones prior to the final investment decision?	Investment preparation
4	a. Are there any other important aspects to consider during the initialization of the investment which I did not address?	Miscellaneous

3. Approval phase

No.	Questions	Key area
1	a. How are investment decisions made? b. How are investment decision authorities distributed? c. How is the approval system designed at your company (e.g. based on the investment volume)? f. Do foreign investment decisions require special approvals?	Investment decision
2	a. What instruments do you use to evaluate investments proposals? b. What kind of qualitative (quantitative) analysis does your company conduct and who is responsible for the preparation? c. How does your company evaluate and consider country risks within the investment proposal? d. How is the physical/technical investment configuration connected to the financial evaluation?	Investment proposals
3	a. Which KPIs/financial figures/ratios or hurdle rates does your company use to evaluate investments? b. Which capital budgeting methods does your company use? c. How does your company modify capital budgeting methods for foreign investments? d. What role does risk analysis play in foreign investment evaluations compared to domestic projects? e. How do you evaluate and select specific investment locations (country, city etc)?	Capital budgeting
4	a. Do you draw on external consultants or local experts (for foreign investments) to prepare investment decisions? If yes, concerning which issues do you consult them?	External consultants
5	a. Are there any other important aspects to consider during the approval of the investment which I did not address?	Miscellaneous

4. Implementation phase

No.	Questions	Key area
1	a. Who is involved in the operational planning for the implementation of investments? b. How are project organizations and teams established? How is the project management set up? c. Does your company use a special project management organization for foreign investments?	Operational planning
2	a. How is the implementation process managed? b. What are typical milestones of the investment implementation? c. How are operational responsibilities and decision authorities allocated? d. What are the main decisions during the investment implementation?	Implementation process
3	a. How is the project reporting designed? b. What kind of information must be reported to the executive board? c. How does your company monitor the project progress (e.g. time, cost, progress etc.)?	Project reporting
4	a. What are the key challenges related to investments in the emerging markets (BRIC, MENA) compared to domestic investments? b. Do you remember a foreign investment of your company where the host country specifics had a major influence on the project progress (e.g. political risks, climate conditions, culture etc.)? If yes, could you please explain the background?	Country specifics
5	a. Are there any other important aspects to consider during the investment implementation which I did not address?	Miscellaneous

5. Start-up and control phase

No.	Questions	Key area
1	a. How does your company document improvement potentials for further investments? b. Has your company established a process for learning and development related to foreign investments, e.g. lessons-learned? If yes, how is it designed?	Learning & development
2	a. Which control mechanisms are used by your headquarter for new foreign subsidiaries (e.g. written company manuals, training of foreign managers at the headquarter, performance reports or transfer of expatriates)?	Control mechanism
3	a. How does your company fill manager vacancies at foreign operations? b. How is the transfer of management know-how organized? c. Please indicate to which degree the headquarter uses expatriates to directly control foreign subsidiaries' operations. d. To which degree does your headquarters provide training for managers before they assume their jobs at the foreign subsidiaries?	Foreign management
4	a. Which type of responsibility centers does your company use to set up foreign subsidiaries (e.g. cost, profit, investment center)? c. What kind of responsibilities does the foreign management board have? d. Who sets strategic directives?	Foreign organization
5	a. What are the key performance indicators (KPI) during and after the start-up of the project? b. Who sets performance targets? c. How does the headquarter evaluate the performance (headquarter's vs. subsidiaries' perspective)? d. How does your company differentiate between different perspectives (e.g. management evaluation vs. project evaluation)?	Performance evaluation

Appendix C: List of interviews

No.	Company	Job position	Nationality	Professional experience
1	TechCo	Management	German	> 15 years
2	TechCo	Management	German	> 15 years
3	TechCo	Management	German	> 15 years
4	TechCo	Management	Brazilian	> 15 years
5	TechCo	Management	Indian	> 15 years
6	TechCo	Management	German	> 15 years
7	TechCo	Management	German	> 15 years
8	TechCo	Management	German	> 15 years
9	TechCo	Management Accounting	Russian	10 - 15 years
10	TechCo	Management Accounting	German	10 - 15 years
11	TechCo	Management Accounting	French	10 - 15 years
12	TechCo	Management Accounting	British	10 - 15 years
13	TechCo	Management Accounting	French	10 - 15 years
14	TechCo	Management Accounting	German	5 - 10 years
15	TechCo	Business Development	German	10 - 15 years
16	TechCo	Business Development	American	10 - 15 years
17	TechCo	Business Development	American	5 - 10 years
18	TechCo	Business Development	Indian	10 - 15 years
19	TechCo	Business Development	German	> 15 years
20	TechCo	Business Development	British	10 - 15 years
21	TechCo	Business Development	German	10 - 15 years
22	TechCo	Business Development	American	10 - 15 years
23	TechCo	Business Development	German	10 - 15 years
24	TechCo	Business Development	German	10 - 15 years
25	TechCo	Business Development	French	10 - 15 years
26	TechCo	Business Development	British	5 - 10 years
27	TechCo	Business Development	Iranian	10 - 15 years
28	GasCo	Management	German	> 15 years
29	GasCo	Management	German	> 15 years
30	GasCo	Management	German	> 15 years
31	GasCo	Management	British	> 15 years
32	GasCo	Management	French	> 15 years
33	GasCo	Management	Indian	10 - 15 years
34	GasCo	Management	French	> 15 years
35	GasCo	Management	Indian	> 15 years
36	GasCo	Management	American	10 - 15 years
37	GasCo	Management Accounting	Dutch	10 - 15 years
38	GasCo	Management Accounting	German	> 20 years
39	GasCo	Management Accounting	German	10 - 15 years
40	GasCo	Management Accounting	German	> 20 years
41	GasCo	Business Development	Indian	> 20 years
42	GasCo	Business Development	German	> 20 years
43	GasCo	Business Development	French	> 20 years
44	GasCo	Business Development	Brazilian	> 20 years
45	GasCo	Business Development	Indian	> 20 years
46	GasCo	Business Development	Chinese	> 20 years
47	GasCo	Business Development	German	10 - 15 years
48	GasCo	Business Development	Indian	> 20 years
49	GasCo	Business Development	Indian	10 - 15 years
50	GasCo	Business Development	German	10 - 15 years
51	GasCo	Business Development	German	> 20 years
52	GasCo	Business Development	Chinese	10 - 15 years

List of references

A

A.T. Kearney (2010): Facts that will shape the world, available at: www.atkearney.de, last revised 5 March 2013.

Agarwal, S./Ramaswami, S. N. (1992): Choice of Foreign Market Entry Mode: Impact of Ownership, Location and Internalization Factors, in: Journal of International Business Studies, 23 (1), p. 1–27.

Aggarwal, A. (2002): Liberalisation, Multinational Enterprises and Export Performance: Evidence from Indian Manufacturing, in: Journal of Development Studies, 38 (3), p. 119–137.

Aggarwal, R. (1980): Corporate Use of Sophisticated Capital Budgeting Techniques: A Strategic Perspective and a Critique of Survey Results, in: Interfaces, 10 (2), p. 31–34.

Agndal, H./Nilsson, U. (2010): Different open book accounting practices for different purchasing strategies, in: Management Accounting Research, 21 (3), p. 147–166.

Agrawal, J./Kamakura, W. A. (1999): Country of origin: A competitive advantage?, in: International Journal of Research in Marketing, 16 (4), p. 255–267.

Aharoni, Y. (1966): The Foreign Investment Decision Process, Boston.

Aharoni, Y. (1971): On the definition of a multinational corporation, in: The Quarterly Review of Economics and Business, 11 (3), p. 27–37.

Aharoni, Y. (1999): The foreign investment decision process, in: Buckley, P. J./Ghauri, P. N. (eds.): The internationalization of the firm, 2nd ed., London, p. 3–13.

Al Qur'an, M. N. (2012): Successful Outward Foreign Direct Investment: Saudi Lessons and Recommendations, in: Ramady, M. A. (ed.): The GCC Economies. Stepping Up To Future Challenges, New York, p. 157–164.

Al Sulaiti, K. I./Baker, M. J. (1998): Country of origin effects: a literature review, in: Marketing Intelligence & Planning, 16 (3), p. 150–199.

Albarran, P./Carrasco, R./Holl, A. (2011): Domestic transport infrastructure and firms' export market participation, in: Small Business Economics, published online (www.springer.com), p. 1–20.

Alfaro, L./Chanda, A./Kalemli-Ozcan, S./Sayek, S. (2004): FDI and economic growth: the role of local financial markets, in: Journal of International Economics, 64 (1), p. 89–112.

Algieri, B. (2011): The Dutch Disease: evidences from Russia, in: Economic Change and Restructuring, 44 (3), p. 243–277.

Al-Laham, A. (1997): Strategieprozesse in deutschen Unternehmungen – Verlauf, Struktur und Effizienz, Wiesbaden.

Alon, I./Lattemann, C./Fetscherin, M./Li, S./Schneider, A. M. (2010): Usage of public corporate communications of social responsibility in Brazil, Russia, India and China (BRIC), in: International Journal of Emerging Markets, 5 (1), p. 6–22.

Amado, G./Brasil, H. V. (1991): Organizational behaviors and cultural context: the Brazilian" jeitinho", in: International Studies of Management & Organization, 21 (3), p. 38–61.

Amann, E./Baer, W. (2012): Brazil as an emerging economy: a new economic miracle?, in: Revista de Historia Económica, 32 (3), p. 412–423.

Amann, E. (2011): A New Brazilian Economic Miracle?, in: CESifo Forum, 12 (1), p. 32–36.

Amann, E./Baer, W. (2005): From the developmental to the regulatory state: the transformation of the government's impact on the Brazilian economy – The Regulation of Development and the Development of Regulation, in: The Quarterly Review of Economics and Finance, 45 (2-3), p. 421–431.

Andersen, P. H./Skaates, M. A. (2004): Ensuring validity in qualitative international business research, in: Marschan-Piekkari, R./Welch, C. (eds.): Handbook of qualitative research methods for international business, Cheltenham, p. 464–485.

Andersen, P. H./Strandskov, J. (1997): International Market Selection – A cognitive mapping perspective, in: Journal of Global Marketing, 11 (3), p. 65–84.

Anderson, C. R./Zeithaml, C. P. (1984): Stage of the Product Life Cycle, Business Strategy, and Business Performance, in: The Academy of Management Journal, 27 (1), p. 5–24.

Anderson, E./Gatignon, H. (1986): Modes of Foreign Entry: A Transaction Cost Analysis and Propositions, in: Journal of International Business Studies, 17 (3), p. 1–26.

Anderson, J. C./Hakansson, H./Johanson, J. (1994): Dyadic Business Relationships within a Business Network Context, in: The Journal of Marketing, 58 (4), p. 1–15.

Andrew, D. (2012): Institutional policy innovation in aviation, in: Journal of Air Transport Management, 21 (1), p. 36–39.

Anfara, V. A./Brown, K. M./Mangione, T. L. (2002): Qualitative Analysis on Stage: Making the Research Process More Public, in: Educational Researcher, 31 (7), p. 28–38.

Antle, R./Eppen, G. D. (1985): Capital Rationing and Organizational Slack in Capital Budgeting, in: Management Science, 31 (2), p. 163–174.

Arbeitskreis Finanzierung der Schmalenbach-Gesellschaft Deutsche Gesellschaft für Betriebswirtschaftslehre e.V. (1994): Investitions-Controlling – Zum Problem der Informationsverzerrung bei Investitionsentscheidungen in dezentralisierten Unternehmen, in: Zeitschrift für betriebswirtschaftliche Forschung, 46 (11), p. 899–925.

Ardichvili, A./Jondle, D./Kowske, B./Cornachione, E./Li, J./Thakadipuram, T. (2012): Ethical cultures in large business organizations in Brazil, Russia, India, and China, in: Journal of Business Ethics, 105 (4), p. 415–428.

Arino, A./Abramov, M. (1997): Partner selection and trust building in West European-Russian joint ventures: A western perspective, in: International Studies of Management & Organization, 27 (1), p. 19–37.

Armijo, L. E. (2007): The BRICs Countries (Brazil, Russia, India, and China) as Analytical Category: Mirage or Insight?, in: Asian Perspective, 31 (4), p. 7–42.

Arnold, G. C./Hatzopoulos, P. D. (2000): The Theory-Practice Gap in Capital Budgeting: Evidence from the United Kingdom, in: Journal of Business Finance & Accounting, 27 (5/6), p. 603.

Aslund, A. (2010): Why doesn't Russia join the WTO?, in: The Washington Quarterly, 33 (2), p. 49–63.

Atherton, A./Elsmore, P. (2007): Structuring qualitative enquiry in management and organization research: A dialogue on the merits of using software for qualitative data analysis, in: Qualitative Research in Organizations and Management, 2 (1), p. 62–77.

Atkinson, R./Flint, J. (2001): Accessing hidden and hard-to-reach populations: Snowball research strategies, in: Social Research Update, 33 (1), p. 1–4.

B

Baines, A./Langfield-Smith, K. (2003): Antecedents to management accounting change: a structural equation approach, in: Accounting, Organizations and Society, 28 (7-8), p. 675–698.

Balabanis, G./Diamantopoulos, A./Mueller, R. D./Melewar, T. C. (2001): The Impact of Nationalism, Patriotism and Internationalism on Consumer Ethnocentric Tendencies, in: Journal of International Business Studies, 32 (1), p. 157–175.

Barkema, H. G./Shenkar, O./Vermeulen, F./Bell, J. H. J. (1997): Working Abroad, Working with Others: How Firms Learn to Operate International Joint Ventures, in: The Academy of Management Journal, 40 (2), p. 426–442.

Barney, J. (1991): Firm Resources and Sustained Competitive Advantage, in: Journal of Management, 17 (1), p. 99–120.

Barney, J. B. (1986): Strategic Factor Markets: Expectations, Luck, and Business Strategy, in: Management Science, 32 (10), p. 1231–1241.

Bartlett, C. A./Ghoshal, S. (1999): Managing across borders – The transnational solution, Boston, Mass.

Bartlett, C. A./Ghoshal, S. (2000): Transnational management – Text, cases, and readings in cross-border management, Boston, Mass.

Barton, H./Brown, D./Cound, J./Marsh, P./Willey, K. (1992): Does top management add value to investment decisions?, in: Long Range Planning, 25 (5), p. 43–58.

Baum, H.-G./Coenenberg, A. G./Günther, T. (2007): Strategisches Controlling, 4th. edn., Stuttgart.

Baum, J. R./Wally, S. (2003): Strategic decision speed and firm performance, in: Strategic Management Journal, 24 (11), p. 1107–1129.

Bäurle, I. (1996): Internationalisierung als Prozeßphänomen, Eichstätt.

Becker, M. (2005): Controlling von Internationalisierungsprozessen, Wiesbaden.

Beena, P. L./Bhandari, L./Bhaumik, S./Gokarn, S./Tandon, A. (2004): Foreign direct investment in India, in: Estrin, S./Meyer, K. E. (eds.): Investment strategies in emerging markets, Cheltenham, p. 124–146.

Behrmann, J. N. : Some patterns in the rise of the multinational enterprise, Research paper 18, Graduate School of of Business Administration, University of North Carolina at Chapel Hill.

Bekaert, G./Harvey, C. R. (2002): Research in emerging markets finance: looking to the future, in: Emerging Markets Review, 3 (4), p. 429–448.

Benito, G. R. G./Gripsrud, G. (1992): The Expansion of Foreign Direct Investments: Discrete Rational Location Choices or a Cultural Learning Process?, in: Journal of International Business Studies, 23 (3), p. 461–476.

Bennett, J. A. (1997): A case for theory triangulation, in: Nursing Science Quarterly, 10 (2), p. 97–102.

Berger, U./Bernhard-Mehlich, I. (2006): Die Verhaltenswissenschaftliche Entscheidungstheorie, in: Kieser, A. (ed.): Organisationstheorien, 6th edn., Stuttgart, p. 168–214.

Betschinger, M.-A. (2010): International trade and investment agreements and foreign direct investment activities in developing and emerging economies – Evidence from Japanese multinational companies, Hamburg.

Betts, P./Hill, A. L. J. (2010): BP's Russian misadventure may be useful experience, available at: www.ft.com, last revised 11 June 2010.

Biggemann, S./Fam, K.-S. (2011): Business marketing in BRIC countries – Business-to-Business Marketing in the BRIC Countries, in: Industrial Marketing Management, 40 (1), p. 5–7.

Bird, R. C./Cahoy, D. R. (2007): Emerging BRIC Economies: Lessons from Intellectual Property Negotiation and Enforcement, in: Northwestern Journal of Technology and Intellectual Property, 5 (3), p. 400–425.

Birkinshaw, J./Hood, N./Jonsson, S. (1998): Building firm-specific advantages in multinational corporations: the role of subsidiary initiative, in: Strategic Management Journal, 19 (3), p. 221–241.

Birkinshaw, J./Hood, N. (2000): Characteristics of Foreign Subsidiaries in Industry Clusters, in: Journal of International Business Studies, 31 (1), p. 141–154.

Bivolaru, E./Andrei, R./Purcaroiu, V. (2009): Branding Romania: A PESTEL framework based on a comparative analysis of two country brand indexes, in: Management & Marketing, 4 (4), p. 101–112.

Blank, S. (2012): The End of Russian Power in Asia?, in: Orbis, 56 (2), p. 249–266.

Blasberg, M./Kotynek, M. (2012): Die versenkten Milliarden. **Die Zeit,** available at: www.zeit.de, last revised 3. February 2013.

Block, S. (2000): Integrating traditional capital budgeting concepts into an international decision-making environment, in: Engineering Economist, 45 (4), p. 309–325.

Block, S. (2005): Are there differences in capital budgeting procedures between industries? – An empirical study, in: Engineering Economist, 50 (1), p. 55–67.

Boddewyn, J. J. (1979): Foreign Divestment: Magnitude and Factors, in: Journal of International Business Studies, 10 (1), p. 21–27.

Boddewyn, J. J. (1983): Foreign and Domestic Divestment and Investment Decisions: Like or Unlike?, in: Journal of International Business Studies, 14 (3), p. 23–35.

Boeh, K. K./Beamish, P. W. (2012): Travel time and the liability of distance in foreign direct investment: Location choice and entry mode, in: Journal of International Business Studies, 43 (5), p. 525–535.

Bonelli, R. (1999): A Note on Foreign Direct Investment and Industrial Competitiveness in Brazil, in: Oxford Development Studies, 27 (3), p. 305–327.

Borchardt, A./Göthlich, S. E. (2009): Erkenntnisgewinnung durch Fallstudien, in: Albers, S./Klapper, D./Konradt, U./Walter, A./Wolf, J. (eds.): Methodik der empirischen Forschung, 3.th edn., Wiesbaden, p. 33–48.

Borensztein, E./Ostry, J. D. (1996): Accounting for China's Growth Performance, in: The American Economic Review, 86 (2), p. 224–228.

Borodina, S. D./Shvyrkov, O. (2010): Investing in BRIC countries – Evaluating risk and governance in Brazil, Russia, India, & China, New York.

Bourgeois, L. J. (1981): On the Measurement of Organizational Slack, in: The Academy of Management Review, 6 (1), p. 29–39.

Bower, J. L. (1970): Managing the Resource Allocation Process – A Study of Corporate Planning and Investment, Boston.

Boynton, A. C./Zmund, R. W. (1984): An assessment of critical success factors, in: Sloan Management Review, 25 (4), p. 17–27.

Brewer, P. (2001): International market selection: developing a model from Australian case studies, in: International Business Review, 10 (2), p. 155–174.

Brewer, P. A. (2007): Operationalizing Psychic Distance: A Revised Approach, in: Journal of International Marketing, 15 (1), p. 44–66.

Brigham, E. F. (1975): Hurdle Rates for Screening Capital Expenditure Proposals, in: Financial Management, 4 (3), p. 17–26.

Bringer, J. D./Johnston, L. H./Brackenridge, C. H. (2004): Maximizing Transparency in a Doctoral Thesis: The Complexities of Writing About the Use of QSR*NVIVO Within a Grounded Theory Study, in: Qualitative Research, 4 (2), p. 247–265.

Broadman, H. G. (2008): China and India Go to Africa: New Deals in the Developing World, in: Foreign Affairs, 87 (2), p. 95–109.

Brod, M./Tesler, L./Christensen, T. (2009): Qualitative research and content validity: developing best practices based on science and experience, in: Quality of Life Research, 18 (9), p. 1263–1278.

Brouthers, K. D./Hennart, J. F. (2007): Boundaries of the firm: Insights from international entry mode research, in: Journal of Management, 33 (3), p. 395–425.

Brühl, R. (2006): Fortschrittskonzeption in der Wissenschaftstheorie, in: Wirtschaftswissenschaftliches Studium, 35 (11), p. 594–599.

Brun, J. F./Combes, J. L./Renard, M. F. (2002): Are there spillover effects between coastal and non-coastal regions in China?, in: China Economic Review, 13 (2-3), p. 161–169.

Brunninge, O./Nordqvist, M./Wiklund, J. (2007): Corporate Governance and Strategic Change in SMEs: The Effects of Ownership, Board Composition and Top Management Teams, in: Small Business Economics, 29 (3), p. 295–308.

Buckley, P. J. (2007): Is the relationship between inward FDI and spillover effects linear? An empirical examination of the case of China, in: Journal of International Business Studies, 38 (3), p. 447–459.

Buckley, P. J./Clegg, J./Tan, H. (2004): Knowledge transfer to China: policy lesson from foreign affiliates, in: Transnational Corporations, 13 (1), p. 31–72.

Buckley, P. J./Clegg J./Wang C. (2002a): The Impact of Inward FDI on the Performance of Chinese Manufacturing Firms, in: Journal of International Business Studies, 33 (4), p. 637–655.

Buckley, P. J./Clegg, J./Tan, H. (2006): Cultural awareness in knowledge transfer to China – The role of guanxi and mianzi, in: Journal of World Business, 41 (3), p. 275–288.

Buckley, P. J./Clegg, J./Wang, C. (2002b): The Impact of Inward FDI on the Performance of Chinese Manufacturing Firms, in: Journal of International Business Studies, 33 (4), p. 637–655.

Burnard, P. (1994): The telephone interview as a data collection method, in: Nurse Education Today, 14 (1), p. 67–72.

Burns, J. O. (1980): Transfer Pricing Decisions in U. S. Multinational Corporations, in: Journal of International Business Studies, 11 (2), p. 23–39.

Butler, K. C./Joaquin, D. C. (1998): A Note on Political Risk and the Required Return on Foreign Direct Investment, in: Journal of International Business Studies, 29 (3), p. 599–607.

C

Calantone, R. J./Tamer Cavusgil, S./Schmidt, J. B./Shin, G.-C. (2004): Internationalization and the Dynamics of Product Adaptation – An Empirical Investigation, in: Journal of Product Innovation Management, 21 (3), p. 185–198.

Carr, C./Tomkins, C. (1996): Strategic investment decisions: the importance of SCM. A comparative analysis of 51 case studies in U.K., U.S. and German companies, in: Management Accounting Research, 7 (2), p. 199–217.

Carr, E. C. J./Worth, A. (2001): The use of the telephone interview for research, in: Journal of Research in Nursing, 6 (1), p. 511–524.

Carrillo, J. E./Franza, R. M. (2006): Investing in product development and production capabilities: The crucial linkage between time-to-market and ramp-up time, in: European Journal of Operational Research, 171 (2), p. 536–556.

Castiglione, C./Gorbunova, Y./Infante, D./Smirnova, J. (2012): FDI determinants in an idiosyncratic country. A reappraisal over the Russian regions during transition years, in: Communist and Post-Communist Studies, 45 (1-2), p. 1–10.

Caves, R. E. (1974): Multinational Firms, Competition, and Productivity in Host-Country Markets, in: Economica, 41 (162), p. 176–193.

Cavusgil, S. T./Zou, S./Naidu, G. M. (1993): Product and Promotion Adaptation in Export Ventures: An Empirical Investigation, in: Journal of International Business Studies, 24 (3), p. 479–506.

Chakrabarti, A. K. (2007): The division of labour in innovation management, in: R&D Management, 19 (2), p. 161–171.

Chakravarthy, B. S./Doz, Y. (1992): Strategy Process Research: Focusing on Corporate Self-Renewal, in: Strategic Management Journal, 13 (1), p. 5–14.

Chamon, M./Mauro, P./Okawa, Y. (2008): Mass car ownership in the emerging market giants, in: Economic Policy, 23 (54), p. 243–296.

Chan, S. (2005): Is There a Power Transition between the U.S. and China? The Different Faces of National Power, in: Asian Survey, 45 (5), p. 687–701.

Chang, S.-J./Rosenzweig, P. M. (2001): The Choice of Entry Mode in Sequential Foreign Direct Investment, in: Strategic Management Journal, 22 (8), p. 747–776.

Chehab, E. G. (2010): A guiding light for investors in Brazil, in: Borodina, S. D./Shvyrkov, O. (eds.): Investing in BRIC countries. Evaluating risk and governance in Brazil, Russia, India, & China, New York, p. 3–23.

Chen, V. Z. (2012): Puzzles and Truths About Indian Outward FDI: Toward a More Relevant and Nuanced Research Agenda on Emerging Market MNEs, in: AIB Insights, 12 (3), p. 10–14.

Cheng, B.-S./Chou, L.-F./Wu, T.-Y./Huang, M.-P./Farh, J.-L. (2004): Paternalistic leadership and subordinate responses: Establishing a leadership model in Chinese organizations, in: Asian Journal of Social Psychology, 7 (1), p. 89–117.

Cheng, H. F./Gutierrez, M./Mahajan, A./Shachmurove, Y./Shahrokhi, M. (2007): A future global economy to be built by BRICs, in: Global Finance Journal, 18 (2), p. 143–156.

Cheng, L. K./Kwan, Y. K. (2000): What are the determinants of the location of foreign direct investment? The Chinese experience, in: Journal of International Economics, 51 (2), p. 379–400.

Cheung, P. T. Y. (2012): China's changing regional development: Trends, strategies and challenges in the 12th Five-Year Plan (2011–2015) period, in: Asia Pacific Viewpoint, 53 (1), p. 1–6.

Child, J. (1981): Culture, contingency and capitalism in the cross-national study of organizations, in: Research in Organizational Behavior, 3 (1), p. 303–356.

Child, J./Rodrigues, S. B./Frynas, J. G. (2009): Psychic distance, its impact and coping modes, in: Management International Review, 49 (2), p. 199–224.

Chiu, J. (2013): Chinese port operators step up investment overseas, available at: www.wallstreetjournal.com, last revised 5 May 2013.

Christopherson, S. (2007): Barriers to "US style" lean retailing: the case of Wal-Mart's failure in Germany, in: Journal of Economic Geography, 7 (4), p. 451–469.

Christy, G. A. (1966): Capital Budgeting – Current Practices and their Efficiency, Oregon.

Cieri, H. de/Cox, J. W./Fenwick, M. (2007): A review of international human resource management: Integration, interrogation, imitation, in: International Journal of Management Reviews, 9 (4), p. 281–302.

Clarke, A. (1999): A practical use of key success factors to improve the effectiveness of project management, in: International Journal of Project Management, 17 (3), p. 139–145.

Coenenberg, A. G./Günther, T. (2011): Grundlagen der strategischen, operativen und finanzwirtschaftlichen Unternehmenssteuerung, in: Busse von Colbe, W./Coenenberg, A. G./Kajüter, P./Linnhoff, U./Pellens, B. (eds.): Betriebswirtschaft für Führungskräfte, 4th edn., Stuttgart, p. 1–28.

Cohen, A. (2006): The North European Gas Pipeline Threatens Europe's Energy Security. **The Heritage Foundation,** available at: www.heritage.org, last revised 8 April 2013.

Contractor, F. J./Kumar, V./Kundu, S. K./Pedersen, T. (2010): Reconceptualizing the Firm in a World of Outsourcing and Offshoring: The Organizational and Geographical Relocation of High-Value Company Functions, in: Journal of Management Studies, 47 (8), p. 1417–1433.

Conway, P./de Rosa, D./Nicoletti, G./Steiner, F. (2006): Product Market Regulation and Productivity Convergence – OECD Economics Department Working Paper No.509, available at: http://papers.ssrn.com/sol3/papers.cfm?abstract_id=929677, last revised 2 March 2013.

Cooper, D. J./Morgan, W. (2008): Case Study Research in Accounting, in: Accounting Horizons, 22 (2), p. 159–178.

Cooper, R. G./Kleinschmidt, E. J. (1985): The Impact of Export Strategy on Export Sales Performance, in: Journal of International Business Studies, 16 (1), p. 37–55.

Copeland, T./Koller, T./Murrin, J. (1990): Valuation – Measuring and managing the value of companies, New York.

Corbin, J. M./Strauss, A. L. (2008): Basics of qualitative research – Techniques and procedures for developing grounded theory, Los Angeles.

Corden, W. M. (1984): Booming Sector and Dutch Disease Economics: Survey and Consolidation, in: Oxford Economic Papers, 36 (3), p. 359–380.

Cray, D. (1984): Control and Coordination in Multinational Corporations, in: Journal of International Business Studies, 15 (2), p. 85–98.

Crespo, N./Fontoura, M. P. (2007): Determinant factors of FDI spillovers – what do we really know?, in: World Development, 35 (3), p. 410–425.

Creswell, J. W./Hanson, W. E./Plano Clark, V. L./Morales, A. (2007): Qualitative Research Designs Selection and Implementation, in: The Counseling Psychologist, 35 (2), p. 236–264.

Creswell, J. W. (1994): Research design – Qualitative & quantitative approaches, Thousand Oaks, Calif.

Crowston, K. (1997): A Coordination Theory Approach to Organizational Process Design, in: Organization Science, 8 (2), p. 157–175.

Cuervo-Cazurra, A./Maloney, M. M./Manrakhan, S. (2007): Causes of the difficulties in internationalization, in: Journal of International Business Studies, 38 (5), p. 709–725.

Cyert, R. M./March, J. C. (1963): A Behavioral Theory of the Firm, Englewood Cliffs.

D

Dahlhaus, C. (2009): Investitions-Controlling in dezentralen Unternehmen – Anreizsysteme als Instrument zur Verhaltenssteuerung im Investitionsprozess, Wiesbaden.

Danmarks Nationalbank (2004): Monetary Review 4th Quarter 2004 – The BRIC Countries, available at: www.royalmint.dk, last revised 3 March 2013.

Davidson, W. H. (1980): The Location of Foreign Direct Investment Activity: Country Characteristics and Experience Effects, in: Journal of International Business Studies, 11 (2), p. 9–22.

Davidson, W. H. (1983): Market similarity and market selection: Implications for international marketing strategy, in: Journal of Business Research, 11 (4), p. 439–456.

Day, G. S./Montgomery, D. B. (1983): Diagnosing the Experience Curve, in: Journal of Marketing, 47 (2), p. 44–58.

Dean, J. W. (1996): Does decision process matter? A study of strategic decision-making effectiveness, in: Academy of Management Journal, 39 (2), p. 368–396.

Dehnen, H. S. (2012): Markteintritt in Emerging market economies – Entwicklung eines Internationalisierungsprozessmodells, Wiesbaden.

Denzin, N. K. (1990): Review essay: Writing the Interpretive, Postmodern Ethnography, in: Journal of Contemporary Ethnography, 19 (2), p. 231–236.

Denzin, N. K./Lincoln, Y. S. (2011): Introduction: The discipline and practice of qualitative research, in: Denzin, N. K./Lincoln, Y. S. (eds.): The Sage handbook of qualitative research, 4. ed., Los Angeles, p. 1–20.

Depner, H./Bathelt, H. (2005): Exporting the German model: the establishment of a new automobile industry cluster in Shanghai, in: Economic Geography, 81 (1), p. 53–81.

Deshpandé, R./Farley, J. U. (1999): Corporate Culture and Market Orientation: Comparing Indian and Japanese Firms, in: Journal of International Marketing, 7 (4), p. 111–127.

Devarajan, S./Lewis, J. D./Robinson, S. (1993): External Shocks, Purchasing Power Parity, and the Equilibrium Real Exchange Rate, in: The World Bank Economic Review, 7 (1), p. 45–63.

Dhanaraj, C./Lyles, M. A./Steensma, H. K./Tihanyi, L. (2004): Managing Tacit and Explicit Knowledge Transfer in IJVs: The Role of Relational Embeddedness and the Impact on Performance, in: Journal of International Business Studies, 35 (5), p. 428–442.

Dierickx, I./Cool, K. (1989): Asset Stock Accumulation and Sustainability of Competitive Advantage, in: Management Science, 35 (12), p. 1504–1511.

Dittmann, I./Maug, E./Schneider, C. (2010): Bankers on the Boards of German Firms: What They Do, What They Are Worth, and Why They Are (Still) There, in: Review of Finance, 14 (1), p. 35–71.

Djankov, S./McLiesh, C./Ramalho, R. M. (2006): Regulation and growth, in: Economics Letters, 92 (3), p. 395–401.

Doney, P. M./Cannon, J. P./Mullen, M. R. (1998): Understanding the Influence of National Culture on the Development of Trust, in: The Academy of Management Review, 23 (3), p. 601–620.

Doz, Y./Prahalad, C. K. (1984): Patterns of Strategic Control within Multinational Corporations, in: Journal of International Business Studies, 15 (2), p. 55–72.

Drews, H. (2008): Abschied vom Marktwachstums-Marktanteils-Portfolio nach über 35 Jahren Einsatz? Eine kritische Überprüfung der BCG-Matrix, in: Zeitschrift für Planung & Unternehmenssteuerung, 19 (1), p. 39–57.

Dückert, T. (2009): Erfolgsfaktoren für das Management strategischer Investitionen – Eine empirische Untersuchung investitionsintensiver Industrien, Chemnitz.

Duncan, R. B. (1972): Characteristics of Organizational Environments and Perceived Environmental Uncertainty, in: Administrative Science Quarterly, 17 (3), p. 313–327.

Dunfee, T. W./Warren, D. E. (2001): Is Guanxi Ethical? A Normative Analysis of Doing Business in China, in: Journal of Business Ethics, 32 (3), p. 191–204.

Dunning, J. H. (1993): The nature of transnational corporations and their activities, in: Dunning, J. H. (ed.): The theory of transnational corporations, New York, p. 1–21.

E

Ebers, M./Gotsch, W. (2006): Institutionenökonomische Theorien der Organisation, in: Kieser, A. (ed.): Organisationstheorien, 6th edn., Stuttgart, p. 247–308.

Eberstadt, N. (2010): The Demographic Future, in: Foreign Affairs, 89 (6), p. 54–63.

Eden, L./Miller, S. R. (2004): Distance matters: Liability of foreignness, institutional distance and ownership strategy, in: Hitt, M. A./Cheng, J. L. C. (eds.): The Evolving Theory of the Multinational Firm. Advances in International Management, Vol. 16, Amsterdam, p. 187–221.

Egelhoff, W. G. (1984): Patterns of Control in U. S., UK, and European Multinational Corporations, in: Journal of International Business Studies, 15 (2), p. 73–83.

Eisenhardt, K. M./Graebner, M. E. (2007): Theory building from cases: Opportunities and challenges, in: Academy of Management Journal, 50 (1), p. 25–32.

Eisenhardt, K. M. (1989a): Agency Theory: An Assessment and Review, in: The Academy of Management Review, 14 (1), p. 57–74.

Eisenhardt, K. M. (1989b): Building Theories from Case Study Research, in: The Academy of Management Review, 14 (4), p. 532–550.

Eisenhardt, K. M. (1989c): Making Fast Strategic Decisions in High-Velocity Environments, in: The Academy of Management Journal, 32 (3), p. 543–576.

Eisenhardt, K. M./Bourgeois III, L. J. (1988): Politics of Strategic Decision Making in High-Velocity Environments: Toward a Midrange Theory, in: The Academy of Management Journal, 31 (4), p. 737–770.

Eiteman, D. K./Stonehill, A. I./Moffett, M. H. (2010): Multinational business finance, 12th. edn., Boston.

Ekeledo, I./Sivakamur, K. (2004): International market entry mode strategies of manufacturing firms and service firms: A resource-based perspective, in: International Marketing Review, 21 (1), p. 68–101.

Elliott, G. R./Cameron, R. C. (1994): Consumer Perception of Product Quality and the Country-of-Origin Effect, in: Journal of International Marketing, 2 (2), p. 49–62.

Epstein, M. J./Roy, M.-J. (2007): Implementing a corporate environmental strategy: establishing coordination and control within multinational companies, in: Business Strategy and the Environment, 16 (6), p. 389–403.

Erickson, F. (2011): A history of qualitative inquiry in social and educational research, in: Denzin, N. K./Lincoln, Y. S. (eds.): The Sage handbook of qualitative research, 4. ed., Los Angeles, p. 43–61.

Eriksson, K./Johanson, J./Majkgard, A./Sharma, D. D. (1997): Experiential Knowledge and Cost in the Internationalization Process, in: Journal of International Business Studies, 28 (2), p. 337–360.

Ernst, D./Aman, T./Großmann, M./Lump, D. (2012): Internationale Unternehmensbewertung – Ein Praxisleitfaden, München.

Ernst, D./Häcker, J. (2012): Applied International Corporate Finance, 2nd. edn., München.

Erramilli, M. K. (1991): The Experience Factor in Foreign Market Entry Behavior of Service Firms, in: Journal of International Business Studies, 22 (3), p. 479–501.

Erzberger, C. (1998): Zahlen und Wörter – Die Verbindung quantitativer und qualitativer Daten und Methoden im Forschungsprozeß, Weinheim.

Estrin, S./Prevezer, M. (2011): The role of informal institutions in corporate governance: Brazil, Russia, India, and China compared, in: Asia Pacific Journal of Management, 28 (1), p. 41–67.

Evans, K. D./Kosec, K. (2012): Early child education: making programs work for Brazil's most important generation – A World Bank Study, Washington.

F

Fabry, N./Zeghni, S. (2002): Foreign direct investment in Russia: how the investment climate matters, in: Communist and Post-Communist Studies, 35 (3), p. 289–303.

Fabry, N./Zeghni, S. (2006): How former communist countries of Europe may attract inward foreign direct investment? A matter of institutions, in: Communist and Post-Communist Studies, 39 (2), p. 201–219.

Fahey, L. (1981): On strategic management decision processes, in: Strategic Management Journal, 2 (1), p. 43–60.

Fan, S./Chan-Kang, C. (2008): Regional road development, rural and urban poverty: Evidence from China, in: Transport Policy, 15 (5), p. 305–314.

Farragher, E. J./Kleiman, R. T./Sahu, A. P. (2001): The association between the use of sophisticated capital budgeting practices and corporate performance, in: The Engineering Economist, 46 (4), p. 300–311.

Farragher, E. J./Kleiman, R. T. (1999): Current Capital Investment Practices, in: Engineering Economist, 44 (2), p. 137–150.

Ferderer, J. P. (1993): The Impact of Uncertainty on Aggregate Investment Spending: An Empirical Analysis, in: Journal of Money, Credit and Banking, 25 (1), p. 30–48.

Fereday, J./Muir-Cochrane, E. (2008): Demonstrating rigor using thematic analysis: A hybrid approach of inductive and deductive coding and theme development, in: International Journal of Qualitative Methods, 5 (1), p. 80–92.

Fey, C. F./Denison, D. R. (2003): Organizational Culture and Effectiveness: Can American Theory Be Applied in Russia?, in: Organization Science, 14 (6), p. 686–706.

Filatotchev, I. (2006): Corporate governance and business strategies in Russia, in: Jain, S. C. (ed.): Emerging economies and the transformation of international business. Brazil, Russia, India and China (BRICs), Cheltenham, Northampton, p. 111–137.

Filbeck, G. (2000): Financial management techniques in family businesses, in: Family Business Review, 13 (3), p. 201.

Financial Times (2008): TNK-BP under renewed Gazprom pressure, available at: www.ft.com, last revised 2 March 2013.

Financial Times (2013): Bosch set to exit solar activities, available at: www.ft.com, last revised 8 April 2013.

Fischer, L. D. (2006): Internationalität der Unternehmung – Aktueller Forschungsstand, Analyse und Konzeptualisierung, Bamberg.

Fischer, T. M. (1993): Kostenmanagement strategischer Erfolgsfaktoren: Instrumente zur operativen Steuerung der strategischen Schlüsselfaktoren Qualität, Flexibilität und Schnelligkeit, München.

Fiss, P. C./Zajac, E. J. (2004): The Diffusion of Ideas over Contested Terrain: The (Non)adoption of a Shareholder Value Orientation among German Firms, in: Administrative Science Quarterly, 49 (4), p. 501–534.

Fitzpatrick, M. (1983): The Definition and Assessment of Political Risk in International Business: A Review of the Literature, in: The Academy of Management Review, 8 (2), p. 249–254.

Fitzpatrick, M. (2000): Blat in Stalin's time, in: Ledeneva, A. V./Lovell, S./Rogachevski, A. (eds.): Bribery and blat in Russia, Basingstoke, p. 166–182.

Flick, U. (1992): Triangulation Revisited: Strategy of Validation or Alternative?, in: Journal for the Theory of Social Behaviour, 22 (2), p. 175–197.

Flick, U. (2008a): Design und Prozess qualitativer Forschung, in: Flick, U./Kardoff, E. von/Steinke, I. (eds.): Qualitative Forschung, Reinbek bei Hamburg, p. 252–265.

Flick, U. (2008b): Triangulation in der qualitativen Forschung, in: Flick, U./Kardoff, E. von/Steinke, I. (eds.): Qualitative Forschung, Reinbek bei Hamburg, p. 309–318.

Flick, U. (2009): Sozialforschung – Methoden und Anwendungen, Reinbek bei Hamburg.

Flick, U. (2010): Qualitative Sozialforschung – Eine Einführung, Reinbek bei Hamburg.

Flyvbjerg, B. (2006): Five misunderstandings about case-study research, in: Qualitative Inquiry, 12 (2), p. 219–245.

Forman, J./Damschroder, L. (2008): Qualitative content analyis, in: Jacoby, L./Siminoff, L. A. (eds.): Empirical methods for bioethics, Amsterdam, London, p. 39–62.

Forsgren, M. (2002): The concept of learning in the Uppsala internationalization process model: a critical review, in: International Business Review, 11 (3), p. 257–277.

Fox, J. (1999): Integration des Controlling in den Entscheidungsprozess bei Auslandsinvestitionen, Frankfurt.

Frank, U. (2007): Wissenschaftstheorie, in: Köhler, R./Küpper, H.-U./Pfingsten, A. (eds.): Handwörterbuch der Betriebswirtschaft, 6th edn., Stuttgart, Sp. 2010–2017.

Fredrickson, J. W. (1984): The Comprehensiveness of Strategic Decision Processes: Extension, Observations, Future Directions, in: The Academy of Management Journal, 27 (3), p. 445–466.

Fredrickson, J. W. (1986): The Strategic Decision Process and Organizational Structure, in: The Academy of Management Review, 11 (2), p. 280–297.

Fredrickson, J. W./Mitchell, T. R. (1984): Strategic Decision Processes: Comprehensiveness and Performance in an Industry with an Unstable Environment, in: The Academy of Management Journal, 27 (2), p. 399–423.

Freund, Y. P. (1988): Critical success factors, in: Strategy & Leadership, 16 (4), p. 20–23.

Froud, J./Haslam, C./Johal, S./Williams, K. (2000): Shareholder value and Financialization: consultancy promises, management moves – Economy and Society, in: Economy and Society, 29 (1), p. 80–110.

Fruhan, W. E. (1979): Financial strategy – Studies in the creation, transfer, and destruction of shareholder value, Homewood.

Frye, T. (2010): Corruption and rule of law, in: Aslund, A./Guriev, S./Kuchins, A. (eds.): Russia after the global economic crisis, Washington, p. 79–94.

Fukumoto, T./Muto, I. (2012): Rebalancing China's Economic Growth: Some Insights from Japan's Experience, in: China & World Economy, 20 (1), p. 62–82.

Fülbier, R. U. (2004): Wissenschaftstheorie und Betriebswirtschaftslehre, in: Wirtschaftswissenschaftliches Studium, 34 (5), p. 266–271.

G

Gaddis, P. O. (1966): Analyzing overseas investment, in: Harvard Business Review, 8 (3), p. 115–122.

Gaida, I. W./Wanner, M./Werners, T.-J. (2008): Investitionsprozesse im Großunternehmen, in: Hirzel, M./Kühn, F./Gaida, I. (eds.): Prozessmanagement in der Praxis, Wiesbaden, p. 119–132.

Gälweiler, A. (2005): Strategische Unternehmensführung, 3rd. edn., Frankfurt am Main.

Gamble, J. (2000): Localizing management in foreign-invested enterprises in China: practical, cultural, and strategic perspectives, in: International Journal of Human Resource Management, 11 (5), p. 883–903.

Gammeltoft, P./Pradhan, J. P./Goldstein, A. (2010): Emerging multinationals: home and host country determinants and outcomes, in: International Journal of Emerging Markets, 5 (3/4), p. 254–265.

Gaur, A. S./Lu, J. W. (2007): Ownership strategies and survival of foreign subsidiaries: Impacts of institutional distance and experience, in: Journal of Management, 33 (1), p. 84–110.

Gemünden, H. G./Walter, A. (1995): Der Beziehungspromoter, in: Zeitschrift für Betriebswirtschaft, 65 (9), p. 971–986.

Gerber, T. P./Schaefer, D. R. (2004): Horizontal Stratification of Higher Education in Russia: Trends, Gender Differences, and Labor Market Outcomes, in: Sociology of Education, 77 (1), p. 32–59.

Gerring, J. (2004): What Is a Case Study and What Is It Good for?, in: The American Political Science Review, 98 (2), p. 341–354.

Ghauri, P. N. (2004): Designing and conducting case studies in international business research, in: Marschan-Piekkari, R./Welch, C. (eds.): Handbook of qualitative research methods for international business, Cheltenham, p. 109–124.

Ghauri, P. N./Santangelo, G. D. (2012): Multinationals and the Changing Rules of Competition, in: Management International Review, 52 (2), p. 145–154.

Giddy, I. H. (1981): The Cost of Capital in the International Firm, in: Managerial and Decision Economics, 2 (4), p. 263–271.

Gilbert, L. S. (2002): Going the distance: 'closeness' in qualitative data analysis software, in: International Journal of Social Research Methodology, 5 (3), p. 215–228.

Gilroy, B. M./Lukas, E. (2006): The choice between greenfield investment and cross-border acquisition: A real option approach, in: The Quarterly Review of Economics and Finance, 46 (3), p. 447–465.

Gitlin, L. N./Fuentes, P. (2012): The Republic of Chile: An Upper Middle-Income Country at the Crossroads of Economic Development and Aging, in: The Gerontologist, 52 (3), p. 297–305.

Gitman, L. J./Mercurio, V. A. (1982): Cost of Capital Techniques Used by Major U.S. Firms: Survey and Analysis of Fortune's 1000, in: Financial Management, 11 (4), p. 21–29.

Gitman, L. J./Vandenberg, P. A. (2000): Cost of Capital Techniques Used by Major US Firms: 1997 vs. 1980, in: Financial Practice and Education, 10 (2), p. 53–68.

Glaser, B. G. (1998): Doing grounded theory – Issues and discussions, Mill Valley.

Glaser, B. G./Strauss, A. L. (1967): Discovery of Grounded Theory – Strategies for Qualitative Research, New York.

Gläser, J./Laudel, G. (2010): Experteninterviews und qualitative Inhaltsanalyse als Instrumente rekonstruierender Untersuchungen, Wiesbaden.

Glaum, M./Grothe, A./Hutzschenreuter, T. (2009): Besonderheiten internationaler Akquisitionen, in: Schmid, S. (ed.): Management der Internationalisierung, Wiesbaden, p. 143–181.

Goldman, M. I. (2004): Putin and the Oligarchs, in: Foreign Affairs, 83 (6), p. 33–44.

Grant, R. M. (1996): Toward a Knowledge-Based Theory of the Firm, in: Strategic Management Journal, 17 (Special Issue Summer), p. 109–122.

Graser, S. (2011): Realwirtschaftliche und finanzwirtschaftliche Internationalisierung – Die besondere Relevanz für Emerging Market Multinationals, Wiesbaden.

Greene, J. C. (2008): Is Mixed Methods Social Inquiry a Distinctive Methodology?, in: Journal of Mixed Methods Research, 2 (1), p. 7–22.

Grochla, E. (1978): Einführung in die Organisationstheorie, Stuttgart.

Gupta, A. K./Govindarajan, V. (2002): Cultivating a Global Mindset, in: The Academy of Management Executive, 16 (1), p. 116–126.

Gupta, S./Navare, J./Melewar, T. C. (2011): Investigating the implications of business and culture on the behaviour of customers of international firms, in: Industrial Marketing Management, 40 (1), p. 65–77.

Guriev, S./Rachinsky, A. (2005): The role of oligarchs in Russian capitalism, in: The Journal of Economic Perspectives, 19 (1), p. 131–150.

H

Haddad, M./Harrison, A. (1993): Are there positive spillovers from direct foreign investment?: Evidence from panel data for Morocco, in: Journal of Development Economics, 42 (1), p. 51–74.

Haka, S. F. (2007): A Review of the Literature on Capital Budgeting and Investment Appraisal: Past, Present, and Future Musings, in: Chapman, C. S./Hopwood, A. G./Shields, M. D. (eds.): Handbook of Management Accounting Research. Volume 2, Amsterdam, p. 697–728.

Haka, S. F./Gordon, L. A./Pinches, G. E. (1985): Sophisticated Capital Budgeting Selection Techniques and Firm Performance, in: The Accounting Review, 60 (4), p. 651–669.

Håkanson, L./Ambos, B. (2010): The antecedents of psychic distance, in: Journal of International Management, 16 (3), p. 195–210.

Han, C. M./Terpstra, V. (1988): Country-of-Origin Effects for Uni-National and Bi-National Products, in: Journal of International Business Studies, 19 (2), p. 235–255.

Handelsblatt (2007): Wo die meisten Produktpiraten hausen, available at: www.handelsblatt.com, last revised 20 January 2013.

Hanushek, E. A./Woessmann, L. (2007): The role of education quality in economic growth, World Bank Working Paper 4122, Washington.

Hanushek, E. A./Woessmann, L. (2008): The role of cognitive skills in economic development, in: Journal of Economic Literature, 46 (3), p. 607–668.

Harris, M./Raviv, A. (1996): The Capital Budgeting Process: Incentives and Information, in: The Journal of Finance, 51 (4), p. 1139–1174.

Harris, M./Raviv, A. (2002): Organization Design, in: Management Science, 48 (7), p. 852–865.

Hartleb, V. (2009): Brand Community Management – Eine empirische Analyse am Beispiel der Automobilbranche, Wiesbaden.

Harzing, A. W. (2002): Of bears, bumble-bees, and spiders: The role of expatriates in controlling foreign subsidiaries, in: Journal of World Business, 36 (4), p. 366–379.

Hastings, D. F. (1999): Lincoln Electric's Harsh Lessons from International Expansion, in: Harvard Business Review, 77 (3), p. 162–178.

Hauschildt, J. (2001): Promotoren – Erfolgsfaktoren für das Management von Innovationen, in: Zeitschrift für Organisation, 70 (6), p. 332–337.

Hauschildt, J./Chakrabarti, A. K. (1999): Arbeitsteilung im Innovationsmanagement, in: Hauschildt, J./Gemünden, H. G. (eds.): Promotoren. Champions der Innovation, 2nd edn., Wiesbaden, p. 66–87.

Hauschildt, J./Kirchmann, E. (1999): Zur Existenz und Effizienz von Prozesspromotoren, in: Hauschildt, J./Gemünden, H. G. (eds.): Promotoren. Champions der Innovation, 2nd edn., Wiesbaden, p. 89–107.

Hauschildt, J./Kirchmann, E. (2002): Teamwork for innovation–the 'troika' of promotors, in: R&D Management, 31 (1), p. 41–49.

Hauschildt, J./Schewe, G. (2000): Gatekeeper and process promotor: key persons in agile and innovative organizations, in: International Journal of Agile Management Systems, 2 (2), p. 96–103.

Hauschildt, J. (2004): Innovationsmanagement, 3rd. edn., München.

He, X./Cao, Y. (2007): Understanding High Saving Rate in China, in: China & World Economy, 15 (1), p. 1–13.

Heenan, D. A./Perlmutter, H. V. (1979): Multinational organization development, Reading (Mass.).

Hellgren, B./Stjernberg, T. (1995): Design and implementation in major investments – A project network approach, in: Scandinavian Journal of Management, 11 (4), p. 377–394.

Henderson, G. V., JR. (1979): In Defense of the Weighted Average Cost of Capital, in: Financial Management, 8 (3), p. 57–61.

Hendley, K. (2009): 'Telephone Law' and the 'Rule of Law' – The Russian Case, in: Hague Journal on the Rule of Law, 1 (2), p. 241–262.

Henisz, W. J./Williamson, O. E. (1999): Comparative economic organization within and between countries, in: Business and Politics, 1 (3), p. 261–277.

Henisz, W. J./Zelner, B. A. (2003): The strategic organization of political risks and opportunities, in: Strategic Organization, 1 (4), p. 451–460.

Hennart, J. F. (2003): Theories of the multinational enterprise, in: Rugman, A. M. (ed.): The Oxford handbook international business, Oxford, p. 127–149.

Hennart, J.-F./Park, Y.-R. (1993): Greenfield vs. Acquisition: The Strategy of Japanese Investors in the United States, in: Management Science, 39 (9), p. 1054–1070.

Hill, H. G., JR. (1955): Capital Expenditure Management, in: The Journal of Business, 28 (4), p. 285–290.

Hirst, M. K./Yetton, P. W. (1999): The effects of budget goals and task interdependence on the level of and variance in performance: a research note, in: Accounting, Organizations and Society, 24 (3), p. 205–216.

Hitt, M. A./Li, H./Worthington, W. J. (2005): Emerging markets as learning laboratories: Learning behaviors of local firms and foreign entrants in different institutional contexts, in: Management and Organization Review, 1 (3), p. 353–380.

Hitt, M. A./Hoskisson, R. E./Hicheon Kim (1997): International Diversification: Effects on Innovation and Firm Performance in Product-Diversified Firms, in: The Academy of Management Journal, 40 (4), p. 767–798.

Hodkinson, P./Hodkinson, H. (2001): The Strenghts and Limitations of Case Study Research – Paper presented at the learning and skills development agency conference, Cambridge.

Hofstede, G. (1983): National cultures in four dimensions, in: International Studies of Management & Organization, 13 (1/2), p. 46–74.

Holtbrügge, D. (2005): Configuration and Co-ordination of Value Activities in German Multinational Corporations, in: European Management Journal, 23 (5), p. 564–575.

Holtbrügge, D./Baron, A. (2011): Markteintrittsstrategien in Emerging Markets. Eine institutionentheoretische Studie in den BRIC-Staaten, in: Puck, J. F./Leitl, C. (eds.): Außenhandel im Wandel, Berlin/Heidelberg, p. 109–130.

Holtbrügge, D./Friedmann, C. B. (2011): Geschäftserfolg in Indien – Strategien für den vielfältigsten Markt der Welt, Berlin, Heidelberg.

Holtbrügge, D./Puck, J. F. (2008): Geschäftserfolg in China – Strategien für den größten Markt der Welt, Dordrecht.

Holtbrügge, D./Welge, M. K. (2010): Internationales Management – Theorien, Funktionen, Fallstudien, Stuttgart.

Hopf, C. (1995): Familie und Rechtsextremismus – Familiale Sozialisation und rechtsextreme Orientierungen junger Männer, Weinheim/München.

Hopf, C. (2008): Qualitative Interviews, in: Flick, U./Kardoff, E. von/Steinke, I. (eds.): Qualitative Forschung, Reinbek bei Hamburg, p. 349–359.

Hopf, C./Nevermann, K./Schmidt, I. (1985): Wie kamen die Nationalsozialisten an die Macht: eine empirische Analyse von Deutungen im Unterricht.

Hopf, C./Hartwig, M. (2001): Liebe und Abhängigkeit – Partnerschaftsbeziehungen junger Frauen, Weinheim.

Hopf, C./Hopf, W. (1997): Familie, Persönlichkeit, Politik – Eine Einführung in die politische Sozialisation, Weinheim.

Hoskisson, R. E./Eden, L./Lau, C. M./Wright, M. (2000): Strategy in Emerging Economies, in: The Academy of Management Journal, 43 (3), p. 249–267.

Howe, K. R. (1988): Against the Quantitative-Qualitative Incompatibility Thesis or Dogmas Die Hard, in: Educational Researcher, 17 (8), p. 10–16.

Hu, A. G. Z./Jefferson, G. H. (2002): FDI Impact and Spillover: Evidence from China's Electronic and Textile Industries, in: World Economy, 25 (8), p. 1063–1076.

Huang, Y./Tang, H. (2012): FDI Policies in China and India: Evidence from Firm Surveys, in: The World Economy, 35 (1), p. 91–105.

Huff, A. S./Reger, R. K. (1987): A Review of Strategic Process Research, in: Journal of Management, 13 (2), p. 211–236.

Hülst, D. (2010): Grounded Theory, in: Friebertshäuser, B./Boller, H./Richter, S. (eds.): Handbuch qualitative Forschungsmethoden in der Erziehungswissenschaft, 3rd edn., Weinheim, p. 281–300.

Humphrey, C./Scapens, R. W. (1996): Methodological themes: Theories and case studies of organizational accounting practices: limitation or liberation?, in: Accounting, Auditing & Accountability Journal, 9 (4), p. 86–106.

Hung, C. L. (2003): The Business of Product Counterfeiting in China and the Post-WTO Membership Environment, in: Asia Pacific Business Review, 10 (1), p. 58–77.

Hunter, W./Power, T. J. (2007): Rewarding Lula: Executive Power, Social Policy, and the Brazilian Elections of 2006, in: Latin American Politics and Society, 49 (1), p. 1–30.

Hutzschenreuter, T./Pedersen, T./Volberda, H. W. (2007): The role of path dependency and managerial intentionality: A perspective on international business research, in: Journal of International Business Studies, 38 (7), p. 1055–1068.

Hwang, K. K. (1998): Guanxi and mientze: Conflict resolution in Chinese society, in: Intercultural Communication Studies, 7 (1), p. 17–38.

Hymer, S. H. (1960): The international operations of national firms: a study of direct foreign investment, Cambridge.

I

International Monetary Fund (2012): World Economic Outlook, available at: http://www.imf.org, last revised 27 November 2012.

Ionascu, D./Meyer, K. E./Estrin, S. (2004): Institutional distance and international business strategies in emerging economies, William Davidson Institue Working Paper No. 728.

Isobe, T./Makino, S./Montgomery, D. B. (2000): Resource Commitment, Entry Timing, and Market Performance of Foreign Direct Investments in Emerging Economies: The Case of Japanese International Joint Ventures in China, in: The Academy of Management Journal, 43 (3), p. 468–484.

Ivarsson, I./Alvstam, C. G. (2005): Technology transfer from TNCs to local suppliers in developing countries: A study of AB Volvo's truck and bus plants in Brazil, China, India, and Mexico, in: World Development, 33 (8), p. 1325–1344.

J

Jahrreiß, W. (1984): Zur Theorie der Direktinvestitionen im Ausland, Berlin.

Jayme, F. G. (2003): Balance-of-Payments-Constrained Economic Growth in Brazil, in: Brazilian Journal of Political Economy, 23 (1), p. 62–84.

Jenkins, R. (2012): China and Brazil: Economic Impact of a Growing Relationship, in: Current Chinese Affairs, 41 (1), p. 21–47.

Jensen, M. C. (1976): Theory of the firm: Managerial behavior, agency costs and ownership structure, in: Journal of Financial Economics, 3 (4), p. 305–360.

Jensen, M. C. (1986): Agency Costs of Free Cash Flow, Corporate Finance, and Take-overs, in: The American Economic Review, 76 (2), p. 323–329.

Jensen, M. C. (1988): Takeovers: Their Causes and Consequences, in: The Journal of Economic Perspectives, 2 (1), p. 21–48.

Jeremias, R. (2012): Germany and Ireland unemployment compared, or why Germany profited from the world economic crisis, in: Working USA - The Journal of Labor and Society, 15 (2), p. 233–265.

Johanson, J. (1966): Swedish special steel in foreign markets, Uppsala.

Johanson, J./Vahlne, J. E. (1990): The mechanism of internationalisation, in: International Marketing Review, 7 (4), p. 11–24.

Johanson, J./Vahlne, J. E. (2009): The Uppsala internationalization process model revisited: From liability of foreignness to liability of outsidership, in: Journal of International Business Studies, 40 (9), p. 1411–1431.

Johanson, J./Wiedersheim-Paul, F. (1975): The internationalization of the firm - four Swedish cases, in: Journal of Management Studies, 12 (3), p. 305–323.

Johanson, J./Vahlne, J.-E. (1977): The Internationalization Process of the Firm – A Model of Knowledge Development and Increasing Foreign Market Commitments, in: Journal of International Business Studies, 8 (1), p. 23–32.

Johansson, J. K./Ronkainen, I. A./Czinkota, M. R. (1994): Negative Country-of-Origin Effects: The Case of the New Russia, in: Journal of International Business Studies, 25 (1), p. 157–176.

Johnson, J./Tellis, G. J. (2008): Drivers of success for market entry into China and India, in: Journal of Marketing, 72 (3), p. 1–13.

Johnson, R. B. (1997): Examining the validity structure of qualitative research, in: Education, 118 (2), p. 282–292.

Jonassen, D. H. (1991): Objectivism versus constructivism: Do we need a new philosophical paradigm?, in: Educational Technology Research and Development, 39 (3), p. 5–14.

Jones, A./Fallon, G./Golov, R. (2000): Obstacles to foreign direct investment in Russia, in: European Business Review, 12 (4), p. 187–197.

Judge, W. Q./Miller, A. (1991): Antecedents and outcomes of decision speed in different environmental context, in: Academy of Management Journal, 34 (2), p. 449–463.

K

Kaiser, U./Sofka, W. : The Pulse of Liability of Foreignness – Dynamic Legitimacy and Experience Effects in the German Car Market, Discussion Paper No. 06-070, Mannheim.

Kajüter, P. (2011): Wertorientierte Unternehmensführung, in: Busse von Colbe, W./Coenenberg, A. G./Kajüter, P./Linnhoff, U./Pellens, B. (eds.): Betriebswirtschaft für Führungskräfte, 4th edn., Stuttgart, p. 27–46.

Kaplan, R. S. (1986): The role for empirical research in management accounting, in: Accounting, Organizations and Society, 11 (4-5), p. 429–452.

Karakaya, F. (1993): Barriers to Entry in International Markets – Journal of Global Marketing, in: Journal of Global Marketing, 7 (1), p. 7–24.

Kedia, B. L./Lahiri, S./Mukherjee, D. (2006): BRIC economies: earlier growth constraints, contemporary transformations and future potential, and key challenges, in: Jain, S. C. (ed.): Emerging economies and the transformation of international business. Brazil, Russia, India and China (BRICs), Cheltenham, Northampton, p. 46–74.

Kee, H. L./Neagu, C./Nicita, A. (2011): Is Protectionism on the Rise? – Assessing National Trade Policies during the Crisis of 2008, World Bank Policy Research Working Paper No. 5274.

Kelle, U. (2008): Computergestütze Analyse qualitativer Daten, in: Flick, U./Kardoff, E. von/Steinke, I. (eds.): Qualitative Forschung, Reinbek bei Hamburg, p. 485–502.

Kelle, U./Laurie, H. (1995): Computer use in qualitative research and issues of validity, in: Kelle, U. (ed.): Computer-aided qualitative data analysis. Theory, methods and practice, London, p. 19–28.

Kelly, M. E. W./Philippatos, G. C. (1982): Comparative Analysis of the Foreign Investment Evaluation Practices by U. S.-Based Manufacturing Multinational Companies, in: Journal of International Business Studies, 13 (3), p. 19–42.

Kern, M. (1979): Klassische Erkenntnistheorien und moderne Wissenschaftslehre, in: Raffée, H./Abel, B. (eds.): Wissenschaftstheoretische Grundfragen der Wirtschaftswissenschaften, München, p. 11–27.

Khambata, D./Ajami, R. A. (1992): International business – Theory and practice, New York.

Khandwalla, P. N. (1972): Environment and its impact on the organization, in: International Studies of Management & Organization, 2 (3), p. 297–313.

Khang, D. B./Myint, Y. M. (1999): Time, cost and quality trade-off in project management: a case study, in: International Journal of Project Management, 17 (4), p. 249–256.

Khanna, T./Palepu, K. (2006): Emerging giants, in: Harvard Business Review, 84 (10), p. 60–69.

Khanna, T./Palepu, K. (2010): Winning in emerging markets: A road map for strategy and execution, Boston.

Khanna, T./Palepu, K./Sinha, J. (2005): Strategies that fit emerging markets, in: Harvard Business Review, 83 (6), p. 63–76.

Kieser, A./Walgenbach, P. (2010): Organisation, 6th. edn., Stuttgart.

Kim, S. H. (1981): An Empirical Study on the Relationship between Capital Budgeting Practices and Earnings Performance, in: The Engineering Economist, 27 (3), p. 185–196.

King, P. (1975): Is the Emphasis of Capital Budgeting Theory Misplaced?, in: Journal of Business Finance & Accounting, 2 (1), p. 69–82.

Klammer, T. (1972): Empirical Evidence of the Adoption of Sophisticated Capital Budgeting Techniques, in: The Journal of Business, 45 (3), p. 387–397.

Klammer, T. (1973): The Association of Capital Budgeting Techniques with Firm Performance, in: The Accounting Review, 48 (2), p. 353–364.

Klesse, H. J./Willershausen, F./Steinkircher, P. (2012): Kraft durch Ausländer, in: WirtschaftsWoche (Issue 25), 18 June 2012, p. 62–67.

Klochikhin, E. A. (2012): Russia's innovation policy: Stubborn path-dependencies and new approaches, in: Research Policy, 41 (9), p. 1620–1630.

Klooß, K./Lirsch, J. (2011) : Wie China deutsche Solarfirmen attackiert, in: Manager Magazin, available at: www.manager-magazin.de, on 17. August 2011.

Kobrin, S. J. (1979): Political Risk: A Review and Reconsideration, in: Journal of International Business Studies, 10 (1), p. 67–80.

Koch, T. (2006): Establishing rigour in qualitative research: the decision trail, in: Journal of Advanced Nursing, 53 (1), p. 91–100.

Kocher, M. G./Sutter, M. (2006): Time is money – Time pressure, incentives, and the quality of decision-making, in: Journal of Economic Behavior & Organization, 61 (3), p. 375–392.

Kochhar, K./Kumar, U./Rajan, R./Subramanian, A./Tokatlidis, I. (2006): India's pattern of development: What happened, what follows?, in: Journal of Monetary Economics, 53 (5), p. 981–1019.

Kokko, A. (1994): Technology, market characteristics, and spillovers, in: Journal of Development Economics, 43 (2), p. 279–293.

Kolbe, C. (1989): Investitionsrechnungen zur Beurteilung von Auslandsinvestitionen, Bergisch Gladbach.

Kornmeier, M. (2007): Wissenschaftstheorie und wissenschaftliches Arbeiten – Eine Einführung für Wirtschaftswissenschaftler, Heidelberg.

Kostova, T. (1999): Transnational Transfer of Strategic Organizational Practices: A Contextual Perspective, in: The Academy of Management Review, 24 (2), p. 308–324.

Kostova, T./Zaheer, S. (1999): Organizational Legitimacy under Conditions of Complexity: The Case of the Multinational Enterprise, in: The Academy of Management Review, 24 (1), p. 64–81.

Kotler, P. (1986): Global standardization—courting danger, in: The Journal of Consumer Marketing, 3 (2), p. 13–15.

Koubek, N. (2010): BRIC-Staaten - Ein neues Zentrum der Weltwirtschaft, in: Koubek, N. (ed.): Jenseits und Diesseits der Betriebswirtschaftslehre. Institutionen - Unternehmenstheorien - Globale Strukturen, Wiesbaden, p. 324–348.

KPMG (2011): Investment in Brazil, Sao Paulo.

KPMG and RSPP (2010): Increasing FDI in Russian Regions, available at: www.kpmg.com, last revised 4 August 2012.

Krefting, L. (1991): Rigor in Qualitative Research: The Assessment of Trustworthiness, in: The American Journal of Occupational Therapy, 45 (3), p. 214–222.

Kremin-Buch, B. (2007): Strategisches Kostenmanagement – Grundlagen und moderne Instrumente, Wiesbaden.

Kuckartz, U. (2010): Einführung in die computergestützte Analyse qualitativer Daten, Wiesbaden.

Kuckartz, U. (2012): Qualitative Inhaltsanalyse – Methoden, Praxis, Computerunterstützung, Weinheim.

Kuijs, L./Wang, T. (2006): China's Pattern of Growth: Moving to Sustainability and Reducing Inequality, in: China & World Economy, 14 (1), p. 1–14.

Kumar, N. (2009): How emerging giants are rewriting the rules of M&A, in: Harvard Business Review, 87 (5), p. 115–121.

Küpper, H.-U. (2008): Controlling – Konzeption, Aufgaben und Instrumente, 5th. edn., Stuttgart.

Kurz, A./Stockhammer, C./Fuchs, S./Meinhard, D. (2004): Das problemzentrierte Interview, in: Buber, R./Gadner, J./Richards, L. (eds.): Applying qualitative methods to marketing management research, Basingstoke, p. 463–475.

Kutschker, M./Schmid, S. (2011): Internationales Management, 7th. edn., München.

Kvint, V. (1994): Don't Give up on Russia, in: Harvard Business Review, 72 (2), p. 62–74.

L

Lamnek, S. (2010): Qualitative Sozialforschung – Lehrbuch, 5th. edn., Weinheim.

Lankes, H.-P./Venables, A. J. (1996): Foreign direct investment in economic transition: the changing pattern of investments, in: Economics of Transition, 4 (2), p. 331–347.

Larimo, J. (1995): The foreign direct investment decision process: Case studies of different types of decision processes in finnish firms, in: Journal of Business Research, 33 (1), p. 25–55.

Leavitt, H. J. (1964): Applied organizational change in industry – Structural, technical and human approaches, in: Cooper, W. W./Leavitt, H. J./Shelly II, M. W. (eds.): New perspectives in organization research, New York, p. 53–71.

Ledeneva, A. V. (1998): Russia's Economy of Favors: Blat, Networking and Informal Exchange, Cambridge.

Ledeneva, A. V. (2011): Telephone justice in Russia, in: The EU-Russia Centre Review, 6 (18), p. 4–22.

Ledeneva, A. (2008): Blat and Guanxi: Informal Practices in Russia and China, in: Comparative Studies in Society and History, 50 (1), p. 118–144.

Lemak, D. J./Bracker, J. S. (2006): A strategic contingency model of multinational corporate structure, in: Strategic Management Journal, 9 (5), p. 521–526.

Lessard, D. R. (1985): International Financial Management: Theory and Application, 2nd. edn., New York.

Levy, O./Schon Beechler/Taylor, S./Boyacigiller, N. A. (2007): What We Talk about When We Talk about "Global Mindset": Managerial Cognition in Multinational Corporations, in: Journal of International Business Studies, 38 (2), p. 231–258.

Lewin, A. Y./Massini, S./Peeters, C. (2009): Why Are Companies Offshoring Innovation? The Emerging Global Race for Talent, in: Journal of International Business Studies, 40 (6), p. 901–925.

Li, G.-H./Yu, C.-M./Seetoo, D.-H. (2010): Toward a Theory of Regional Organization, in: Management International Review, 50 (1), p. 5–33.

Li, X./Liu, X./Parker, D. (2001): Foreign direct investment and productivity spillovers in the Chinese manufacturing sector, in: Economic Systems, 25 (4), p. 305–321.

Lieberman, E. S. (2005): Nested Analysis as a Mixed-Method Strategy for Comparative Research, in: The American Political Science Review, 99 (3), p. 435–452.

Lieberman, M. B./Montgomery, D. B. (1988): First-mover advantages, in: Strategic Management Journal, 9 (1), p. 41–58.

Lilienthal, D. (1960): Management of the multinational corporation, in: Anshen, M./Bach G. (eds.): Management and corporations. A symposium held on the occasion of the 10th anniversary of the Graduate School of Industrial Administration, Westport, p. 119–158.

Lincoln, Y. S. (1995): Emerging Criteria for Quality in Qualitative and Interpretive Research, in: Qualitative Inquiry, 1 (3), p. 275–289.

Lincoln, Y. S./Guba, E. G. (1990): Judging the quality of case study reports – International Journal of Qualitative Studies in Education, in: International Journal of Qualitative Studies in Education, 3 (1), p. 53–59.

Liu, X./Buck, T./Shu, C. (2005): Chinese economic development, the next stage: outward FDI?, in: International Business Review, 14 (1), p. 97–115.

Liu, Y./Chen, D. (2012): Why China Will Democratize, in: The Washington Quarterly, 35 (1), p. 41–63.

Liu, Z. (2002): Foreign Direct Investment and Technology Spillover: Evidence from China, in: Journal of Comparative Economics, 30 (3), p. 579–602.

Locatelli, C./Rossiaud, S. (2011): A neoinstitutionalist interpretation of the changes in the Russian oil model, in: Energy Policy, 39 (9), p. 5588–5597.

Lorie, J. H./Savage, L. J. (1955): Three Problems in Rationing Capital, in: The Journal of Business, 28 (4), p. 229–239.

Lovett, S./Simmons, L. C./Kali, R. (1999): Guanxi versus the Market: Ethics and Efficiency, in: Journal of International Business Studies, 30 (2), p. 231–247.

Luk, C.-L./Yau, O. H. M./Sin, L. Y. M./Tse, A. C. B./Chow, R. P. M./Lee, J. S. Y. (2008): The Effects of Social Capital and Organizational Innovativeness in Different Institutional Contexts, in: Journal of International Business Studies, 39 (4), p. 589–612.

Luk, S. T. K./Fullgrabe, L./Li, S. C. Y. (1999): Managing Direct Selling Activities in China: A Cultural Explanation, in: Journal of Business Research, 45 (3), p. 257–266.

Luo, Y. (1997): Partner Selection and Venturing Success: The Case of Joint Ventures with Firms in the People's Republic of China, in: Organization Science, 8 (6), p. 648–662.

Luo, Y. (1998): Timing of Investment and International Expansion Performance in China, in: Journal of International Business Studies, 29 (2), p. 391–407.

Luo, Y. (2001): Determinants of local responsiveness: perspectives from foreign subsidiaries in an emerging market, in: Journal of Management, 27 (4), p. 451–477.

Luo, Y. (2003a): Market-Seeking MNEs in an Emerging Market: How Parent-Subsidiary Links Shape Overseas Success, in: Journal of International Business Studies, 34 (3), p. 290–309.

Luo, Y. (2003b): Industrial Dynamics and Managerial Networking in an Emerging Market: The Case of China, in: Strategic Management Journal, 24 (13), p. 1315–1327.

Luo, Y. (2007): Guanxi And Business, Singapore.

Luo, Y./Mezias, J. M. (2002): Liabilities of foreignness: Concepts, constructs, and consequences, in: Journal of International Management, 8 (3), p. 217–221.

Luo, Y./Park, S. H. (2001): Strategic alignment and performance of market-seeking MNCs in China, in: Strategic Management Journal, 22 (2), p. 141–155.

Luo, Y./Peng, M. W. (1999): Learning to Compete in a Transition Economy: Experience, Environment, and Performance, in: Journal of International Business Studies, 30 (2), p. 269–295.

Luo, Y./Shenkar, O./Nyaw, M. K. (2002): Mitigating liabilities of foreignness: Defensive versus offensive approaches, in: Journal of International Management, 8 (3), p. 283–300.

Luo, Y./Shenkar, O. (2006): The Multinational Corporation as a Multilingual Community: Language and Organization in a Global Context, in: Journal of International Business Studies, 37 (3), p. 321–339.

Luo, Y./Tung, R. L. (2007): International Expansion of Emerging Market Enterprises: A Springboard Perspective, in: Journal of International Business Studies, 38 (4), p. 481–498.

Luong, P. J./Weinthal, E. (2004): Contra coercion: Russian tax reform, exogenous shocks, and negotiated institutional change, in: The American Political Science Review, 98 (1), p. 139–152.

M

Macharzina, K./Wolf, J. (2010): Unternehmensführung, 7th. edn., Wiesbaden.

Madhok, A. (2006a): How Much Does Ownership Really Matter? Equity and Trust Relations in Joint Venture Relationships, in: Journal of International Business Studies, 37 (1), p. 4–11.

Madhok, A. (2006b): Revisiting Multinational Firms' Tolerance for Joint Ventures: A Trust-Based Approach, in: Journal of International Business Studies, 37 (1), p. 30–43.

Maisonrouge, J. G. (1974): The mythology of multinationalism, in: Columbia Journal of World Business, 9 (1), p. 7–12.

manager magazin (2003): Appell an die Sachlichkeit, available at: www.manager-magazin.de, last revised 13 February 2013.

Manigart, S. (2000): Venture Capitalists, Investment Appraisal and Accounting Information: A Comparative Study of the USA, UK, France, Belgium and Holland, in: European Financial Management, 6 (3), p. 389–403.

Mao, J. C. T. (1970): Survey of Capital Budgeting: Theory and Practice, in: The Journal of Finance, 25 (2), p. 349–360.

March, J. G./Simon, H. A. (1958): Organizations, New York.

Marcus, A. C./Crane, L. A. (1986): Telephone Surveys in Public Health Research, in: Medical Care, 24 (2), p. 97–112.

Maritan, C. A. (2001): Capital Investment as Investing in Organizational Capabilities: An Empirically Grounded Process Model, in: The Academy of Management Journal, 44 (3), p. 513–531.

Marr, J./Reynard, C. (2010): Investing in emerging markets – The BRIC economies and beyond, Chichester.

Marschan-Piekkari, R./Reis, C. (2004): Language and languages in cross-cultural interviewing, in: Marschan-Piekkari, R./Welch, C. (eds.): Handbook of qualitative research methods for international business, Cheltenham, p. 224–243.

Marschan-Piekkari, R./Welch, C. (2004): Qualitative research methods in international business: The state of the art, in: Marschan-Piekkari, R./Welch, C. (eds.): Handbook of qualitative research methods for international business, Cheltenham, p. 5–24.

Marshall, C./Rossman, G. B. (1989): Designing qualitative research, Newbury Park, Calif.

Martinez, J. I./Jarillo, J. C. (1989): The Evolution of Research on Coordination Mechanisms in Multinational Corporations, in: Journal of International Business Studies, 20 (3), p. 489–514.

Mascarenhas, B. (1984): The Coordination of Manufacturing Interdependence in Multinational Companies, in: Journal of International Business Studies, 15 (3), p. 91–106.

Mathison, S. (1988): Why Triangulate?, in: Educational Researcher, 17 (2), p. 13–17.

Mayring, P. (2002): Einführung in die qualitative Sozialforschung – Eine Anleitung zu qualitativem Denken, 5th. edn., Weinheim.

Mayring, P. (2008a): Neuere Entwicklungen in der qualitativen Forschung und der Qualitativen Inhaltsanalyse, in: Mayring, P./Gläser-Zikuda, M. (eds.): Die Praxis der qualitativen Inhaltsanalyse, Weinheim, p. 7–19.

Mayring, P. (2008b): Qualitative Inhaltsanalyse, in: Flick, U./Kardoff, E. von/Steinke, I. (eds.): Qualitative Forschung, Reinbek bei Hamburg, p. 468–475.

Mayring, P. (2010): Qualitative Inhaltsanalyse – Grundlagen und Techniken, Weinheim.

McCarthy, D. J./Puffer, S. M. (2008): Interpreting the ethicality of corporate governance decisions in Russia – Utilizing integrative social contracts theory to evaluate the relevance of agency theory norms, in: Academy of Management Review, 33 (1), p. 11–31.

McCarthy, D./Puffer, S./Dunlap, D./Jaeger, A. (2012): A Stakeholder Approach to the Ethicality of BRIC-firm Managers' Use of Favors, in: Journal of Business Ethics, 109 (1), p. 27–38.

McManus, J./Ardly, B./Floyd, D. (2012): Fostering Chinese firms through entrepreneurship, globalization, and international finance, in: Strategic Change, 21 (3-4), p. 179–191.

McMillan, J./Naughton, B. (1992): How to reform a planned economy: Lessons from China, in: Oxford Review of Economic Policy, 8 (1), p. 130–143.

Melin, L. (1992): Internationalization as a Strategy Process, in: Strategic Management Journal, 13 (2), p. 99–118.

Mendoza, E. G. (1995): The Terms of Trade, the Real Exchange Rate, and Economic Fluctuations, in: International Economic Review, 36 (1), p. 101–137.

Meuser, M./Nagel, U. (2010): Experteninterviews - wissenssoziologische Voraussetzungen und methodische Durchführung, in: Friebertshäuser, B./Boller, H./Richter, S. (eds.): Handbuch qualitative Forschungsmethoden in der Erziehungswissenschaft, 3rd edn., Weinheim, p. 457–471.

Meyer, K. E./Estrin, S. (2001): Brownfield Entry in Emerging Markets, in: Journal of International Business Studies, 32 (3), p. 575–584.

Meyer, K. E./Thu Tran, Y. T. (2006): Market Penetration and Acquisition Strategies for Emerging Economies, in: Long Range Planning, 39 (2), p. 177–197.

Mezias, J. M. (2002): Identifying liabilities of foreignness and strategies to minimize their effects: the case of labor lawsuit judgments in the United States, in: Strategic Management Journal, 23 (3), p. 229–244.

Michailova, S./Worm, V. (2003): Personal Networking in Russia and China: Blat and Guanxi, in: European Management Journal, 21 (4), p. 509–519.

Miles, M. B./Hubermann, A. M. (1986): Qualitative data analysis – A sourcebook of new methods, Beverly Hill.

Mintzberg, H. (1973): Strategy making in three modes, in: California Management Review, 16 (2), p. 44–53.

Mintzberg, H./Raisinghani, D./Théorêt, A. (1976): The Structure of "Unstructured" Decision Processes, in: Administrative Science Quarterly, 21 (2), p. 246–275.

Mitchell, W. (1989): Whether and When? Probability and Timing of Incumbents' Entry into Emerging Industrial Subfields, in: Administrative Science Quarterly, 34 (2), p. 208–230.

Mittermüller, B./von Nitzsch, R. (2008): Empirische Analyse der Erfolgsfaktoren im Investitionscontrolling, in: Finanz Betrieb, 10 (12), p. 769–779.

Mohammad, S./Whalley, J. (1984): Rent Seeking in India: Its Costs and Policy Significance, in: Kyklos, 37 (3), p. 387–413.

Mohan, R. (2002): Small-scale industry policy in India: A critical evaluation, in: Krueger, A. O. (ed.): Economic policy reforms and the Indian economy, Chicago, p. 213–267.

Mohr, L. B. (1982): Explaining organizational behavior – The limits and possibilities of theory and research, San Francisco.

Moore, J. S./Reichert, A. K. (1983): An analysis of the financial management techniques currently employed by large U.S. corporations, in: Journal of Business Finance & Accounting, 10 (4), p. 623–645.

Moore, J. S./Reichert, A. K. (1989): A Multivariate Study of Firm Performance and the Use of Modern Analytical Tools and Financial Techniques, in: Interfaces, 19 (3), p. 79–87.

Morgan, G./Smircich, L. (1980): The case for qualitative research, in: The Academy of Management Journal, 5 (4), p. 491–500.

Morrison, A./Roth, K. (1994): Relating Porter's configuration/coordination framework to competitive strategy and structural mechanisms: analysis and implications, in: Journal of Management, 19 (4), p. 797–818.

Morschett, D./Schramm-Klein, H./Zentes, J. (2010): Strategic International Management, 2nd. edn., Wiesbaden.

Mrotzek, R. (1989): Bewertung direkter Auslandinvestitionen mit Hilfe betrieblicher Investitionskalküle, Wiesbaden.

Müller, S./Kornmeier, M. (1997): Motive und Unternehmensziele als Einflussfaktoren der einzelwirtschaftlichen Internationalisierung, in: Macharzina, K./Oesterle, M.-J. (eds.): Handbuch Internationales Management, Wiesbaden, p. 71–101.

Müller-Ibold, T. (2010): Foreign Investment in Germany: Restrictions Based on Public Security Concerns and Their Compatibility with EU Law, in: Herrmann, C./Terhechte, J. P. (eds.): European Yearbook of International Economic Law 2010, Berlin/Heidelberg, p. 103–122.

Murphy, J. D. (1995): Plunder and preservation – Cultural property law and practice in the People's Republic of China, Hong Kong, New York.

Mutinelli, M./Piscitello, L. (1998): The entry mode choice of MNEs: an evolutionary approach, in: Research Policy, 27 (5), p. 491–506.

Myers, S. C./Majluf, N. S. (1984): Corporate financing and investment decisions when firms have information that investors do not have, in: Journal of Financial Economics, 13 (2), p. 187–221.

N

Newburry, W./Zeira, Y. (1997): Generic differences between equity international joint ventures (EIJVs), international acquisitions (IAs) and international greenfield investments (IGIs): Implications for parent companies, in: Journal of World Business, 32 (2), p. 87–102.

Newman, I./Ridenour, C. S./Newman, C./DeMarco, G. (2003): A typology of research purposes and its relationship to mixed methods, in: Tashakkori, A./Teddlie, C. (eds.): Handbook of mixed methods in social & behavioral research, Thousand Oaks, California, p. 167–188.

Ngai, P. (2003): Subsumption or Consumption? The Phantom of Consumer Revolution in "Globalizing" China, in: Cultural Anthropology, 18 (4), p. 469–492.

Norton, F. E. (1955): Administrative Organization in Capital Budgeting, in: The Journal of Business, 28 (4), p. 291–295.

Novick, G. (2008): Is there a bias against telephone interviews in qualitative research?, in: Research in Nursing & Health, 31 (4), p. 391–398.

Noy, C. (2008): Sampling knowledge: The hermeneutics of snowball sampling in qualitative research, in: International Journal of Social Research Methodology, 11 (4), p. 327–343.

O

Oblak, D. J./Helm, R. J. (1980): Survey and Analysis of Capital Budgeting Methods Used by Multinationals, in: Financial Management, 9 (4), p. 37–41.

O'Donnell, S. W. (2000): Managing foreign subsidiaries: agents of headquarters, or an interdependent network?, in: Strategic Management Journal, 21 (5), p. 525–548.

OECD (2010a): OECD Economic Surveys: China 2010, available at: www.oecd-ilibrary.org, last revised 6 August 2012.

OECD (2010b): OECD Factbook 2010, available at: www.oecd-ilibrary.org, last revised 3 March 2013.

OECD (2011a): OECD Economic Surveys: Brazil 2011, available at: www.oecd-ilibrary.org, last revised 3 March 2013.

OECD (2011b): OECD Economic Surveys: India 2011, available at: www.oecd-ilibrary.org, last revised 3 March 2013.

OECD (2011c): OECD Economic Surveys: Russian Federation 2011, available at: www.oecd-ilibrary.org, last revised 3 March 2013.

O'Grady, S./Lane, H. W. (1996): The Psychic Distance Paradox, in: Journal of International Business Studies, 27 (2), p. 309–333.

Ohno, K. (2009): Avoiding the Middle Income Trap, in: ASEAN Economic Bulletin, 26 (1), p. 25–43.

Oliver, D. G./Serovich, J. M./Mason, T. L. (2005): Constraints and opportunities with interview transcription: Towards reflection in qualitative research, in: Social Forces, 84 (2), p. 1273–1289.

Ondrack, D. A. (1985): International human-resources management in European and North-American firms, in: International Studies of Management & Organization, 15 (1), p. 6–32.

O'Neill, J. (2001): Building Better Global Economic BRICs. (Goldman Sachs, Global Economics Paper No. 66).

O'Neill, J./Wilson, D./Purushothaman, R./Stupnytska, A. (2005): How solid are the BRICs? (Goldman Sachs, Global Economics Paper No. 134).

Ong, L. L. (1997): Burgernomics: the economics of the Big Mac standard, in: Journal of International Money and Finance, 16 (6), p. 865–878.

Osipian, A. (2012): Who is Guilty and What to Do? Popular Opinion and Public Discourse of Corruption in Russian Higher Education, in: Canadian and International Education, 41 (1), p. 81–95.

Oswald, H. (2010): Was heißt qualitativ forschen? Warnungen, Fehlerquellen, Möglichkeiten, in: Friebertshäuser, B./Boller, H./Richter, S. (eds.): Handbuch qualitative Forschungsmethoden in der Erziehungswissenschaft, 3rd edn., Weinheim, p. 183–201.

Ott, F. M. (2000): Strategisches Investitionscontrolling in internationalen Konzernen – Konzeption und Umsetzung in der chemischen Industrie, Wiesbaden.

Ozawa, T. (1992): Foreign direct investment and economic development, in: Transnational Corporations, 1 (1), p. 27–54.

P

Panagariya, A. (2007): Why India lags behind China and how it can bridge the gap, in: World Economy, 30 (2), p. 229–248.

Papadakis, V. M. (1998): Strategic Investment Decision Processes and Organizational Performance: An Empirical Examination, in: British Journal of Management, 9 (2), p. 115–132.

Papadopoulos, N./Chen, H./Thomas, D. R. (2002): Toward a tradeoff model for international market selection, in: International Economic Review, 11 (2), p. 165–192.

Payne, A. (2008): The G8 in a changing global economic order, in: International Affairs, 84 (3), p. 519–533.

Pearce II, J. A. (2000): Cultivating guanxi as a foreign investor strategy, in: Business Horizons, 43 (1), p. 31–38.

Peng, M. W./Wang, D. Y. L./Jiang, Y. (2008): An institution-based view of international business strategy: A focus on emerging economies, in: Journal of International Business Studies, 39 (5), p. 920–936.

Peng, M. W./Zhou, J. Q. (2005): How Network Strategies and Institutional Transitions Evolve in Asia, in: Asia Pacific Journal of Management, 22 (4), p. 321–336.

Pensel, J. (1977): Die Produktions- und Investitionspolitik der internationalen Unternehmung, Berlin.

Perlmutter, H. V. (1971): Toward research on and development of nations, unions, and firms as worldwide institutions, in: International Studies of Management & Organization, 1 (4), p. 419–449.

Perlmutter, H. V. (1969): The Tortuous Evolution of the Multinational Corporation, in: Columbia Journal of World Business, 10 (1), p. 9–18.

Peteraf, M. A. (1993): The cornerstones of competetive advantage: A resource-based view, in: Strategic Management Journal, 14 (3), p. 179–191.

Petersen, B./Pedersen, T. (2002): Coping with liability of foreignness: Different learning engagements of entrant firms, in: Journal of International Management, 8 (3), p. 339–350.

Peterson, R. B. (2004): Empirical research in international management: A critique and future agenda, in: Marschan-Piekkari, R./Welch, C. (eds.): Handbook of qualitative research methods for international business, Cheltenham, p. 25–55.

Peterson, R. A./Jolibert, A. J. P. (1995): A Meta-Analysis of Country-Of-Origin Effects, in: Journal of International Business Studies, 26 (4), p. 883–900.

Pfaff, D./Bärtl, O. (1999): Wertorientierte Unternehmenssteuerung – Ein kritischer Vergleich ausgewählter Konzepte, in: Zeitschrift für betriebswirtschaftliche Forschung (Special issue 41/99), p. 85–115.

Piercy, N./Giles, W. (1989): Making SWOT analysis work, in: Marketing Intelligence & Planning, 7 (5/6), p. 5–7.

Pike, R. (1996): A longitudinal survey on capital budgeting practices, in: Journal of Business Finance & Accounting, 23 (1), p. 79–92.

Pinches, G. E. (1982): Myopia, Capital Budgeting and Decision Making, in: Financial Management, 11 (3), p. 6–19.

Pittman, R. (2004): Russian Railways Reform and the Problem of Non-discriminatory Access to Infrastructure, in: Annals of Public and Cooperative Economics, 75 (2), p. 167–192.

Pittman, R. (2007): Make or Buy on the Russian Railway? Coase, Williamson, and Tsar Nicholas II, in: Economic Change and Restructuring, 40 (3), p. 207–221.

Pittman, R./Diaconu, O./Sip, E./Tomova¡, A./Wronka, J. (2007): Competition in freight railways: "Above-the-rail" operators in central Europe and Russia, in: Journal of Competition Law and Economics, 3 (4), p. 673–687.

Poland, B. D. (1995): Transcription quality as an aspect of rigor in qualitative research, in: Qualitative Inquiry, 1 (3), p. 290–310.

Popova, M. (2012): Post-Communist Courts, in: Problems of Post-Communism, 59 (5), p. 3–5.

Popper, K. R. (1994): Logik der Forschung, 10th. edn., Tübingen.

Porter, M. E. (2007): Towards a dynamic theory of strategy, in: Strategic Management Journal, 12 (Special Issue 2), p. 95–117.

Porter, M. E. (1986): Changing patterns of international competition, in: California Management Review, 28 (2), p. 9–40.

Porter, M. E. (1998): Capital disadvantage: America's failing capital investment, in: Porter, M. E. (ed.): On Competition, Boston, p. 431–468.

Pratt, M. G. (2009): From the editors – For the lack of a boilerplate: Tips on writing up (and reviewing) qualitative research, in: Academy of Management Journal, 52 (5), p. 856–862.

PricewaterhouseCoopers (2008): The World in 2050: Beyond the BRICs: a broader look at emerging market growth prospects, available at: www.pwc.com, last revised 3 March 2013.

Puffer, S. M./McCarthy, D. J./Boisot, M. (2010): Entrepreneurship in Russia and China: The Impact of Formal Institutional Voids, in: Entrepreneurship Theory and Practice, 34 (3), p. 441–467.

Puffer, S./McCarthy, D./Jaeger, A./Dunlap, D. (2012): The use of favors by emerging market managers: Facilitator or inhibitor of international expansion?, in: Asia Pacific Journal of Management, published online (www.springer.com), p. 1–23.

Q

Qiu, L. D./Tao, Z. (2001): Export, foreign direct investment, and local content requirement, in: Journal of Development Economics, 66 (1), p. 101–125.

R

Rabbiosi, L./Elia, S./Bertoni, F. (2012): Acquisitions by EMNCs in Developed Markets, in: Management International Review, 52 (2), p. 193–212.

Raffée, H./Abel, B. (1979): Wissenschaftstheoretische Grundfragen der Wirtschaftswissenschaften, München.

Rahman, Z./Bhattacharyya, S. K. (2003): First mover advantages in emerging economies: a discussion, in: Management Decision, 41 (2), p. 141–147.

Ramamurti, R. (2012): Competing with emerging market multinationals, in: Business Horizons, 55 (3), p. 241–249.

Rappaport, A. (2006): Ten ways to create shareholder value, in: Harvard Business Review, 84 (9), p. 66–80.

Rappaport, A. (1986): Creating shareholder value – The new standard for business performance, New York.

Ray, G./Barney, J. B./Muhanna, W. A. (2004): Capabilities, Business Processes, and Competitive Advantage: Choosing the Dependent Variable in Empirical Tests of the Resource-Based View, in: Strategic Management Journal, 25 (1), p. 23–37.

Reger, G. (2004): Coordinating globally dispersed research centres of excellence – The case of Philips Electronics, in: Journal of International Management, 10 (1), p. 51–76.

Reichertz, J. (2007): Qualitative Sozialforschung – Ansprüche, Prämissen, Probleme, in: Erwägen – Wissen – Ethik, 18 (2), p. 1–14.

Reichmann, T. (2011): Controlling mit Kennzahlen, 8th. edn., München.

Rettie, R./Robinson, H./Radke, A./Ye/X. (2008): CAQDAS: a supplementary tool for qualitative market research, in: Qualitative Market Research: An International Journal, 11 (1), p. 76–88.

Reuters (2013): Beijing's toxic smog was years in the making, had many sources, available at: www.reuters.com, last revised 21 January 2013.

Richardson, S. (2006): Over-investment of free cash flow, in: Review of Accounting Studies, 11 (2-3), p. 159–189.

Riege, A. (2004): Gültigkeit und Zuverlässigkeit von Fallstudien, in: Buber, R./Gadner, J./Richards, L. (eds.): Applying qualitative methods to marketing management research, Basingstoke, p. 285–296.

Roberts, C. (2010): Russia's BRICs Diplomacy: Rising Outsider with Dreams of an Insider, in: Polity, 42 (1), p. 38–73.

Roberts, C. (2011): Building the New World Order BRIC by BRIC, in: The European Financial Review (Spring), p. 4–8.

Roberts, K./Wilson, R. (2002): ICT and the Research Process: Issues Around the Compatibility of Technology with Qualitative Data Analysis, in: Forum Qualitative Social Research, 3 (2), Rn. 1–52.

Robson, M. J./Katsikeas, C. S. (2005): International strategic alliance relationships within the foreign investment decision process, in: International Marketing Review, 22 (4), p. 399–419.

Rodrik, D. (2006): What's So Special about China's Exports?, in: China & World Economy, 14 (5), p. 1–19.

Rogoff, K. (1996): The Purchasing Power Parity Puzzle, in: Journal of Economic Literature, 34 (2), p. 647–668.

Rolfe, G. (2006): Validity, trustworthiness and rigour: quality and the idea of qualitative research, in: Journal of Advanced Nursing, 53 (3), p. 304–310.

Rolfe, S. E. (1970): The international corporation in perspective, in: Rolfe, S. E./Damm, W. (eds.): The multinational corporation in the world economy. Direct investment in perspective, 2. printing, New York, p. 5–34.

Roll, R. (1986): The Hubris Hypothesis of Corporate Takeovers, in: The Journal of Business, 59 (2), p. 197–216.

Rosenblatt, M. J./Jucker, J. V. (1979): Capital Expenditure Decision-Making: Some Tools and Trends, in: Interfaces, 9 (2), p. 63–69.

Rösgen, K. (2000): Aufgabenfelder des Investitionscontrollings, in: Kostenrechnungspraxis, 44 (4), p. 251–261.

Ross, M. (1986): Capital Budgeting Practices of Twelve Large Manufacturers, in: Financial Management, 15 (4), p. 15–22.

Roth, K. (1992): International Configuration and Coordination Archetypes for Medium-Sized Firms in Global Industries, in: Journal of International Business Studies, 23 (3), p. 533–549.

Roth, K./Morrison, A. J. (1990): An Empirical Analysis of the Integration-Responsiveness Framework in Global Industries, in: Journal of International Business Studies, 21 (4), p. 541–564.

Rothlauf, J. (2012): Interkulturelles Management – Mit Beispielen aus Vietnam, China, Japan, Russland und den Golfstaaten, München.

Ryan, P. A./Ryan, G. P. (2002): Capital Budgeting Practices of the Fortune 1000: How Have Things Changed?, in: Journal of Business & Management, 8 (4), p. 355–364.

S

Sachs, J. D. (2008): The rise of TNCs from emerging markets: the global context, in: Sauvant, K. P./Irmak, I./Mendoza, K. (eds.): The rise of transnational corporations from emerging markets. Threat or opportunity?, Cheltenham, Northampton, p. 15–19.

Samuelson, P. A. (1952): The Transfer Problem and Transport Costs: The Terms of Trade When Impediments are Absent, in: The Economic Journal, 62 (246), p. 278–304.

Sandelowski, M. (1995): Sample size in qualitative research, in: Research in Nursing & Health, 18 (2), p. 179–183.

Sangster, A. (1993): Capital investment appraisal techniques: A survey of current usage, in: Journal of Business Finance & Accounting, 20 (3), p. 307–332.

Sapper, R. (2007): Kriterien und Elemente zum spezifischen Projektmanagement von Investitionsprojekten im chemischen und pharmazeutischen Anlagenbau, Kassel.

Sauvant, K. P. (2006): Inward and outward FDI and the BRICs, in: Jain, S. C. (ed.): Emerging economies and the transformation of international business. Brazil, Russia, India and China (BRICs), Cheltenham, Northampton, p. 313–409.

Savvides, S. (1994): Risk analysis in investment appraisal – Project Appraisal, in: Project Appraisal, 9 (1), p. 3–18.

Scapens, R. W. (1990): Researching management accounting practice: The role of case study methods, in: The British Accounting Review, 22 (3), p. 259–281.

Schaefer, C. (2004): Steuerung und Kontrolle von Investitionsprozessen – Theoretischer Ansatz und Konkretisierung für das öffentliche Beteiligungscontrolling, Wiesbaden.

Schäfer, T. (1995): Auslandsinvestitionen und Währungsrisiken, Wiesbaden.

Schäffer, U./Brettel, T. (2005): Ein Plädoyer für Fallstudien, in: Zeitschrift für Controlling & Management, 49 (1), p. 43–46.

Schall, L. D./Sundem, G. L./Geijsbeek, W. R., JR. (1978): Survey and Analysis of Capital Budgeting Methods, in: The Journal of Finance, 33 (1), p. 281–287.

Schierenbeck, H./Lister, M. (2002): Value Controlling – Grundlagen wertorientierter Unternehmensführung, 2nd. edn., München.

Schmid, S. (2013): Strategien der Internationalisierung, 3rd. edn., München.

Schmidbauer, R. (1998): Konzeption eines unternehmenswertorientierten Beteiligungs-Controlling im Konzern, Frankfurt am Main.

Schnell, R./Hill, P. B./Esser, E. (2011): Methoden der empirischen Sozialforschung, 9th. edn., München.

Scholz, J. (1996): Auslandsinvestitionsrechnung – Möglichkeiten zur Berücksichtigung der Unsicherheit, Wiesbaden.

Schoppe, S. G. (1998): Kompendium der Internationalen Betriebswirtschaftslehre, 4th. edn., München.

Schuh, A. (2009): Fallstudien in der Strategieforschung, in: Buber, R./Holzmüller, H. H. (eds.): Qualitative Marktforschung, 2nd edn., Wiesbaden, p. 999–1017.

Schuster, C. P. (2006): Negotiating in BRICs: business as usual isn't, in: Jain, S. C. (ed.): Emerging economies and the transformation of international business. Brazil, Russia, India and China (BRICs), Cheltenham, Northampton, p. 410–427.

Schweiger, D. M./Sandberg, W. R./Ragan, J. W. (1986): Group Approaches for Improving Strategic Decision Making: A Comparative Analysis of Dialectical Inquiry, Devil's Advocacy, and Consensus, in: The Academy of Management Journal, 29 (1), p. 51–71.

Schweitzer, M. (1978): Wissenschaftsziele und Auffassungen in der Betriebswirtschaftslehre – Eine Einführung, in: Schweitzer, M. (ed.): Auffassungen und Wissenschaftsziele der Betriebswirtschaftslehre, Darmstadt, p. 1–14.

Scott, W. R. (2003): Institutional carriers: reviewing modes of transporting ideas over time and space and considering their consequences, in: Industrial and Corporate Change, 12 (4), p. 879–894.

Seale, C./Silverman, D. (1997): Ensuring rigour in qualitative research, in: The European Journal of Public Health, 7 (4), p. 379–384.

Shapiro, A. C. (1978): Capital Budgeting for the Multinational Corporation, in: Financial Management, 7 (1), p. 7–16.

Shih, F.-J. (1998): Triangulation in nursing research: issues of conceptual clarity and purpose, in: Journal of Advanced Nursing, 28 (3), p. 631–641.

Shimizu, K./Hitt, M. A./Vaidyanath, D./Pisano, V. (2004): Theoretical foundations of cross-border mergers and acquisitions: A review of current research and recommendations for the future, in: Journal of International Management, 10 (3), p. 307–353.

Shleifer, A./Vishny, R. W. (1989): Management entrenchment: The case of manager-specific investments, in: Journal of Financial Economics, 25 (1), p. 123–139.

Shoham, A./Rose, G. M./Albaum, G. (1995): Export Motives, Psychological Distance, and the EPRG Framework – Journal of Global Marketing, in: Journal of Global Marketing, 8 (3-4), p. 9–37.

Shotter, J. (1990): Knowing of the third kind, Utrecht.

Sierke, B. R. A. (1989): Investitions-Controlling im Controlling-System – Darstellung eines integrierten Ansatzes mit Hilfe ausgewählter linearer Dekompositionsverfahren, Göttingen.

Simon, H. A. (1957): A Behavioral Model of Rational Choice, in: Simon, H. A. (ed.): Models of man: Social and rational, New York, p. 161–241.

Simon, H. A. (1976): Administrative Behavior, 3rd. edn., New York.

Simon, H. A. (1955): A Behavioral Model of Rational Choice, in: The Quarterly Journal of Economics, 69 (1), p. 99–118.

Simon, H. A. (1979): Rational Decision Making in Business Organizations, in: The American Economic Review, 69 (4), p. 493–513.

Simon, H. (2007a): Hidden Champions des 21. Jahrhunderts – Die Erfolgsstrategien unbekannter Weltmarktführer, Frankfurt/Main.

Simon, M. C. (2007b): Der Internationalisierungsprozess von Unternehmen, Wiesbaden.

Singhal, S. (2011): The significance and performance of infrastructure in India, in: Journal of Property Research, 28 (1), p. 15–34.

Sinkovics, R. R./Penz, E./Ghauri, P. N. (2008): Enhancing the Trustworthiness of Qualitative Research in International Business, in: Management International Review, 48 (6), p. 689–714.

Sirmon, D. G./Hitt, M. A./Arregle, J. L./Tochman Campbell, J. (2010): The dynamic interplay of capability strengths and weaknesses: investigating the bases of temporary competitive advantage, in: Strategic Management Journal, 31 (13), p. 1386–1409.

Smith, D. E. (1974): The Social Construction of Documentary Reality, in: Sociological Inquiry, 44 (4), p. 257–268.

Sörensen, J. B. (2002): The Strength of Corporate Culture and the Reliability of Firm Performance, in: Administrative Science Quarterly, 47 (1), p. 70–91.

Stake, R. E. (1995): The art of case study research, Thousand Oaks et al.

Steinke, I. (1999): Kriterien qualitativer Forschung – Ansätze zur Bewertung qualitativ-empirischer Sozialforschung, Weinheim.

Steinke, I. (2008): Gütekriterien qualitativer Forschung, in: Flick, U./Kardoff, E. von/Steinke, I. (eds.): Qualitative Forschung, Reinbek bei Hamburg, p. 319–331.

Stern, J. (2005): The future of Russian gas and Gazprom, Oxford.

Strauss, A. L./Corbin, J. M. (1990): Basics of qualitative research – Grounded theory procedures and techniques, Newbury Park, California.

Strübing, J. (2002): Just do it?, in: Kölner Zeitschrift für Soziologie und Sozialpsychologie, 54 (2), p. 318–342.

Strübing, J. (2004): Grounded theory – Zur sozialtheoretischen und epistemologischen Fundierung des Verfahrens der empirisch begründeten Theoriebildung, Wiesbaden.

Sturges, J. E./Hanrahan, K. J. (2004): Comparing telephone and face-to-face qualitative interviewing: a research note, in: Qualitative Research, 4 (1), p. 107–118.

Subacchi, P. (2008): New power centres and new power brokers: are they shaping a new economic order?, in: International Affairs, 84 (3), p. 485–498.

Suddaby, R. (2006): From the editors: What grounded theory is not, in: Academy of Management Journal, 49 (4), p. 633–642.

Sutton, R. I./Staw, B. M. (1995): What Theory is Not, in: Administrative Science Quarterly, 40 (3), p. 371–384.

Swoboda, B. (2001): Dynamische Prozesse der Internationalisierung – Management-theoretische und empirische Perspektiven des unternehmerischen Wandels, Wiesbaden.

T

Talaulicar, T./Grundei, J./von Werder, A. (2005): Strategic decision making in start-ups: the effect of top management team organization and processes on speed and comprehensiveness, in: Journal of Business Venturing, 20 (4), p. 519–541.

Tan, J./Peng, M. W. (2003): Organizational slack and firm performance during economic transitions: two studies from an emerging economy, in: Strategic Management Journal, 24 (13), p. 1249–1263.

Tashakkori, A./Teddlie, C. (2003): Major issues and controversies in the use of mixed methods in the social and behavioral sciences, in: Tashakkori, A./Teddlie, C. (eds.): Handbook of mixed methods in social & behavioral research, Thousand Oaks, California, p. 3–50.

Tayeb, M. (1994): Organizations and national culture: Methodology considered, in: Organization Studies, 15 (3), p. 429–446.

Taylor, A. M. (2002): A Century of Purchasing-Power Parity, in: The Review of Economics and Statistics, 84 (1), p. 139–150.

Taylor, D. H. (1994): Problems of Food Supply Logistics in Russia and the CIS, in: International Journal of Physical Distribution & Logistics Management, 24 (2), p. 15–22.

Technische Universität München (2012): Chinese Champions – Patente made in China, available at: www.chinese-champions.de, last revised 8 April 2013.

Teddlie, C./Tashakkori, A. (2003): Major issues and controversies in the use of mixed methods in the social and behavioral sciences, in: Tashakkori, A./Teddlie, C. (eds.): Handbook of mixed methods in social & behavioral research, Thousand Oaks, California, p. 3–50.

Teddlie, C./Tashakkori, A. (2011): Mixed Methods Research: Contemporary issues in an emerging field, in: Denzin, N. K./Lincoln, Y. S. (eds.): The Sage handbook of qualitative research, 4. ed., Los Angeles, p. 285–300.

Teece, D. J. (1986): Profiting from technological innovation: Implications for integration, collaboration, licensing and public policy, in: Research Policy, 15 (6), p. 285–305.

The Boston Consulting Group (2013): Allies and Adversaries, available at: www.bcg.de, last revised 21 January 2013.

The Economist (2009): Brazil takes off, available at: www.economist.com, last revised 3 March 2013.

The Economist Intelligence Unit (2009): China – country profile 2009, available at: www.economist.com, last revised 7 August 2012.

The United Nations (2012): Human Development Report 2011, available at: www.undp.org, last revised 26 November 2012.

The World Bank (2010): Russian economic report, available at: www.worldbank.org, last revised 2 August 2012.

The World Bank (2011): Multipolarity: The New Global Economy, Washington.

The World Bank (2012a): China country overview, available at: www.worldbank.org, last revised 6 August 2012.

The World Bank (2012b): How we classify countries, available at: www.worldbank.org, last revised 26 November 2012.

The World Bank (2012c): India country overview, available at: www.worldbank.org, last revised 31 July 2012.

The World Bank (2012d): Russia country overview, available at: www.worldbank.org, last revised 2 August 2012.

Tolley, G. S./Olson, E. (1971): The Interdependence between Income and Education, in: Journal of Political Economy, 79 (3), p. 460–480.

Tosi, H. L./Gomez-Mejia, L. R. (1989): The Decoupling of CEO Pay and Performance: An Agency Theory Perspective, in: Administrative Science Quarterly, 34 (2), p. 169–189.

Toyne, B. (1989): International Exchange: A Foundation for Theory Building in International Business, in: Journal of International Business Studies, 20 (1), p. 1–17.

Transparency International (2011): Corruption Perception Index 2011, available at: www.transparency.de, last revised 3 March 2013.

Tsang, E. W. K. (1998): Can guanxi Be a Source of Sustained Competitive Advantage for Doing Business in China?, in: The Academy of Management Executive, 12 (2), p. 64–73.

Tsoukas, H. (1989): The Validity of Idiographic Research Explanations, in: The Academy of Management Review, 14 (4), p. 551–561.

Tucker, C. (1983): Interviewer Effects in Telephone Surveys, in: The Public Opinion Quarterly, 47 (1), p. 84–95.

U

UNCTAD (2012): World Investment Report 2012 – Towards a new generation of investment policies, available at: www.unctad.org, last revised 3 March 2013.

UNCTAD (2013): Country fact sheets: Germany, available at: www.unctad.org, last revised 19 February 2013.

V

van de Ven, A. H./Huber, G. P. (1990): Longitudinal Field Research Methods for Studying Processes of Organizational Change, in: Organization Science, 1 (3), p. 213–219.

van de Ven, A. H./Delbecq, A. L./Koenig, R., JR. (1976): Determinants of Coordination Modes within Organizations, in: American Sociological Review, 41 (2), p. 322–338.

van den Bergh, J. (2009): The GDP paradox, in: Journal of Economic Psychology, 30 (2), p. 117–135.

Velthuis, L. J./Wesner, P./Hebertinger, M. (2005): Value Based Management – Bewertung, Performancemessung und Managemententlohnung mit ERIC®, Stuttgart.

Vernon, R. (1966): International Investment and International Trade in the Product Cycle, in: The Quarterly Journal of Economics, 80 (2), p. 190–207.

Verschuren, P. J. M. (2003): Case study as a research strategy: some ambiguities and opportunities, in: International Journal of Social Research Methodology, 6 (2), p. 121–138.

Victor, C. R. (1988): Some methodological aspects of using postal questionnaires with the elderly, in: Archives of Gerontology and Geriatrics, 7 (2), p. 163–172.

W

Walsh, I. J./Bartunek, J. M. (2011): Cheating the fates: Organizational foundings in the wake of demise, in: Academy of Management Journal, 54 (5), p. 1017–1044.

Wang, S./Tong, T. W./Chen, G./Kim, H. (2009): Expatriate Utilization and Foreign Direct Investment Performance: The Mediating Role of Knowledge Transfer, in: Journal of Management, 35 (5), p. 1181–1206.

Webb, C. (1999): Analysing qualitative data: computerized and other approaches, in: Journal of Advanced Nursing, 29 (2), p. 323–330.

Wei, W. (2005): China and India: Any difference in their FDI performances?, in: Journal of Asian Economics, 16 (4), p. 719–736.

Weinstein, A. (2006): A strategic framework for defining and segmenting markets, in: Journal of Strategic Marketing, 14 (2), p. 115–127.

Welge, M. K./Amshoff, B. (1998): Internationales Controlling: Aufgaben – Techniken – Organisation, in: Lachnit, L./Lange, C./Palloks, M. (eds.): Zukunftsfähiges Controlling, München, p. 445–480.

Welge, M. K. (1982): Planning in German Multinational Corporations, in: International Studies of Management & Organization, 12 (1), p. 6–37.

Welge, M. K./Al-Laham, A. (2012): Strategisches Management, 6th. edn., Wiesbaden.

Welge, M. K./Holtbrügge, D. (1998): Internationales Management, Landsberg am Lech.

Wernerfelt, B. (1984): A resource-based view of the firm, in: Strategic Management Journal, 5 (2), p. 171–180.

West, R./Frumina, E. (2012): European Standards in Russian Higher Education and the Role of English: A case study of the National University of Science and Technology, Moscow (MISiS), in: European Journal of Education, 47 (1), p. 50–63.

Wicher, H. (1995): Das Promotorenkonzept - Eine Problemanalyse, in: Das Wirtschaftsstudium, 24 (10), p. 820–832.

Wilson, D./Purushothaman, R. (2003): Dreaming with the BRICs. The path to 2050. (Goldman Sachs, Working Paper No. 99).

Wilson, M. (1993): Empirical evidence of the use of a framework of risk and return in capital budgeting for foreign direct investment, in: Managerial Finance, 16 (2), p. 25–34.

Wind, Y./Douglas, S. P./Perlmutter, H. V. (1973): Guidelines for Developing International Marketing Strategies, in: The Journal of Marketing, 37 (2), p. 14–23.

Witte, E. (1973): Organisation für Innovationsentscheidungen, Göttingen.

Witte, E. (1977): Power and innovation: A two-center theory, in: International Studies of Management & Organization, 7 (1), p. 47–70.

Witte, E. (1999): Das Promotoren-Modell, in: Hauschildt, J./Gemünden, H. G. (eds.): Promotoren. Champions der Innovation, 2nd edn., Wiesbaden, p. 9–41.

Witzel, A. (2000): The problem-centered interview, in: Forum Qualitative Social Research, 1 (1), Article 22, p. 1–9.

Witzel, A. (1982): Verfahren der qualitativen Sozialforschung – Überblick und Alternativen, Frankfurt am Main.

Wood, V. R. R. N./Gopalakrishna, P. (2012): Higher education in the Middle East and India – Overview and two programs created to educate global business leaders in emerging markets, in: China-USA Business Review, 11 (1), p. 143–159.

Wrona, T. (2005): Die Fallstudieanalyse als wissenschaftliche Forschungsmethode, ESCP-EAP Working Paper No. 10.

X

Xiao, Y./Wang, F./Liu, Y./Wang, J. (2012): Reconstructing Gravitational Attractions of Major Cities in China from Air Passenger Flow Data, in: The Professional Geographer, 65 (2), p. 265–282.

Xu, D./Shenkar, O. (2002): Institutional Distance and the Multinational Enterprise, in: The Academy of Management Review, 27 (4), p. 608–618.

Y

Yan, T./Yi Qian, W. (2004): Environmental Migration and Sustainable Development in the Upper Reaches of the Yangtze River, in: Population & Environment, 25 (6), p. 613–636.

Yin, R. K. (2008): Applications of case study research, 2nd. edn., Thousand Oaks, California.

Yin, R. K. (2009): Case Study Research – Design and Methods, 4th. edn., Los Angeles, London, New Delhi.

Z

Zaheer, S. (1995): Overcoming the Liability of Foreignness, in: The Academy of Management Journal, 38 (2), p. 341–363.

Zaheer, S. (2002): The liability of foreignness, redux: a commentary, in: Journal of International Management, 8 (3), p. 351–358.

Zalan, T./Lewis, G. (2004): Writing about methods in qualitative research: towards a more transparent approach, in: Marschan-Piekkari, R./Welch, C. (eds.): Handbook of qualitative research methods for international business, Cheltenham, p. 507–528.

Zhang, K. H./Song, S. (2001): Promoting exports: the role of inward FDI in China, in: China Economic Review, 11 (4), p. 385–396.

Zhang, Y./Zhang, Z./Liu, Z. (2007): Choice of entry modes in sequential FDI in an emerging economy, in: Management Decision, 45 (4), p. 749–772.

Zheng, P. (2009): A comparison of FDI determinants in China and India, in: Thunderbird international Business Review, 51 (3), p. 263–279.

Münsteraner Schriften zur Internationalen Unternehmensrechnung

Herausgegeben von Peter Kajüter

Band 1 Daniela Barth: Prognoseberichterstattung. Praxis, Determinanten und Kapitalmarktwirkungen bei deutschen börsennotierten Unternehmen. 2009.

Band 2 Tobias Dickmann: Controllingintegration nach M&A-Transaktionen. Eine empirische Analyse. 2010.

Band 3 Simon Esser: Produktorientiertes Kostenmanagement in der chemischen Industrie. Eine empirische Analyse. 2011.

Band 4 Christian Reisloh: Influence of National Culture on IFRS Practice. An Empirical Study in France, Germany and the United Kingdom. 2011.

Band 5 Matthias Moeschler: Cost Accounting in Germany and Japan. A Comparative Analysis. 2012.

Band 6 Martin Merschdorf: Der Management Approach in der IFRS-Rechnungslegung. Implikationen für Unternehmen und Investoren. 2012.

Band 7 Kristian Bachert: Fair Value Accounting. Implications for Users of Financial Statements. 2012.

Band 8 Daniel Blaesing: Nachhaltigkeitsberichterstattung in Deutschland und den USA. Berichtspraxis, Determinanten und Eigenkapitalkostenwirkungen. 2013.

Band 9 Christina Voets: Kulturelle Einflüsse auf die Anwendung des Impairment-Tests nach IAS 36. Eine experimentelle Untersuchung in Asien und Europa. 2013.

Band 10 Thomas Poplat: Foreign Investments in BRIC Countries. Empirical Evidence from Multinational Corporations. 2014.

www.peterlang.de